Theodore Dreiser

Beyond Naturalism

Edited by

Miriam Gogol

NEW YORK UNIVERSITY PRESS
New York and London

NEW YORK UNIVERSITY PRESS
New York and London

Cover art: From a photograph of Theodore Dreiser looking at a bust of John Cowper Powys. Hollywood, 1942. Reprinted with the permission of the University of Pennsylvania, Department of Special Collections.

Library of Congress Cataloging-in-Publication Data
Theodore Dreiser: beyond naturalism / edited by Miriam Gogol.
    p. cm.
    Includes index.
    ISBN 0-8147-3073-6 (cloth : alk. paper). — ISBN 0-8147-3074-4 (paperback : alk. paper)
    1. Dreiser, Theodore, 1871–1945 — Criticism and interpretation. 2. Naturalism in literature. I. Gogol, Miriam, 1949– .
PS3507.R55Z848   1995   95-14447
    813'.52–dc20   CIP

New York University Press books are printed on acid-free paper, and their binding materials are chosen for their strength and durability.

Manufactured in the United States of America

Contents

Acknowledgments

I extend special thanks to Florian Stuber, Albert Ashforth, and Madelyn Larsen, all of whom gave very generously of their time in reading and revising portions of this book.

My gratitude is extended as well to the library staff of the Theodore Dreiser papers, Department of Special Collections, the University of Pennsylvania. Quotations from unpublished Dreiser manuscripts were used with the permission of The Trustees and copyrighted by them. Grateful acknowledgment is made to the University of Calgary Press for granting permission to reprint material in Irene Gammel's essay, "Sexualizing the Female Body: Dreiser, Feminism and Foucault" (*Sexualizing Power in Naturalism* [Calgary, 1994]) and to the University of North Carolina Press for permission to reprint sections of James Livingston's "*Sister Carrie's* Absent Causes" (*Pragmatism and the Political Economy of Cultural Revolution, 1850–1940* [Chapel Hill, 1994]).

I also thank Zanvel A. Liff for his encouragement and inspiration over the years. Without his help, this volume would not have come into existence. I dedicate my portions of this book to D. Fred, Ariella, and F. Gogol.

Miriam Gogol

Introduction

Miriam Gogol

To his contemporaries, Theodore Dreiser was best known for his "naturalism" and for his defiance of the genteel tradition of American letters. For most of his career, he was surrounded by notoriety, and after the publication, in 1925, of *An American Tragedy*, his name was a household word. Fifty thousand people bought copies in the first few years, many more read the book, and still more read of attempts in Boston to have the book banned.[1] With time, though, naturalism became absorbed within the larger tradition of American writing, the genteel literary establishment lost its power to sway readers, and the controversies that swirled about Dreiser in his lifetime were largely resolved. Dreiser's reputation, however, has not merely survived; it continues to grow. Hardly a year passes that does not see the appearance of a new edition of Dreiser's writings, including such volumes as the unexpurgated *Sister Carrie* (1981), *American Diaries, 1902–1926* (1982), *An Amateur Laborer* (1983), *Dreiser–Mencken Letters* (1986), *Newspaper Days* (1991), and the restored *Jennie Gerhardt* (1992). And the works keep coming. New editions are planned from the University of Pennsylvania, the Library of America, and Oxford University Press.[2]

Today Dreiser is considered a classic American writer and has a global following. His fiction is required reading in many American literature courses in colleges and universities in the United States and abroad, including universities in India, Japan, China, Germany, Hungary, and the former Communist-bloc countries. His work is also heavily anthologized.

To a large extent, Dreiser's strength of character has contributed to his enduring popularity with readers. Where other writers succumb to the urge to judge and censor, Dreiser merely describes. He told the truth as he saw it, and in doing so, he focused on subjects that have become primary concerns in modern American fiction. Even his life inspires readers: As the son of a poor immigrant, he struggled for social recognition; as an unskilled worker, he fought for a salary that would provide the necessities for survival; as a young author, he strove to make his voice heard above the cacophony of a robust democratic society. If readers identify with Clyde Griffiths in *An American Tragedy* and Hurstwood in *Sister Carrie*, it is because they identify with Dreiser himself. Dreiser's honesty is the source of the power in his writing; that honesty makes it possible for readers to understand the powerful desires that drive his characters to crimes of passion. Without judgment, without censorship, Dreiser reports what he sees and what he knows. As we are learning through overwhelming media coverage of sensational trial cases—description does yield explanation and insight.

In many ways, Dreiser is a greater author than Henry James, against whom he was pitted in Lionel Trilling's essay "Reality in America" (1950).[3] Like James, Dreiser gives us in-depth studies of the psychic struggles of his characters but, unlike James, Dreiser is willing to get his hands dirty. The world of Dreiser's fiction is so much larger than that of James. He shows us the external forces that shape his characters' lives and provides some of the first authentic portrayals of working-class people.

But Dreiser's fiction goes beyond these evident truths. He was drawn to ideas and subjects that continue to engage readers' imaginations. Take, for example, the question of feminism. Contemporary feminists have interestingly ambivalent feelings toward Dreiser.[4] On the one hand, they are repulsed by some of his own relationships with women. He was a known womanizer, who was not above writing identical love letters to two different women; in fact, he often wrote to at least two lovers at the same time. By his own account, to have to remain faithful to any woman would almost have "killed" him (6 June 1917, *Diaries*). Later in life he confided to his niece Vera Dreiser that he was in love a thousand times, or "most likely never at all."[5]

On the other hand, in the first decades of this century Dreiser was one of the few American authors—male or female—who in creating characters defied many of the culture's stereotypes of the "working girl."[6] If he was often callous to women in his life, Dreiser was gently sympathetic to them in his books. Although not true of all his female characters, many of them exhibit characteristics that we would call feminist: primarily their independence in social, economic, and vocational spheres. They pursue worldly goals and through their drive succeed in obtaining them. This is just one of the many paradoxes that fascinate readers and is beginning to perplex scholars.

Even though Dreiser was a forerunner in accurately describing the often squalid conditions in which struggling young women had to work, their depressing domestic surroundings, and their assorted job-related trials, the historical significance of these descriptions is only now being studied. Although scholars have traditionally shied away from intimate biographical questions, frowning on what Joyce Carol Oates labeled "pathography,"[7] a growing number of scholars find it impossible to avoid considering a writer's private life. This volume includes essays that bring this and other such current issues to a discussion of Dreiser and his *oeuvre*.[8]

It is remarkable that so few critical books and no recent collections of critical essays have been published that reflect current thinking about Dreiser's canon. This collection, which presents new essays that treat his work as a whole and raises contemporary theoretical questions about his canon, is the first to appear in 24 years.[9]

Here is a writer of extraordinarily wide-ranging interests, whose work draws global attention, but who until recently has had virtually one aspect of his art be the principal focus of professional studies. More than any other American novelist, Theodore Dreiser has been associated with naturalism.[10] And much of the significant writing about him since the mid-1960s has focused on the issue of whether he is a naturalist, which suggests that this controversy has become one of the permanent centers of Dreiser criticism.[11]

This collection, however, goes "beyond naturalism," hence the title. But what does that mean, and what is "naturalism" anyway? In this time of radical changes in ways of looking at literature and especially of classifying it, all terms have come under new scrutiny. And certainly "naturalism," which has been defined and redefined particularly since the late 1940s, has been viewed with suspicion. George J. Becker (1949), defining all naturalism, including American, considered it "no more than an emphatic and explicit philosophical position taken by some realists," the position being a "pessimistic materialistic determinism."[12] Lars Ahnebrink (1950), in the first major study of the naturalist movement in America, defined it largely in terms of its European antecedents, as found in Flaubert, Zola, Turgenev, and Hardy. Charles Child Walcutt (1956) analyzed its roots as indigenous to American Transcendentalism or realism and argued that its major themes involved determinism, survival, violence, and taboo.[13] Donald Pizer (1984) agreed that naturalism derived from previous American movements and described the naturalist novel as primarily populated with the poor, the uneducated, and the unsophisticated. Pizer also suggested "a compensating humanistic value in [the naturalist's] characters or their fates which affirms the significance of the individual and of his life."[14]

We owe an enormous debt to critics such as Donald Pizer, Charles Walcutt, Ellen Moers, and Richard Lehan.[15] Without them we might be left with the attempts of a literary establishment (as represented by Trilling's previously cited essay) to dismiss or suppress a writer who so clearly challenged many of its genteel assumptions about life and art.[16] As an early reader of these essays pointed out, the early Dreiserians "defined an inviolate place for Dreiser in American literary history, pointed out his distinctive and distinguishing qualities, the direction of his influence" — in brief, created and sustained a critical interest in Dreiser that is a rationale for this book.

Clearly, at one time, the term "naturalism" was a useful way of letting people perceive certain characteristics of Dreiser's art and helped to account for some of its impact. But there remains a problem with the term "naturalism." Dreiser himself mocked the term,[17] and recent theorists on literary realism, such as Eric Sundquist and Amy Kaplan, bypass it altogether.[18] Walter Benn Michaels does use the term in the title of his powerful, albeit controversial, book, *The Gold Standard and the Logic of Naturalism* (1987), but importantly, he uses the term, he says, "*not* to help breathe new life into the old debate over what naturalism is and how exactly it differs from realism," but to map out the historic reality in which this literature finds its place and to identify its set of interests and activities.[19] Indeed, he and the other new historicists try to avoid not only that "old debate" but also the assumptions that govern it.

The works of several new critics have led us to look at turn-of-the-century American culture in very different ways. And Dreiser has provided a definitive case study for this scholarship. For these critics, Dreiser's fiction is a repository of the era's literary and cultural developments: the spectacle of a consumer culture, of urban aesthetics; theories of bodies, machines, and technology; forms of market culture; and others.[20]

This surge of interest has brought readers and scholars to look "beyond naturalism" in their approach toward Dreiser. In this collection, for example, the ten essayists offer original interpretations of Dreiser's works from such disparate points of view as new historicism, poststructuralism, psychoanalysis, feminism, film studies, and canon formation. Indeed, the first six essays concentrate on gender studies and on psychoanalysis, areas that have been virtually neglected in Dreiser criticism. Several essays in this group focus on Dreiser's ambivalent relationships to women in his life and his presentation of them in his fiction. Until now, only a handful of women scholars have written on Dreiser, and scarcely anyone has written on women in Dreiser.[21] It is time that women, bringing with them new concerns and an interest in new issues, enter the debate about Dreiser's work, and I am pleased that among the young generation of critics represented in this book half are women.

The essayists write about Dreiser's fiction and autobiographical pieces — not only his two autobiographies, but also his diaries and letters. One essay brings new attention to *A Gallery of Women* (1929), Dreiser's collection of nonfictional and semifictionalized sketches of his female friends and acquaintances. Two essays consider the new University of Pennsylvania edition of *Jennie Gerhardt*, which restores some 16,000 words deleted from the first-edition text printed in 1911 by Harper and Brothers. Although most of his novels are discussed at length, *Sister Carrie* and *An American Tragedy* are referred to by almost every essayist in large part because they are Dreiser's most popular works. *An American Tragedy* was his only bestseller, and *Sister Carrie* is still required reading in colleges around the world. It seems appropriate that essays in this volume, which introduces Dreiser in new ways, focus on the books that readers know and feel they are familiar with. But all of these essays will surprise, intrigue, and disturb readers who have reached foregone conclusions about Dreiser and his art.

These essays make Dreiser harder to pigeonhole and harder to define. In fact the major significance of this collection is that despite this elusiveness the scholars presented here are beginning to understand the complexity of his vision and the largeness of his landscape, and they are able to establish connections that reveal his strengths as well as his weaknesses. In one fashion or another, all the essayists discuss paradoxes in Dreiser's life and work in the context of modern cultural criticism; in so doing, they raise new questions about enduring aspects of his art. The first four essays discuss Dreiser in relation to feminism, men's studies, and poststructuralism. In the lead essay, "Dreiser and the Discourse of Gender," Shelley Fisher Fishkin explores Dreiser's attitude toward women and the extent to which he represents the contradictions in the culture of his day. Irene Gammel in "Sexualizing the Female Body" takes a similar stand. Despite the undeniable truth that Dreiser firmly established sex as a discursive fact in modern American fiction, this deconstructive essay undermines the perception that Dreiser waved the banner of sexual liberation in his battle against American literary "puritanism."

Viewing Dreiser from an opposing position, Nancy Warren Barrineau in her essay, "Recontextualizing Dreiser," uses the University of Pennsylvania edition of *Jennie Gerhardt* to argue that Dreiser's novel is radical in its historical veracity about working-class women's difficulties at the turn of the century. Scott Zaluda also defends Dreiser's gender presentations in "Secrets of Fraternity." Zaluda focuses on what he perceives as Dreiser's uneasiness with the dominant male ethos and men's social power in late nineteenth-century America.

The next two essays discuss Dreiser's fiction in relation to psychoanalysis. Surprisingly few psychoanalytical essays have been published on Dreiser's fiction, yet Dreiser would seem to invite such readings. As Saul Bellow astutely commented years ago, more than most authors, Dreiser invites such readings because "Dreiser has more open access to primary feelings than any American writer of the twentieth century."[22] My essay, "'That oldest boy don't wanta be here,'" analyzes the emotional polarities of shame and pride that dominate much of Dreiser's fiction. In another essay, "Lacanian Equivocation in *Sister Carrie, The "Genius,"* and *An American Tragedy*," Leonard Cassuto applies the psychoanalytic theories of Jacques Lacan to analyze the contradictory wants and alienations of some of Dreiser's major characters.

Paul Orlov's "On Language and the Quest for Self-Fulfillment" allies Dreiser's thinking with the philosophy of Martin Heidegger. The similarities Orlov discerns expose misconceptions in the traditional view of Dreiser, expanding his purely naturalistic worldview, while affirming his fictional artistry and his strengths as a thinker.

Lawrence Hussman discusses Dreiser's paradoxical relation to popular culture in his essay, "Squandered Possibilities: The Film Versions of Dreiser's Novels." Hussman notes that many of Dreiser's novels have been adapted by some of the world's most illustrious directors—Sergei Eisenstein, Joseph von Sternberg, William Wyler, George Stevens. But Hussman questions why the results have never matched the complexity of vision of the source texts, even though something approaching that complexity is attainable in cinema.

The final essays concentrate on *Sister Carrie* from generic, new historic, and modern philosophical perspectives "beyond naturalism." In "Carrie's Library," M. H. Dunlop defines the differences between popular and serious fiction. She focuses on a seemingly minute but extremely significant contradiction in the references to popular novels in two different editions of *Sister Carrie* (Norton, 1970; University of Pennsylvania Press, 1981).

The collection culminates with James Livingston's *"Sister Carrie's* Absent Causes." His essay addresses yet another paradox in Dreiser's novel: Why Dreiser situated a realistic style within the apparently archaic form of romance. Livingston's response reveals important aspects of modern American consumer culture.

The many disparate approaches in this collection reflect the reality of a richly multilayered Theodore Dreiser. By definition paradox suggests views that contradict each other but which contain truth. It is clearly possible to view all of the different and sometimes contradictory perspectives offered by these essays as true and at the same time reflective of each other, thus creating a better picture of Dreiser as a whole. These essayists show that it is possible to view Dreiser from such vastly different angles that a new Dreiser emerges, one of extraordinary depth and complexity, one who not only goes "beyond naturalism" but who clearly has all the enduring qualities of a classic American writer.

Notes

1. The controversy that surrounded Dreiser began with his first novel, *Sister Carrie*, in 1900, and includes *The "Genius,"* in 1915, whose banning was protested by almost five hundred American writers. *An American Tragedy* was barred in Boston in 1927 along with a number of other books. In protest, an anticensorship rally was held, and Margaret Sanger appeared with her mouth taped shut in a gesture of opposition against the city's ban on birth control. The rally drew much newspaper coverage, and the participants were portrayed as advocates of "dirty" books. See Richard Lingeman, *Theodore Dreiser: An American Journey, 1908–1945* (New York: Putnam's Sons, 1990), pp. 138–9, 141, 288, 321–2.

2. I particularly wish to thank Albert Ashforth for his extensive editing of this essay. I also wish to thank Florian Stuber, Madelyn Larsen, and Leonard Cassuto for their many suggestions.

3. Lionel Trilling's essay on Dreiser was probably the most damaging article on Dreiser ever written and probably the one most often read. See Lionel Trilling, "Reality in America," in *The Liberal Imagination* (New York: Viking, 1950).

4. See Laura Hapke, *Tales of the Working Girl: Wage-Earning Women in American Literature, 1890–1925* (New York: Twayne, 1992), pp. 69–85. She provides a compelling, historically based argument about Dreiser's ambivalence regarding work and the feminine character.

Also see Miriam Gogol's review of her volume, "At Long Last: 'Tales of the Working Girl,'" *Dreiser Studies* 23 (Fall 1992): 43.

5. Vera Dreiser, *My Uncle Dreiser* (New York: Nash, 1976), p. 185. Dreiser's *Diaries* are filled with telling statements. In a typical encounter, Dreiser tells one of his lovers, Bert, that "she must accept me as I am. I am to come or go as I choose. I refuse to dine with her or sleep with her every night unless I want to" (November 11, 1917). In another, Dreiser generalizes about his inner state: "Feel very sad to think affection is always jealous and painful, in myself and everyone" (November 21, 1917). In yet another: "Tired of my various girls and wish I had a new love" (November 2, 1917).

Also, see his entries on February 8, 1916, February 10, 1916, February 11, 1916, and October 17, 1916. *Theodore Dreiser: The American Diaries, 1902–1926*, ed. Thomas P. Riggio (Philadelphia: University of Pennsylvania Press, 1982).

There is ample evidence that many of the women in Dreiser's life were made extremely unhappy and felt abandoned by him. To cite a few, Anna Tatum took to drink shortly after becoming involved with him. Louise Campbell wanted to marry him but knew that he never would. Kirah Markham, whom some have argued wanted her freedom, said "What's the good of a freedom I don't want and can't use?" Estelle Kubitz's hysterics at finding traces of other women led her to cry in her sleep. She said she could not live with those unknown rivals whose letters she occasionally discovered and Dreiser could not give them up. But even more than them, she could not compete with the phantom of that "impossible she": "You want me to compete with a wraith, an illusion. . . . Well it can't be done and I don't propose to try" (quoted in Richard Lingeman, *Theodore Dreiser: An American Journey*, pp. 155, 134).

6. The other early exception who comes to mind is the iconoclastic Anzia Yezierska, that "sweatshop Cinderella," who created self-transforming heroines in *Bread Givers* (1925), *Children of Loneliness* (1923), *Hungry Hearts and Other Stories* (1920–1927), and so on. For an excellent discussion of her contributions, see Laura Hapke, *Tales of the Working Girl: Wage-Earning Women in American Literature, 1890–1925*, pp. 111–8.

7. Karen J. Winkler, "Seductions of Biography," *The Chronicle of Higher Education* 27 (October 1993): A6.

8. Biographers have always perceived Dreiser's life as relevant, current, and contemporary with contradictions and conflicts that we can recognize in ourselves. Studies keep appearing about his life and his relationships with people. Note *The New York Times Book Review*'s cover

story (March 8, 1992) on Dreiser and H. L. Mencken and numerous other articles, and consider the large number of biographies that have been published to date: Richard Lingeman, *Theodore Dreiser: At the Gates of the City, 1871–1907* (New York: Putnam's Sons, 1986) and *Theodore Dreiser: An American Journey, 1908–1945*; W. A. Swanberg, *Dreiser* (New York: Charles Scribner's Sons, 1965); Helen Dreiser, *My Life with Dreiser* (New York: World Publishing, 1951); Dorothy Dudley, *Forgotten Frontiers: Dreiser and the Land of the Free* (New York: H. Smith and R. Haas, 1932); and H. L. Mencken, "Theodore Dreiser," in *A Book of Prefaces* (New York: Knopf, 1920). We also have critical studies that include biography: Lawrence E. Hussman, *Dreiser and His Fiction: A Twentieth-Century Quest* (Philadelphia: University of Pennsylvania Press, 1983); Yoshinobu Hakutani, *Young Dreiser: A Critical Study* (Rutherford, N.J.: Fairleigh Dickinson University Press, 1980); Donald Pizer, *The Novels of Theodore Dreiser: A Critical Study* (Minneapolis: University of Minnesota Press, 1976); Robert Penn Warren, *Homage to Theodore Dreiser* (New York: Random House, 1971); Richard Lehan, *Theodore Dreiser: His World and His Novels* (Carbondale: Southern Illinois University Press, 1969); Ellen Moers, *Two Dreisers* (New York: Viking, 1969); Philip Gerber, *Theodore Dreiser Revisited* (New York: Twayne, 1992); and F. O. Matthiessen, *Theodore Dreiser* (New York: W. Sloane Associates, 1951). But, as Donald Pizer indicates, these accounts provide only a fraction of the rich biographical material available, for much of it was written by his contemporaries. See Donald Pizer, Richard W. Dowell, and Frederic E. Rusch, *Theodore Dreiser: A Primary Bibliography and Reference Guide* (Boston: G. K. Hall, 1991), p. 94.

9. The last collection of original essays on Dreiser's canon appeared in 1971 (John Lydenberg, ed., *Dreiser: A Collection of Critical Essays* [Englewood Cliffs, N.J.: Prentice-Hall, 1971]). In 1981, Donald Pizer published *Critical Essays on Theodore Dreiser*. The purpose of that volume, however, was not to provide new original essays on Dreiser's canon, but rather to reprint articles of literary or historical significance dating from 1901 (W. M. Reedy) to 1977 (Pizer). See Donald Pizer, ed., *Critical Essays on Theodore Dreiser* (Boston: G. K. Hall, 1981). The only recent collection of essays pertains exclusively to one novel, *Sister Carrie*, and includes such excellent essays as Alan Tractenberg's "Who Narrates: Dreiser's Presence in *Sister Carrie*." See Donald Pizer, ed. *New Essays on SISTER CARRIE* (Cambridge and New York: Cambridge University Press, 1991).

10. For some of the important discussions of the significance of the term "naturalism," see Alfred Kazin, *On Native Grounds: An Interpretation of Modern American Prose Literature* (New York: Harcourt, 1942);

Lars Ahnebrink, *The Beginnings of Naturalism in American Fiction: A Study of the Works of Hamlin Garland, Stephen Crane, and Frank Norris with Special References to Some European Influences, 1891–1903* (Cambridge: Harvard University Press, 1950); Charles C. Walcutt, *American Literary Naturalism, A Divided Stream* (Minneapolis: University of Minnesota Press, 1956); Larzer Ziff, *The American 1890s: Life and Times of a Lost Generation* (New York: Viking, 1968); Haskell M. Block, *Naturalistic Triptych: The Fictive and the Real in Zola, Mann, and Dreiser* (New York: Random House, 1969); Richard Lehan, *Theodore Dreiser: His World and His Novels*; Donald Pizer, *Realism and Naturalism in Nineteenth-Century American Literature* (Carbondale: Southern Illinois University Press, 1966; rev. ed., 1984). Also see June Howard, *Form and History in American Literary Naturalism* (Chapel Hill: University of North Carolina, 1985) and Lee Clark Mitchell, *Determined Fictions: American Literary Naturalism* (New York: Columbia University Press, 1989). See Mitchell, pp. vii–xvii and 131–4 (notes 2, 6, and 7), for a summary of studies that have defined historical influences on American naturalism and for a discussion of scholars' sometimes contradictory definitions of the movement (from 1942–1987).

11. Donald Pizer, Richard W. Dowell, and Frederic E. Rusch, *Theodore Dreiser: A Primary Bibliography and Reference Guide*, p. 93.

12. Donald Pizer, *Realism and Naturalism in Nineteenth-Century American Literature*. (Quotation, p. 10.)

13. Walcutt, p. 20.

14. Pizer, *Realism and Naturalism in Nineteenth-Century American Literature*, pp. 10, 11.

15. See note 10 for titles of some of the works by Walcutt, Lehan, and Pizer. Also see Ellen Moers, *Two Dreisers*.

16. The well-documented efforts at dismissing Dreiser began in 1915 with Stuart P. Sherman's famous essay, "The Naturalism of Mr. Dreiser," which Sherman later retitled, "The Barbaric Naturalism of Theodore Dreiser."

17. Throughout his career, Dreiser regarded himself as a realist not a naturalist. See his letters to H. L. Mencken, March 22, 1915, and March 29, 1915. Thomas P. Riggio, ed., *Dreiser-Mencken Letters: The Correspondence of Theodore Dreiser and H. L. Mencken, 1907–1945*.

18. Amy Kaplan, *The Social Construction of American Realism* (Chicago: University of Chicago Press, 1988); Eric J. Sundquist, ed., *American Realism: New Essays* (Baltimore: Johns Hopkins University Press), 1982.

19. Walter Benn Michaels. *The Gold Standard and the Logic of Naturalism* (Berkeley: University of California Press, 1987), pp. 26, 27; emphasis added.

20. For example, see Walter Benn Michaels, *The Gold Standard and the Logic of Naturalism*; Philip Fisher, *Hard Facts: Setting and Form in the American Novel* (New York: Oxford University Press, 1985); Mark Seltzer, *Bodies and Machines* (New York: Routledge and Kegan Paul, 1992); Howard Horwitz, *By the Laws of Nature: Form and Value in Nineteenth-Century America* (New York: Oxford University Press, 1991); Louis J. Zanine, *Mechanism and Mysticism: The Influence of Science on the Thought and Work of Theodore Dreiser* (Philadelphia: University of Pennsylvania Press, 1993); *Papers on Language and Literature* 27 (Spring 1991); Michael Davitt Bell, *The Problem of American Realism: Studies in the Cultural History of a Literary Idea* (Chicago: University of Chicago Press, 1993).

21. Among a few others, see Amy Kaplan, *The Social Construction of American Realism*; Rachel Bowlby, *Just Looking: Consumer Culture in Dreiser, Gissing and Zola* (New York and London: Methuen, 1985); Susan Wolsterholme, "Brother Theodore, Hell on Women," in *American Novelists Revisited: Essays in Feminist Criticism*, ed. Fritz Fleischmann (Boston: G. K. Hall, 1982); Mary A. Burgan, "*Sister Carrie* and the Pathos of Naturalism," *Criticism* 15 (Fall 1973): 336–49; Cathy N. Davidson and Arnold E. Davidson. "Carrie's Sisters: The Popular Stereotypes for Dreiser's Heroines," *Modern Fiction Studies* 23 (Autumn 1977): 395–407; Dorothy Dudley, *Forgotten Frontiers: Dreiser and the Land of the Free*, 1932; Ellen Moers, *Two Dreisers*, 1969; Helen Dreiser, *My Life with Dreiser*, 1951.

22. Saul Bellow, "An Interview with Saul Bellow" *Publishers Weekly* 204 (October 22, 1973): 74.

Dreiser and the Discourse of Gender[1]

Shelley Fisher Fishkin

As feminist critics have trained their eyes on the masculinist prism through which American culture filtered so much of women's experiences, they have focused on the work of Cooper, Emerson, Thoreau, Hawthorne, James, Twain, Hemingway, Faulkner, and many others—but not Dreiser. The one feminist essay on Dreiser, published in 1982, concludes with the verdict that he is, "if not a feminist, at least a fellow traveller, allied with feminists in a struggle against patriarchy."[2] When Theodore Dreiser has been charged with "uncaring womanizing," as he was by male critics at an MLA panel in 1983, two of the women in his life, Marguerite Tjader Harris and Yvette Eastman, leaped to his public defense.[3]

Dreiser has fared well at the hands of both women critics and women in his life for good reasons. Compared with many of his fellow writers, Dreiser's efforts to craft believable women characters in his fiction were often exemplary, a fact that has drawn talented women critics to his work. And compared with many of his male contemporaries, Dreiser's empathy for the emotional and psychological needs and intellectual aspirations of real-life women was legendary, inspiring positive testimonials in person and in print. Dissent from this ringing consensus—such as that of biographer William Swanberg—came to be thought of as suspect, given the prudish standards of behavior that inspired the attack.

It would be naive, however, to take feminists' silence on Dreiser as proof of his unfailing ability to extricate himself from the culture's ideology of gender. He was both ahead of his time and a creature of his time, a knot of contradictions as intricate and complicated as the culture itself. Through him one can read that culture's ambivalences and tensions regarding women. A man and writer as complex as Dreiser requires a second look—on this,

1

as on virtually any other subject. This essay (along with Irene Gammel's in this volume) is a first step in this reexamination.

The current critical climate encourages more subtle and complex readings of the discourse of gender than those that characterized the first wave of feminist criticism in the 1970s and early 1980s. Essay collections such as Nancy Miller's *The Poetics of Gender* (1986) and Elaine Showalter's *Speaking of Gender* (1989) foreground such issues as "the contingency of the dominant male tradition," the differences between male and female writers' treatments of a subject, and "the social conditions of literary production" (including the study of "the conditions necessary for writing at all.")[4] They also problematize, in complex ways, the means by which gender shapes the power dynamics that operate in a culture. And recent books by and about male feminists[5] reveal the diversity of perspectives held by men who are openly committed (as Dreiser never was) to a feminist agenda.

These books and others suggest questions that critics have never asked of Dreiser's work. For example, feminist critics' concern with the "contingency of the dominant male tradition" might lead us to ask how Dreiser's sources shaped the gender dynamics of his fiction. *An American Tragedy* was based on newspaper reports of the Chester Gillette trial, reports that reiterated uncritically a range of gender stereotypes that dominated turn-of-the-century journalism. To what extent did Dreiser reinscribe those stereotypes in his fiction? Critics' call for comparative investigation of male and female imaginative models might lead us to ask what a feminist writer might have made from the same raw materials. Contemporary interest in the "the social conditions of literary production" and "the conditions necessary for writing" suggest questions about the role women played in the creation of Dreiser's work, and the opportunities open to young women writers in the early twentieth century. What did the aspiring women writers who linked their lives to Dreiser's gain from what was clearly a symbiotic relationship, and what did they lose? What were they willing to give up, and why? These questions suggest that there is still much we need to learn about the sexual politics of the culture that shaped Dreiser and that his art, in turn, helped shape.

To what extent did Dreiser transcend the gender discourse of his time, and to what extent did he reinscribe it in new ways? This question is the backdrop for this essay. Given the limitations of time and space, this essay is of necessity a case study, a piece of a bigger puzzle, one small approach to this large question, a beginning. As it weaves together elements of Dreiser's art and biography, feminist theory, and popular culture to understand both the conventions that dominated representations of women in the early part of the twentieth century and Dreiser's adherence to or departure from them, it marks some potentially fruitful directions for future research.

Critics have devoted much attention to Dreiser's best-known imaginative representations of women, Carrie and Jennie. This essay will turn the spotlight on some Dreiser women who have remained largely in the shadows. First and foremost is the central female character in the Dreiser novel which received the greatest critical and popular acclaim, *An American Tragedy*.[6] Roberta Alden has been generally ignored by critics in their rush to comment on Dreiser's larger themes in the book and on his masterful characterization of Clyde Griffiths, the central consciousness of the novel. Just as Roberta has been overshadowed by Clyde, the women Dreiser pulled into his orbit in real life have been overshadowed by Dreiser: we have attended to them solely as they reflect and illuminate aspects of the male figure that has been our main focus of interest. An examination of Dreiser's relation to the discourse of gender of his time demands that we move these figures from the periphery to the center of our attention.

Before she achieved immortality as Dreiser's "Roberta Alden," Billy Brown[7] (who was murdered in upstate New York in 1906) came to national attention through the journalists' accounts of her during the Gillette murder trial. I will begin by exploring the ways in which the newspaper reporters' representations of Billy Brown conformed to the dominant culture's ideology of gender and will then examine the ways in which Dreiser reiterated or expanded on their representations in his account of this woman's life in his novel. Both the reporters' and Dreiser's versions of Billy Brown will be compared with information about her that emerges from the trial transcript and other historical sources. Dreiser's representations of Billy Brown and of other real-life women, in both his published writing and his private letters, are the result of his shaping and selection (both consciously and unconsciously) of a range of historical materials and cultural conventions. I will examine this shaping process to gain insight into the culture's ideology of gender in the first part of this century, and Dreiser's response to it.

Billy Brown

Dreiser's first encounter with Billy Brown was in the pages of the *New York World,* and newspaper accounts remained his major source throughout his work on the novel.[8] In all of the press coverage of the Gillette murder trial, Billy Brown was made to play her assigned role in the courtroom melodrama: victim. It was a familiar role for women under popular Victorian conceptions of womanhood.[9] For the purposes of the press, the most important thing about Billy Brown was that she was dead. Beyond that, reporters were eager to tap into their readers' readiness to read yet another story of innocence wronged, a story dripping with all the pathos that could be wrung from it, with roots in the cautionary tales that had played such a prominent role in both folk and literary traditions in this country for more than a century.

For this reason, all that the readers of the *New York World* learned about Billy Brown was that she had been an innocent, respectable farmer's daughter—not unlike thousands of other farmers' daughters in upstate New York—who had been cruelly murdered by a cold-blooded, social-climbing young man who had first violated her sexually and then refused to marry her. District Attorney Ward, for example, noted: "It will not take me long to tell you who Grace Brown was. She was a clean, pure, honest girl" (*New York World,* November 17, 1906). The paragraphs devoted to Billy Brown in the newspaper were primarily of two sorts: those describing her corpse, and those quoting from the pleading letters she wrote to Gillette.

It is understandable why these particular elements would dominate the newspaper accounts. Dreiser's own memories of his experiences as a newspaper reporter in St. Louis suggest the central role murder and seduction played in turn-of-the-century journalism. Of his editor at the St. Louis *Republic*, Dreiser wrote, in *Newspaper Days*:

> Deaths, murders, great social or political scandals or upheavals and the like, those things which presented the rough, raw facts of life, as well as its tenderer aspects, seemed to throw him into an ecstasy—not over the woes of others but over the fact that he was to have an interesting paper tomorrow. . . . "Ah, it was a terrible thing, was it? He killed her in cold blood, eh? You say there was a great crowd out there, do you? . . . Well! Well! Well, write it all up. Write it all up. Looks like a pretty good story to me—doesn't it to you?. . . You can have as much space as you want for that—column, a column and a half, or two—just as it runs. Let me look at it before you turn it in." Then he would begin whistling or singing . . . or would walk up and down in the city-room rubbing his hands in obvious satisfaction.[10]

Dreiser noted that when no story "of immediate import was supplied by the daily news," his editor "created new ones himself, studying out interesting phases of past romances or crimes in the city which he thought it would be worthwhile for me to work up. . . . "[11]

The murder of Billy Brown had all the qualities Dreiser's editor in St. Louis sought so avidly: it was long on graphic gore and it was long on heartrending emotions. And if there was one paper in the country that was equipped to sensationalize a naturally sensational story like this one, it was Pulitzer's *World*. Two of the most prominent headlines on January 1, 1894, for example, the year Dreiser took a short-lived job on the *World*, were "Shot His Bride Dead" and "Done by a Fiend." The kind of journalism the *World* had come to represent was satirized in an 1897 cartoon in the comic magazine *Life* titled "In the Old Pit Shaft": as two gentlemen descend through an old mine shaft into the snake-infested belly of the earth, one excursionist asks the other, "Doesn't it terrify you—the depths to which we are descending?" "Oh, no!" replies his friend, "I'm a reporter for the New York *World*."[12]

The *World*'s artists had a heyday with illustrations for the stories of the Gillette trial, often filling a full quarter of the paper's front page, and occasional full pages inside, with drawings of "Chester Gillette as He Appears on Trial for His Life, and the Girl with Whose Murder He is Charged," "Chester Gillette as He Appeared in Court and His Senior Counsel," "Chester Gillette as He Appeared on the Witness Stand Telling His Version of Grace Brown's Death," and so on. In these artists' pictures, Billy Brown is portrayed as a woman who stepped out of a Victorian cameo: beautiful, chaste, with her hair in the current Gibson-girl fashion (a style that the real Billy Brown could never persuade her hair to follow—as photographs of her reveal).[13]

The *World* covered the gory coroner's report in loving detail and also quoted extensively from the letters Billy Brown had sent to Gillette. The letters of Billy Brown that drove the jurors to tears were sold on the courtroom steps in a specially published pamphlet and were hungrily bought by the scores of spectators at the trial. The helpless, pleading tone of those documents, the sense of innocence wronged, of good faith betrayed, of young womanhood tarnished and destroyed, rang oddly familiar: it was a not-so-distant cousin of the sentimental fiction against which realist and naturalist novelists at the end of the nineteenth century rebelled. Parts of them resemble bestsellers from the end of the eighteenth century, such as Susanna Rowson's *Charlotte Temple* or Hannah Webster Foster's *The Coquette*, both cautionary tales in which the seduced and abandoned woman, like Billy Brown, dies before the story's end.[14]

But the entrepreneur who published Billy Brown's letters and the reporters, as well, expressed no interest in another batch of letters that surfaced at the trial: those from Chester Gillette. The letters he wrote to Billy Brown, during a period when she went home suddenly to comfort a bereaved sister, are pleading in their own special key. "You don't know how lonesome it is now with less work for me and nothing to do evenings. . . . Hurry back as you don't know how lonesome it is here," Gillette wrote in one of them. "Dear how I miss you," he wrote in another.[15] (It is ironic that these letters—which were never quoted in the papers and which Dreiser probably never saw—bear a distinct resemblance to innumerable letters Dreiser himself would send over the course of his life to innumerable young women, all of whom—for the moment, at least—he had great trouble doing without. To Marguerite Tjader Harris, for example, he wrote, "I'm so truly lonely"; and on another occasion, "I miss you so painfully you may not guess how much."[16]) Billy Brown's letters, unlike Gillette's, fit the paradigm: they fleshed out the image of her as victim. Gillette's letters did not. In the melodrama at hand, he was to be portrayed as a monster. The letters made him sound vulnerably human. Therefore they were excised from the journalists' records.

Several other points did not make it from the courtroom into the press for the same reason: they were extraneous to the gendered morality play that was being presented in the media. (The prosecutor, of course, was enacting a drama not vastly different from that featured in the press. The difference is that the lawyers did not control everything that witnesses said in the courtroom, but the journalists did control all that they wrote in the newspapers. In other words, material that did not "fit" the arguments being made managed to slip into various testimonies during the trial, but were largely edited out by the lawyers in their summaries and by journalists in their reports.) In each of these areas, the elements of Billy Brown's character challenge the weak, passive, feminine "victim" role in which she was cast during the trial.

First is the issue of professional competence. According to the representations of her in the *World*, Billy Brown worked in the factory alongside the other "girls" in unexceptional ways. In fact, as Craig Brandon has noted, "she proved to be such a good worker that she seems to have filled in at a number of jobs for other workers who went on vacation."[17] In addition, she was soon advanced to a position of some responsibility as an inspector.[18] Billy Brown's versatile skills as a worker and inspector (possibly a source of some personal satisfaction and pride as well) gave her a measure of mobility in the factory, which in turn made it easier for her to meet Gillette.

Second is the issue of intellectual curiosity. The Billy Brown of the newspaper reports never opens a book, but evidence indicates that reading was a key part of Billy Brown's life — and that it may have been precisely her thirst for intellectual stimulation that attracted her initially to Gillette. As fellow workers testified at the trial, Chester Gillette and Billy Brown shared an affection for popular magazines and newspapers of the day and both spent a great deal of their free time reading.[19] Craig Brandon notes that Billy "also showed an interest in more literary subjects, a love for which was probably instilled by her friend and teacher Maude Kenyon," who had ignited her love of books during high school.[20]

As a coworker recalled, Billy "was trying to educate herself to be (Gillette's) equal." She noted that Grace was always proud that Chester had been to "college."[21] In fact, Chester had not been to college: he *had* attended Oberlin, but it was the Oberlin preparatory school. He did nothing, however, to disabuse friends of the image of him as a "college man." Instead, he encouraged it, telling tales about his adventures "in college" and in the West.[22] Despite all his dissembling about "college," Chester *was*, in fact, better educated than anyone else Billy knew in Cortland, and was the only person with whom she could discuss the books, newspapers, and magazines she read.

Third is the subject of Billy's sexual drive. The prosecuting attorney at the trial was determined to characterize Billy Brown's first sexual encounter with Chester Gillette as an experience as close to rape as he could make it. Reporters covering the trial made clear how shocked the jurors, the public, and they themselves were by Chester Gillette's initial intimation, on the witness stand, that he may not have forced himself on Billy. The following exchange transpired in the courtroom:

Q. Gillette; whose house were you in when [improper relations] first occurred?
A. I was at her sister's house.
Q. Where were you?
A. In Cortland.
Q. Where were you in the house?
A. In the parlor I guess it is called.

Q. Did you struggle with the girl?
A. No sir.[23]

His questioner then rephrases the question in several ways until Chester gives him the "yes" answer that he seeks. "Did she say 'No; no' many times?" he asks; and "Before you accomplished the purpose of having sexual intercourse with this girl did she struggle and resist you?" Chester eventually assents.

The *World* reported this exchange as follows:

Before you succeeded in overcoming "Billy" Brown did she resist you?

No.

And as Gillette gave that answer he realized what he had done. There was menace in the face of every man in the courtroom. He tried his best to overcome the resentment he had aroused. . . . (November 29, 1906)

If Billy Brown had not resisted Chester Gillette in their initial sexual encounter, "every man in the courtroom" — and presumably in the reading public — did not want to know about it.

I suggest that Billy Brown's competence at her work, her desire to have someone to talk to about what she read, and her potential sense of her own sexual autonomy ran counter to the dominant ideology of gender of her day. The masculinist prism through which the reporters viewed her life prevented them from seeing her as a complex and whole woman, and led them to cast her, instead, as a weak, passive, dependent — i.e., stereotypically "feminine" — victim. Dreiser, as we will see, did the same.[24]

Gender Stereotypes at the Turn of the Century

Work outside the home for a woman was viewed, throughout most of the culture, as a sometimes necessary and always unfortunate way station along the road to marriage.[25] For this reason, whether a woman was good at her work simply did not matter. Marriage was really the only plot women could enact in literature as well as life.

Charlotte Perkins Gilman bemoaned the pervasiveness of the tyrannous love plot as the only story women could tell or enact: "Love and love and love — from 'first sight' to marriage. There it stops — just the fluttering ribbon of announcement, 'and lived happily ever after.' Is that kind of fiction any sort of picture of a woman's life?"[26] William Dean Howells, as well, recognized the ubiquitousness of the love plot: "A love intrigue of some sort," he wrote, "is all but essential to the popularity of any fiction."[27]

The love plot was no less pervasive in life—particularly for working-class women. In *The Long Day: The Story of a New York Working Girl Told by Herself* (1905), Dorothy Richardson writes of a woman worker, "She has become successful in the only way a woman can, after all, be successful. Minnie is married."[28] Mary McDowell, a labor organizer, cited the dominance of the love plot as the key obstacle to organizing "wage-earning women to better their economic conditions," and noted that the same dreams animate young women of all economic classes: "The workers are young—they dream of marriage, of giving up the world of wages to make a home for 'that not impossible he, wrapped up in mystery.' The girls do not differ from the young in any walk of life. They no more consider the welfare of that mysterious future than does the daughter of their boss."[29]

In popular culture, as well as in the testimony of organizers, social workers, and fiction writers, the love plot loomed large in young women's imaginations, as this turn-of-the-century Yiddish folk song sung in New York makes clear:

Day the same as night, night the same as day.
And all I do is sew and sew and sew.
May God help me and my love come soon.
That I may leave this work and go.[30]

A headline that ran next to the lead headline, "Gillette Found Guilty of First Degree Murder" in the *World* was, "Factory Girls, 14 of 'Em, Wed in a Day." The factory owner was glad to "wish them all happiness," but was worried about how to replace them; obviously, there was no question of their returning to work after marriage.[31] If work was something to be left for marriage as soon as possible, there was no point in developing any pride about it. Absent, for the most part, from both popular culture and high culture were stories in which women took pride in a job well done.[32]

A woman's thirst for intellectual stimulation was also, as far as the dominant paradigms of the culture were concerned, beside the point. Popular pseudoscientific discourse argued that women had "inferior brain weight" or "a tendency to brain fever if educated."[33] The president of Harvard proclaimed that American women "should recognize that the most satisfying intellectual pursuits of women are those associated with marriage, childrearing, and the schooling of young children."[34] Although by the end of the century more than 5,000 women were graduating yearly from the nation's colleges and the majority were moving into the labor force,[35] popular stereotypes still generally ignored women's interest in things of the mind and focused on their concern with fashion or domesticity, as the women's pages in the nation's newspapers during this period testify.

As for women's sexual drive, despite challenges from Free Love advocates like Victoria Woodhull and Emma Goldman, the message from mainstream popular culture at the turn of the century was fairly clear: respectable women didn't have it.[36] Or if they did, they channeled it quietly into their marriages and certainly did not talk about it. In the pervading popular paradigm, women were divided into two classes, those who were "pure" and those who were "impure." A popular nineteenth-century advice book to young women, for example, prints sketches of the two paths women might take on two opposite sides of the page, and accompanies them with verbal descriptions. There is a direct progression from sketches labeled "At 15, In questionable company" to "At 20, Idle and immodest," to "At 26, Immoral and outcast," to "At 40, In poverty and wretchedness." On the opposite side of the page there is a direct progression from "At 15, Studious and modest," to "At 20, Virtuous and intelligent," to "At 26, A happy mother," to "At 70, An estimable grandmother."[37] When sexual relations took place outside of marriage—even if marriage was the result—the popular assumption was that the woman had been seduced and betrayed, not that she might have been expressing her own sexual desires.[38]

Roberta Alden

The fact that Dreiser's initial encounter with Billy Brown came mediated through the formulaic sensationalism of the turn-of-the-century popular press was a key factor shaping the representation of her that he wrote into his 1925 novel. In many ways, Dreiser simply passed along to readers of his novel the stereotyped Billy Brown the reporters had presented in the press. In his version, as in theirs, her competence at her job and any intellectual curiosity she may have had, are largely erased. Roberta Alden takes no special pride in her work. Her mind is empty of all but inarticulate yearnings—yearnings after affection, love, social status, and material goods[39]—and the only book she opens in the course of the novel is a seed catalogue (294).[40]

Her attitudes towards sex may be more complex than those which the reporters ascribed to Billy Brown in the newspapers, but ultimately she is characterized as passive, reactive, and weak.[41] Roberta Alden fantasizes, for example, that she and Clyde "might sit and talk and hold hands perhaps. He might even put his arms around her waist, and she might let him." But she checks herself in the next sentence: "That would be terrible, as some people here would see it, she knew. And it would never do for him to know that—never. That would be too intimate—too bold" (262). Later, when Clyde escalates physical contact, Dreiser tells us, in words that could have come straight out of the mouth of the District Attorney, "he held her while she resisted him," but then adds, "although it was almost impossible for her to do so" (274). Ultimately, Dreiser has Clyde succeed with Roberta over her protests, after weeks of calculated psychological manipulation.

It is worth noting, however, that the prose with which Dreiser limns the change in their relationship is as lacking in active verbs as the murky ambiguous prose he uses to describe the drowning: "The wonder and delight of a new and more intimate form of contact, of protest gainsaid, of scruples overcome! Days, when both, having struggled in vain against the greater intimacy which each knew that the other was desirous of yielding to, and eventually so yielding, looked forward to the approaching night with an eagerness which was as a fever embodying a fear" (299). Floating noun clusters and exclamations replace active verbs. As in the drowning sequence, the absence of a subject and verb in the sentence makes it hard to assign responsibility for activities that transpire.[42] Roberta's tendency to be demanding, victimizing, and self-victimizing are natural extensions of her own victimization: the essence of her character is still that of pure, passive, vulnerable, pitiable victim.

One should not assume that *all* of Dreiser's characterizations of women fit this mold. On other occasions—in works that earned him less popular acclaim, such as *Sister Carrie* and *A Gallery of Women*—Dreiser departed from these gender stereotypes in notable ways. Dreiser's Carrie (an actress), his Olive Brand (a poet), and his Ellen Adams Wrynn (an artist) are examples of women who took pride in their work. Carrie reads a little; Olive Brand reads a lot. Both are portrayed (sympathetically) as intellectually curious. And all three of these women are more sexually autonomous, as Dreiser paints them, than was Roberta.[43] The fact that Dreiser was capable of writing against the culture's gender stereotypes on these occasions does not negate the fact that in *An American Tragedy*, his most famous and most widely read novel, for the most part he accepted them. It is even possible that his adherence to the culture's stereotypes in this book may help explain the novel's stunning commercial viability. As Philip Gerber has noted, the popular success of *An American Tragedy* was immediate and unprecedented. Despite its having been issued in two volumes (at a whopping five dollars a set), by the end of 1926 the novel had sold more than 50,000 copies, and its publisher, Horace Liveright, had negotiated the sale of screen rights to Famous Players for $90,000, in that day a startling sum for residuals.[44]

It is interesting, by way of contrast, that the books in which Dreiser departed from or challenged the culture's ideology of gender (such as *Sister Carrie* or *The "Genius"*) were, commercially speaking, largely unsuccessful.[45]

Stereotypes are rooted in realities; most likely there were real-life women in Dreiser's world who resembled, on occasion, the stereotypical Billy Brown painted in the press. Dreiser clearly had sympathy for their plight and empathized with their pain. But the fact that stereotypes about women may have their roots in reality does not negate the power of these stereotypes. Once reified and interpreted by the culture to define the condition of most women most of the time, they confine and constrict a woman's sense of herself and her possibilities.

At times, Dreiser simply accepted the reporters' accounts. Thus, in describing Billy Brown, he chose not to reshape that material in significant ways. In the process, he naturalized the assumptions that informed the accounts in the press. That is different from the choices he made regarding Chester Gillette, as a number of critics have established.[46] Dreiser changed the facts of Gillette's life to make his character a more sympathetic "everyman" figure. This was part of his project of underscoring the normality underlying the criminal in American life.[47] "The crime in the novel is truly the creative product of the author's philosophy and experience," Kathryn M. Plank noted, commenting on the changes Dreiser made in Gillette's story to fit his preconceived paradigm and "observations of American society."[48] To render "the tragic reality at the center of the American dream," Donald Pizer has observed, Dreiser felt it necessary to reshape a man represented in the press as "a shallow-minded murderer" into "any one of us."[49] Dreiser did not find it necessary to reshape a woman who had been represented in the press in equally stereotypical terms: that characterization fit his artistic needs.

The gender stereotypes that emerge in Dreiser's representation of Billy Brown reflect those that obtained in the culture at large at the time of her death in 1906. But by the time Dreiser was writing the novel—the 1920s—they had begun to change. Dissident voices were more audible and alternative images of gender more readily available, both in the real world and in literature. Although Dreiser allowed the automobile culture of the 1920s to creep into his novel, which was set around 1906 and earlier, he kept the changing images of women out of it.

Alternate Realities

How might another kind of imagination have reinterpreted Billy Brown? The tragic reality at the center of the American dream for Dreiser was, on this occasion, a tragic reality seen from a masculinist perspective. What might a feminist contemporary of Dreiser's—a Charlotte Perkins Gilman or an Edna St. Vincent Millay, for example—have done with the same raw material? Gilman was interested in the special attraction to women of men who took them seriously intellectually or professionally, who engaged them in spirited conversation. Millay was intrigued by the satisfaction women took in the erotic dimension of their lives. How might someone not content with the stereotypical portrayal of Billy, much as Dreiser was not content with the stereotypical portrayal of Chester Gillette, have reshaped her story? Might there be another Billy Brown lurking underneath the stereotype—one we can never exhume, but whom we might imagine?

This Billy Brown may have taken pride in her work, in the quickness with which she learned her job, the ease with which she related to coworkers, the intelligence with which she mastered her new environment. This Billy Brown thirsted for conversation about books and magazines and newspapers she read. She loved to talk about literary characters as if they were living, breathing human beings. She liked brief excursions into philosophy, psychology—she didn't use those terms, of course; she simply liked talking about what made people tick. After her teacher and friend Maude Kenyon married and after Billy moved to Cortland, there was no one she could share these thoughts with, no one she could talk with about what she read. Then Chester Gillette came along. He was the one person in the factory who could carry on a conversation about books, who thought about what he read, who had been to college, who liked hearing her ideas. He was a good listener. It was such a relief to break through that loneliness, to find someone else as anxious as she was to read the next installment of the latest popular novel in the local paper. They would talk over lunch break in the factory, and she would give him candy she'd brought as a treat. She had longed for someone to talk to like this, ever since Maude had gone. She liked the way he made her feel. She liked touching him. She liked it when he touched her. . . . She wanted those talks in the parlor late at night to go on forever. . . .

The foregoing fiction is, of course, my own; I am not asking it of Dreiser. I have drawn it merely to suggest some alternative ways in which this same raw material might have been molded; it is designed to emphasize the malleability of the "facts" on which Dreiser's novel was based.

We can never meet *this* Billy Brown. We can only imagine her. Did Dreiser meet her in a new incarnation as he worked on his novel in the 1920s? It is true that challenges to the dominant paradigm did, by this time, exist.[50] "New Women" of the 1920s, like Edna St. Vincent Millay, were forthright in asserting their right to be sensual, sexual beings on their own terms. Victories won by Margaret Sanger (to whose *Birth Control Review* Dreiser contributed) helped clear the way for women to maintain and express more sexual autonomy. Charlotte Perkins Gilman and others argued that it was important for women to lead fulfilling, independent lives beyond the confines of the domestic sphere. However, while the 1920s did bring challenges to the ideology of gender that had dominated at the turn of the century, many of them remained relatively muted. For example, despite the fact that by the 1920s women had moved into the workforce in unprecedented numbers and had made their way into many professions, popular images of women who took pride in their work lagged far behind. As June Sochen has noted, "[Zona] Gale herself was sympathetic to the women's movement, had written for feminist publications, and understood the positions of such New York City feminists as Crystal Eastman and Henrietta Rodman. But neither she nor Fannie Hurst dared to portray a woman who led a rich, purposeful life independent of a husband and marriage. Both authors were themselves independent, but both upheld traditional values in their writing."[51]

If we cannot meet the "other" Billy Brown in Dreiser's text or in the text the reporters have given us, there is one place where we *can* meet her — or at least her very close cousin: in Dreiser's life. The Billy Brown we can imaginatively exhume from beneath those layers of cultural iconography bears a striking resemblance to the many real-life young women who were so important to Dreiser's work and well-being. Why did he seek out such women, and why were they attracted to him? How did he respond to their thirst for intellectual growth, to their professional ambitions, to their sense of themselves as sexually autonomous beings? What did they gain from their relationships with Dreiser? What did they lose? The answers to these questions, as to nearly all other questions involving Dreiser, are contradictory and convoluted.

A subject that has remained on the fringes of both mainstream and feminist scholarship is the complex role male mentors and models have played for aspiring women writers. The influence of male writers on women writers in American literary history is beginning to be explored;[52] the influence of women writers on men is also being investigated in preliminary ways.[53] Generally neglected, however, is the often vexed and complex relationship these men and women had to each other in their lives, particularly in those instances when these initially intellectual relationships took on sexual dimensions as well. Perhaps the distastefulness of the sexist stereotype of the woman who "sleeps her way to the top" has discouraged feminist scholars from investigating this ambiguous and complex subject; having fought so long to define women by something other than their sexuality, even broaching this subject may seem to be a "step backward." Underneath that stereotype, however, some fascinating chapters of social history and gender relations remain to be uncovered.

Simultaneously empowering and threatening, influential male writers had the capacity to nurture, exploit, stifle, guide, encourage, terrify, and embolden women with literary aspirations; they probably did all these things. Our understanding of the intricacies of Dreiser's role in this process will be enriched by forthcoming publications on the subject by Lawrence Hussman and Thomas P. Riggio, both of whom are editing unpublished primary documents that illuminate Dreiser's relationship with women.[54]

Time and again, young women from around the country would read one of Dreiser's books and find themselves writing the author a letter. They would share a bit of themselves with him: their questions, their responses to his work, their thoughts on literature, their ideas. And he would write back. Often he would invite them to visit him. And many did. What drew these young women to Dreiser was a thirst for intellectual stimulation and sympathy that he seemed exceptionally willing to provide.

One such woman, Clara Jaeger, was lured to New York to work for Dreiser by a letter that began, "Clara, Clara — intense, aesthetic, poetic, your letter speaks to me . . . from Philadelphia, where, once, for a time, I dwelt . . . would you come to see me here in New York, and we can talk? . . . "[55] (It was always the promise of talk that lured women to him, the sense that he understood their questions, hopes, dreams — and that he had the knowledge and experience to stimulate their thinking as no one else they had ever met could. "We talked easily," Clara Jaeger recalled thinking, soon after she and Dreiser met, "I felt completely at home with him. . . . I knew we would never have to make conversation." Over a "seven-course dinner and a bottle of red wine," Jaeger remembers, "on and on we talked. We talked of Plato and Greek art, of astronomy, of Leonardo da Vinci, and we talked about Dreiser. . . . "[56] And Marguerite Tjader Harris recalled, "From the beginning our friendship was based on a love of things outside of ourselves [the work of John Cowper] Powys, Russian literature, a probing into the mysteries beyond life; an impersonal element, sometimes chilling—like the thought of interplanetary space."[57])

Swanberg, puzzling over the roots of women's attraction to Dreiser, concludes that "his magnetic power over women was composed of something more than sex attraction. For as long as his interest lasted, it was often intense, kindly, flattering, truly sympathetic and wonderfully understanding—indeed, perhaps too powerful to last very long."[58] Marguerite Harris called him "super-sensitive, a doctor of souls, knowing them and seeing their secrets."[59] Lawrence Hussman, borrowing a phrase Molly Haskell used to describe Woody Allen, recently called Dreiser a "Casanova of conversational empathy."[60]

Dreiser's empathy and rapport certainly played a key role in many young women's responses to him, but his willingness to talk about books and ideas, to point them towards new intellectual adventures, to take them seriously as thinking human beings, was as seductive as his attentive listening. "Dreiser keeps giving me books to read," Clara Jaeger writes. "He is certainly determined to educate me. I have now read Dostoyevsky thoroughly: *The Idiot*, adored by T. D., *The Brothers Karamazov, Crime and Punishment.* Then Thomas Hardy, Somerset Maugham, especially *Of Human Bondage*, Zola's *Nana* and *Madame Bovary*, and John Cowper Powys."[61]

As they struggled to make a place for themselves in a literary market that was unfamiliar and somewhat frightening to them, a number of ambitious, bright young women found in Dreiser a supportive and encouraging ally. The correspondence might begin with comments about one of Dreiser's books; the woman might send some work of her own; in the end she would ask for Dreiser's help in marketing her writing.[62] Dreiser would urge colleagues to be on the lookout for jobs for some of these young women.[63] For others he would offer to write a "blurb."[64] For some who went to work for him, the experience of being taken seriously as a person who could think, write, edit, and be of help to a great writer, was intoxicating.[65] "I have found a wonderful friend and champion," Clara Jaeger wrote, ". . . And to top it all, I have a job and a salary, doing work that can only be intensely interesting. I am confident that I can edit those long sentences."[66]

Dreiser placed Jaeger's novel with an agent, and she was thrilled to be offered a $300 advance. But her mentor gave her some cautionary advice: "He suggests that I hold the novel, not necessarily accept this offer which has come so easily, and aim to give the book more 'social' emphasis. After I have polished it, I can try one of the really first-class publishing houses; he says he will help me with the revision."[67] Although Dreiser was a literary and intellectual mentor for many women, he was, in turn, dependent on their professional competence. Yet he was also known to exploit and betray bright, talented women who made the mistake of trusting him, thereby revealing a curiously ambivalent attitude towards their professional role.

As Thomas Riggio has observed,

> women came to be his major prepublication readers. . . . The diaries find Dreiser constantly submitting his writing to the scrutiny of one or another of his close female friends. Many of his intimate and long-term relations—with Louise Campbell, Anna Tatum, Lillian Rosenthal, to name a few—began with letters that soundly criticized one of his books. The best part of the large correspondence he maintained with women, often for years without meeting them or for decades after their intimacies ended, revolves around their consideration of his work. As his writing became less accessible to old friends like Arthur Henry and Mencken, he came to rely more on the talented women he knew to judge his initial drafts."[68]

Did Dreiser view the advice he was getting from these women as a professional service that deserved compensation? The women on whose advice he relied most—such as Anna Tatum and Marguerite Tjader Harris—may have sometimes worked for him as unpaid editors and secretaries.[69] On those occasions when Dreiser did pay a woman a salary to work as his secretary, he often assumed that her sexual favors were part of the bargain.[70] (Clara Jaeger does not seem to have objected; at least her memoir treats the episode without resentment, and with equanimity. Without questioning her right or ability to make her own choices, one might nonetheless underline the power differential that obtained between the middle-aged, confident, established man of letters and the vulnerable, insecure, confused young woman. This asymmetry, combined with the fact that the intimacies were treated—along with the bottle of wine and seven-course dinner—as part and parcel of the unwritten contract whereby Dreiser had just that day secured her services as a secretary, give one pause. Her choice may have been her own, but its context may have been somewhat coercive.[71])

The professionally competent, ambitious, and bright women who connected themselves to Dreiser found that there were other risks as well. Clara Jaeger made a note of the fact, for example, that Helen Dreiser had "dropped everything, given up her career as an actress, to follow him."[72] While he was attracted to ambitious women who took their work seriously, they had to be willing single-mindedly to put him first.

The loyalty Dreiser demanded from the professional women on whose literary and editorial judgment he relied seems to have been rather one-sided. Dreiser wrote a secretary connected with the Little Theatre whom he had met in Chicago, "to arrange for her to come to New York and serve as his helpmate and literary assistant." When she did, he "dropped her cold." His friend Floyd Dell was shocked by his brutal abandonment of her.[73] The literary agent Flora Mai Holly was another victim of Dreiser's double standard. After persuading her to take a cut in her commission, Dreiser summarily discharged her. It was an ungrateful blow to the woman who had persuaded B. W. Dodge and Co. to reissue *Sister Carrie*.[74]

Exploitation and abandonment were not the only risks a woman undertook by working for Dreiser; there was always the chance that he would plagiarize from her as well. As Swanberg notes:

> He was apt to steal ideas without realizing it, or indeed caring very much. Miss [Sally] Kussell had written a short story about a poor dressmaker who fell in love with a struggling artist, which she showed him. He shrugged, saying it was not bad. Later, he wrote a story on that identical theme, giving it to her to edit. He was surprised when she pointed out that it was her idea, having forgotten that entirely.[75]

What did Dreiser think of the idea that women had sexual drives not unlike those of men? He thought it was terrific—if it drove them into his bed. If it did not, however, he could be shamelessly insulting about—what else?—their commitment to literature![76] "Forceful women who kept their distance," Swanberg notes, "could reduce him to erotic frenzy,"[77] for Dreiser's own sexual drive was uncontrollable. While Swanberg's prudery has discredited some of his judgments of Dreiser,[78] no one has accused him of putting words in the mouths of the friends and family members he interviewed in his biography. Dreiser's wife Jug commented to a male lawyer and friend who visited her bedside when she was sick,

> I have been interested in watching you as you have sat by my bedside. You have not tried to touch me. Theo could no more have done that than he could have stopped breathing. All his life he has had an uncontrollable urge when near a woman to lay his hand upon her and stroke her or otherwise come into contact with her.[79]

Dreiser was laconic about his problem: "It's not my fault," he once told a friend. "You walk into a room, see a woman and something happens. It's chemical. What are you going to do about it?"[80]

Dreiser preferred women who responded to his passion with passion of their own. He was fond of paying lip service to the beauties of "free love." But as for sexual freedom in the concrete, while Dreiser embraced "varietism" for himself, he demanded total faithfulness from his women. Kirah Markham recalled, "If a man so much as sat by the fire with me while [Dreiser] was off of an evening with another woman there were horrible scenes the next morning. . . . With his own promiscuous code, he could not believe in my faithfulness."[81]

Ironically, the qualities Dreiser valued most in a real-life companion—within limits—turn out to be precisely those qualities that Billy Brown herself may have had, qualities that the *World*'s reporters, and then Dreiser himself, erased from their representations of her. What precisely those limits were become apparent if we examine Dreiser's letters to Marguerite Tjader Harris—secretary, editor, and lover during his later years. Harris struggled to push those limits while Dreiser struggled to contain her. In the end, he would see Harris through the same gendered blinders that he saw Billy Brown.

From the start of their relationship Marguerite Tjader Harris's intellectual curiosity and openness attracted Dreiser intensely. "I think of you as active, resourceful, brave, interested in so many things, and so *intelligently*," he wrote.[82] Later on he would write, in a similar vein, "Whether you know it or not you are always somewhere in my mind shining brightly as a mental and tempera mental prodigy. The girl with a wild heart and a free mind—one actually driven by the creative force of nature itself."[83]

As Marguerite Tjader Harris proved her skills as his assistant and helpmate, Dreiser expressed his awe at her competence:

Marguerite Dear:
    Wasn't that a hectic week! And you the swell, loving indus-
trious, capable and clever secretary and hostess and sweetheart
and bed-fellow—doing not only everything on the dot but *getting
it done*. Truly it was delightful having you so near me and taking
care of so many things [crossouts] I have never known a more
capable and diplomatic and socially and mentally fit person. I
can only think of Lord Nelson and his gifted and guiding Lady
Hamilton. *You should have been a general's or a statesman's wife
or sweetheart*. You'd be famous either way.[84]

Dreiser's comment that the best that this enormously capable
woman might have aspired to be was a "general's or a statesman's
wife or sweetheart"—rather than a general or a statesman herself—
might seem to run counter to the many other occasions when
Dreiser urged women to become achievers in their own right.
It is oddly reminiscent, however, of a conversation he had with
Harris the evening they first met.

As Harris recalls the occasion, "After dinner we sat on a stiff
studio couch and talked casually for a time. But then Dreiser
asked me what I was doing. It did not seem enough to him that I
was married and took part in the rushing social life of New York.
'Nothing but a parasite,' he teased, 'I can put you to work.' "[85]
Dreiser did, in fact, put Harris to work. He asked her to comb
New York galleries for illustrations that "might fit into the mood"
of the prose-poem he had just completed, "My City," which was
to be published in a special art edition. As Harris recalls,

> I promised to do so, since I frequently made the rounds of the
> New York galleries. He told me that there was also literary work
> with which I might help. His hand was on my knee in a way
> which was both paternal and confident.[86]

While someone who "was married" (to someone else) and
"took part in the rushing social life of New York" might be, from
Dreiser's perspective, "a parasite," someone who let him put his
hand on her knee and who was willing to rush around New York
on his errands was in a different category entirely. As Dreiser
came to rely more and more on the panoply of "wifely" and other
services Harris performed for him, he does not seem to have been
struck by any inconsistency on this front. He initially pulled her
into his orbit by accusing her of being a "parasite," but his ploy
was only too transparent. It was not putting her to work for her
own sake that concerned him—it was getting her to work *for him*.
    Dreiser offered Harris a "way out" of the tug of war that pulled
so many women of her time in opposite directions. Women, like

Harris, who wanted more than conventional married life offered, but less than all-out rebellion against the culture's norms, were caught in a bind. How could they reconcile the desire to be intellectually stimulated and professionally challenged with the desire to retain one's attraction to men, to be feminine, to not challenge directly the ubiquitous "marriage plot" that women had been socialized into from birth? I suspect that it is precisely the contested nature of that territory in the culture that helped Dreiser live with his own contradictory tendencies to push women out into the world, on the one hand, and to pull them into his own personal sphere (as lover, assistant, helpmate, hostess, etc.) on the other. For Dreiser, it was easy for a woman to "have it all": all she had to have was a preternatural devotion to *him*.

As for Harris's sexual drive, Dreiser celebrated it blissfully during those periods when it was directed towards him. He did an about-face, however, when he responded to a letter from her stipulating that she would come out to California to work on *The Bulwark* with him only if he agreed to follow what he referred to as certain "school marmish instructions" she had set forth regarding his conduct. His comment—a revisionist version of their past involvement—was clearly designed to infuriate her. He wrote: "As it were you were so driven by your own desires as to be compelled to continuously explore all phases of the sex act—almost to the exclusion of the literary creative act."[87]

Once Marguerite Tjader Harris made it clear she was not interested in being involved sexually with Dreiser, he tried to deny the value of the intellectual and creative work she had performed for him professionally. His claim that she had been so absorbed in sex—deviantly so—as to almost overshadow or neglect the job she had been hired to do simply does not hold up. His letters from the period she was working with him tell a different story. They document the care and competence with which Harris performed the professional tasks Dreiser assigned her. Dreiser was simply rewriting the past in light of his frustrations in the present.

As he took seriously the intellectual aspirations of the young women who came to him for guidance, as he nurtured and supported their careers, and as he urged them to express their sexual passions, Dreiser challenged the dominant ideology of gender of his time. Yet his challenge was neither consistent nor truly subversive.

While he may have unwittingly reinforced the reporters' erasure of Billy Brown's intellectual curiosity, her pride in her work, and her natural interest in sex, it was with all his wits about him that he endeavored to erase those same qualities in his representations of Marguerite Tjader Harris. Dreiser's progressive theories and practices were stymied by his obsessive jealousies and sexual compulsions. His empathy and understanding were limited by his egotism and self-absorption. The sexual politics that informed Dreiser's personal relationships and his work mirror the tensions that inhered in the culture itself—and are as contradictory and complex. Dreiser both challenged and reinscribed the discourse of gender of his day in his art and in his life, in ways we may never, perhaps, fully disentangle.

Notes

1. I am grateful to Robert Crunden, Milton Fisher, Miriam Gogol, Lawrence Hussman, Thomas P. Riggio, Lillian Robinson, and Jeffrey Rubin-Dorsky for conversations, comments, and criticism that helped shape my thinking about Dreiser in this essay.

2. Susan Wolsterholme, "Brother Theodore, Hell on Women," in Fritz Fleischmann, ed., *American Novelists Revisited: Essays in Feminist Criticism* (Boston: G. K. Hall, 1982), pp. 243–264. (Quotation, p. 264.) Although other women critics have written on Dreiser, they have not generally done so from a feminist perspective.

3. I am grateful to Thomas P. Riggio for recounting to me this incident, at which he was present. Thomas P. Riggio, personal correspondence.

4. Elaine Showalter, *Speaking of Gender* (New York: Routledge, 1989) pp. 6, 9–10; Nancy K. Miller, ed., *The Poetics of Gender* (New York: Columbia University Press, 1986), p. xiii.

5. These include Harry Brod, *The Making of Masculinities* (Newbury, Calif.: Sage, 1987); Michael Kimmel, *Changing Men: New Directions in Research on Men and Masculinity* (Cambridge: Unwin Hyman, 1987); and Joseph Boone and Michael Cadden, *Engendering Men: The Question of Male Feminist Criticism* (New York: Routledge, 1990).

6. This essay does not claim that the female character Dreiser created in this novel is representative of all of Dreiser's fictional females. Dreiser is wildly inconsistent. There are elements of Roberta Alden (her sexual passivity, for example), however, that Irene Gammel finds echoed in other of Dreiser's female characters, including Carrie Meeber and Jennie Gerhardt. See Irene Gammel, "Sexualizing the Female Body: Dreiser, Feminism, and Foucault," in Miriam Gogol, ed., *Theodore Dreiser: Beyond Naturalism* (New York: New York University Press, 1995), pp. 31–54.

7. Grace Brown was the woman's formal name. Her nickname, and the name she was called most often, was "Billy." Throughout this paper she will be referred to as Billy Brown.

8. Both Ellen Moers and Donald Pizer acknowledge the difficulty of determining precisely which factual material Dreiser drew on for the novel. Pizer makes a fairly convincing case, however, for the idea that despite Dreiser's own reference to "testimony introduced at the trial," Dreiser in fact relied exclusively on stories that appeared in the *New York World* "for his verbatim material and for almost all other explicit detail." Donald Pizer, "An American Tragedy" in Harold Bloom, ed., *Theodore Dreiser's "An American Tragedy"* (New York: Chelsea House, 1988), pp. 45–67. (Quotation, p. 57.) See also Ellen Moers, *Two Dreisers* (New York: Viking, 1969), p. 44. If Dreiser did, by some chance, actually examine the trial transcript and read testimony introduced at the trial, that would only strengthen the significance of his adherence to the journalists' omission of material that did not fit the paradigms of the melodramas they were narrating in their daily stories.

9. For a complex reading of this myth, see "The Myth of Womanhood: Victims," in Nina Auerbach, *Woman and the Demon: The Life of a Victorian Myth* (Cambridge: Harvard University Press, 1982), pp. 7–34.

10. Theodore Dreiser, *Newspaper Days* (Philadelphia: University of Pennsylvania Press, 1991), pp. 261–62. For more on Dreiser's background in journalism, see Shelley Fisher Fishkin, *From Fact to Fiction: Journalism and Imaginative Writing in America* (Baltimore: Johns Hopkins University Press, 1985; New York: Oxford University Press, 1988), pp. 86–134.

11. Dreiser, *Newspaper Days,* p. 263.

12. R. F. Bunner, "In the Old Pit Shaft" (Cartoon). *Life* 29 (no. 733) (January 7, 1897): 32.

13. New York *World,* November 14, 1906; November 18, 1906; and November 29, 1906. For a photograph of Billy Brown, see Joseph W. Brownell and Patricia A. Wawrzaszek, *Adirondack Tragedy: The Gillette Murder Case of 1906* (Interlaken, N.Y.: Heart of the Lakes Publishing, 1986), p. 36.

14. Hannah Webster Foster, *The Coquette* (1797), Introduction by Cathy Davidson (New York: Oxford University Press, 1986); Susannah Rowson, *Charlotte Temple* (1791), Introduction by Cathy Davidson (New York: Oxford University Press, 1986).

15. Quoted by lawyers. The People of the State of New York vs. Chester Gillette. State of New York Court of Appeals. Appeal Book, vols. I, II and III (Ilion, Herkimer and Frankfort, N.Y.: Citizen Print), pp. 70–4. Cited hereafter as "Trial Transcript." Exhibits 5, 6, 7. Original trial transcript pp. 1007–9.

16. Dreiser to Harris, June 12, 1944 and June 19, 1944. I am grateful to Lawrence Hussman for making me aware of sixty uncatalogued letters from Dreiser to Marguerite Tjader Harris in the Harry Ransom Humanities Research Center at the University of Texas at Austin, which proved invaluable in my research. All citations in this essay from letters between Dreiser and Harris refer to letters at the Harry Ransom Humanities Research Center.

17. Craig Brandon, *Murder in the Adirondacks: An American Tragedy Revisited* (Utica: North Country Books, 1986), p. 56

18. See Theresa Harnishfager's testimony in the trial transcript. While Billy Brown's job as an inspector was still likely to be a fairly low-level factory job, it won her a freedom of movement that assignment to a single workstation would have denied her. Presumably her ability to learn new tasks quickly played some role in her being called on frequently as a substitute.

19. Brandon, *Murder in the Adirondacks,* p. 60.

20. Brandon, *Murder in the Adirondacks,* p. 60.

21. Brandon, *Murder in the Adirondacks,* p. 60.

22. Brandon, *Murder in the Adirondacks,* p. 67.

23. Trial transcript, pp. 78–9.

24. The newspaper reporters and Dreiser may have erased the pride Billy Brown took in her work, her love of reading and stimulating conversation, and her potential sense of her sexual autonomy, but it is worth noting that these traits are often absent from Dreiser's characters in general (particularly in *An American Tragedy*). This does not, however, change the fact that the real-life model for his character may have had them, while the fictional creation did not. It merely makes the point that Dreiser was rarely willing to grant *any* of his characters more than a limited sense of autonomy or initiative (with key exceptions — Frank Cowperwood, for example). Rather, personal identity, for many of Dreiser's characters, tends to be a mirror box of reflected images, imagined associations, longings, gazes, desires, auras, mirages, clothes, objects, performances, and anticipations. See, for example, Philip Fisher, *Hard Facts: Setting and Form in the American Novel* (New York: Oxford University Press,

1985); Amy Kaplan, *The Social Construction of American Realism* (Chicago: University of Chicago Press, 1988); Walter Benn Michaels, *The Gold Standard and the Logic of Naturalism* (Berkeley: University of California Press, 1987); Rachel Bowlby, *Just Looking: Consumer Culture in Dreiser, Gissing, and Zola* (New York: Methuen, 1985).

25. Counterexamples to this general trend can be found as well. Thomas P. Riggio has pointed, for instance, to *Hill's Manual,* an immensely popular book with which Dreiser was familiar. First published in 1873 (and remaining in print until 1960), it asserted, "The sphere of woman's action and work is so widening that she can to-day, if she desires, handsomely and independently support herself. She need not, therefore, marry for a home" (personal correspondence). Nonetheless, many women writers of the period bemoaned the fact that views like these were more the ideal than the reality. As Elaine Showalter notes, "by the *fin de siècle* a post-Darwinian 'sexual science' offered expert testimony on the evolutionary differences between men and women. While women's 'nurturant domestic capabilities fitted them for home and hearth,' . . . men had evolved aggressive, competitive abilities 'that fitted them for public life' " (Elaine Showalter, *Sexual Anarchy: Gender and Culture at the Fin de Siècle* [New York: Viking Penguin, 1990], p. 8.)

26. Charlotte Perkins Gilman, "Masculine Literature" [Part V. *Our Androcentric Culture; or The Man-Made World*], *The Forerunner* 1 (March 1910): 21.

27. William Dean Howells, *"Criticism and Fiction" and Other Essays*, ed. by Clara Marburg Kirk and Rudolf Kirk (New York: New York University Press, 1959), p. 71.

28. Dorothy Richardson, *The Long Day: The Story of a New York Working Girl Told by Herself* (New York: Century Co., 1905).

29. Mary McDowell, "Our Proxies in Industry," 11. Quoted in Leslie Woodcock Tentler, *Wage-Earning Women: Industrial Work and Family Life in the United States, 1900–1930* (New York: Oxford University Press, 1979), p. 214, n. 31.

30. Quoted in Alice Kessler-Harris, "Organizing the Unorganizable: Three Jewish Women and Their Union," 7. Cited in Tentler, *Wage-Earning Women*, 210, note 97.

31. *New York World,* December 5, 1906.

32. There were, of course, notable exceptions to this rule. Most importantly Charlotte Perkins Gilman endeavored to create a body of fiction that directly challenged the "love plot" as the only plot available to women. See Shelley Fisher Fishkin, " 'Making a Change':

Strategies of Subversion in Charlotte Perkins Gilman's Journalism and Fiction," in Joanne Karpinski, ed., *Critical Essays on Charlotte Perkins Gilman* (Boston: G. K. Hall, 1992).

33. This characterization of a wide range of arguments is Nina Auerbach's in *Woman and the Demon*, p. 12. See also Elizabeth Janeway, *Man's World, Woman's Place: A Study in Social Mythology* (New York: Morrow, 1971) and Janeway, *Between Myth and Morning: Women Awakening* (New York: Morrow, 1975).

34. Charles W. Eliot quoted in Theodore Penny Martin, *The Sound of Our Own Voices: Women's Study Clubs 1860–1910* (Boston: Beacon Press, 1987), p. 26. Martin cites such sources as Sally Schwager, "'Harvard Women': A History of the Rounding of Radcliffe College" (Ed.D. thesis, Harvard Graduate School of Education, 1982), p. 18.

35. Jean E. Friedman and William G. Shade, *Our American Sisters: Women in American Life and Thought*, 3d ed. (Lexington, Mass.: D.C. Heath and Co., 1982), p. 323.

36. For a description of Victorian ideology of "passionlessness," see Nancy Cott, "Passionlessness: A Reinterpretation of Victorian Sexual Ideology, 1790–1850," *Signs* 4 (1978): 219–36. According to Barbara Hobson, it was not until the 1920s that the widespread belief that women were passionless began to disappear. Barbara Meal Hobson, *Uneasy Virtue: The Politics of Prostitution and the American Reform Tradition* (New York: Basic Books, 1987), p. 185.

37. Facsimile page of advice book reproduced in June Sochen, *Herstory: A Record of the Women's Past*, 2d ed. (Palo Alto: Mayfield Publishing Co., 1982), p. 198.

38. Kathryn Tovo makes this point in her study of the Berachah Home, a turn-of-the-century residence for unwed mothers and "fallen" women in Arlington, Texas. Kathryn Tovo, "Rescue Homes at the Turn of the Century: The Berachah Home Experience," unpublished paper, University of Texas, Austin.

39. Dreiser tells us that Roberta strikes Clyde as "more intelligent" than the other factory girls, but there is no further comment on the nature of her intelligence or on her intellectual interests. Dreiser, *An American Tragedy* (New York: New American Library, 1981), p. 241.

40. One might note that many of these qualities apply to Clyde, as well. But what is at issue here is not the oft-noted twinning Dreiser evokes in his characterization of Clyde and Roberta, but rather the ways in which the press and Dreiser fit Billy Brown into a certain very gender-specific, narrow mold. (When Dreiser "lowers" Chester Gillette's

educational and social status in the novel, making Clyde Griffiths less sophisticated and well traveled, he is making Clyde conform to another gender-specific stereotype dominant in the culture, that of the Horatio Alger hero [see Fishkin, *From Fact to Fiction*, pp. 122–5].)

41. The fact that Dreiser portrayed Roberta Alden's sexuality in this way does not mean that he was incapable of depicting women with strong sexual drives. (Note, for example, his character Angela Blue in *The "Genius."*)

42. For an analysis of Dreiser's elimination of active verbs to add ambiguity to the drowning, see Fishkin, *From Fact to Fiction*, pp. 130–4.

43. In *A Gallery of Women*, vol. I (New York: Horace Liveright, 1929), for example, Dreiser addresses the issue of work on pp. 113, 138, and 156–71, of books and reading on pp. 81, 82, 87, and 96, and of sexual autonomy on pp. 77–8.

44. Philip Gerber, "'A Beautiful Legal Problem': Albert Levitt on *An American Tragedy." Papers on Language and Literature* 27 (Spring 1991): 214–42. (Quotation, p. 216.)

45. To be fair, this difference may well be the result, in large part, of Dreiser's greater success as a novelist in *An American Tragedy*. Older, more accomplished, and more confident in his art, Dreiser may simply have written a better book in 1925 than he had written earlier.

46. As Donald Pizer commented, for example, "Dreiser relied on the Gillette case but was not bound by it. His intent was not to retell a story but to recast Gillette's experience into . . . a story which would render the tragic reality at the center of the American dream. He therefore made a large number of changes in his sources, all of which are related to two basic impulses: to shift the unavoidable impression of the documentary evidence that Gillette was a shallow-minded murderer to the impression that Clyde might be any one of us caught in the insoluble conflict between our deepest needs and the unyielding nature of experience; and to transform the shapeless, repetitive, and superficial manifestation of life in an actual trial into the compelling revelation of human nature and experience present in fiction at its best" (Pizer, "An American Tragedy," p. 58). See also Fishkin, *From Fact to Fiction*, pp. 121–34.

47. Fishkin, *From Fact to Fiction*, p. 125.

48. Interestingly, Plank found that Dreiser "alters" the facts of the other murder cases he describes as well:

In order to add a sense of historical verifiability to the social and economic forces that he offers as the motivation for the crime in *An American Tragedy,* Dreiser creates a tradition of similar crimes. Although this tradition is not factually accurate, it is a valuable extension of the novel. The errors in "I Find the Real American Tragedy" are not evidence of a careless researcher, but of an imaginative writer who borrows from history to support his fiction. It reveals that Dreiser depended less on historical events and factual details than many people have argued. . . .

See Kathryn M. Plank, "Dreiser's Real American Tragedy," *Papers on Language and Literature* 27 (Spring 1991), 268–87.

49. Pizer, "An American Tragedy," p. 58.

50. Indeed, they had existed earlier, as well, as the work of Charlotte Perkins Gilman amply demonstrates. See Fishkin, " 'Making a Change.' "

51. June Sochen, *Herstory,* p. 35.

52. A case in point is Emily Budick, *Engendering Romance: Women Writing in the Hawthorne Tradition* (New Haven: Yale University Press, 1994).

53. See for example Gregg Camfield, *Sentimental Twain: Samuel Clemens in the Maze of Moral Philosophy* (Philadelphia: University of Pennsylvania Press, 1994).

54. Lawrence Hussman is editing Marguerite Tjader Harris's memoir for publication. Thomas P. Riggio has been working with Yvette Eastman on her memoirs and with the 230 unpublished letters she has from Dreiser; he is also editing a book of Dreiser's letters to women.

55. Clara Jaeger, *Philadelphia Rebel: The Education of a Bourgeoise* (Richmond: Grosvenor, 1988), p. 68.

56. Jaeger, *Philadelphia Rebel,* pp. 74–6.

57. Marguerite Tjader Harris, *Theodore Dreiser: A New Dimension* (Norwalk: Silvermine, 1965), p. 4.

58. Swanberg, *Dreiser* (New York: Charles Scribner's Sons), p. 233.

59. Harris, *Theodore Dreiser,* p. 1.

60. Lawrence Hussman, Comments, panel on "Theodore Dreiser in the Nineties: Lacan, Foucault and Feminist Readings." American Literature Association Conference. Sunday, May 26, 1991. Washington, D.C.

61. Jaeger, *Philadelphia Rebel,* p. 88.

62. One woman who sought help from Dreiser in marketing her writing was Louise Ann-Miller. See Swanberg, *Dreiser,* p. 141.

63. He wanted Mencken to help find Anna Tatum an editorial job (Swanberg, *Dreiser,* 211).

64. Dreiser to Harris, April 13, 1931.

65. Jaeger, *Philadelphia Rebel,* p. 79.

66. Jaeger, *Philadelphia Rebel,* pp. 78–9.

67. Jaeger, *Philadelphia Rebel,* p. 105.

68. Thomas P. Riggio, ed., *Theodore Dreiser: The American Diaries, 1902–1926* (Philadelphia: University of Pennsylvania Press, 1982), Introduction, p. 25.

69. Often the relationship was more informal—such as when he took Lillian Rosenthal's advice about changing the plot of *Jennie Gerhardt* (Swanberg, *Dreiser,* p. 143). Although Swanberg calls Anna Tatum Dreiser's "unpaid secretary" (171), Thomas P. Riggio affirms that no proof exists one way or the other that Tatum was not paid (personal communication). The correspondence with Marguerite Tjader Harris reveals that she often worked in an unpaid capacity.

70. Jaeger, *Philadelphia Rebel,* p. 77.

71. This is not meant to imply that all such interactions involving Dreiser were coercive; some, presumably, were not.

72. Jaeger, *Philadelphia Rebel,* p. 96.

73. Swanberg, *Dreiser,* p. 169, n. 25.

74. Swanberg, *Dreiser,* 150, n. 42; 117, 161.

75. Thomas P. Riggio has criticized Swanberg's account of Dreiser's plagiarism as simplistic. He notes that Dreiser "had an unbelievable memory: he could recite whole chapters verbatim, years after he had written them. Kussell wouldn't have gotten the piece back to edit if he had been a cheap plagiarist" (Personal communication). While Dreiser's habit of plagiarizing may not have been "cheap" or conscious, it was, nonetheless, a potential hazard for the aspiring young women writers who shared their work with him. One might add that Dreiser plagiarized from men as well—the roster includes George Ade, Poe, and Sherwood Anderson. It is the asymmetry of power that fell along gender lines, however, that makes his plagiarizing from women perhaps more troubling.

76. Dreiser to Harris, July 5, 1944.

77. Swanberg, *Dreiser,* p. 237.

78. Thomas P. Riggio, personal communication.

79. Swanberg, *Dreiser,* p. 137.

80. Swanberg, *Dreiser,* p. 375, n.7.

81. Swanberg, *Dreiser,* p. 197.

82. Dreiser to Harris, n.d., 1 p. ms. "Dear Marguerite . . . "

83. Dreiser to Harris, March 8, 1944.

84. Dreiser to Harris, April 9, 1941 (emphasis added).

85. Harris, *Theodore Dreiser,* p. 2.

86. Harris, *Theodore Dreiser,* p. 2.

87. Dreiser to Harris, July 5, 1944.

Sexualizing the Female Body: Dreiser, Feminism, and Foucault

Irene Gammel

Surrounded by an aura of what Dreiser often calls a "pagan" sensuality, many of his female characters paradoxically also exude a strange sense of sexual abstinence, almost chastity. Philip Fisher has commented on Carrie Meeber's absence of sexual desires and eroticism in her love relationships at the same time that she enacts desires and eros very successfully on the theater stage.[1] In *An American Tragedy* (1925), Roberta Alden briefly electrifies the protagonist Clyde Griffiths with her "poetic sensuality," only to haunt him and the reader for the rest of the novel in the image of the corpse recovered from the depths of Big Bittern Lake, whose sexuality and desires are re-created in strangely intimate detail by pathologists and prosecutors in a spectacular murder trial.

Aileen Butler in the *Trilogy of Desire* (1912, 1914, 1947) is presented in the first volume as the incarnation of sensual vitality indulging in a short-lived, clandestine carnival of sex with her partner, only to turn into a neglected wife in the next two volumes. There, her mature, untapped sexuality is reduced to occasional pleasureless adulteries with men who turn out to be lesser doubles of her husband, leaving a sense of waste, ruin, and sterility in her life. This impression is further emphasized by the slow decay of her body. Leslie Fiedler, commenting on the chastity of the "unchurched nun," Sister Carrie, and on Jennie Gerhardt's almost asexual mothering of her two lovers, irreverently draws the conclusion that Dreiser "could never portray, for all his own later hectic career as a lover, any woman except the traditional seduced working girl of sentimental melodrama."[2]

Yet, despite this penchant for the gender stereotypical seduction theme, Dreiser has gained the stature of a literary French Marianne, who, by waving the flag of sexual liberation in his battle against the bulwarks of American literary "puritanism," has firmly established sex as a discursive fact. In his works, Dreiser celebrates sexuality as the major driving force in life, holding it up as a force of progress endlessly engaged in battles against sexually repressive social conventions and institutions. As Charles Glicksberg has put it in his *Sexual Revolution in American Literature* (1971), sex, according to Dreiser, is the "primal source of beauty, the mother of the arts, it provides the vital incentive that makes for progress and achievement."[3] Alfred Kazin uses a very similar language in the introduction to the unexpurgated edition of *Sister Carrie* (1981): "To the always alienated and radical Dreiser, Carrie represents the necessity of transformation, sex as revolution."[4]

Elevated to the level of a canonized critical "fact," Dreiser's discourse of sexual frankness and liberation, is, nonetheless, problematic — not only because it may reinscribe old stereotypes in a new language, as Fiedler's critique implies, but also because it innocently assumes the existence of sexuality as an innate, bodily fact, a fact that is presumed to be recoverable — like a *Ding an sich* — underneath layers of psychological repressions and literary censorship. Dreiser's discursive scientificity is underlined by his characteristic use of materialistic imagery, such as "magnetism" and "chemism." Especially in his evocation of sexuality, he strengthens the impression of the body as an easily graspable, physical or natural entity, whose existence is presumed to have been hidden behind veils of conventions. The tacit implication behind such language is that "lifting the veil" and transcending conventions with a discourse of "frankness" will make the "real thing" automatically appear "as it is" and grant it a place in literature in its own right.

Since Dreiser has come to epitomize the discursive explosion on sexuality in early twentieth-century American literature, a postmodern perspective on sexuality, as it is expressed for example in *The History of Sexuality* (1980) by French philosopher Michel Foucault, presents a springboard for reexamining the accepted views on Dreiser's eulogy of sex and desire. Foucault rejects, debunks, and caricatures discourses of sexual liberation. He argues that what is nowadays subsumed under the term "sexuality" is by no means "innate" or "natural," but rather a complex historical construct created over the last two centuries in our discursive practices. Since the eighteenth century, Foucault argues, people have not really shaken off sexual "repressions" and become more active sexually, but they have become obsessed with the pleasure of talking and writing and theorizing about sexuality, with putting sexuality in linguistic and scientific categories: "[S]ex was taken charge of, tracked down as it were, by a discourse that aimed to allow it no obscurity, no respite."[5] Even more importantly, in this process of transforming sex into discourse, sexuality has been policed, because talking about sexuality in regulated, "authorized" discourses helps control it.

It is here that Foucault's theory intersects with important concerns of (post)modern feminism, and these points of intersection will be useful in drawing attention to the power effects inherent in Dreiser's inscription of the female body in his texts.[6]

Turning to Dreiser's *A Gallery of Women* (1929), a collection of nonfictional and semifictionalized sketches on the author's female friends and acquaintances—here, especially, to the sketch of "Emanuela"—we find not only an excellent starting point, but also a true touchstone to evaluate Dreiser's inscription of female sexuality as well as the underlying gender-based ideologies in his fiction. "Emanuela" presents an account of a beautiful and gifted woman artist, whom the thirty-year-old narrator–author meets in New York's artistic circles. According to Dreiser's first-person account, she repeatedly initiates contact with him only to retreat with an almost physical repulsion from his sexual advances. "I don't like you that way!," she tells him, also confessing candidly that the "muddy depths" of sex are not for her, that she in fact does not want any sexual relationship.[7] The narrator, irritated at being led by the nose, excels at exposing Emanuela's duplicity, namely, the fact that she "pursues" him for years, never tires of "luring" him into accepting tantalizing *tête à têtes*, but each time almost ritually thwarts what he longs for most—the sexual contact.

But as Emanuela oscillates between her attraction for the narrator and her physical repulsion, so the narrator himself oscillates between irresistible attraction and angry, frustrated retreat—an interplay that is paralleled by the oscillating discourses he adopts to describe and evaluate Emanuela. Describing his role as a briskly advancing Don Juan, the narrator lovingly weaves the threads of his idealizing love–romance tapestry, evoking Emanuela in terms of Minerva, Diana, and Venus, and mythologizing her "white," "seraph"-like, virginal body, only to intersperse in his romance a cooler, scientific–analytical thread when it comes to dealing with her "freezing recessions." This discursive oscillation, better than anything else, illustrates the narrator's duplicity in his relationship with the young woman whose body strikes him as "beautiful and voluptuously formed," but who refuses to fulfill what he sees as the "natural" functions of such a "perfect" body, namely, to have intercourse with a man.

"Was she not a clear illustration of some of Freud's prime contentions?" (693), the narrator asks, taking recourse in a psychoanalytic authority—sanctioned as truthful by himself and the intellectual forerunners of his contemporary society. It matters little that Emanuela rejects this discourse for herself: "Oh, yes, she had read Freud, and had been impressed in part, but could not accept him fully. No. His analysis was too coarse and too domineering, left no place for anything but itself. And there was nothing that was the whole truth about anything" (695). Despite her protests— sex cannot possibly be "the base of *all* dreams"—Dreiser imposes the Freudian discourse as truthfully revealing the secrets about her character, namely, her sexual repression, her "sex inhibition," and "the obvious pathologic fact in her case, that she was frigid" (687). After establishing the "fact" of Emanuela's "frigidity," he does not, however, abandon the chase as useless; on the contrary, despite his better judgment he continues it sporadically for more than a decade, as if his realization of the woman's "frigidity" made the chase all the more intense, the sexual object all the more desirable.

Dreiser's Freudian discourse implies that frigidity is partly rooted in the organic and partly in childhood repressions.[8] Simone de Beauvoir, in contrast, gives a very persuasive definition of frigidity that refrains from making any biological assumptions and from speculating about a far-away childhood. At the same time, it locates the roots of frigidity in gender relationships of power. De Beauvoir writes that "resentment is the most common source of feminine frigidity; in bed the woman punishes the male for all the wrongs she feels she has endured, by offering him an insulting coldness."[9] Dreiser's excursion into amateur psychoanalysis reveals more about his own motivations than Emanuela's. One is reminded here of de Beauvoir's recognition that "antifeminists" have used "science—especially biology and experimental psychology"—to prove women's inferiority.

Here, Foucault's theory, and with it poststructuralist feminism, intersects with de Beauvoir's critique to demonstrate how much the body is in fact "constructed" through scientific, especially (socio)biological and psychoanalytic, discourses. Drawing on Foucaultian theory, Chris Weedon has pointed out that "biological theories of sexual difference" have been used to create social gender definitions, with the result that social roles have become fixed on the basis of the argument that these roles are deeply rooted in an "unchanging natural order."[10] From a poststructuralist perspective, to be sure, there is no such thing as a purely biological, "natural" body that exists prior to culture. The body, always already submerged in and imbued with culture, is in fact "constructed" through discourses, social practices, and norms that the individual inscribes on his/her body. The notion of the existence of a "natural" body is, however, ideologically supported by what we have come to accept as empirical "truths" (or as "common sense"), which Weedon quickly disqualifies as "tautological," as illustrated in the following example. In most societies, she argues, "women have primary responsibility for childcare," an empirical fact that is often used to back up the (socio)biological (and patriarchal) claim that women are "naturally suited to these roles," a claim which in turn helps to perpetuate the social status quo.[11]

If anything, "Emanuela" emphasizes the narrator's painful efforts to prove the truth value of his analysis: "For what was the real truth about her?" (702), he asks not once but repeatedly, subjecting—even though rarely—his own conclusions to a skeptical requestioning: "Or am I misreading you, and are you really moved by something which I cannot feel?" (703). But the text also turns against its author–narrator–analyst by exposing that it is indeed his discourse of truth—his use of sanctified Freudian theory—that not only aids but makes possible the narrator's dominant position in this relationship. It culminates in several problematic scenes in which he indulges in the fantasy of taking his victim by force. But as he slips into the role of an imaginary rapist, his theory helps him to shift the desire for enforced intercourse from himself to his victim: "Unquestionably, in some errant, repressed and nervous way, she was thinking that I would assail and overcome her, cave-man fashion, and so free her once and for all of her long and possibly,—how should I know—torturing self-restraint" (698).

At the same time, the narrator becomes obsessed with demonstrating "scientifically" that Emanuela's "mental opposition" and "muscular rejection" are indeed pathological, uncontrollable bodily reactions. Drawing on Freud's theory, he reads and writes her as a typical case of pathological frigidity, of desiring sex but having built up a "wall of reserve" (707) against it. She has therefore crossed the boundary into "abnormal" sexual behavior—stubborn sexual resistance. "I think you must be mad [crazy]. In fact, I'm sure you are" (709), he closes his "analysis," stomping off more like the rejected and disappointed lover than the impassioned psychologist.

Throughout the sketch, the narrator is concerned with supporting his analysis with observable, biological facts. He goes so far as to trace what seems to him nature's inscription of Emanuela's "abnormal" psychological history on her body: "in her face was a trace of something—could it be a shadow of grossness?—her repressed emotions or desires at last gaining headway?" (718–9). Furthermore, it is not so much that the asexual friendship Emanuela offers does not count for much, but according to the narrator-author, a "happy camaraderie" with a woman like Emanuela is *biologically* impossible for a male:

> What nonsense! What lunacy! And I told her so. Men were not like that. I was not. She would not like me that way if I were. She was indulging in some unnatural, hopeless, futile dream. In God's name, what was all her physical beauty for? (687).

Repeatedly, he demonstrates (with himself as the only example) that discussions about art and literary styles in the presence of her physically "perfect" body are at best boring and pointless for a male, at worst a torture. Thus, biology and psychoanalysis not only serve the narrator–author to inscribe female sexuality in terms of a compulsory heterosexuality, but also to pathologize a behavior that is not in tune with "normalized" sexual behavior.

When Dreiser wrote *Sister Carrie* (1900), he was not yet familiar with Freudian psychoanalysis. As Ellen Moers points out, Freud's theory probably became known to Dreiser after 1909, after Abraham Brill—a Dreiser friend from 1918 on—had translated some of Freud's major writings into English. According to Moers, it was mainly Freud's *Theory of Sex* that influenced Dreiser. In that work, Dreiser found the basis for the concept of sexual "chemism" that he uses so obsessively in *An American Tragedy* to describe the sexual drive.[12] Nevertheless, the sketch of "Emanuela" highlights how much Dreiser's reading of Freudian psychoanalysis converges with his own private experiences and with what he sees as the basis of life, namely, biology and the laws of nature. The later sketch, in fact, functions as a condensed *roman à clef* that helps unravel Dreiser's presuppositions about the psychosexual nature of his earlier heroines.

Above all, the sketch of "Emanuela" draws attention to the problematics and power politics of Dreiser's tacit assumptions about female sexual passivity, which is also a striking feature of *Sister Carrie, Jennie Gerhardt* (1911), and *An American Tragedy*. It draws attention to the intense power play of Dreiser's euphoric celebration of the inner "magnetism" of the beautiful female body, which the author thematizes in the Cowperwood trilogy and *The "Genius"* (1915). But even more importantly, the sketch shows the power effects inherent in any claim that a specific sexuality is "normal" or "abnormal," claims that are made in almost all of Dreiser's major works, either through overt commentary or through clever manipulation of narrative form.

To discuss Dreiser's inscription of "normalized" sexuality, let us briefly recall Foucault's *History of Sexuality*:

Thus, in the process of hysterization of women, "sex" was defined in three ways: as that which belongs in common to men and women; as that which belongs *par excellence*, to men, and hence is lacking in women; but at the same time, as that which by itself constitutes woman's body, ordering it wholly in terms of the functions of reproduction and keeping it in constant agitation through the effects of that very function.[13]

Dreiser's fiction inscribes this sexualization of the female body in different forms. *Jennie Gerhardt, An American Tragedy,* and *The "Genius"* explore the problem of unwanted pregnancies, whereby women are shown to be deterministically entrapped within the biological logic of a reproductive womb. Although apparently "undersexed," Emanuela's body is shown to be filled with sex, albeit with a "repressed" and thus hidden and concealed sexuality. It surfaces, according to Dreiser's analysis, in her "mothering" of the author–narrator – her cooking for him, her tucking him into bed. In other works, this hysterization appears in sublimated forms. Like Emanuela, all of Dreiser's major female characters are assumed to be endowed with bodies saturated with sex, so that they cannot escape a sexual destiny. But being saturated with sex in Dreiser's world does not imply sexual activity for the female, but the contrary. The sex-filled female is a rather static target that prompts the male to move, attracting the males like a honeypot does the buzzing flies.

Not only is Carrie's sexual initiation with her first lover Charles Drouet described in terms of her "yielding" and his "victory," but so is Roberta Alden's with Clyde Griffiths in *An American Tragedy,* and so is almost every other sexual relationship in Dreiser's works. "She struggled but in vain," is how the narrator describes Carrie's seduction by her second lover, Charles Hurstwood: "Instantly there flamed up in his body the all-compelling desire."[14] The language surrounding the sexual act with Hurstwood is submerged in tropes of male power and dominance. At the same time, it is embedded in a discourse that supports the "normalcy" of this sexuality.

Earlier in the novel when Carrie is even more firmly resisting the middle-aged saloon manager's advances, her lack of passion for Hurstwood is explained by "a lack of power on his part, a lack of that majesty of passion that sweeps the mind from its seat."[15] This discourse implies that in order to be sexually aroused a woman has to be taken possession of completely, has to be usurped completely, has to be overwhelmed both in spirit and in body.[16] In Dreiser's works, beginning with *Sister Carrie,* but also in *An American Tragedy* and the *Trilogy of Desire*, sexual relations almost automatically create relationships of power. The male inevitably dominates the female by imposing a form of sexuality that anticipates the conquering sexuality from which Emanuela retreats with so much horror in the later work.

Emanuela's stubborn sexual resistance is interpreted as an indicator of her "abnormal" psychological makeup, which provokes the narrator's irritation, puzzlement, and impotent anger. Its "flip side" — Carrie's passive acceptance of sexual intercourse — is sanctified by the main narrative voice as having a biological basis, thereby excusing her transgressions against society's prohibition of premarital sex. Critics have commented that in crucial moments Carrie displays a striking passivity, which seems to absolve her from any responsibility for her actions, a passivity that ultimately protects her "virtue."[17] This is typically Dreiserian, we might argue, characteristic of both men and women in his fiction. After all, passively wavering, Hurstwood turns into a thief, Clyde Griffiths into a "murderer." Yet the important difference is that Carrie's passivity extends mainly into the sexual realm, a realm in which Hurstwood storms ahead with the passionate single-mindedness of the enamored lover.

From the omniscient narrator's point of view, Carrie is never a subject of the sexual act. Rather, sexuality, apart from being innate and constituting her body, is something that happens to her. The narrator easily accepts this as a "normal" bodily reality, in tune with biology and nature, and ultimately sanctioned by the fact that it is pleasurable for the male. When Drouet invites Hurstwood to his newly established "house," thus signaling to his friend the fact of his sexual success, Carrie, as Drouet's kept woman, is only present in the gap of the male characters' dialogue.[18] "I'll introduce you," is all Drouet tells Hurstwood about her, while the object of the introduction remains suspended in a linguistic silence, not even given a name but somehow magically attached as a sexual body to Drouet and his "house."

In this instance, the effect of this gap is that the woman's sexuality is activated through others; it comes into being and gains a life not by itself, but detached from her own body. It is activated not in the sex act, but in the pleasurable discourse of two males. This conversational gambit, in which Carrie connects the two men through her very absence, occurs significantly in a club that is "for men only," Chicago's prestigious Fitzgerald and Moy's. This reenforces the impression that the woman has no control over her sexuality. In this instance, female sexuality is part of a male network, easily conjured up as a gap, a hole to be filled by the male desire which it generates.

And yet, Dreiser's narrative should not be completely identified with its narrator, as the narrative itself occasionally counters and subverts its omniscient voice, for example, by presenting a second voice that implicitly calls into question the narrator's comments. For instance, the only passage in the novel where Carrie is portrayed as being a subject of the sexual act is filtered significantly through the mind of a woman, Carrie's sister Minnie, who dreams during the night of Carrie's initiation that Carrie is descending into a black pit:

> There was a deep pit, into which they were looking; they could see the curious wet stones far down where the wall disappeared in vague shadows. An old basket, used for descending, was hanging there, fastened by a worn rope.
> "Let's get in," said Carrie.
> "Oh, no," said Minnie.
> "Yes, come on," said Carrie.
> She began to pull the basket over, and now, in spite of all protest, she had swung over and was going down.[19]

This dream takes the place of a description of the sexual act itself.[20] In her sister's eyes, Carrie is not only sexually active, but even invites Minnie to join her. The narrator, in contrast, wishes to absolve Carrie of any responsibility for her action, as he surrounds her sexuality with a deliberate discourse of passivity and determinism.

And so does the author, who is partly complicitous with his narrator. After all, Minnie's dream is filtered through the mind of a woman who has been set up earlier as thoroughly "conventional." This is a clever authorial manipulation, as it quickly disqualifies Minnie as an "unreliable" narrative "consciousness" when it comes to judging Carrie's "unconventional" sexual actions. And yet, by presenting this "second" voice as subconscious – it is the voice of Minnie's dream – and by presenting it as female, Dreiser inevitably creates a classical discourse of the other, a discourse that not only speaks of female sexual activity, but that also erupts into and thoroughly disrupts the narrative's male, rational monologue, a voice that speaks of the normality of female sexual passivity.

By contradicting the narrator's voice, Dreiser's text implicitly questions the "normalized" standard of female sexual passivity. Also, the fact that Dreiser chooses as his protagonist a female character who moves from one sexual relationship to the next, apparently planning to "give up" sexual contacts when she becomes rich, is an obvious critique of the sexual practices that the narrator presents as "normal." If anything, the narrative implicitly exposes the fact that these "normal" sexual practices are not satisfying for women, although they appear to be highly pleasurable for men. Thus the narrative's critique of "normalized" sexual practices is mainly inscribed into the margins of the text, with a contradictory voice erupting occasionally to "poke holes" in the dominating male narrative voice.

The male narrator strongly manipulates the reader's responses, and yet cannot help but reveal his own gender bias in the process. Although the narrators in *Sister Carrie* and "Emanuela" profess to argue against the sexual "conventions" of their society, much of their discourse in fact affirms a conventional gender-specific sexual behavior. Given the early heroine's involuntary slippage into sex and the notion that Emanuela's body needs not so much to act in order to be "freed" but to be acted upon by a male in order to connect with life, it is not astonishing that most of Dreiser's fictional women are described as sexually passive creatures. If sex in Dreiser's fictional world is an inevitable factor in the constitution of a healthy body and an inseparable part of a person's subjectivity, then the Dreiserian sexual economy is also ruled by a gender-based "equation inevitable," a calculation of gain and loss, of power and impotence, which shifts the credit/power balance between male and female to the male side through the fact of the sexual initiation.

As the narrator–author is obsessed with Emanuela's virginal state, so the moment of sexual initiation, in every novel ritually delayed and endowed with a titillating suspension, takes on a special significance all the more important as the sexual act itself is usually relegated into the gaps of the text and thus silenced. As a female has the power to hold the male in a powerful suspension before the sexual initiation—we only need to recall the melancholic, masochistic yearnings of Clyde for Roberta, of Eugene for Angela, of Cowperwood for Berenice—so the sexual initiation in Dreiser's texts inevitably reverses the relationship of power between male and female. This pattern explains the narrator's helpless and frustrated anger at Emanuela, who, by successfully and eternally delaying the sexual contact, never allows him to place her on the "debit" side of the equation.

In Dreiser's sexual world, women inevitably lose by "giving" themselves to a partner, while the man wins: "how delicious is my conquest," is Drouet's reaction, while Carrie reflects, "What is it I have lost?," after the first sexual contact has been established.[21]

Similarly, in *An American Tragedy*, Clyde Griffiths' sense of self grows as a result of his seduction of the factory worker Roberta; from a "simpleton" he turns into a conquering Don Juan in his own (and her) eyes, and thus becomes capable of even grander tasks and ready for the sexual conquest of rich women, the Sondra Finchleys of this world. Roberta, in contrast, feels she has given him "everything" and as a result further belittles herself in his eyes and flatters him, since her future depends on "her ultimate rehabilitation via marriage."[22]

Thus it is the first sexual contact which not so much introduces but reverses a gender imbalance "always already" present in Dreiser's sexual world. Granted, the narrator in *Sister Carrie* is careful to link this phenomenon critically to society's "arbitrary" sexual conventions,[23] but the fact remains that the narrator simultaneously eulogizes precisely those sexual courtship patterns that grow out of society's prohibitions. In Dreiser's narratives, it is in the crucial moment of the conquest of the female that the man is born into "masculinity," and in which ideal "femininity" is constituted as passive, yielding and sacrificial, based on a biological body that is presumed to be ruled by the economy of the gift, the womb that accepts and nourishes.

As Dreiser argues in his autobiography, *A Book about Myself* (1922), the female tends to be more monogamous, and hence more "moral" and conventional than the male. The monogamous standard is linked to what the autobiographer Dreiser interestingly qualifies not as a law of nature but as the societal convention of the propagation of the race, a convention that Dreiser rejects in his life, but to which women, through their reproductive roles, are more strongly attached.[24] Dreiser's fiction and nonfiction are not only saturated with the narrators' tirades against marriage, an institution that entraps and enchains the male, they are also saturated with dramatizations of powerful female sexual monogamy, an obsessive attachment of the woman to one male. This often takes the form of an almost psychological fixation, but it also turns the women into powerfully resisting creatures, paradoxically without seriously subverting the ideal of the sacrificial female.

We recall the intimidating effect of Aileen's physical fight against one of Cowperwood's mistresses, as we recall the strength and nagging passion of Angela, which impresses the unfaithful Eugene not a little, and we recall the superior strength of the pregnant Roberta, who firmly demands that Clyde marry her when she becomes pregnant. The women's strength, partly based on the pressures of social conventions, is also attached to a psychological bond: by "giving" themselves to their partners, these women have given up "everything," so that their "gift" in fact attaches them sexually and emotionally to one man, with whose body they have come to establish a symbiotic relationship. Dreiser excels at dramatizing the helpless pathos of, and in fact his sympathy with, these women who are attached in a slave–master dependency to husbands and lovers who yearn to desert them for other women.

In contrast to women, Dreiser argues in the autobiography of his early years, *Dawn* (1931), "men [are] at heart apparently varietists."[25] In the life of a male the "monogamous standard" is "entirely wrong,"[26] he argues, which inevitably entails the "law" of gender conflict, given the penchant for "female monogamy." The sexual reality principle of sensual peace that Aileen, Roberta, and Jennie offer to their lovers cannot sustain the early ecstasy so cherished by Dreiser's male, an ecstasy that dies with "real" sexual contact, when the supreme fantasy of desire dies in the reality of pleasurable sexual satisfaction. What keeps men such as Cowperwood and Witla from breaking with their wives is the consciousness of the women's ultimate "gift," which attaches the men through a chain of guilt, although one also has to wonder whether these men are not as much attached through the (never really acknowledged) motherly services and home that these women offer.

Dreiser presents the complementary "flip side" of such monogamous female attachment in Emanuela and Carrie Meeber. These women are not attached to any man but, unlike the monogamously bound female, they are desired by all men and have the gift of "eternally" arousing anew the male desire. Although the male's interest in the truly sensual woman is bound to die in the sexual contact, the body of the eternally tempting, yet sexually aloof, woman holds Dreiser's male forever in ecstatic suspension. Even though the narrator-author of "Emanuela" is no longer interested in his aging friend, her sexual elusiveness inscribes itself forever in his memory, as she continues to preoccupy him as a "temperament and a life that cannot be driven from one's mind" (662). Similarly, the mature Carrie, weary of men's advances, seems almost timelessly desirable in her lethargic and unreachable sexual aloofness as a famous Broadway actress.

It is women who are ultimately nonsacrificial and nonyielding who are allocated negative subject positions in Dreiser's texts, generally as the cold status-oriented, castrating female, who is judged and condemned by the narrative's "master" discourse as the ultimately undesirable. Mrs. Hurstwood, whose struggle for independence from her husband is fought with superior strategy and cleverness, can hardly call forth the reader's admiration, as she is submerged in an imagery of coldness that turns her into a money-hungry "python," who devours her husband, spitting him out (metaphorically) castrated, a half-man. Furthermore, truly promiscuous women who are not necessarily "yielding" — a typical example is Hortense Briggs in *An American Tragedy* who knows how to "capitalize [on] her looks"[27] — are generally presented as cold, calculating, and aggressively exploitative, at best the classical honey trap for the male.

When Clyde Griffiths is sexually initiated in a brothel, the female prostitutes appear through Clyde's eyes as stereotypical, "scarlet" women, who take the initiative sexually with the ulterior motive of getting at the customer's money. In striking contrast, the main narrative voice deploys all the registers of sympathy when it comes to male prostitution, as in the case of the bellhops in the Green–Davidson Hotel, who are presented as entrapped victims seduced by the "wiles and smiles and the money" of lustful, rich, elderly women and male homosexuals.[28]

Because the moment of the first sexual contact presents the most intense and titillating interpenetration of sex and power for Dreiser's male, and because the dominating sexual economy in Dreiser's works is so obsessively ruled by sanctified male promiscuity which multiplies this magical first moment, it seems to be the pleasure of sexualized power rather than the pleasure of the mutual contact of two bodies that proves most desirable for Dreiser's males. Dreiser's males, who are ruled by a penchant for promiscuity, are in fact not interested, occasionally even retreat in horror, from sexually promiscuous women. Falling in love with the young actress Stephanie Platow, Cowperwood immediately abandons her when he learns that she also seeks sexual pleasures with other men, just as Clyde Griffiths, who admittedly longs for a "free pagan girl," quickly dismisses as vulgar the sexually free Rita Dickerman and the sexually jocular factory women.

In his autobiographical writings, Dreiser, moreover, describes his younger self as not interested in sex when it is given too freely, a confession that is embedded in an indicative language of power: "My conquest was so easy that it detracted from the charm. The weaker sex, in youth at least, has to be sought to be worth while."[29] Indeed, the "sweetly feminine" should be "in no wise aggressive or bold,"[30] because a woman who is "too assertive and even aggressive or possessive"[31] can easily alienate a man, as she stirs up deep-seated male fears of impotence, fears that Dreiser dramatizes with an authentic urgency. And conversely, women are enticing when they play the courtship game of "mock-helplessness" and become involved in a "mock-defensive wrestling match,"[32] which not only allays deep-seated male fears, but also increases the male illusion of conquest.

Michel Foucault separates sexual behavior into three parts: "acts," that is, actual intercourse; "pleasure," or sexual enjoyment and satisfaction; and "desire," or the sexual yearning which precedes intercourse. Foucault argues that desire has taken center stage in modern Western culture, while the act itself and pleasure have been marginalized: "Acts are not very important, and pleasure—nobody knows what it is!"[33] This polemical critique can be applied to most of Dreiser's texts, and recent Dreiser critics have in fact shifted their focus from a discussion of sexuality to the more specific role of desire in Dreiser's writing.[34] Walter Benn Michaels has argued that for Dreiser Carrie Meeber embodies insatiability, and thus becomes the epitome of desire: "Carrie's body, infinitely incomplete, is literary and economic, immaterial and material, the body of desire in capitalism."[35] It is her desire that makes Carrie a success story in her society, Michaels argues, while Hurstwood's body and life disintegrate because he has stopped desiring and only lives to fulfill his basic needs.

Although Michaels' identification of feminine desire with capitalism may be persuasive, it glosses over the gender configuration of the microcosmic power play that regulates the economy of desire in *Sister Carrie*. After all, how much is Carrie's desire her own desire? "Where there is desire, the power relation is already present," Foucault reminds us,[36] while contemporary feminist critics highlight how much women in patriarchal cultures have been taught to "mimic" male desires.[37]

Very few of Dreiser's female characters experience a direct, spontaneous desire for sex, or are sexually attracted by the sight or the touch of an attractive male body. Female sexual desire does not exist as such in Dreiser's writing; it is generally attached to another medium. Emanuela, for example, has a strong interest in art, which the narrator analyzes as a sublimated desire for sex. Carrie's desire appears to be not for sex but for clothes, but in the novel she has to travel the road of sex—she has to sleep with Drouet and Hurstwood—in order to fulfill her sensualized desire for a nice appearance. Jennie's desire is the altruistic desire to help her family, but she can only help her family by becoming a sexualized kept woman. And Aileen is primarily in love with Cowperwood's "powerful spirit" and his social status, not with his body. The effect is that in Dreiser's fiction every aspect of female life becomes thoroughly sexualized, because every desire can be read as rooted in sex. A woman's social ambitions, her altruism, her artistic desires, everything becomes sexual, supposedly emanating from a sex-filled body, and thus offering numerous angles through which her body may be seduced. As a result, the male can only establish sexual contact with the female body after engaging in the hermeneutical task of reading and interpreting the nature of her desire. Finding the right medium for fulfilling her desire is essential to gain access to her body.

Yet underneath its overt eulogy of desire, Dreiser's fiction also presents a critique. He emphasizes that Carrie's desire for beauty and clothes is not her own, but is always already mediated in her society's power structures. It is usually male lovers who play powerful roles in the "mediation" of female desire, illustrating Foucault's point that power resides not so much in repression but in pleasurable seduction. Carrie's body, for example, undergoes a true metamorphosis under the tutelage of Drouet, who sets himself up as "a good judge" and a "teacher" for Carrie. He continually points out superior feminine "models," who indicate that Carrie is "lacking."[38] Carrie imitates the body language and the dressing styles of those women whom Drouet points out to her, thus inscribing on her body not only Drouet's but also society's conventional ideals of femininity and perfect beauty.

In contrast to women's mediated arousal of sexual desire, it is the act of looking at women that arouses spontaneously the male sexual desire and propels "man" forward in his chase for the ultimate sexual "possession." In *Dawn,* Dreiser argues that "the form of a woman, and its energizing force is communicated through the eye," as he makes a case for the "naturality" or the biological basis of the male obsession with gazing at "her form, that mystic geometric formula" that "inflames his passions."[39]

"As long as the master's scopophilia (i.e., love of looking) remains satisfied, his domination is secure," writes feminist theorist Toril Moi,[40] a critique that applies to Dreiser's work not only because of its obsessive inscription of pleasurable male scopophilia, but also because many of Dreiser's narratives involve the reader in a duplicitous voyeurism. In "Emanuela," the narrator repeatedly savors the magical moments of the heroine's "undressing," her "slipping out of a heavy, blood-red velvet coat" (684), an act that he celebrates as the pleasurable revelation of the female body underneath, "for me as alluring as ever" (684). In *Sister Carrie* this voyeuristic pleasure of "undressing" the woman is given a twist in that Drouet enjoys the sensual moments of "dressing" Carrie with new clothing in a department store, moments that already anticipate the future "undressing."

Dreiser emphasizes that women like Carrie and Jennie no longer "keep their eyes down," but look back at men and thus challenge the social conventions of looking.[41] And yet, the play of gazes is a double-edged sword in Dreiser's fiction that does not lead to the women's claiming their subject status, but to its opposite. In *Sister Carrie*, Hurstwood woos Carrie with his eyes in a theater, and she becomes the object of specular penetration when she looks back at him: "Several times their eyes accidentally met, and then there poured into hers such a flood of feeling as she had never before experienced."[42] Standing on the upper landing of a hotel staircase, Senator Brander in *Jennie Gerhardt* initiates Jennie's seduction, when she looks up at him from downstairs.[43]

Dreiser presents another facet of this power play of desire in *The Titan* (1914), in which Cowperwood's wife Aileen Butler appears like "a truly beautiful, a vibrating objet d'art,"[44] whose beauty is presented to the "spectators" of Chicago, the socially prominent who comment and judge her like a representation. Not only does the novel interweave the motifs of sex, art, and power, but to emphasize the notion of the female as "art object" even further, Cowperwood has Aileen's picture painted "while still young" and in the prime of her beauty. This picture becomes part of his art collection, hung opposite "a particularly brilliant Gérôme, then in the heyday of his exotic popularity—a picture of nude odalisques of the harem, idling beside the highly colored stone marquetry of an oriental bath."[45]

Gérôme's nudes are a very apt mirror image of Aileen's picture as well as the real Aileen. (The picture also evokes Carrie, who, in one of her roles, parades on the stage as a harem girl.) Just as Gérôme's harem suggests a potential cornucopia of sex for the male potentate, so its complementary mirror image, the picture of Aileen, celebrates sexual vitality and draws a whole number of male spectators. They dream of sexual pleasure with her, but are simultaneously made conscious of the "lack" of this pleasure in their own lives; they are "chained" into "conventional" relationships with "cold" and "possessive" wives.

The juxtaposition of the two visual representations in the same gallery—of Aileen and the harem—work together to draw attention to what is really absent in both pictures: the male as owner of the picture as well as "master" over the female body. Cowperwood triumphs over all of the male spectators, who are aware that he is the only one to have access to the beautiful body they admire in the picture. As the owner of the gallery, Cowperwood presents himself as a lover of beauty. At the same time, his role as a powerful master–accumulator–owner is inscribed in the gaps of the representations he owns.

But *The Titan* also draws attention to the danger of being the center of a representation, as Aileen is in the beginning of the novel. After Cowperwood's first social event in Michigan Avenue, in which Aileen is offered as the representational "center-piece," it is in fact Aileen who is dismissed by Chicago society as "too showy" and "vulgar." The Cowperwoods' social failure is repeatedly attributed to Aileen; she is sacrificed not only by the socially prominent in Chicago but also by Cowperwood, who distances himself from her.

Whereas Aileen is dismissed by conventional society, Carrie is the ultimate triumph as an art object, albeit through the authorial manipulation of filtering her stage acting exclusively through the gaze of yearning male spectators. Acting on the amateur and professional stage, Carrie's success is not so much explained by her outstanding artistic performances, but by the fact that she is an art object into which can be read any desire, all the better as she is not monogamously attached to anyone, as is Aileen. As Carrie and Aileen are turned into sexualized art objects, so the sketch of "Emanuela" is characterized by Dreiser's mythologizing of the beauty of his loved-one, of evoking her so blatantly in terms of Greek goddesses and other idealized images that Emanuela is thoroughly transformed into a fictional creature. In front of our eyes, she becomes a product of the artist's mind, a fiction of beauty rather than a creature of flesh and blood, an art object, rather than the artist she yearns to be.

This Pygmalion motif is most clearly thematized (and satirized) in *The "Genius"* (1915), the novel about the rise and fall and subsequent rise of the artist–painter Eugene Witla. His self-confessed ideal of feminine beauty is the woman at eighteen, an ideal he supports with century-old social practices as proof of the naturality of such male desire: "That was the standard, and the history of the world proved it."[46] The last third of *The "Genius"* focuses on Eugene's love for what he perceives to be his ultimate ideal, Suzanne Dale, who is half his age and who is willing to (but never does) give herself to him with no marriage chains attached, the ultimate "gift" of the female to the male in Dreiser's fiction. "You changed me, made me over into the artist again," he exclaims enthusiastically.[47]

But when Eugene celebrates the "pathos of [Suzanne's] voicelessness," the reader realizes the irony and the power play of a relationship in which a middle-aged man reads his own dreams and ideals into her blank smile. Suzanne constitutes an intense energy, which she offers as a "gift" to be formed and rewritten by the artist–Pygmalion Eugene. The power play becomes most evident when Eugene—eulogizing change, activity, movement in his own life and art—expects Suzanne not to change. When she does and turns away from him, she stirs up deep aggressions in Eugene. She is cast out of his life like an evil witch, but his memory of her is transformed into art, leaving traces in his paintings.

This is the same movement that Dreiser enacts in the sketch of "Emanuela," in which the woman, after having been cast out of his life, is transformed into art, whereby her name, turned into the title of his artistic production, becomes an integral part of the "Gallery of Women" he has created and owns. It is interesting that the narrator–author writes about Emanuela after her beauty has faded and after the "real" woman has "died" in his life. There is no doubt that the narrator's friendship has ended with the fading of Emanuela's physical charms: "But from that day to this I have never seen nor heard of Emanuela. It may be that she is dead—although I doubt it" (721).

Emanuela's figurative "death" in the narrator's life is important. In Dreiser's fictional world, creation and life are almost inevitably linked to sacrifice and death. Through the eyes of the male protagonists (and the narrators), Angela and Aileen appear to be aging and fading quickly. This prompts Eugene and Cowperwood to cast them aside and to "replenish" their own youth and creativity in new relationships with younger women. In *The "Genius,"* Angela's birthgiving, the dramatic climax of the novel and the archetypal image of female production, ends in Angela's death, thus setting the artist free from the yoke of marriage. We recall the death of the pregnant Roberta as well as the fact that Jennie's child Vesta dies and that Lillian's children from Cowperwood are relegated into the margins of the text, their existence silenced, so that we almost forget that they were ever born.

Indeed, in Dreiser's world the female's role as productive and creative icon has been usurped by the male. In *The "Genius,"* the female is sacrificed and displaced as "producer" by the male artist, as Eugene carries his destiny as "producer" even in his name and the epithet, the "genius."[48] Despite Dreiser's distance from Eugene—he deliberately puts the "genius" in quotation marks— the sexual economy celebrated by the narrator makes it almost impossible for female characters to be artists. Granted, the singer Christina Channing in *The "Genius"* is a successful artist with her own reverse philosophy of promiscuity, but the fact remains that she is present in the narrative only to be sexually initiated by Eugene, after which she conveniently disappears from the text.

Moreover, the sketch of "Ellen Adams Wrynn" in *A Gallery of Women* presents a woman painter with promising talent but who, monogamously attached to a painter-lover who cannot live with her competition, is no longer capable of painting after her lover leaves her. Her artist's career disintegrates into nothingness, while her former lover, promiscuously happy, establishes himself as a successful painter. Although Dreiser's sympathies in this sketch are without doubt with the woman–painter, he seems to struggle with the same problem of a woman's artistic competition in the sketch of "Emanuela." As the narrator–author of the sketch, Dreiser appears to be driven by an obsession to reestablish his power over a woman who not only rejects him sexually, but who has been more successful as a young writer than he was.

Grudgingly acquiescing that Emanuela is a successful popular writer and, as an editor, even publishing her stories in his magazine, he nevertheless ridicules her writing as "conservative" and "conventional." Infuriated that she should criticize his novels, it is indeed with sadistic pleasure that the narrator insists on convincing the reader of his aging friend's bodily disintegration, which is accompanied by her creative stagnation. The latter is inevitable because she has "never functioned properly as a woman" (719). He would like to see himself as the initiator of Emanuela into true art—not by discussing art with her on an intellectual level, but by initiating her into sexuality, thus establishing her contact with "real life" and giving birth to her capacity to reproduce life in literature. Yet the fact remains that, given the narrator's understanding of sexual economy, sexual contact with Emanuela would give him a double, albeit a somewhat paradoxical, advantage: that of becoming a midwife in her artistic career and of awakening in her the monogamously yielding woman, that sacrificial spirit which she lacks, but which would most certainly kill her as an artist, as it does in the case of Ellen Adams Wrynn.

Alas, in the sketch of "Emanuela," the narrator's sexual success is thwarted, which means, however, that he has only lost a sexual battle, not the war. With the support of Freud's theoretical weapons, he is eventually in a position to pronounce his "victory." When Emanuela, as a mature and no longer "beautiful" woman, turns to him for help in an artistic and personal crisis, he pronounces a vindictive judgment on her whole life: "Emanuela, you have never really expressed yourself as a woman, and so you do not know men and women or life" (719). The fact that Emanuela refused to be sexually active "castrates" her as an artist in his eyes. Only through the experience of sex might Emanuela have "better understood life, acquired that grip on reality which would have vitalized the literary or narrative gift that she had" (720), even though sex for her would have to involve a submission to rape.

Finally, like the narrator–author of "Emanuela," most of Dreiser's fictional narrators and most of his male characters not only celebrate but claim as their right the disruption of sexual conventions. At the same time, they claim to speak the "truth" of sex, a truth that promises to liberate the body from repressive social constraints. And yet, for most of the female characters, this celebrated sexual liberation is an illusion, as their bodies and sexualities are evoked only in terms of a goal that prompts the males to impose their own sexualities and to search in women's bodies for what D. H. Lawrence—another problematic sexual "liberator"—has described as the "bedrock" of her nature. Insisting on imposing the norms of what they claim to be a "normal" sexuality, Dreiser's narrators and male characters elevate their own male sexuality to the "true" standard, which not only erases any notion of a woman's sexuality but also marginalizes female sexual activity into the "abnormal." To a large extent Dreiser's fiction affirms, even celebrates, this masculine sexuality, as it affirms the Don Juan philosophy of most of its male characters with all its misogynistic implications.

And yet, what makes Dreiser's fiction rewarding—even from a feminist perspective—is that it simultaneously exposes the gender bias, the duplicity, and the arbitrary power politics of its male characters and narrators. Dreiser's writing is full of contradictions and tensions between the male narrators' omniscient voices on the one hand and the erupting female voices on the other; between the narrators' rejection of conventions and their embracing of biological normality; between the female characters' claims for independence and their subjection to male sexual conquests. It is the internal contradictions and tensions of the texts that inevitably expose the inherent gender bias, and thus the texts themselves partly critique their narrators' misogyny from within.

Not only are our sympathies drawn to "Emanuela," we cannot help but admire her apparently Quixotic resistance against "normalization." Yet through Emanuela, we also witness the tragic fact that it is "normalization" that triumphs in the end. As a mature woman, Emanuela confesses to the narrator: "I should have married or given myself to you" (721), a confession that stands out as a sad reminder that she has "failed" to become sexually "normalized" and pays the price in human isolation, once her "beautiful" body of eighteen has metamorphosed into mature womanhood. Still, the narrator ends his sketch on a deliberately ambiguous note: "It may be that she is dead—although I doubt it" (721). He does not dare close the door completely, and thus there remains a slim chance that Emanuela may have discovered a new life, a life that is, however, far beyond the narrator's realm and imagination, a life that he is not capable of writing and that is therefore relegated into the gaps of his text.

Notes

1. Philip Fisher, *Hard Facts: Setting and Form in the American Novel* (New York: Oxford University Press, 1985), pp. 165–6.

2. Leslie Fiedler, "Dreiser and the Sentimental Novel," in *Dreiser: A Collection of Critical Essays*, ed. John Lydenberg (Englewood Cliffs, N.J.: Prentice-Hall, 1971), p. 47.

3. Charles Glicksberg, *The Sexual Revolution in Modern American Literature* (The Hague: Martinus Nijhoff, 1971), p. 35.

4. Alfred Kazin, "Introduction," *Sister Carrie* by Theodore Dreiser (New York: Penguin American Library, 1983), p. ix.

5. Michel Foucault, *The History of Sexuality*, vol. 1, trans. Robert Hurley (New York: Vintage, 1980), p. 20.

6. For a theorizing of this fruitful intersection of Foucault's and feminist theories, see especially Chris Weedon, *Feminist Practice and Poststructuralist Theory* (Oxford: Basil Blackwell, 1987), pp. 107–35, as well as the collection of essays edited by Irene Diamond and Lee Quinby, *Feminism and Foucault: Strategies for Resistance* (Evanston, Ill.: Northwestern University Press, 1988). For a feminist argument against the linkage of feminism with Foucault's philosophy, see Nancy Hartsock, "Foucault on Power: A Theory for Women?" in *Feminism/Postmodernism*, ed. and intro. Linda Nicholson (New York: Routledge, 1990), pp. 157–75 .

7. Theodore Dreiser, "Emanuela," in *A Gallery of Women*, vol. 2 (New York: Horace Liveright, 1929), p. 683. Further references will appear parenthetically in the text.

8. I do not mean to suggest that the narrator's reading of Emanuela and Freud's theory are identical, as the narrator occasionally misreads Freud as much as he misreads Emanuela. Nevertheless, Kate Millett has criticized Sigmund Freud for accepting female frigidity to some degree as evidence of women's lesser libidinal energy, and she has criticized him for suggesting that frigidity may be partially rooted in the "organic," in *Sexual Politics* (Garden City, N.Y.: Doubleday, 1970), p. 194.

9. Simone de Beauvoir, *The Second Sex*, trans. and ed. H. M. Parshley (New York: Vintage, 1974), p. 439.

10. Weedon, *Feminist Practice*, p. 128.

11. Weedon, *Feminist Practice*, p. 128.

12. Ellen Moers, *Two Dreisers* (New York: Viking, 1969), pp. 262–3.

13. Foucault, *History of Sexuality*, p. 153.

14. Theodore Dreiser, *Sister Carrie* (New York: Modern Library, n.d.), p. 307.

15. Dreiser, *Sister Carrie*, p. 241.

16. Although the unexpurgated edition is sexually more explicit and daring (Carrie and Hurstwood for example make love before they are married), the sexual roles are not essentially different from the 1900 edition of *Sister Carrie*.

17. For a discussion of Carrie's moral ambiguity, see Terence J. Matheson, "The Two Faces of Sister Carrie: The Characterization of Dreiser's First Heroine," *Ariel* 11 (October 1980): 71–85.

18. Dreiser, *Sister Carrie*, p. 91.

19. Dreiser, *Sister Carrie*, pp. 89–90.

20. See Joseph Church's discussion of Minnie's dream as a reflection of her "own frustrated desires," in "Minnie's Dreams in *Sister Carrie*," *College Literature* 14 (1987): 184.

21. Dreiser, *Sister Carrie*, p. 101.

22. Theodore Dreiser, *An American Tragedy* (New York: New American Library, 1981), p. 344.

23. Dreiser, *Sister Carrie*, p. 101.

24. Theodore Dreiser, *A Book about Myself, His Autobiography 2: Newspaper Days* (Greenwich, Conn.: Fawcett, 1965), p. 272.

25. Theodore Dreiser, *Dawn, His Autobiography 1: The Early Years* (Greenwich, Conn.: Fawcett, 1965), p. 509.

26. Dreiser, *A Book about Myself*, p. 272.

27. Dreiser, *An American Tragedy*, p. 102.

28. Dreiser, *An American Tragedy*, p. 49.

29. Dreiser, *Myself*, p. 280.

30. Dreiser, *Myself*, p. 26.

31. Dreiser, *Dawn*, p. 224.

32. Dreiser, *Dawn*, p. 225.

33. Michel Foucault, "Afterword (1983): On the Genealogy of Ethics: An Overview of Work in Progress," in *Michel Foucault: Beyond Structuralism and Hermeneutics* by Hubert L. Dreyfus and Paul Rabinow (Chicago: University of Chicago Press, 1983), p. 243.

34. See Walter Benn Michaels, "*Sister Carrie*'s Popular Economy," *Critical Inquiry* 7 (Winter 1980): 373–90; Lawrence E. Hussman, *Dreiser and His Fiction: A Twentieth-Century Quest* (Philadelphia: University of Pennsylvania Press, 1983); June Howard, *Form and History in American Literary Naturalism* (Chapel Hill: University of North Carolina Press, 1985); Fred G. See, *Desire and the Sign* (Baton Rouge: Louisiana State University Press, 1987).

35. Walter Benn Michaels, "Critical Response III. Fictitious Dealing: A Reply to Leo Bersani," *Critical Inquiry* 8 (Autumn 1981): 165–71.

36. Foucault, *History of Sexuality*, p. 81.

37. See especially Luce Irigaray's argument that women play at experiencing a desire which is really not theirs: "Elles s'y retrouvent, proverbialement, dans la mascarade. Les psychanalystes disent que la mascarade correspond au désir de la femme. Cela me parait pas juste. Je pense qu'il faut l'entendre comme ce que les femmes font pour recuperer quelque chose du désir, pour participer au désir de l'homme, mais au prix de renoncer au leur. Dans la mascarade elles se soumettent a l'économie dominante du désir," *Ce sexe qui n'en est pas un* (Paris: Les Editions de Minuit, 1977), p. 131.

38. See Dreiser, *Sister Carrie*, p. 112.

39. Dreiser, *Dawn*, p. 409.

40. Toril Moi, *Sexual/Textual Politics: Feminist Literary Theory* (London and New York: Methuen, 1985), p. 134.

41. On reciprocal looking in *Sister Carrie*, see also June Howard, *Form and History*, pp. 149–51.

42. Dreiser, *Sister Carrie*, p. 121.

43. Dreiser, *Jennie Gerhardt* (Cleveland: Dell Publishing, 1963), p. 20. Also, in the *Trilogy of Desire* Dreiser stresses Cowperwood's "magnetic" eyes in the seduction of women, just as Clyde in *An American Tragedy* seduces women with his sensitive gaze.

44. Theodore Dreiser, *The Titan, Trilogy of Desire*, vol. 2 (New York: Thomas Y. Crowell, 1974), p. 36.

45. Dreiser, *The Titan*, p. 68.

46. Theodore Dreiser, *The "Genius,"* (New York: John Lane Company,

1915), p. 296.

47. Dreiser, *The "Genius,"* p. 542.

48. "Eugene," "Geni" and "genius" are etymologically linked to Latin *gigno, genui, genitum*, which means to beget, to bring forth, to produce.

Recontextualizing Dreiser: Gender, Class, and Sexuality in *Jennie Gerhardt* [1]

Nancy Warner Barrineau

Theodore Dreiser has not often been labeled a feminist, and I do not intend here to claim this designation for him. When it comes to honest, realistic treatment of American women, there is admittedly much that a late twentieth-century critic (especially a feminist) might wish to see in his work which is plainly beyond its scope. For instance, lesbians and women of color are all but invisible in Dreiser's fictional world, as they were, in essence, in his social world. But Dreiser's major novels do offer a vital portrayal of the world of white heterosexual women of the laboring classes, that group of women dubbed "working girls" by their real-life contemporaries, a group until then severely underrepresented in American fiction. Even here, Dreiser is not polemic, and he does not hammer home a thesis. In fact, his presentation of "women's issues" mirrors what critics have always recognized about his work: it is, in the words of Stanley Fish, not a "rhetorical" but a "dialectical presentation," one that stimulates its readers to provide their own conclusions rather than offering them a clear synthesis. [2] Nonetheless, Dreiser's willingness to represent this much of the spectrum of American women's lives should stimulate us to refocus our attention on issues that his books raise but that our readings usually leave submerged.

On its publication in 1911, *Jennie Gerhardt,* Dreiser's second novel, received this notice in the Washington *Evening Star* from an anonymous reviewer (who later in the piece identified herself as a woman):

> At its close one cries, out of an absorbing urgency to help: "Everyone must read this book!" Then in a minute one settles back. What is the use? Who can help Jennie Gerhardt? No one. Men cannot; their help always hurts. Women will not. In

> 10,000 years from now, Mr. Dreiser, when the animosities of sex, mayhap, are somewhat mollified, put out this book again. Then we will see what can be done for your Jennie Gerhardts.[3]

Two things stand out most distinctly in this review (and in others like it): the writer's blatant identification of Jennie with her real-life contemporaries — an association that Dreiser himself also made — and her assumptions that the position of these women is all but hopeless and attempts to remedy it futile. The review suggests that women's history is not merely an embellishment for Dreiser's readers, but instead an indispensable context if we are to grasp fully either the text or subtext of *Jennie Gerhardt*. I would in fact argue that, given recent debate about the canon of American literature and the place of "traditional" white male writers within it, we must reevaluate Dreiser's fiction in the context of the lives of real working-class women in the late nineteenth and early twentieth centuries in order to read and teach his novels effectively.

In *Jennie Gerhardt*, even more so than in *Sister Carrie*, Dreiser dramatizes without a shadow of a doubt that for working-class women (both fictional characters like Jennie and real women, such as his own mother and sisters, who served as models for these characters), gender, social class, and sexuality determine economic success or failure. Despite her remarkable intellectual and economic progress, Jennie remains a part (sometimes in subtle ways) of an underclass — defined by her status as an essentially uneducated, unskilled, and underpaid working-class woman from a not yet entirely assimilated immigrant family — from which she cannot ever completely escape. And, ironically, her willingness to exploit the sexuality she exudes in order to escape this underclass (combined with her lack of control over the consequences of her sexual choices) guarantees that she will never quite break loose from it.

Jennie's social class and her family's desperate financial straits ensure at least two things: that she must work to live and that the working world will be linked inextricably to her sexual initiation. In fact, from the time her story begins, it is clear that Jennie is a commodity (often sexual merchandise) passed from one "owner" to another. From the time the novel opens with its account of her first paying job — where she and her mother together earn three dollars for three days of back-breaking, demeaning work each week — it is clear that their inadequate wages help determine Jennie's fate. For just as Sarah Dreiser had supplemented the family income in Sullivan, Indiana, when Dreiser was a child, the Gerhardt women begin to take in laundry at the hotel to make ends meet. In the process, Jennie is introduced to George Sylvester Brander, the well-educated, successful U.S. senator who quickly begins a sexual flirtation with her.

Jennie's job and her ensuing relationship with Brander underscore her value as a commodity. Brander, it seems, is attracted to her mostly because she makes him feel rich, powerful, and even young again (although he is fifty, only seven years younger than Jennie's father). Very suddenly, apparently unaware of the irony in his choice of words, he claims sexual ownership of Jennie. He tells her, "You're my girl anyhow. . . . I'm going to take care of you in the future."[4] Later, after he has become the family's benefactor, he tells her mother, "Here is your finest treasure, Mrs. Gerhardt. . . . I think I'll take her." Both his statement and her (also ironic) reply—"Well, I don't know. . . whether I could spare her or not" (38)—make it clear that Jennie is also a commodity to her family, an important component of the family economy which her parents can choose to "sell" or withhold. The family's desperation and Brander's generosity combine to convince Mrs. Gerhardt (like Dreiser's mother, who did the same with his sister Mame) to accept his money and look the other way while Brander seduces her daughter. By the time he decides that he "can't do without [her]" (48–9), Jennie is a "kept" woman and Brander is supporting the entire Gerhardt family. Although he proposes to marry her and send her away to school (presumably to conceal her until she can be transformed into a member of the rising middle class), Brander dies before he can marry her and just before Jennie discovers she is pregnant.

By allowing Jennie to suffer the natural consequences of her first youthful experience with sex, Dreiser in this novel explores territory barely glimpsed in *Sister Carrie*. We know, mainly by inference, that Carrie (like Jennie) engages in two long-term sexual relationships. But while writing his first novel, Dreiser censored himself much more stringently, eager to have it published despite the standards of censorship that he knew others would impose on the novel. There is no mention of birth control, and Carrie does not get pregnant or even, apparently, worry that she may.[5] But *Jennie Gerhardt* makes a quantum leap, for Dreiser was willing this time to dramatize realistically what would most likely happen to a young woman in Jennie's situation. Even with the censorship, this novel reveals Dreiser's awareness that to women like Jennie—regardless of their wishes—pregnancy is the probable consequence of sex. Dreiser's ability to imagine and dramatize the full implications of a working woman's sexuality had advanced considerably since his first novel. Here Dreiser acknowledges that, in an age when unhampered access to birth control is still woefully inadequate, women must often pay a high price for their half of the sexual contract.

Dreiser was, indeed, expanding the boundaries of realism. This attempt, I would contend, can be compared to the radical struggle during those same years of Margaret Sanger, a prime mover in the American birth-control movement, who "first presented birth control as a free-speech issue," insisting that "the most urgent need was to establish the right of birth control advocates to write and speak openly on the subject."[6] In fact, when the First American Birth Control Conference (which Sanger organized) took place in New York in November 1921, Dreiser was sufficiently interested in the topic to be one of the official international sponsors.[7]

It is easy to understand Dreiser's reticence in dealing with the same issue in *Sister Carrie*. When he began his career as a novelist, Dreiser, like most other Americans, especially writers, was well aware of the role that Anthony Comstock and others like him played in the late-nineteenth century politics of authorship. In 1873, maneuvered by Comstock, Congress passed a law that had extensive and long-term ramifications at every level of American society. This most famous of the federal Comstock laws prohibited the mailing of information about contraception, written material about sex, and pornography—all lumped together as "obscene." Conviction carried a penalty of six months to five years of "hard labor in the penitentiary," combined with a fine ranging from one hundred to two thousand dollars.[8] Congress subsequently appointed Comstock a special agent of the post office, in which position he diligently enforced the law until his death in 1915. He claimed that in his first six months in this capacity he confiscated "194,000 obscene pictures and photographs, 134,000 pounds of books, 14,200 stereopticon plates, 60,300 'rubber articles,' 5,500 sets of playing cards, and 31,150 boxes of pills and powders, mostly "aphrodisiacs" (and, surely, abortion remedies). He also bragged that he had the power to drive his targets to suicide (fifteen women in all, according to later accounts).[9]

Of course, because the law criminalized the distribution of pamphlets about sex and birth control as well as contraceptive devices, its greatest impact was on those women (and men) seeking to limit their fertility. The 1873 Act was not overturned until 1938. Only then could contraceptive information be mailed legally in the United States. Even twenty years later, in 1957, Alfred C. Kinsey's research material on female sexuality was seized by U.S. Customs (although ultimately the courts cleared Kinsey).

Comstock's power was so great that Margaret Sanger held him personally responsible for the inability of poor women in the United States to receive contraceptive information, as well as for her own arrest for distributing her book *Family Limitation* through the mail.[10] In fact, when she resigned her position as a public health nurse in order to dispense birth control information full time, doctors warned her that she would not succeed (even if she could locate reliable information, a possibility about which they were skeptical). They told her, "Comstock'll get you if you don't watch out."[11]

Comstock profoundly affected the literary world, especially those realistic writers who were daring, increasingly, to write more openly about sex and its consequences. His personal slogan— "Morals, not Art or Literature"—announced baldly that medical publications were not his only targets. In fact, he once "pronounced foreign literary classics to be more harmful than the crudest pornography. He hammered home his point by attempting to banish the *Decameron*, *Arabian Nights*, and Rousseau's *Confessions* from the United States."[12] Certainly Dreiser wrote *Sister Carrie* with an eye tipped toward the forces of Comstock; and in 1911, while he was finishing *Jennie Gerhardt*, the 1873 Comstock law still prohibited honest literary treatment of sexual issues, as well as open discussion and dissemination of birth control information.

But attitudes were gradually beginning to change. Just around the corner—in 1915—Sanger and her colleagues would coin the term "birth control."[13] In addition, writers were gradually managing to slip past the censors, especially, it seems, in magazine articles. The *Reader's Guide to Periodical Literature*, which began indexing articles in 1900, provides a wealth of information on the changes taking place in these decades. In Volume 1 (1900–1904) the heading "sex" does appear, but it includes no controversial titles. Instead, the articles deal with rather innocuous gender issues or sex traits in plants. Even by Volume 3 (1910–1914), there is, of course, not yet a subject heading for "birth control," because the word had still not worked its way into common usage. However, related categories, like "sex (psychology)," "sex determination," and "sexual hygiene" were proliferating rapidly. The heading "sex instruction" encompasses 65 entries, most dealing with what children should learn about sex and whether they should learn it from their mothers or public school teachers. Many of the 18 entries under "sexual ethics"—articles with titles like "What Is Your Daughter's Chum Whispering to Her?," "Sex O'Clock in America," and "Necessary Evil is Not Necessary"—illustrate how controversial these subjects remained, but they also confirm that more open discussion, even in the press, had begun. By Volume 4 of the *Reader's Guide* (1915–1918), the added category "birth control" listed 46 articles, many of which used the new term in their titles.[14] A perusal of the *Reader's Guide*, along with other evidence, helps support the theory of some historians that the sexual revolution (which greatly affected women, probably much more than it did men) did not begin in the 1920s, as conventional wisdom has fixed it, but was already well underway in the teens (Gordon, *Woman's Body* 188).

But even considering this slowly changing social climate, *Jennie Gerhardt* is remarkably forthright, although some of its early reviewers missed the sexual implications. An anonymous reviewer for the New Orleans *Times-Democrat* wrote, "Let no one turn to 'Jennie Gerhardt' with the expectation of finding scenes of passion. The author is essentially reticent in dealing with the great facts of life" (Salzman 73). Admittedly, there are no explicit sex scenes in this novel. Nevertheless, Dreiser does indeed deal with "the great facts of life." For one thing, the novel considers Jennie's pregnancy from a number of angles. The practical and the moralistic realms merge immediately when her father discovers she is pregnant, for his rigid attitude toward her pregnancy cuts her off instantly from her family's support. Mr. Gerhardt responds in a conventional and predictable way: he labels her a "street-walker" who "has set herself right to go to hell" (84) and that same evening throws her out onto the streets to fend for herself.

No doubt because Dreiser was anxious to prevent the similarly conventional reader from identifying with Mr. Gerhardt, the narrator sardonically explains, " 'Conceived in iniquity and born in sin,' is the unnatural interpretation put upon the process by the extreme religionist, and the world, by its silence, gives assent to a judgment so marvelously warped" (92). Then, arguing from the evidence of modern science, he continues: "Surely there is something radically wrong in this attitude. The teachings of philosophy and the deductions of biology should find more practical application in the daily reasoning of man. No process is vile, no condition unnatural" (93). Jennie, he points out, is the "helpless victim" of an "unreasoning element of society" which could see nothing but "a vile and premeditated infraction of the social code, the punishment of which was ostracism" (94). So much, Dreiser says, for received morality.

H. L. Mencken, on reading the completed manuscript of *Jennie Gerhardt*, wrote Dreiser, "If anyone urges you to cut down the book bid that one be damned. . . . Let it stand as it is."[15] However, the terms of Dreiser's agreement with Harper and Brothers, which first published the novel in 1911, included a stipulation that the publisher would fully revise the manuscript and expurgate what the editors found "offensive," all at Dreiser's own expense. And so Ripley Hitchcock, along with his staff, managed to cut 16,000 words from the typescript. James L. W. West III argues that, as a result, "a blunt, carefully documented piece of social analysis" became "a love story merely set against a social background." In particular, profanity, slang, and references to alcohol disappear, and "virtually all mention of sex is muted or removed."[16] Thus, in the first edition, some of Dreiser's commentary about Jennie's sexuality, including her pregnancy, is lost to the reader.

Nonetheless, despite the censorship, Dreiser does confront openly at least some of the medical and social issues surrounding Jennie's pregnancy, which instantly completes her transformation into the maternal being which she will remain throughout the novel. She thinks that it is "a wonderful thing to be a mother—even when the family [is] shunned" and "that she would love this child, would be a good mother to it if life permitted" (95–6). Her new worries about "hygiene and diet" send her quickly to Dr. Ellwanger, the family physician, who (despite being a Lutheran) knows the ways of the world. He addresses Mrs. Gerhardt's fears about social opinion (confirming that the stance of Jennie's father is an "unnatural interpretation") and the physical threat to Jennie's well-being. He says,

> "Well, you mustn't worry. These things happen in more places than you think. If you knew as much about life as I do, and about your neighbors, you would not cry. There are few places I go that there is not something. Your girl will be all right. She is very healthy. She can go away somewhere afterward, and people will never know." (96)

Jennie listens to the doctor's "sound and practical advice" with rapt attention, "anxious to do whatever she [is] told," and readily answers when he probes into the identity of the baby's father. When she tells him, he answers, "That ought to be a bright baby" (96). At this point the two editions diverge, because an editor at Harper and Brothers deleted some of the exchange. As Dreiser first wrote it (and as the passage appears in the restored text), the doctor also said, "I think it will be a girl," and the narrator explained, "He was judging by a peculiar conformation of the muscles of the back which at this period was to him an invariable sign. Then the doctor added, 'You need not worry,' . . . . 'You will have an easy time. You are a strong girl'" (96).

Both versions of this short scene raise crucial questions about the relationship between working-class women and the medical establishment. Perhaps the most obvious ones touch on the competence of the family physician. What kind of doctor is he? Can he indeed predict IQ and gender? Does he really know Jennie will have no trouble with childbirth, or is he merely responding as a man to whom childbirth appears "easy"? Perhaps most intriguing of all, how did Dreiser and the editors who censored the text view the folksy German doctor?

West argues that the scene as it was originally cast paints Dr. Ellwanger as "little more than a practitioner of folk medicine," more evidence that the Gerhardts are "people trapped by ignorance and poverty, helpless before figures of authority."[17] The attitudes of Jennie and her mother toward the doctor apparently confirm this speculation; for Jennie regards the doctor as if he were a god, and Dr. Ellwanger "preside[s]" over the birth, only "assisted" by Mrs. Gerhardt, though she has survived childbirth six times and knows "exactly what to do" (97). But given what we know of the medical status quo in the 1880s, when Jennie has her baby, the passage raises other issues as well, among them why a family of the Gerhardts' position turns to a doctor rather than to a midwife (if, indeed, Mrs. Gerhardt herself is not capable of providing Jennie with prenatal care and attending at her labor).

In "Forgotten Women: American Midwives at the Turn of the Twentieth Century," Judy Barrett Litoff points out that during this period immigrants and members of the lower classes generally hired midwives to deliver their babies at home, rather than pay a doctor (whose services were much more restricted than a midwife's, as they often still are) or be confined in a charity hospital. However, most American midwives received little or no training and were not considered reputable practitioners by the native-born middle and upper classes or by the medical establishment.[18] By the end of the century a major struggle had evolved between midwives and physicians (almost all male) who specialized in the new field of obstetrics. As Carroll Smith-Rosenberg demonstrates, the male medical profession had fought intensely to take from women the power to regulate all those medical concerns that had in the past been assumed to be characteristically "female" — gynecology and obstetrics, including birth control, abortion, and childbirth.[19] On the basis of late-nineteenth century evidence, G. J. Barker-Benfield argues that the rise of gynecology was simply a powerful expression of the male need to control women and that "gynecologists treated their patients as if they were rebels or criminals."[20]

This struggle may explain why the Gerhardts turn to a family doctor rather than to a midwife.

That the Gerhardts' doctor is Dr. Ellwanger, rather than a different kind of doctor, also makes sense in historical context; for a parallel struggle between "regular" doctors and those who practiced folk medicine — the "homeopaths, hydropaths, eclectics, [and] the large number of rural-born physicians who remained marginal to the world of urban medical schools and medical societies" (that is, the "irregulars") — was also taking place in the late-nineteenth century. The "regulars" gradually won this battle with the passage of medical licensure laws by individual states (Smith-Rosenberg 228–33; Gordon, *Woman's Body* 159). Traditionally, however, most Americans of the Gerhardts' (and Dreiser's) social stratum had turned to the "irregulars," and Dr. Ellwanger is no doubt this kind of doctor.

Perhaps, as West argues, Dr. Ellwanger does represent the exclusion of the Gerhardts — especially the women of the family — from the structures of social power. But since he is clearly an "irregular" physician, himself excluded by the powerful medical establishment, he may really be their ally. And just perhaps, despite the disclaimers of the "regular" physicians, he knows what he is talking about. After all, Jennie does give birth — with no complications — to an intelligent girl. His assumption about the child's IQ is based on a theory of heredity firmly ingrained in the nineteenth century: that "the father was responsible for a child's external musculature and skeletal development, the mother for the internal viscera, the father for analytical abilities, the mother for emotions and piety."[21] Even with the excised sentences restored, the conflicting strands of evidence make it difficult to identify conclusively Dreiser's attitude toward Dr. Ellwanger,[22] especially because Ellwanger's theories were not limited to folk practitioners but were probably shared by the "regulars" and by Dreiser himself. But what Dreiser preserves for us is a lively cultural debate (still unresolved more than eighty years later) about the relationship between women's health issues, including reproduction, and the medical establishment.

A vast textual gap lies between this scene with Dr. Ellwanger, which takes place early in Jennie's pregnancy, and the next major scene, when her child is born. Most significantly, the novel all but ignores the physical realities of Jennie's pregnancy or the work she performs during it. Dreiser tells us only that

> Going about her household duties, she was content to await without murmur the fulfillment of that process for which, after

all, she was but the sacrificial implement. When her duties were lightest, she was content to sit in quiet meditation, the marvel of life holding her as in a trance. When she was heaviest pressed to aid her mother, she would sometimes feel herself quietly singing, the pleasure of work lifting her out of herself. (94–5)

We learn of the "many things to be done" to prepare for the baby: "clothes to be made, secrecy to be observed, care in her personal conduct of hygiene and diet observed" (96), but somehow Dreiser fails to convince me that he has fully visualized Jennie's pregnancy.

The description of Jennie's labor, limited to a single paragraph, is similarly censored by the author. Glossing over the dangers and pain of childbirth, still very real in the 1880s, Dreiser writes, "the child was ushered into the world" (96–7) — a rather euphemistic way to describe a passive childbirth. Then, abruptly, the scene shifts to Jennie's relationship with her baby:

There was no difficulty, and at the first cry of the new-born infant, which came with its appearance, there awakened in Jennie a tremendous yearning toward it which covered all phases of her responsibility. This was *her* child! It was weak and feeble — a little girl, as Dr. Ellwanger had predicted, and it needed her care. She took it to her breast, when it had been bathed and swaddled, with a tremendous sense of satisfaction and joy. This was her child, her little girl. She wanted to live and be able to work for it, and she rejoiced, even in her weakness, that she was so strong.

She is "up and about" in only ten days, exceeding the "quick recovery" anticipated by the doctor, further evidence to Dreiser that Jennie was "born with strength and with that nurturing quality which makes the ideal mother" (97). Once again, it is possible that Dreiser was incapable of dramatizing this event realistically and convincingly. But it is also feasible that he is intentionally avoiding the censor's pen in his discussion of a subject that still could not be discussed candidly.

Without grappling with this section of the novel, the reader cannot fully understand Dreiser's view of Jennie. Clearly, motherhood is essential to Jennie's nature. Thus, Dreiser may be quite simply reflecting the prevailing medical (and social) opinion that a woman's sole purpose was childbearing. Many commentators, in fact, felt compelled to argue that this role was determined absolutely by biology. As one physician framed it in 1870, it seemed to many observers "as if the Almighty, in creating the female sex, had taken the uterus and built up a woman around it" (Smith-Rosenberg and Rosenberg 335).

If this were Dreiser's implication, then we could reasonably infer that he had become significantly more conservative in his assumptions about the nature of women during the last decade. After all, Carrie is a "nonreproductive woman" (as Smith-Rosenberg phrases it)[23] — presumably by choice — who seems to have no maternal instincts whatsoever. But other readings of these two parallel texts are possible. It may be that Dreiser could not yet meld both attributes in the same character, or perhaps he is merely reflecting a society that has not yet allowed women to combine the variant sides of their nature. Thus, Carrie and Jennie may simply function as the opposite ends of a dialectic for which an adequate synthesis has not yet emerged. A reviewer for the *Bookman* adopted this stance when he wrote that "if all womankind could. . . be divided into two groups" the two characters "would stand as representatives of these opposite types, the woman whose pleasure lies in receiving, and the woman whose joy it is to give." Jennie, in contrast to Carrie, he wrote, "has the inborn instinct of motherhood; she must have, always, something or somebody to whom she may make sacrifice" (Salzman 77). Although Kate Chopin, in *The Awakening*, takes pains to establish that not every woman (certainly not Edna Pontellier, who has two young children) is a "mother–woman" (26), most voices in that generation were not so tolerant. But Dreiser, like Chopin, refused to insist that motherhood is essential to every woman or that all women are fulfilled by motherhood alone — or by motherhood at all. Instead, he conveys to the reader that Jennie, with her "supreme motherly instincts" is the exception among women, not the rule.

If Jennie were middle class, motherhood would almost automatically mean her withdrawal from the working world. But since Brander's death has eliminated her chance to join the middle class and thus enjoy the luxury of full-time motherhood, when Vesta is born, the novel turns its attention once more to the curious intersection of work and sex. Jennie becomes part of the paid workforce once more, and we are quickly reminded that she is still a firmly entrenched part of an underclass, clinging only barely, in fact, to working-class status. Her education, economic status, family position, and role as mother determine where she will turn; for Jennie is trained for nothing but domestic work. Although she looks for work in both the department stores and the factories first, she is almost fated to return to a domestic job, though a less grueling position than her earlier one at the Columbus House. Hired as a lady's maid for four dollars a week plus room and board (benefits she does not enjoy because she returns at night to her family), Jennie begins working in the Bracebridge mansion, the scene of her encounter with Lester Kane.

Jennie's peculiar position in the Bracebridge household confirms how well Dreiser understands the quandary that young working-class American women faced at the end of the century. She needs a job not only to support her child (whom she feels she must hide), but also to raise her status as well as that of her extended family. Yet taking the only job she is trained for virtually guarantees, because of its nature, that she will never really escape her class after all; for the position of women employed as domestic workers was in some ways even worse than that of other menial laborers, even factory workers. Working conditions were often harsh, and domestic workers' wages averaged between two and five dollars per week. Since those who "lived in" could not punch out at the end of a shift, their hours were typically half again as long as the factory worker's.[24] And domestic workers had little hope of earning the respect of the middle class, much less of presuming to rise to it. Consequently, as the century progressed, domestic work was left more and more to immigrants (or the daughters of immigrants) and women of color. After extensively surveying domestic workers in the 1890s, historian Lucy Maynard Salmon determined that most other American women resisted this work because of its dull, unchallenging nature; the unlikelihood of promotions; the long hours which reduced their independence; and the necessity of working beside immigrant and minority women.[25]

Dreiser also depicts another kind of bias faced by these workers. More than other lower-class menial workers, domestic employees were assumed to be sexual adventurers. Family members often treated servants as "a source of moral contagion,"[26] and wives and mothers watched the female hired help with a sharp eye lest they initiate sexual liaisons with the family's sons and husbands. In fact, the middle class as a whole held a "widespread hostility" toward working-class women, especially domestics, which according to Charles E. Rosenberg "might well have mirrored middle-class repression of the sexuality which the lower orders were presumed to enjoy."[27] In the nineteenth and into at least the early twentieth century, it was widely believed that anyone wishing to climb into the middle class must sublimate sexual energy and use it for other, more capitalistic pursuits. Race and social class (not just gender) were presumed to determine one's sex drive. Lower-class women, especially women of foreign descent and women of color, so the hypothesis went, were more sexual than middle- and upper-class white women, who were increasingly expected by their very nature to be oblivious to sexual matters. A body of convincing evidence suggests that the historic distinction between "'good' and 'bad' women has. . . been coded in class and racial terms"—that is, that the moral lines have traditionally been drawn between the "pure" sexuality of middle-class white women and the promiscuity of ethnic and lower-class women.[28]

Given this late-nineteenth century conventional wisdom, the unwelcome sexual attention that Jennie receives in her new domestic job is not surprising. Dreiser makes it plain that male visitors to the Bracebridge mansion approach her routinely "with a view to luring her into some unlicensed relationship" (119). And Jennie, because of her family situation and the outcome of her encounter with Brander, is likely to fulfill the stereotype of the sexual underclass. At first she resists, but rather than continue to question these men's prerogative to make demands of her or reject the stereotype, Jennie begins to reflect that perhaps she was "innately bad and wrong herself" (120). Thus, when Lester Kane shows up, she is ripe for the picking; although "she did not bear any outward marks of her previous experience" and "there were no evidences of coquetry about her, . . . still he 'felt that he might succeed'" (122). Some would assume that Lester magically intuits something about Jennie's past or about her essential nature, but given his socialization, he probably merely assumes that a young female domestic servant is fair game for what he thinks of as the "browsing" of the upper-class male (122).

Jennie's sexual dilemma confirms her place in the working class, but it also shows Dreiser pushing the boundaries of censorship. Even in the expurgated first edition, Jennie is a far more sexual woman than Carrie is, her sexuality a much more dangerous commodity than is Carrie's. Like Brander before him, Lester is attracted at first sight by her sexuality alone; and, also like Brander, he claims her by saying, "You belong to me." And, also like her first lover, he all but forces her into a dangerous liaison which offers no more ultimate security than did her first affair. Although Dreiser's first novel does not explore fully the consequences of Carrie's sexual choices, *Jennie Gerhardt* breaks new ground in daring to expose the controversy over women's control of their own reproductive functions.

The issue is only implicit early in the novel, but in retrospect it is clear that Brander, who seems to love Jennie, sins by omission when he fails to provide her with birth control (to which he certainly must have had access) or to marry her before he dies. He thereby denies her the legal and financial status that would have protected her later on. Jennie's subsequent experience raises the issue of birth control—still under the control of the Comstock law — more explicitly. When Lester, unaware of her previous affair or the existence of a child, decides that he, too, must "have" her, Jennie initiates a discussion of birth control with him. Jennie approaches the subject quite timidly, but the exchange is, nonetheless, remarkable, considering her personality as well as the prevailing standards of censorship. In the first edition, after hearing his proposal, Jennie realizes that a "relationship with him meant possible motherhood for her again. The tragedy of giving birth to a child — ah, she could not go through that a second time, at least under the same conditions." Finally, she tells him, "I couldn't have a baby." Lester replies, cryptically, "You're a great girl, Jennie. . . . You're wonderful. But don't worry about that. It can be arranged. You don't need to have a child unless you want to, and I don't want you to." He reiterates a moment later: "It's so. . . . You believe me, don't you? You think I know, don't you?" Although she "falter[s]," she answers "Yes."[29]

A careful reader of even the first edition can grasp what Ripley Hitchcock, Dreiser's editor at Harper and Brothers, tried to expunge: a dialogue which marks a crucial change in Dreiser's treatment of sexual material. First, Dreiser is willing to move beyond *Sister Carrie* (where sexual exchanges are always handled covertly), this time signaling openly the sexual nature of Jennie and Lester's illicit relationship and admitting that for both of them it is a calculated move. More importantly, both Dreiser and his protagonist seem to be newly cognizant of the perils of female sexuality, so much so that both are brazen enough to discuss it — Jennie with Lester, Dreiser with the reader, although his attempt is mediated by the editorial censor. Their conversation confirms that Jennie, who has had one affair and given birth to a child, knows little or nothing about birth control, while Lester, the single, wealthy, sophisticated man-about-town, knows a great deal.

It also suggests that Lester feels in control of the issue, because he does not offer to explain to Jennie what she desperately needs to know and because he makes it plain that he will probably use contraceptives as a matter of course — not from any desire to protect Jennie, but because he is reluctant to father a child. Later in the passage he adds: "But anyway, I wouldn't let any trouble come to you. . . . Besides, I don't want any children. There wouldn't be any satisfaction in that proposition for me at this time. I'd rather wait. But there won't be — don't worry." Jennie answers faintly, but "not for worlds could she have met his eyes" (Viking 165).

All these implications are clearer yet in the typescript version altered by Hitchcock, now restored in the Pennsylvania edition. There, after telling Jennie not to worry, Lester adds, "You don't need to. I understand a number of things that you don't yet" (158). Later on the narrator tells us that Jennie "half-wondered what it was he knew and how he could be so sure, but he did not trouble to explain" (159). These passages, deleted in the first edition, reinforce the impression that Lester is making sure that Jennie feels the chasm which age, gender, and social class place between them. To put it bluntly, his remarks (as Dreiser was surely well aware) are chauvinistic and paternalistic, sure to make Jennie uncomfortable. At the end of Lester's remarks, Dreiser added, "He stopped and she opened her eyes in wonder and a kind of shame. She had never known that" (158). His editors excised these sentences,[30] but they confirm that Dreiser wanted the reader to know that Jennie is ignorant about contraception and embarrassed about having to rely on Lester for vital information about her own body.

Since Jennie does not become pregnant again and the subject never resurfaces, Lester apparently does have access to effective contraceptives. With the exception of the birth control pill, most forms of contraception used today were already available in the late-nineteenth century, with similarly mixed results. Withdrawal and the "safe period" method—limiting intercourse to the time when a woman was ostensibly unable to conceive—were common practices carried over from earlier centuries. The latter, however, was even more unreliable then than now, for the "safe period" was calculated based on misguided information about when ovulation occurs. It was in fact the 1920s before the medical profession discovered precisely when women ovulated (Smith-Rosenberg 231; Degler 214). Thus medical guides and marriage manuals frequently instructed women in precisely how and when to *get* pregnant in the guise of teaching them how *not* to. Some marriage guides even claimed that a woman could not become pregnant unless she experienced sexual desire or orgasm (Smith-Rosenberg 138).

Domestically manufactured condoms were made possible by the invention of vulcanized rubber around the mid-nineteenth century. However, at a cost of approximately $3.00 per dozen, they may still have been too expensive for laborers, who earned an average annual wage of $500 in 1865.[31] Their use, of course, depended on male compliance. However, condoms had one major advantage: a loophole in the law allowed them to be sold for the prevention of venereal diseases in men, but not to men or women who admitted wanting them for contraception.[32]

Douches and diaphragms (called "womb veils," "pessaries," or, in the case of one 1846 prototype, "The Wife's Protector") were also available (Degler 346). Diaphragms, in fact, were the choice of public health clinics once they finally began distributing contraceptives. By 1920, a "new lactic acid paste," developed by Sanger's clinic, was being used with diaphragms with a 98 percent success rate (Douglas 185). But as some historians point out, the diaphragm had serious drawbacks for the very population which needed it most. Its use (especially with the lactic acid paste or, later, spermicidal jelly) was difficult for women who lived in tenements without private bathrooms. In addition, many women failed to use it reliably simply because they did not understand "how conception takes place." For these women, some writers point out, the condom was probably a much more reliable method (Hymowitz and Weissman 297–8).

And, of course, there was abstinence, a strategy widely advocated by strange bedfellows from both the left and right. On moral grounds, conservatives promoted abstinence even for married couples who wanted to limit the size of their families. Some radical feminists argued that women could truly control their own bodies only by abstinence and that using birth control would allow them one fewer rationale for controlling their own sexuality (Degler 257–8). Even most doctors remained skeptical of birth control. Dr. H. S. Pomeroy wrote in 1888 that there was only "one prescription which is both safe and sure—namely, *that the sexes shall remain apart*" (Rosenberg 138); and the American Medical Association did not endorse birth control until 1937 (Taft 222).

By whatever means women regulated their fertility, the declining birth rate confirms that couples were employing birth control methods more reliably than they had in the past. And, when all else failed, a large body of evidence suggests that abortion was also a common means of birth control, although it was illegal in most states by 1880 (Smith-Rosenberg 218). As Gordon points out, the increasing sexual freedom available to women made birth control "important for women," not just married ones. She argues that "the possible impermanence of love made birth control an absolute necessity. It was not a solution to the problem of sexual equality, but it was a small help" (*Woman's Body* 158).

The real problem for Jennie is not the lack of birth control technology, but her dearth of knowledge about how to control her own fertility. The disparity which Dreiser draws between Jennie's and Lester's knowledge about birth control makes a great deal of sense in the context of the mid-1880s (when this part of the novel is set) as well as in the decade or so during which Dreiser drafted the manuscript. Strong evidence substantiates the fact that in those decades information about birth control, despite the efforts of the Comstock forces, was readily available to the middle and upper classes. One doctor, for instance, reported around the turn of the century that "there was 'hardly a single middle-class family' among his clients. . . that did not expect him to implement their 'desire to prevent conception"; and the American journalist Lydia Commander wrote in 1907 that "among the upper classes some kind of contraceptive knowledge was 'practically universal.' "[33]

But the same was not true of women in the lower classes, who routinely found the reproductive process beyond their control. In 1903 an article in *Popular Science Monthly* asserted smugly that "outside our immigrant classes. . . women have learned the art of preventing pregnancy." Historians have documented that members of the working class in the United States and immigrants have always had birth rates significantly higher than the middle and upper classes and that not all social groups practice birth control with equal effectiveness. There are probably several reasons for this difference – among them, the beliefs held within classes or ethnic groups about the relative advantages and disadvantages of having large families, as well as the cost of contraceptive devices (Kennedy 44; Degler 220–1).

Abraham Jacobi (known as "the father of pediatrics") un-leashed an unpopular topic when he used his 1912 inaugural address as president of the AMA to rally support for the dissem-ination of birth control to all women. His address underscored the inequality of a system in which the wealthy but not the poor could obtain contraceptives (Gordon, *Woman's Body* 169). Then as now, education was also a key factor: the poor have always been the last to get contraceptive information. As late as 1921 Emma Goldman wrote to Margaret Sanger, "Tell me how it is the wealthier class of people can get information like that and those that really need it, can't?"[34] According to Degler, interviews of working women around the turn of the century suggest that immigrant women knew how to limit their fertility to a greater degree than observers like Sanger knew, but they had few reliable resources besides abstinence and abortion (22).

The difference in the number of their respective children is one fundamental difference between Jennie and her mother. Mrs. Gerhardt dies not only from overwork, but also from a lifetime of childbearing, as did many women of her day. In 1900, the average life span for women was approximately 48 years. This rose to more than 65 years by 1940, in large part because women were having fewer children and because childbirth had become much safer.[35] Early in the novel Mrs. Gerhardt tells Senator Brander she has six children. His reply—"You've certainly done your duty to the nation" (14)—may seem somewhat peculiar to modern readers, but in 1911, it must have signaled a familiar debate.

The controversy belongs, in fact, to the period in which Dreiser was composing *Jennie Gerhardt,* not to the decades when Brander (who dies in 1880) was a Washington politician. By the late 1890s, Theodore Roosevelt's concern about the nature of population growth had brought the issue to national attention. In well-publicized speeches he warned about the conjunction of the declining birth rate of native-born American women with increasing immigration and high birth rates among immigrant women. Between 1905 and 1910, the "race suicide" scare, linked to Roosevelt's imperialistic designs for the "white" race, became particularly ugly. It reflected and intensified cultural anxiety about the inherent conflict between the immigrant and native populations. It attacked women who "strayed from their proper sphere," especially college educated women (who tended to have the lowest birth rates) and middle-class women who joined the workforce. Native-born women who chose to have no children (or to have significantly fewer than did their mothers and grandmothers) Roosevelt labeled "criminal against the race. . . the object of contemptuous abhorrence by healthy people" (Gordon, *Woman's Body* 132–6). Roosevelt expounded, "If the women do not recognize that the greatest thing for any woman is to be a good wife and mother, why, that nation has caused [sic] to be alarmed about its future."[36]

There is one odd element in Brander's comment to Mrs. Gerhardt about the number of childen she had borne. He seems to consider them strong "native" stock whose proliferation is a credit to the nation. Although it is not clear whether Mrs. Gerhardt is native born, Mr. Gerhardt was born in Germany. The family is thus a poor immigrant family of the kind whose fertility Roosevelt and his supporters would gladly have limited. Perhaps Mrs. Gerhardt is a first-generation American, or perhaps Brander is more progressive than others in Washington. But it is evident, at any rate, that Mrs. Gerhardt's patterns of reproduction are far different from the next generation's.

In his personal life Dreiser surely was, as Robert Penn Warren tagged him, "hell on women."[37] But in his novels, particularly in *Jennie Gerhardt,* he exposes his empathy for women—especially members of the working classes—and his understanding of their plight. The novel's engagement with turn-of-the-century women's issues has always resonated with scattered readers, such as the Washington *Evening Star*'s reviewer, who "close[d] this book strengthened in her belief that this world is no place for women" (Salzman 75). Eighty-odd years later, reestablishing the complex and vital historical context out of which Dreiser wrote *Jennie Gerhardt* can help readers grasp just how realistic and radical this novel really is.

Notes

1. This essay was made possible by a 1992 Summer Stipend from the National Endowment for the Humanities.

2. Stanley Fish, *Self-Consuming Artifacts: The Experience of Seventeenth-Century Literature* (Berkeley: University of California Press, 1972). Quoted by Ross Murfin in "What Is Reader Response Criticism?" *The Awakening* by Kate Chopin (New York: Bedford, 1993), p. 299.

3. Jack Salzman, *Theodore Dreiser: The Critical Reception* (New York: David Lewis, 1972), p. 76. For the reference to the writer's gender, see the conclusion of the review quoted above, p. 73.

4. *Jennie Gerhardt*. The University of Pennsylvania Dreiser Edition, ed. James L. W. West III (Philadelphia: University of Pennsylvania Press, 1993), p. 35. Unless otherwise indicated, internal page citations correspond to this edition.

5. In the 1952 Paramount film version of the novel, *Carrie*, starring Jennifer Jones and Lawrence Olivier, she does become pregnant by Hurstwood, only to miscarry in their squalid flat. My theory is that the movie included several changes that were contrived to domesticate a Carrie who was still too threatening to the social order even fifty years after Dreiser created her.

6. Carol Hymowitz and Michaela Wesman, eds., *A History of Women in America* (New York: Bantam Books, 1978), pp. 297–8.

7. Ellen Chesler, *Woman of Valor: Margaret Sanger and the Birth Control Movement in America* (New York: Simon and Schuster, 1992), p. 200.

8. "Comstock Law, 1873." Rpt. in *Women's America: Refocusing the Past*, 3d ed., ed. Linda K. Kerber and Jane Sherron De Hart (New York: Oxford University Press, 1991), p. 537.

9. Edward DeGrazia, *Girls Lean Back Everywhere: The Law of Obscenity and the Assault on Genius* (New York: Random House, 1992), pp. 4–5. For my information on Comstock and literary censorship, I have also relied heavily on Alec Craig, *Suppressed Books. A History of the Conception of Literary Obscenity* (Cleveland: World Pub., 1963).

10. Margaret Sanger, *My Fight for Birth Control* (New York: Farrar and Reinhart, 1931). Rpt. in Kerber and De Hart, 342–9. (Quotation, p. 346.)

11. Margaret Sanger, *Margaret Sanger: An Autobiography* (New York: Dover, 1971), rpt. of 1938 ed., p. 93.

12. Richard Lingeman, *Theodore Dreiser: An American Journey 1908–1945* (New York: Putnam's Sons, 1990), p. 128.

13. Linda Gordon, *Woman's Body, Woman's Right: Birth Control in America* (New York: Viking Penguin, 1990), p. 221.

14. In "The Dating of the American Sexual Revolution: Evidence and Interpretation," Daniel Scott Smith points out that more articles on subjects related to sexuality—especially such topics as divorce and prostitution—appeared in the *Reader's Guide* between 1910 and 1914 than in the years 1919 to 1924 or 1925 to 1928. (Michael Gordon, ed., *The American Family in Socio-Historical Perspective*, 2d ed. [New York: St. Martin's Press, 1978], 426–38.) (Quotation, p. 434.) Smith's discussion is fascinating, and his claim is technically correct. But in truth the 1910–1914 volume includes more entries under *most* headings than these later volumes; it is 700 pages longer than the next volume. Whether a boom in periodical literature or more fastidious indexing accounts for the difference, I do not know.

15. Thomas P. Riggio, ed., *Dreiser-Mencken Letters: The Correspondence of Theodore Dreiser and H. L. Mencken, 1907–1945*, (Philadelphia: University of Pennsylvania Press, 1986), p. 69.

16. "The Composition of *Jennie Gerhardt*," in *Jennie Gerhardt*, The University of Pennsylvania Dreiser Edition, pp. 421–60. (Quotation, p. 442.)

17. James L. W. West III, "Editorial Theory and the Act of Submission," *Papers of the Bibliographic Society of America* 83 (1989): 169–85. (Quotation, p. 184.)

18. *The Historian* 40 (February 1978): 235–51. As Litoff points out, American midwives were held in ill favor in part because they did not receive the same training offered to their European counterparts (many of whom, of course, emigrated to the United States). However, during this period a few schools, such as New York City's College of Midwifery and the Playfair School of Midwifery in Chicago, did provide rigorous training for American midwives (242–3). Midwives were distrusted further because many people thought that they acted as abortionists, which indeed they often did.

19. Carroll Smith-Rosenberg, *Disorderly Conduct: Visions of Gender in Victorian America* (New York: Oxford University Press, 1985), p. 228 and *passim*. See also G. J. Barker-Benfield, *Horrors of the Half-Known Life: Male Attitudes Toward Women and Sexuality in Nineteenth-Century America* (New York: Harper and Row, 1976), p. 62; and Linda Gordon, *Woman's Body, Woman's Right: Birth Control in America*, p. 157.

20. "The Spermatic Economy: A Nineteenth-Century View of Sexuality," in Michael Gordon, pp. 374–425. (Quotation, p. 389.)

21. Carroll Smith-Rosenberg and Charles Rosenberg, "The Female Animal: Medical and Biological Views of Woman and Her Role in Nineteenth-Century America," *Journal of American History* 60 (September 1973): 332–56. (Quotation, p. 337.)

22. See West, "Editorial Theory," pp. 184–5.

23. Carroll Smith-Rosenberg argues that during this period the woman who refused to reproduce generated a great deal of cultural anxiety. (See *Disorderly Conduct*, p. 23.) This theory may shed light on the early critical hostility toward Carrie.

24. Barbara Mayer Wertheimer, *We Were There: The Story of Working Women in America* (New York: Pantheon Books, 1977), pp. 209–10.

25. Lucy Maynard Salmon, *Domestic Service* (New York: Macmillan, 1897), rpt. as "Objections to Domestic Service" in *Early American Women: A Documentary History 1600-1900*, ed. Nancy Woloch (Belmont, Calif: Wadsworth, 1992), pp. 419–22.

26. Charles E. Rosenberg, "Sexuality, Class and Role in 19th-Century America," *American Quarterly* 25 (May 1973): 131–53. (Quotation, p. 143.)

27. Rosenberg, "Sexuality, Class and Role," p. 143. There is evidence also, of course, that some working-class women confirmed these stereotypes when they replaced or supplemented their low wages by working as prostitutes. Of the 2,000 New York prostitutes surveyed by William Sanger, 37 were factory workers, 39 housekeepers, and 933 servants of other descriptions. See *The History of Prostitution: Its Extent, Causes and Effects Throughout the World* (New York: Medical Pub. Co., 1913), p. 524.

28. Kathy Peiss and Christina Simmons, *Passion and Power: Sexuality in History* (Philadelphia: Temple University Press, 1989), p. 6. See also Rosenberg, "Sexuality, Class and Role," *passim*.

29. *Jennie Gerhardt*, ed. Donald Pizer (New York: Viking Penguin, 1989), pp. 164–5. Further references to this edition will be cited within the

text as Viking.

30. See West, "The Composition of *Jennie Gerhardt*," p. 443, for a detailed comparison of this passage in the two texts.

31. Carl L. Degler, *At Odds: Women and the Family in America from the Revolution to the Present* (New York: Oxford University Press, 1980), pp. 210–7; and Smith-Rosenberg and Rosenberg, "The Female Animal," p. 346.

32. Emily Taft Douglas, *Margaret Sanger: Pioneer of the Future* (New York: Holt, Rinehart and Winston, 1970), p. 101.

33. David Kennedy, *Birth Control in America: The Career of Margaret Sanger* (New Haven: Yale University Press, 1970), p. 45.

34. Linda Gordon, "Birth Control and Social Revolution," in *A Heritage of Her Own: Toward a New Social History of American Women*, ed. Nancy F. Cott and Elizabeth H. Pleck (New York: Simon and Schuster, 1979), pp. 445–75. (Quotation, p. 466.)

35. Susan Householder Van Horn, *Women, Work, and Fertility, 1900-1986* (New York: New York University Press, 1988), p. 46.

36. Van Horn, *Women, Work, and Fertility*, p. 1. The 1905–1909 volume of the *Reader's Guide* indexed 34 articles under "race suicide," which had for the first time earned a separate subject heading. In the next volume (1910–1914), only 12 titles (two by Theodore Roosevelt) appear. Some—like Seth Low's "Is Our Civilization Dying?," which appeared in the April 1913 *Fortnightly Review*—warned about the dangers of the declining native birth rate, but others pointed out the fallacies of this popular argument.

37. Robert Penn Warren, *Homage to Theodore Dreiser: On the Centennial of His Birth* (New York: Random House, 1971), p. 6.

The Secrets of Fraternity: Men and Friendship in *Sister Carrie*

Scott Zaluda

Little critical attention has been paid to references Theodore Dreiser made in *Sister Carrie* to the Elks fraternity, an important element of Hurstwood's and Drouet's social and commercial world during the Chicago portion of the novel. Early on, Dreiser sketches Drouet's "type" with, among other markings, "the secret insignia of the Order of Elks" suspended from his watch chain (5).[1] At one point, Drouet recognizes "the value of lodge standing and the great influence of secret insignia" for success in business (152). Hurstwood's "considerable influence, owing to his long standing with the Elks, who were rather influential locally," helps assure a full house of Chicago political and commercial luminaries for Carrie's acting debut in an Elks' theatrical benefit (174). But while these and other allusions to the Elks may be few and far between, they nonetheless offer important clues for interpreting the novel within a discourse of gender in late nineteenth-century American cities.

This essay examines how *Sister Carrie* represents a fraternity of men gathered in bars and restaurants or for events sponsored by the Elks; the essay also identifies ways that the novel, in the terms of Amy Kaplan, creates and criticizes white, middle-class masculinity and men's social power in late nineteenth-century commercial society. "Against contradictory representations"[2] of fraternities and male fellowship, such as those that appeared in authorized fraternal publications, or those that have appeared in historical accounts of American fraternities, Dreiser, I argue, represents a self-serving and aggressive middle-class, American male type who finds his identity both among and against a community of other men who look, talk, and act just like him — referred to ironically as a "better social order" (47) — and against a variety of

77

others, men and women, whose interests contradict his own and his community's.

In reading *Sister Carrie*, I direct my attention to these defining relationships between different men of the dominant social group and between those men and others in the industrial city. Men's relations as represented in the novel appear often to bear out social historian Mary Ann Clawson's observation that fraternalism "is above all about boundaries, in both their institutional and symbolic aspects — their construction, their bridging, and occasionally their dismantling." Notably, Clawson says, membership in an organized group of any kind creates a boundary between members and nonmembers.[3]

The lodge brothers milling around in the street outside the Avery Hall theater on the night of the Elks benefit create boundaries between themselves and their wives, the city's working women, and others of the surrounding working-class neighborhoods; between themselves and the homeless as well as other new urban types, that is, European immigrants and African–Americans, whose presence in *Sister Carrie*, while merely allusive, still helps define the social boundaries and identities of white, middle-class businessmen. The ways these men fraternize, either outside theaters or inside resorts and restaurants, also suggest that social boundaries may be constructed (or dismantled) internally as well; in other words, boundaries formed against types and groups of the external society are often mirrored within the relationship of lodge brother to lodge brother.

To shed light on the boundaries men create to define themselves against other types and groups, while exploring Dreiser's dis-ease with the proscriptions surrounding nineteenth-century American men, I read *Sister Carrie* in part through sociologist Georg Simmel's turn-of-the-century monograph, *The Secret Society* (1906).[4] Simmel sees the secret society, historically and contemporaneously, as constituted by external pressures within societies in transformation. Secrecy itself, Simmel wrote, has an "external" sociological significance; that is, secret gatherings, rituals, and symbols such as those which attracted men to American fraternal societies signify an uneasy "relationship between the one who has the secret and another who does not."[5]

Simmel suggests a useful framework for interpreting intersections of internal and external tensions that give rise to and compose the male world of Hurstwood and Drouet. In the secret society, he remarks, "as everywhere else, the intensified seclusion against the outside is associated with the intensification of the cohesion internally."[6] "Associated" here does not imply a direct proportion, per se, but a kind of interpenetration by which a social group's sense of itself is inextricable from its sense of those from which it secludes itself.

But Simmel's rendering of the internal/external oppositions that generate and sustain secret societies of men does not account for the entire complex of tensions by which the men in Dreiser's novel construct themselves, and their relations within and outside the exclusive, at times secret, circle of males-only discourse. Thus, I argue that the internal cohesion of "gentlemen Elks" who lounge about chattering in Hurstwood's resort is at once intensified and contested by internal tensions of eroticized fellowship and mutual aggression. Finally, although Simmel develops a broad perspective on the social dynamics that attract men to and hold them in groups within changing societies, Dreiser is finely tuned in to the shifting boundaries of urban, white, middle-class male fellowship and, thus, to details of instability marking transformations in American social life.

In *The Secret Society,* Georg Simmel noted that the essential purpose of certain secret orders among men in Africa and India was "to emphasize the differentiation of men and women."[7] Without engaging that point specifically, I would nonetheless employ Simmel's concept to argue that the vast proliferation of fraternal orders in the United States after the Civil War, along with eating and drinking places catering exclusively to men, occurred as part of an increasing separation of the gendered spheres of home and work, and as part of a response to the increased presence of women, outside the home and in the workplace.[8]

Gunther Barth (1980) has argued that although women's salaries and working hours were generally oppressive, new forms of employment in the factory and department store "opened up a major female avenue into the male-dominated urban job market. The total effect was to introduce women as a new social force in city life."[9] Still, this new proximity of men and women in the center city tended often to reinforce strictures of segregation, official and unofficial, within both economic and social arenas. For instance, Robert Thorne has shown in his study, "Places of Refreshment in the Nineteenth-Century City" (1980), that men could "venture in public where women could not and might, it was supposed, be educated or toughened by contact with the varieties and extremes of urban life. [Men's] freedom of action offered possibilities of either immorality or improvement, where for women they lay only in disgrace."[10]

Simmel views the secret society's "flight into secrecy" as a "ready device for social endeavors and forces that are about to be replaced by new ones."[11] To carry that idea through constructions of history, such as Barth's and Thorne's, at this point in the history of American cities, when an industrial system had already gone far to isolate work from home and men from women, millions of American men, perceiving a need to reinforce their separation against a complicating presence of women within the spheres of male-dominated work and recreation, enacted a kind of flight into forms of ritual behavior intended in part to preserve ideals of masculinity. For example, calling themselves knights and guards, the Elks, like the Masons upon whom they modeled themselves, through formal, secret rituals conjured up an imaginary medieval manhood.

But reaction to the changing status of women must be understood as having formed only part of the context for a widespread flight of men toward fraternal orders during the thirty years following the Civil War. Indeed, contrasting African and Indian societies, Simmel grounds his explanation of the contemporary secret society—his main Western example is the Freemasons—with a reading of the social consequences of Western industrialism, emphasizing throughout the monograph that the secret society emerges as a consequence of desires to accommodate and to resist extensive cultural change.

To make the argument that male fellowship in *Sister Carrie* is represented as a response to forces of social and cultural change, it is necessary to demonstrate that such change is also a concern of the narrative. In fact, the narrator is noticeably eager to suggest the transience of the novel's representations between its opening moment in 1889 and the moment the story is being told in 1899–1900, in view of the rapidity of social transformation. Several examples will serve at this point to indicate the novel's characteristic qualifying note that social forces and endeavors have either already raced well past the life conditions decribed or that they are about to.

First, the city itself is constantly in flux, constantly looking forward. Chicago's population, expanding at the rate of 50,000 a year, thrives, the narrator tells us, not "upon established commerce," but "upon the industries which prepared for the arrival of others" (12, 16). "Anticipation of rapid growth" has even been inscribed upon future suburbs in the form of streetcar lines which "extended far into open country" (16). A closer perspective indicates that within the city's central districts, department stores, at the time a brand new institution, and factories have begun introducing women by the thousands as both workers and consumers (18, 22)—just as Barth has noted. Looking inside one of those factories, the narrator mitigates his description of the "hard contract" faced by women working in 1889 factories by educating his 1900 reader to the fact that "the new socialism which involves pleasant working conditions for employees had not then taken hold upon manufacturing companies" (39).

Moreover, changes such as these seem to be linked to the disruption and instability of basic social elements such as family life. Hurstwood's "perfectly appointed" North Side household, the book's main example of middle-class domestic life, "can scarcely be said to be infused with" a home atmosphere "calculated to make strong and just the natures cradled and nourished within it" (81). Absent fathers are increasingly alienated from their profligate sons and daughters, ambitious husbands from their desexualized wives (82–3). Although a man in Hurstwood's position as manager still needs to have "a respectable home anchorage," the masculine world of the "resort which he managed was his life" (85). Home and family relations are in the process in 1889 of becoming superficial, burdensome, and increasingly separated from men's interests.

In the suggestion that secret societies formed in reaction to something, Simmel echoes points of view many nineteenth-century fraternal orders had of themselves as settings of seclusion. Historian Carey McWilliams (*The Idea of Fraternity in America* [1973]) has written that an American man in the "great age of fraternal orders," the Gilded Age, could find "safe retreat from his daily life of competition, insecurity, and hostility" in a "world of pure affection, a momentary place of romance" promised by the the the fraternity.[12] According to a 1931 organizational publication, the Benevolent and Protective Order of Elks "was born in the minds and hearts of a small group of devoted friends, whose only selfish desire was for fraternal companionship."[13]

Nevertheless, the first order of any secret gathering, Simmel says, is "protection."[14] In fact, the Protective Order of Elks had been founded after the Civil War by a group of social outcasts, white minstrel show performers, performing in blackface. Originally calling themselves the Jolly Corks, after the substance used to blacken their faces on stage, these men, who first met in the corner of a downtown Manhattan saloon, according to another Elks historian,

> were made up of the stratum of humanity—the theatrical profession —which for proceeding generations had been stigmatized

as "vagabonds" — those children of genius who have done so much to beautify and enrich the world. . . . . It has only been in later years that the general public has come to understand the great fraternity which sprang from the loins of this once despised theatrical profession.[15]

By the turn of the century, however, the Elks had grown so large that their status as a secret society had greatly changed. Indeed, they were now publishing accounts of themselves for the general public and enjoying such publicity as came from local newspaper columns devoted to the activities of fraternities. The nature of Elks protectiveness would change, too, as the society expanded and as its stigmatized theatrical ranks were replaced by a conventional middle class. Once secrecy was no longer necessary for protecting a despised group, once the secrets had been "limited" to the "formalities" of society meetings,[16] the need felt by Elks for protection was being influenced by other concerns — to use McWilliams's terms, other hostilities, new sorts of competition, new insecurities.

McWilliams's big, unwieldy study, a kind of romance in itself, captures with affection the fraternity's own expressed dream of creating a "protective order" within a threatening or problem-ridden society, a secret environment for acting out a romance or nostalgic fantasy of ideal social relations. But except in recognizing that there was at one time something other against which a "faint, romantic echo of fraternity,"[17] articulated through secret speech and behavior, offered at least momentary seclusion, McWilliams shows little interest in the social tensions themselves which produced desires for exclusive male companionship, or in what Simmel saw as the "association" of those tensions with fraternal companionship.[18]

In *Sister Carrie,* Charles Drouet, a typical Chicago salesman of his age and a member of the Benevolent and Protective Order of Elks, identifies with the romantic, somewhat erotic symbol of the wild male animal suspended from his watch chain (5), a symbol chosen originally by the founders of the Elks in 1867 for its attractive physical characteristics and, importantly, for its fidelity with other males. But contrary to the official story that the Elks' only selfish desire for gathering was companionship,[19] as the bearer of that symbol on a gold chain attached to his vest pocket, "a secret sign that stands for something," Drouet also marks himself eligible to rise "way-up" the social scale (152). For Drouet, then, the secret of the symbol is its association with success and with things that the group associates with specifically male success.

Merely being among men in certain public places, immersed in the music of what Dreiser calls their "pointless phraseology" (46), connotes for Drouet success and sensory pleasures as indistinguishable. Drouet is virtually seduced by the romance of the carnival-like setting of the restaurant, resort, or theater. He is "lured as much by his longing for pleasure as by his desire to shine among his betters" (47). The most seductive element of the gathering appears to be the nearness of other men: "here men gather, here chatter, here love to pass and rub elbows" (47).

> The many friends [Drouet] met here dropped in because they craved, without perhaps consciously analyzing it, the company, the glow, the atmosphere, which they found. One might take it after all as an augur of the better social order, for the things which they satisfied here, though sensory, were not evil. No evil could come out of the contemplation of an expensively decorated chamber. The worst effect such a thing could have would be perhaps to stir up in the material-minded an ambition to arrange their lives upon a similarly splendid basis. (47)

Moralizing is not this narrator's descriptive style, though irony often is; considering Hurstwood's disastrous fate, the "worst effect" of this juxtaposition of influential elements will be, we know, far worse. Auguring a better social order, the image given here for ironic contemplation is one of businessmen glowing within a sphere of gaudy light.

Like other elements of the social world Dreiser imagines, the splendid surface that draws these men toward each other has another side, that is a discourse of business and sexual gain. Drouet's ability to turn pointless phrases has, in fact, a point when he is talking with the well-connected resort manager. Drouet has

> what was a help in his business, a moderate sense of humor, and could tell a good story when the occasion required. He could talk races with Hurstwood, tell interesting incidents concerning himself and his experiences with women, and report the state of trade in the cities which he visited, and so managed to make himself almost invariably agreeable. . . .
>
> "Come around after the show. I have something I want to show you," said Hurstwood. . . .
>
> "Is she a blonde?" said Drouet, laughing.
>
> "Come around about twelve," said Hurstwood, ignoring the question. (44, 48)

Hurstwood ignores the question because he understands more acutely than his less socially "way-up" friend that certain questions need not be asked; that is, the invitation to "come around" must, among initiated men, conceal its secret of illicit sexuality.

This blending of commerce and sexuality, their "chatter," along with their passing and rubbing of elbows must, the narrator says, "be explained upon some grounds. It must be that a strange bundle of passions and vague desires gives rise to such a curious social institution or it would not be" (47). A term the narrator may have been searching for here to characterize those passions, one which comes out of late twentieth-century feminist theory, is homosocial. That is, these relations are political in nature but they are also sexualized, without being explicitly homosexualized.

I am suggesting that one way to interpret relations in the setting of saloon and fraternal society is to utilize Eve Kosofsky Sedgwick's term homosociality, referring to the difference made "when a social or political relationship is sexualized."[20] Sedgwick's conception of "the play of desire and identification by which individuals negotiate with their societies for empowerment," sees an "active congruence" among constructions of gender, heterosexuality, homosexuality, and homosociality.[21] Such a congruence is present in *Sister Carrie*'s Chicago where male bonds are constituted and cemented by relations that value eroticized desire for the physical pleasure of being among men, narratives of sexual exploitation of women told to other men, and sexual and business success acknowledged and advanced by other men.

Of course, in *Sister Carrie*, women also wield social power which disrupts the restricted homosocial circle of male relations. A very uneroticized wife, Hurstwood's for example, in the separate sphere of the home, is an outsider, indeed a threat, to male pleasure, who must nonetheless be accommodated within Victorian communal arrangements. Family, a wife and children, to use the terms of Simmel, is associated in *Sister Carrie* with the internal cohesion of the male group as both a necessity for upward mobility within Hurstwood's economic class and as a standard of morality within and against which these male relations are formed.

The craving for the type of male relations available within fraternal societies may have resulted from a need either to substitute for something lacking in domestic life or to resist something about American domestic life in the Gilded Age that was in transformation and which threatened male power and autonomy. Moreover, nineteenth-century men in saloons and protective orders, in offering homosocial reinforcement to one another, as a result may have rendered less interesting the companionate, sexual, and parental bonds within the family. In his survey of late nineteenth-century secret societies, W. S. Harwood blames, among other things, a "peculiar fascination in the unreality" of fraternal mysticism and ritual along with "conviviality" associated with drinking, for a deterioration of family relationships.[22]

When in the company of his family, the *Sister Carrie* narrator says, a man may visit a Wisconsin resort where he must spend these "stiff, polished days, strolling about conventional places doing conventional things" (85). In *Sister Carrie*'s male culture, segregated male relationships are sought after because they give a context to the unconventional possibility of unresponsible sexuality, at least in discourse when not in actuality. Such notably secret pleasure is presumably enjoyed by Hurstwood and other men during a so-called "alderman's junket" to Philadelphia. "Nobody knows us down there," one of the men tells Hurstwood. "We can have a good time" (86). Additionally, the body of Carrie generates for Hurstwood fantasies of sexual abandon, a kind of liminality inconceivable within the family but not within the protective order of fictive brotherhood.

For Dreiser, then, male secrecy becomes a device of unconventional sexuality, a seclusion from the stiff and barren connotations of domestic life. Signing what cannot and need not be spoken aloud, Hurstwood's friend gives "just the semblance of a wink" to punctuate this invitation to "have a good time" with "several who were his friends" on the ten-day junket (86).

Within the circle of male secrets, an eroticized figure like Carrie, who is not a wife, like the "blonde" Drouet anticipates for his midnight liaison with Hurstwood, functions for men to delineate their private and public sexual power. Carrie is the "little peach" Drouet "struck" on a train whom Drouet mentions to Hurstwood, "trying to impress his friend" (49), and whom he eventually shares with Hurstwood, feeling, then, "closer to him than ever before" (95). Here, too, clichés of silent, secret understanding translate the true meaning of Drouet's invitation to Hurstwood. "I want you to come out some evening," Drouet says to Hurstwood, who "looked up quizzically, the least suggestion of a smile hovering about his lips" (80).

But obviously Carrie has a more complex and important role in the novel than as a sexual object bonding men. As Dreiser's principal character, she is central to his critique of constructions of male power. Carrie's performance in the Elks' theatrical benefit, for example, creates a focus for exposing an intense homosocial contest of two male friends, Drouet and Hurstwood, not only against an external factor, women, as they struggle for control of their privilege to deceive both wives and lovers, but internally between each other—as they struggle to maintain their backslapping fellowship against raging competition from their sexual desires.

Given the occurrence of these tensions, the meaning of the ubiquitous word "friend" in *Sister Carrie* may be held in place as follows: for a man to be a friend of other men means that he can fit himself into a publicly heterosexual and often commercial discourse and that he feels a strong pleasure based upon physical intimacy with other men among bright objects, including young, unmarried women. Male friendship also means that a man agrees to maintain what Erving Goffman (1959) has called "a veneer of consensus" as to how the situation of his coming together with other men or with women is to be defined and controlled. He agrees, that is, to openly express his affinities with other men and to suppress or conceal his aggressiveness as a desiring economical and sexual being, the "worst effect" (47) resulting from his envy and ambition.[23]

Dreiser exposes these dynamics of male togetherness most fully through the relationship of Hurstwood and Drouet. Compared with Hurstwood's social situation, his friend Drouet's position in the group is marginal. Unaware of Hurstwood's envy of his relations with Carrie, Drouet looks toward Hurstwood with a kind of narcissistic arousal. When Hurstwood visits the apartment Drouet shares with Carrie, who, to amplify Drouet's social position, is presented as Mrs. Drouet, Drouet exacts great pleasure from seeing himself being admired and appreciated by another man for his choice of a woman—like the choice of a pair of shoes—and from noting what he takes for an increasing intimacy with the admiring man, actually his rival. On the other hand, in the course of the story Hurstwood's thoughts, words, and deeds concerning Drouet range from being sympathetic to patronizing to jealous to violently destructive. At one point, Hurstwood "mastered himself only by a superhuman effort," as he wishes for an "end of Drouet" (193).

Meanwhile, the "object of this peculiarly involved comedy," as Dreiser describes Carrie, her attractiveness and value on the increase, sorely strains the fraternal balance of arousal, shows of comraderie, and rivalry tinged with violence. Nevertheless, both men, in their own ways, are manipulating Carrie, the "little peach" Drouet "struck" on the train (48), in order to have their secret pleasure without sacrificing their fellowship as members of the group or the larger community. To recoup Simmel's terms, then, Carrie, an outsider to the male community, like the communally sanctioned domestic sphere which she displaces, is associated with both the seclusion against the outside and the intensification of the group's internal cohesion. As the excluded "other," as well as the secret object of desire, she is made to inform much of the novel's male discourse.

As an outsider to both the fraternity and family, Carrie is linked to several other insidious social types in Dreiser's late nineteenth-century American city, with whom the Elks may have felt sharp differences. She is one of the factory workers, for example, whose ubiquitous presence in the city calls into question the affability of the men who manage manufacturing shops and display their Elk medallions. And she is linked to others of the nondominant culture who crowd the expanding city about whom the men of the resort display no apparent awareness.

In a defining scene, when Carrie, Drouet, and Hurstwood are all together one evening, they encounter a ragged man on the street outside a theater begging for the price of a bed. Here the writer juxtaposes three men, two "old friends," Drouet and Hurstwood, and a gaunt-faced stranger, described as a "picture of privation and wretchedness" (139). The two friends are lodge brothers in Chicago's Elk's Club, but the third man, without a home, let alone a club, is wholly outside of any fraternity or community. He is hardly human; belonging to a mass, he is merely a "picture" of his condition. The stranger is someone in whose face these men cannot see the likes of themselves as they see themselves reflected in the resort's ornate mirrors; he is someone whose desperate phraseology is both foreign and antithetical to their "pointless" chatter. Except for a wholly anomalous moment of discovery by Drouet, the third man seems not to exist at all.

The meaning of friendship among the men of the resort is reinforced here as an agreement not to disrupt the community with social adversity; oblivious of adversity or concealing its existence, male coherence in *Sister Carrie* is, in Simmel's terms, associated with its seclusion from all representations of a pathologic national mass of poverty and homelessness.[24]

But masculine identity and the coherence of male relations are intensified, in the novel, not only by obliviousness to adverse social conditions, but by feeling what Simmel calls the "aristocratizing motive": the desire of a group to let others "feel their superiority."[25] For a second, Drouet has felt a stranger's plight, handing over a dime "with an upwelling feeling of pity in his heart" (139). Still, several moments earlier Drouet has been handing over a line to his "little peach" about his plans to marry her, and he has also recently bragged about having lied to "Burnstein—a regular hook-nosed sheeny," in selling him "a complete line" (135).

The "line" Drouet is always selling is his apparent goodwill. But whether he hands it out or sells it, as he does to women and to Jewish merchants respectively, for his commission he gains feelings of social superiority.

At the same time that Hurstwood feels a certain amount of "injustice" (138) about the game he is playing with his Elks brother, the tense dynamic of Drouet's and Hurstwood's homosocial politics of male fraternity struts its power in manipulating women, the homeless, and the Jew—another dehumanized figure, whose presence in 1900, resulting from waves of recent immigration, was perceived as threatening to the "better social order" that middle-class lodge brothers of American cities and towns dreamed they were creating.

The Elks's own revised history (1931) articulates that social order as "the Order" itself:

> Non-Sectarian, non-political, drawing its members from all sections, from all denominations, and from all political parties, the Order was naturally a medium through which those of differing creeds and political affiliations and sectional viewpoints would reach a better understanding of each other.
>
> Organized at a time when the aftermath of the civil war was still apparent in sectional bitterness and prejudice which retarded the healing of old wounds and delayed the restoration of real national accord, the Order of Elks may justly claim a foremost place among the agencies which aided in the final destruction of those barriers and speeded the happy consummation of a truly united people.[26]

The early twentieth-century membership records of Charles Edward Ellis's Elks history include photographic images of a post-Civil War new national Order of middle-class men who, based on their names and faces, apparently found neither common ground nor "better understanding" with Jews, African–Americans, or with Catholic immigrants such as Dreiser's father. Clawson points out that while the major orders never "openly barred admission to members of any ethnic minority," nevertheless the "changing character of immigration, the increasing articulation of nativist sentiment and the polarization created by the interaction of fraternal anti-Catholicism and Catholic anti-fraternalism led the fraternal movement to abandon the model of cultural pluralism that had characterized its earlier years."[27]

"Policies toward race," Clawson notes, "were much more consistent; indeed, racial exclusion was a hallmark of mainstream American fraternalism throughout its history. This was accomplished not simply on a de facto basis, but by formally requiring that prospective members must be white."[28]

One measure of how the Elks, founded by a group of white showmen who performed in blackface, had changed their position within the changing society, is that the 1931 account referred to above wholly omits mentioning the founders' line of work.[29] In *Sister Carrie*, when an Elks officer mentions to Drouet that a fellow Elk, Harry Burbeck, "does a fine black-face turn" (153), the burnt-cork mask donned by jolly corks like Harry for comic effect no longer symbolizes by irony the status of the socially despised performer and Elks' founder. Indeed, the secret of the blackface mask referred to in passing in *Sister Carrie* is that it mocks and dehumanizes only the real blacks, against whose social degradation, along with that of Jews and women, these kinds of businessmen–impressionists, like their fraternal forebears, have elevated themselves.

Tensions of inner cohesion intensified through seclusion from insidious social others are subtly articulated the night of the Elks Club benefit, when all the men come together in a carnival scene that magnifies the world of restaurant and resort.   In the first place, Dreiser concocts this scene to present a contest between the two male friends; at least one of them, Hurstwood, while watching Carrie's stage performance is able just "fairly" to maintain "his standard of good fellowship" (188) — to keep in balance, that is, homosocial male fellowship, powerful erotic desires, and an overall communal sense of order.   But there are other things happening, particularly outside the theater, that suggest how the better social order organizes the boundaries of its existence.

The scene takes place before Avery Hall. Fallen into disuse, Avery Hall exemplifies the secret society's penchant for protecting social endeavors and forces in rapid transformation. Avery Hall had once connoted a pastoral escape from the city. Originally, the narrator tells us, it had been built

> as part of a larger summer garden, when the ground upon which it was located was not more than a mile from the city limits. The city had grown so rapidly and extended its borders so far that the summer garden idea had been abandoned and the surrounding ground parceled out into one-story store buildings which were largely vacant. The hall itself, like much other Chicago property, was not in demand. (172)

But where no lights have burned for some time, lamps from the "patched and repaired" theater (172) now draw "the fascinated gaze of children and shopkeepers and people living in flats across the way." That gaze is drawn specifically toward

> the lights of a certain circle. . . of small fortunes and secret order distinctions. . . gentlemen Elks [who] knew the standing of one another. . . [who] had regard for the ability which could amass a small fortune, own a nice home, keep a barouche or carriage perhaps, wear fine clothes and maintain a good mercantile position. Anyone who did this and belonged to their lodge was quite a figure. (177, 178)

For the occasion, the Elks are animated by their "aristocratizing motive." The men of the club and resort are basking in the gaze of the shopkeepers and flat dwellers in a blighted, depressed neighborhood. Brightly illuminated at the focal center of shadowed social multiplicity, these men seem to imagine that they form a kind of a colony which, by feeling superior to what surrounds and supports it, asserts a typical colonialist's prerogative to define a better social order. Nevertheless, the veneer of consensus is penetrated by conflict both from within and from outside the focal center of the carnival.

Some of that conflict is generated by the invasive presence of women. Although convention dictates that wives be present at this gathering, not one of them speaks throughout the scene. Still, the men remain wary of their presence. Dreiser represents the secrecy cloaking what men say to one another by having them whisper or speak in asides. One woman in particular, Carrie, creates an intensification of eroticized tensions within the male group. Erotic desire, resulting from Carrie's performance in the amateur production, initiates a dangerous fantasy, Hurstwood's passionate dream of escape from normal communal constraints, including the constraint to be just to a male friend and thus to preserve the unspokenness of an agreement that cements male-to-male relations.

At the same time, the people living in flats and working in shops across the way, or the factory girls whose eyes haunt the borders of other glittering theater crowds, have a quiet, ironic presence in the novel, which penetrates the borders of homogeneous male inclusion. That the modern American city was pluralistic and defined by its class, gender, and race differences, both accounted for and contradicted the professed communal "distinctions" of proliferating middle-class secret orders. Again, in Simmel's terms, the seclusion against the people gazing in from the flats across the way "is associated with" — it both generates and penetrates — the intensification of the circle's internal cohesion.

Expressions of fellowship within this Chicago business community may not, on the surface at least, seem aggressive or even oppressive. Indeed, businessmen in *Sister Carrie* cling together in a bundle of erotic passions. But taking together everything that the narrator tells us about these men, and in particular their coarse treatment of and language for women and wives, the conditions of work in their factories, their dehumanization of the homeless, Jews, and African–Americans through blackface comedy, and their aggressiveness towards each other, we must ask whether such a represented claim of fraternity, no matter how secluded its enactment, can have been meant to be seen as "benevolent," let alone romantic.

The secret society, Simmel remarked, is above all defined by its consciousness of having a consensus surrounding particular interests, interests which over time change to resist and to accommodate other, at times contradictory, interests.[30] From the critical perspective Dreiser developed in his first novel, the representative late nineteenth-century romantic moment of male togetherness is actually a conscious political gathering of an interest group, which in secret and public ways consents to seek protection from and to protect "social endeavors and forces that are about to be replaced by new ones."[31] Dreiser's scattered allusions to the Elks in the first part of the novel, his images of men in saloons and restaurants, and the relations he depicts between men and between the sexes, may be read together as a narrative of American male culture, dreaming of order as it resists and accommodates breaches and changes in the boundaries of its imagined domain.[32]

Notes

1. Theodore Dreiser, *Sister Carrie* (Harmondsworth: Penguin Books, 1981, published by arrangement with the University of Pennsylvania Press). All page references in the text are to this edition of the novel.

2. Amy Kaplan, *The Social Construction of American Realism* (Chicago: University of Chicago Press, 1988), pp. 5–7.

3. Mary Ann Clawson, *Constructing Brotherhood: Class, Gender, and Fraternalism* (Princeton: Princeton University Press, 1989), p. 248. Insight into the fraternal impulses of nineteenth-century American men is most cogently articulated by scholars whose work has come to be labeled as men's studies. See, for example, in addition to Clawson, Mark C. Carnes, *Secret Ritual and Manhood in Victorian America* (New Haven: Yale University Press, 1989); Carnes, "Middle-Class Men and the Solace of Fraternal Ritual" in *Meanings for*

Manhood: Constructions of Masculinity in Victorian America, eds. Mark
C. Carnes and Clyde Griffen (Chicago: University of Chicago Press,
1990); E. Anthony Rotundo, *American Manhood: Transformations
in Masculinity from the Revolution to the Modern Era* (New York:
Basic Books, 1993). See, also, recent studies such as T. J. Jackson
Lears' *No Place of Grace: Antimodernism and the Transformation of
American Culture, 1880–1920* (New York: Pantheon Books, 1981)
and Carroll Smith-Rosenberg's *Disorderly Conduct: Visions of Gender
in Victorian America* (New York: Knopf, 1985), which use literary
works as textual evidence for criticizing cultures of nineteenth-century
manhood.

I find the appellation "men's studies" neither helpful nor descriptive of the critical work I carry out. Recently, men's studies, seen
as a critical movement, has been assailed by Eve Kosofsky Sedgwick
as a depoliticized compensation for women's or feminist studies.
See Sedgwick, "Gender Criticism," in *Redrawing the Boundaries,* eds.
Stephen Greenblatt and Giles Gunn (New York: Modern Language
Association, 1992) pp. 271–302. However, to support her argument,
Sedgwick unjustly totalizes the men's studies movement as having
very limited goals. Although her critique may have bearing in individual instances, especially where efforts have been made to define
men as though women were not also in the world, Sedgwick's dis-
missal of men's studies as merely "compensatory" and intellectually
"stultifying" ignores any possibilities that studies of gender focused
on men or masculinity can be a necessary angle of inquiry for the
larger project of cultural criticism (a project to which Sedgwick has
made important contributions, including one I refer to later in this
essay).

4. Georg Simmel, *The Secret Society,* trans. Albion W. Small, *American
Journal of Sociology,* XI (January 1906). The translation I use was
made in 1950 by Kurt H. Wolff in an edition intended to reacquaint
English readers with the scope of Simmel's thinking. *The Sociology
of Georg Simmel* (Glencoe, Ill.: Free Press, 1950), pp. 345–76.

The first Dreiser critic to articulate a connection between Simmel's writing and American realism was Philip Fisher. In *Hard Facts:
Setting and Form in the American Novel* (New York: Oxford University Press, 1985), Fisher alludes to Simmel's characterizations of
relationships formed by reactions to what Fisher calls the "too various and demanding" city (p. 136). Giving my attention to writings
other than the ones referred to by Fisher, I also examine Simmel's
formulations of reactive social behavior in the city, but use Simmel's
language more directly than Fisher has to frame a reading of *Sister
Carrie.*

5. Simmel, p. 345. Carnes, *Secret Ritual and Manhood in Victorian America*, Introduction, emphasizes that secret rituals, above all else, seem to have attracted men to fraternal orders.

6. Simmel, p. 369.

7. *Ibid*, p. 364.

8. W. S. Harwood, "Secret Societies in America," *North American Review* 164 (May 1897): 617–24, gives the figure of 32,000 for the national membership of the Benevolent and Protective Order of Elks (B.P.O.E.), three years before *Sister Carrie*'s publication. The fifty-plus fraternal societies he surveys had a total membership of five and one half million men. The Elks were a mid-sized group at the time, compared, for example, with the Masons (750,000 members) and the Order of Scottish Clans (4,000 members). The Elks are also one of a handful of groups on Harwood's list which still prosper. Clawson notes that orders such as the Elks, which experienced the greatest growth in the twentieth century, "de-emphasized ritual and offered a more couple-oriented sociability to their members" (p. 263).

9. Gunther Barth, *City People: The Rise of Modern City Culture in Nineteenth-Century America* (New York: Oxford University Press, 1980), p. 145.

10. Robert Thorne, "Places of Refreshment in the Nineteenth-Century City," *Buildings and Society: Essays on the Social Development of the Built Environment,* ed. Anthony D. King (London: Routledge and Kegan Paul, 1980), p. 235.

11. Simmel, p. 347.

12. Carey McWilliams, *The Idea of Fraternity in America* (Berkeley: University of California Press, 1973), p. 80.

13. *The Elks National Memorial* (Chicago: Authorized by the Grand Lodge of the Benevolent and Protective Order of Elks of the United States of America and Published Under the Supervision of the Elks National Memorial and Publication Commission, 1931), p. 8.

14. Simmel, p. 345.

15. Charles Edward Ellis, *An Authentic History of the Benevolent and Protective Order of Elks* (Chicago: by the author, a member of Lodge #4, 1910), p. 7.

16. Simmel, p. 356.

17. McWilliams, p. 380.

18. Simmel, p. 369.

19. *Elks National Memorial*, p. 8.

20. Eve Kosofsky Sedgwick, *Between Men: English Literature and Male Homosocial Desire* (New York: Columbia University Press, 1985), p. 1.

21. *Ibid*, pp. 5, 27.

22. Harwood, p. 621.

23. Erving Goffman, *The Presentation of Self in Everyday Life* (Garden City, N.Y.: Doubleday Anchor Books, 1959), p. 9. Discussing in the 1920s what he defined as essentially male group relations, Sigmund Freud noted that the sexualized feelings which hold men in a circle "turn into an expression of tenderness as easily as into a wish for someone's removal." *Group Psychology and the Analysis of the Ego*, 1922, trans. James Strachey (New York: Norton, 1959), pp. 37–8.

24. Ellis notes that "Charity" is emblazoned upon the Elks' banner, along with "Justice," "Fidelity," and "Brotherly Love." The Chicago chapter's yearly theatrical benefits during the late nineteenth century raised money for the social security of the lodge members as well as for outside causes (Ellis).

25. Simmel, p. 364.

26. *Elks National Memorial*, pp. 12–13.

27. Clawson, p. 131.

28. *Ibid*, p. 132. One consequence of barring blacks, Clawson notes, was a separate black fraternal movement, including an Improved Benevolent and Protective Order of Elks of the World, which has survived into the late twentieth century (p. 132).

29. *Elks National Memorial*.

30. Simmel, p. 363.

31. *Ibid*, p. 347.

32. For readings, comments, and suggestions that have helped me to shape this discussion, I am grateful to Jane Collins, Jean Gallagher, Barbara Shollar, and Miriam Gogol.

"That oldest boy don't wanta be here": Fathers and Sons and the Dynamics of Shame in Theodore Dreiser's Novels

Miriam Gogol

As every reader of Theodore Dreiser knows, his novels are moving and powerful human documents, containing as they do characters and situations which etch themselves — often permanently — into the consciousness of readers. Despite the fact that among American writers Dreiser has had many imitators, none has ever possessed his unique ability to move readers. And even his most perceptive critics find the source of this power elusive and difficult to explain.[1]

Recently, in reading *An American Tragedy* (Boni and Liveright, 1925) and *Jennie Gerhardt* (University of Pennsylvania, 1992),[2] I was struck by two aspects of Dreiser's fiction: how his characters regard themselves and how they relate to others, particularly other family members. In focusing on these features, I have come to realize that many of Dreiser's characters are shame ridden, both in their view of themselves and in their relationships with others. Invariably, they feel unable to measure up, to meet the standards of behavior set for them, with the result that they suffer under a burden of inadequacy. In their dealings with others, they feel that these inadequacies have become public and affect the way other people regard them. With few exceptions in Dreiser's novels, it is the male characters who are plagued most deeply and poignantly by feelings of shame.[3] Because shame weakens the image of autonomy that many males strive to project, they fight to keep the shame hidden; and they suffer excruciatingly when it becomes public, as it inevitably does. These portrayals are extremely realistic and persuasive, reflecting accurately the way a sense of shame and fear of exposure exert influence in the real lives of men, depriving them of the respect of others and making them weak and ineffectual.

Sharing these values and fears, readers identify strongly with these characters and sympathize with their dilemmas at a deep emotional level. Particularly moving in Dreiser's novels are the relationships between fathers and sons, relationships nearly always characterized by a searing sense of shame in the son, who feels himself burdened by his father's inadequacies and failures. There is, I feel, no question that much of Dreiser's power as a writer stems from this ability to portray shame-wracked males in such an affecting way.

This sense of shame comes through most powerfully in the novels' early vignettes: the unforgettable opening pages of *An American Tragedy* that set the stage for the mortification which Clyde Griffiths wrestles with for the rest of his life. Standing on a corner with his street-preaching parents, the adolescent Clyde feels humiliated by the pitying glances of passersby, one of whom remarks: "That oldest boy don't wanta be here. He feels outa place, I can see that. It ain't right to make a kid like that come out unless he wants to." Interestingly, that person in the crowd not only observes how ashamed Clyde is but also places the blame on others, presumably the parents: "It ain't right *to make* a kid like that come out unless he wants to."[4] This passage suggests that the parents are a cause of the shame felt by the children.

Shame as the novelistic keynote is also struck in the opening pages of the restored *Jennie Gerhardt*. Jennie's brother, Bass, feels "mortification" (12)[5] at the thought that his cronies might see Jennie and his mother cleaning floors in the Columbus House Hotel. Bass cautions his sister: "Don't you ever speak to me if you meet me around there. . . . Don't you let on that you know me . . . you know why" (12). When he concocts a ploy to steal coal to heat their home, he repeats: "Don't any of you pretend to know me . . . do you hear?" (28). Like Clyde in *An American Tragedy*, Bass here bespeaks a shame experienced by all members of his family.

Similar to the fathers in *Jennie Gerhardt* and *An American Tragedy*, Dreiser's own father was torn between the worldly demands of his family and his own personal need to adhere to otherworldly standards and values. Just as the Gerhardts and the Griffiths, the Dreiser family perpetuated an overpowering legacy of shame, one that haunted Dreiser throughout his life and provided the firsthand experience that he carried into his novels. The legend of Dreiser's father's economic failure in America would throw a long shadow over Dreiser and his family. Some of the striking similarities between Dreiser's family and that of his characters, especially between John Paul, Senior (Dreiser's father), and Old Gerhardt (Jennie's father), have been noted by biographers.[6] But I would like to go beyond biographical parallels and suggest that Dreiser's ability to depict shame-bound families so forcefully comes from his own inherited experience of family shame.

My contention—that a family like the Dreisers could carry such a legacy through the generations—is supported by the findings of family systems theorists (Bowen [1988], Kerr [1988], Fossum and Mason [1986], Nathanson [1987], Morrison [1989], H. B. Lewis [1987, 1971], Osherson and Klugman [1990] et al.). Before the development of family systems theory, psychoanalytic theory had evolved through the study of individual patients and, as a result, viewed the family as a collection of relatively autonomous people each motivated by his or her own particular psychological mechanisms and conflicts.[7] Family systems theorists reverse that perception. Rather than being seen as autonomous, the individual is perceived as a part of the family emotional unit.[8] As family systems analyst Carl Whitaker states: "I don't believe . . . in individuals anymore; I think they're only fragments of a family."[9] In other words, we are all part of a larger system and play only a part in its history. To understand the part that we play, it is not only helpful, but also necessary, to analyze the individual in the context of his or her larger family system. Perhaps this is why family theory potentially holds greater appeal for literary scholars than psychoanalysis, or rather the "psyche" camp of psychoanalysis— Freudians, Kleinians, object-relations theorists, and Winnicottian interpreters. It accords more closely with the "analysis" camp, especially the Lacanians—which directs attention away from the individual mind existing before or outside the act of analysis from which we deduce its existences.[10]

Family systems theory posits that the functioning of any individual in a family can be understood only in the social context of the family and in relation to the other people closely involved with him or her. When the founder of family systems theory, Murray Bowen, defined the emotional unit of the family as an "undifferentiated ego mass," he helped to explain how the troubled individuals he encountered as a clinical psychiatrist derived their behavior from their family systems.[11] Families who develop an "undifferentiated ego mass" establish vague or tenuous emotional boundaries among family members. They encourage members to become emotionally entangled or enmeshed with one another and accordingly (and in some instances unconsciously) block attempts by an individual to differentiate himself or herself emotionally from other family members. Children in such families become entangled in the "family relationship process" as soon as they are born; their self-images are formed in "reaction to the anxieties and emotional neediness of others," of parents in particular, and family members tend to define children through their own "emotionally distorted perceptions."[12]

Although a detailed analysis of the nature of shame in men as considered by family theorists is beyond the scope of this essay, an overview will be helpful in understanding what follows. Shame is a poorly understood affect, as contemporary Harvard shame psychologists Samuel Osherson and Steven Klugman explain, in part because it is so aversive and associated with infantile states: "Shame refers to a sense of inadequacy or exposure, often of a public nature, in which the sense of self feels in danger of being flooded or overwhelmed with [negative] feeling."[13] Aptly called the "judging companion" by William James (in *The Principles of Psychology*) in 1890, shame is the self judging the self as an internalized "other."[14] It has to do with an image you have of yourself and the resulting sense of deficiency or deficit, when you do not measure up.[15]

Even though it has been argued that women are shame prone, psychologists have come to believe that men are more shame vulnerable.[16] It may well be that feelings of shame are central to what leave men feeling bad about themselves. Many men deny themselves self-expression of their own vulnerability, perhaps when most needed. According to Osherson and Klugman, if men do not acknowledge their difficulty with dependency, they can be left struggling with problems of love and intimacy. Men then feel confused and inadequate. They experience a profound sense of social isolation, with defenses that have a narcissistically hardened aspect.[17]

From Dreiser's autobiographies, published and unpublished, as well as from his diaries and letters, we know that he struggled with extreme feelings of inadequacy and self-doubt, especially throughout the first half of his life. These caused such emotional and physical symptoms as neurasthenia, bad dreams, and sleeplessness. He also struggled in his personal relationships, most notably with women, with many of whom he became intensely involved and then dropped.[18] In the various versions of *Dawn*, he describes his "war" with shame: "All through the first half of my life, I felt this—*this war* with age and death and degradation—less desperately . . . as I neared maturity . . . [But] all through my youth *I ran* —. . . . Ah, the horror. . . , disgrace, . . . [the] shame, of being shut out, ignored, forgotten, left to wander friendless. . . . "[19]

And, to Dreiser, his father, in large part, was the villain. Dreiser viewed him as tyrannical and fanatically religious. Dreiser wrote in *Dawn* that he had "never known a man more obsessed by a religious belief" (*Dawn*, ch. I, 5–6). When his family was hungry, his children without shoes, John Paul, Sr., continued to pay tithes to the church and send his children to parochial school. He believed "that his soul's salvation depended upon paying dollar for dollar" each expense incurred, even those not fully his responsibility (typescript, ch. I, 2). For John Paul, Sr., accepted "literally the infallibility of the Pope, the immaculate conception of the Virgin . . . the dogmatic interpretation of mass . . . and the like" (typescript, ch. I, 3). According to Dreiser, his father condemned anything pleasurable—candy, parties, good clothes, dancing—all the things Dreiser and his siblings craved.[20]

Dreiser writes repeatedly of the clashes between his father and the children who were "bursting with animal impulses" and who "did not, . . . could not, accept his version of how their lives should be lived" (transcript, ch. IV, 28). When Dreiser and the other children would not listen to him, his father "beat . . . or abused" them[21] and charged that they were all "plunging straight to hell." John Paul, Sr. had come to the "grim realization" that "his children would not do right. They would not go to church as he wished. They would not obey the laws of sobriety and virtue as he conceived them to be" (typescript, ch. IV, 28). Shame psychologists say that the church is often appropriated in this way and used by control figures within the family system as a rule maker and supporter justifying an impossible set of injunctions.[22] Members of such families, unable to measure up, live with the hounds of shame in hot pursuit.[23]

And Dreiser lived with such hounds. As an adolescent, he was perceived by an unkind contemporary as a "gawk . . . [who] kept to himself, had no dealings with the other boys; [who] went along the street with his head down as if afraid to look anyone in the eye. We boys thought he was 'queer,' and in the main were as ready to avoid him as he was to keep away from all companionship."[24] Describing himself as a "lank, spindly youth,"[25] Dreiser was intensely self-conscious about the perceived deficiencies of his body: "Someone had once said for instance that my ears were too large, or my teeth, or my mouth. I had been commented on as ungainly or bashful. *Now these burned in my brain*" (typescript, *Dawn*, ch. XLVII, 434; emphasis added).

Inevitably, having incorporated a part of his father and his father's ideals, Dreiser became a self-conscious and withdrawn adolescent. With his voracious appetite for sex, beautiful girls, and gorgeous clothes, he was adhering to standards he could never hope to achieve. Because feelings do not exist unalloyed (for there is no pure hatred just as there is no pure love), Dreiser struggled with both shame and guilt (as he himself described): Guilt about his sexual desires and his hostile feelings toward his father, shame that somehow despite all he could not maintain his father's impossible standards, standards which he had internalized as his own ego ideal.

No aspect of his character remained unaffected by these feelings of guilt — about his physical appearance, his inadequacies, his appetites: "In all my life, I never knew a man more interested in women from the sex point of view" (*Dawn*, ch. XII, 122), he observed about his brother, Paul, and that other notable exception, himself. Dreiser believed his appetites were too much, that *he* was too much: "For I was born to want too much, and to long too much, and to think too keenly or comparatively — and perhaps even too erotically [*sic*]" (typescript, ch. LVII, 524).

Much of his guilt apparently stemmed from early injunctions and manifested itself most extremely in years of depression and bouts of illness and nightsweats because of his "self-abuse" (typescript, ch. IL, 447), as he referred to his masturbation, which "became a habit which endured until I married, at twenty-eight" (typescript, ch. IL, 441): "I cannot tell you how seriously all this affected me — how horribly it depressed me. For a period of at least four or five years, I was thrown into the most gloomy mental state whenever I thought of my condition" (typescript, ch. IL, 448). Dreiser believed that he would be punished for his "self-abuse" by the "los[s]" of his "manhood" (typescript, ch. LVII, 522). For his "self-defilement" and "sin," he would suffer "hell-fire and the like" (typescript, ch. IL, 450). He was troubled by the phrase, "the wages of sin is death," and that other, "broad is the way and straight the gate which leadeth to destruction" (typescript, ch. LXXVI, 724). In other words, his fears were couched in the biblical language of his accusing father.

For plainly and inescapably, no matter how much he would "run," Dreiser was his father's son, as he explains about his youthful state of mind: "I took my opinions of life and morals from what I heard my father and mother say and what they declared I must believe. Thus, my faith in the Catholic church . . . sprang largely from my father. What people would think and what was right or wrong morally or socially I took jointly from my mother and father. . . . Between them, however, they had managed to build up for me a *gloomy moral code which must be adhered to*, I thought and yet against which I was always *sinning*" (typescript, ch. XLVIII, 441; emphasis added).

According to pioneer shame psychoanalyst Helen Block Lewis, shame and guilt coexist as internalized mechanisms. Shame with its focus on the evaluation of the self can be contrasted with guilt, in which the self is not the central object of negative evaluation, but rather its central focus is *the thing* done or undone.[26] In other words, shame is about an individual's feelings of inadequacy. Guilt is about *the deed* done, the forbidden pleasure taken or at least wanted. Shame results from an inability to comply with the internalized rules, regulations, and standards (mirrored from the father in Dreiser's case). And guilt in Dreiser's case, from his hating his father and having murderous feelings toward him, and from his overwhelming sexual desires. Just as this tension between aggression and deep mortification is a strong dynamic in Dreiser's psyche, so it is in the lives of his most compellingly drawn characters, significantly placed in families with all the trappings of shame.

Through this lens, it is possible to view *Jennie Gerhardt* and *An American Tragedy* as classic studies of multigenerational family shame. Both Asa Griffiths in *An American Tragedy* and Old Gerhardt in *Jennie Gerhardt* are prototypes of Dreiser's own father. As the narrator in *Jennie Gerhardt* repeatedly tells us, Old Gerhardt has no sense of how the world is organized (a *sine qua non* in the Dreiser corpus). With him, "religion was a consuming thing" (117). He sought perfection in this world, always trying to be so "honest and upright . . . that the Lord would have no excuse for ruling him out. He trembled not only for himself but for his wife and children. Would he not some day be held responsible for them? Would not his own laxity and lack of system in inculcating the laws of eternal life to them end in his and their damnation? He pictured to himself the torments of hell, and wondered how it would be with him and his in the final hour" (52–3).

Such deep torment, such self-lacerating questions about damnation, leads the father to even greater sternness. His children were punished with ostracism and expulsion, when they did not comply with his rules. They and their mother responded with greater secrecy and concealment of deeds they knew would provoke his disapproval. According to shame psychologists, the cardinal rule of the shame-bound family *is* control, to be in control of all behavior and interaction. All of the other rules (perfectionism, blame, denial, secrecy) flow from it and support it. This control is rigidly held by one or more family members over the others in tyrannical fashion. The shame generated by Old Gerhardt seems to operate on all the younger members of his family, who begin to feel they individually inherited some kind of curse[27] and have anxiety and fears. Ultimately the family disbands and those who can, take flight, having no further contact with the other members.

In many ways, the story of *Jennie Gerhardt* is recapitulated in *An American Tragedy*: Again, we see a cursed family with a father who lives by otherworldly standards and shame bound children who perpetuate the shame. Like William Gerhardt, Asa Griffiths is a prototype of Dreiser's own father. At the novel's opening, Asa, the "confused brother of the Door of Hope" (I, 158), is presented as a "most unimportant-looking person" (I, 3), a "figure [who] bespoke more of failure than anything else" (I, 3), who nonetheless not only tries to live by celestial standards and to impose them on his immediate family, but who also insists on "evangelizing the world" (I, 11).

In fact, *An American Tragedy* can be seen as a study of *four* generations of familial shame, beginning with Asa's father (and Clyde's grandfather), Joseph Griffiths, down to little Russell, who, on the closing page of this circular novel, looks and acts ominously like Clyde. We are told on page 177 of volume one of the Boni and Liveright edition that Joseph Griffiths had a "prejudice" against his youngest son, Asa, and had "harried" (178) him from his home without his share of the family inheritance. Through this shame-inducing process of expulsion and disinheritance, we see set in motion a possible source of the shame that is passed down from generation to generation — from Joseph to Asa, from Asa to his son, Clyde, and from Clyde's family to Clyde's clone, Russell, the illegitimate son of Esta, whom Clyde's family adopted after fictionalizing him as an orphan. Russell shows all the markings of being another Clyde and following in his shame-filled steps. He is indoctrinated into the same "fundamental verities" (III, 213) that had so tormented Clyde in his own childhood. In that famous final scene Russell refuses to go home but asks for money to buy an ice cream cone instead, signaling his own craving for this world's carnal pleasures.

The focus of the family shame, however, is on Clyde, a classic case. For shame is a sense of having failed to live up to one's own projected image of success, which for Clyde is to dress correctly, talk correctly, know the right people, and maintain the image other people respect. Not only does he ultimately fail to do all this, but his disgrace becomes a matter of public record. The newspapers day in and day out expose the embarrassing details of his familial and social background and the scandal of his criminal record.

The family shame is passed down to Clyde and his siblings through Asa and his wife,[28] who unrealistically require that the children live by "the straight and narrow" (II, 168).[29] Thus shame is perpetuated, for the material values by which the children live lead them to hunger for pleasures that are forbidden. Asa and his wife heighten their children's feelings of inadequacy by exposing them to street meetings where the father is jeered at ("Here comes old Praise-the-Lord Griffiths") and Clyde is taunted ("Hey, you're the fellow whose sister plays the organ. Is there anything else she can play?" [I, 6]).

But Clyde yearns to be another kind of son, pride filled, like Gilbert Griffiths, his cousin, to whom he bears such an uncanny resemblance that Gilbert's own mother is "startled" (II, 221). Clyde ruminates: "How wonderful it must be to be a son, who, without having to earn all this, could still be so much, take oneself so seriously, exercise so much command and control" (II, 223).

Interestingly, this prideful side of Gilbert is all that we see of him. Shame psychologists Merle Fossum and Marilyn Mason define pride as the obverse of shame. They maintain that "pride is related to a fantasy of oneself rather than to one's actual behavior." Whereas shame is the inner experience of being looked down upon by the social group, "pride is maintaining the fantasy, the delusion of grandeur, the fantasy of being the envy of other people."[30] And Gilbert in his prideful state is the opposite of the unassuming but seeking Clyde.

This excessively proud man is the other prototypical male in the Dreiser corpus. For example, in contrast to the ineffectual Asa Griffiths, his brother Samuel, Gilbert's father, exudes such extreme pride. He is a patriarch, a remote grand organizer, totally in control, rich, masterful, judicious but unyielding. Aptly and repeatedly called the "governor" (II, 197, 215, 232) by his son, he is a "kind of Croesus" (I, 14). In characteristic fashion, Samuel Griffiths, the wise arbiter, when confronted with Clyde's alleged crime, holds off judgment. We quickly hear the chorus of admiration for him from his attorney, his son, et al., who think: "The power of him! The decision of him! The fairness of him in such a deadly crisis!" (III, 178).

In the same way, Archibald Kane and his son, Lester, the key male in *Jennie Gerhardt*, are contrasted with the pathetic William Gerhardt. Archibald, the founder of a manufacturing company, is as wise and masterful as Samuel Griffiths, his son as distant and pride filled. These and other such characters make one think of so many other curiously egotistical males in Dreiser, the most extreme being Frank Algernon Cowperwood, the "I satisfy myself" superman of the *Trilogy of Desire*.

Helen Block Lewis describes the three aspects of the internal monitoring system as shame, guilt, and pride. In fictionalizing these concepts, Dreiser presents these interrelated aspects of the self largely as disengaged entities each epitomized by a particular person. He often characterizes someone as "shame-bound" or having a combination of "guilt" and "shame" in contrast to a brother or another family member who has the polar opposite, pride. Although Dreiser presents these different aspects dueling within a character as complex as Clyde, they are most often presented as separate dramatic renderings of mutually exclusive states of mind.

Despite his wishes to be the "son" of Samuel Griffiths, Clyde clearly is shaped in his own father's likeness. Like his father who was "harried" from his home, Clyde is exiled early on, after the hit-and-run accident that kills a child. Born into the shame of his parents' miserable makeshift life, Clyde is further reduced by his sister's illegitimate child. His life becomes one of secrecy, concealment and lies: after running from the car accident, he hides the impermissible relationship with his employee, Roberta (which he regards as "a dark secret" [II, 308]), her pregnancy (to him an even darker secret), and his involvement in her "murder" (the most "horrible, destructive secret" [III, 137] of them all).

Clyde's constant lies and cover-ups stem from his deep-seated feeling of inadequacy, of being a "nobody" (II, 194), but with a strong desire to "rise up and be somebody" (II, 175). The central drama of the novel emerges from this double image, this struggle between his sense of inadequacy (shame) and his desire to break out of this image. Roberta's pregnancy brings this struggle to a peak. Feeling trapped by her predicament (and thus the "dark" chance of becoming a father as hapless as his own), Clyde fears that marriage to Roberta "would spell complete ruin for him" (II, 425). He yearns for the alternative, marriage to Sondra, which would mean the realization of his "splendid dreams" (II, 16), an escape from his own shame-based image, really an abdication of it, for he significantly rewrites his past to measure up to her and her friends' social and economic standards.

To Clyde, murdering or not murdering Roberta is the choice between a life of shame (married to a "nobody"—"For after all, who was she? A factory girl!" [I: 309]) and a life of nonshame (pride)—with Sondra. His own "evil voice" articulates this dilemma: "But she will not let you go or go her way unless you accompany her. And if you go yours, it will be without Sondra and all that she represents, as well as . . . your standing with your uncle, his friends, their cars, the dances, visits to the lodges on the lakes. And what then? A small job! Small pay! Another such period of wandering as followed that accident at Kansas City. Never another chance like this anywhere. Do you prefer that?"

(II, 50). This voice, threatening him with shame, offers him the option of a life of pride. All these elements — guilt, shame, and pride — war within him.

Clyde's suffering is further intensified by the sudden emergence of another more punitive father figure who replaces Asa, who has become virtually wordless and is "not expected to live" (III, 360), for he cannot withstand the public disgrace of Clyde's conviction for murder.[31] At this juncture Orville W. Mason, a father in his own right and the district attorney of the county, steps in as the most dramatically cast, shaming "father" in the novel. Permanently disfigured by a fall when he was an adolescent, Mason is "exceedingly sensitive to the fact of his facial handicap" (III, 92). He has a "psychic sex scar," Dreiser tells us, which resulted in "youthful sexual deprivations" (III, 108), for his acute sense of self-shame made it difficult for him to function sexually.

And as is typical in a shaming "family," shame begets shame: Shamed literally by the nose on his face, Mason becomes the shaming father to the "son" who breaks rules which he, the father, never got a chance to break. Because of his "youthful . . . deprivations," Mason immediately and intensely identifies with Roberta, the victim. She comes from a family "which on sight struck him as having perhaps like himself endured the whips, the scorns and contumelies of life" (III, 98). His identification with the victim exacerbates his rage against Clyde, the assumed aggressor: "He conceived an enormous personal hate for the man. The wretched rich! The idle rich! . . . If he could but catch him" (III, 104).

And catch him he does. Armed with his shame-filled rage and the injunctions of the law, Mason, the hunter, is in hot pursuit. He eyes Clyde "as one might an unheard-of and yet desperate animal" (III, 148). And Clyde with his "frozen-faced terror" (III, 150) becomes the "harried animal, deftly pursued by hunter and hound" (II, 429). In one of the most humiliating scenes in the novel, Mason toys with Clyde, threatening to publicly expose him by taking him back to face his well-connected friends if he does not confess.

But the hot pursuit began long before Mason: It started with Clyde's grandfather who shamed his son, Asa, who then maintained the family shame by filling his children with impossible injunctions. Overwhelmed by desire, Clyde's struggle had always been between guilt and shame. A clue to guilt is the way it is phrased as "things" that are "bothering" the person. With Clyde, once he becomes involved with Sondra, he is perpetually "bothered" by the problem of Roberta and her pregnancy. Before that infamous scene on Big

Bittern in which Roberta is drowned, a bitter battle rages within Clyde between his destructive aggression ("to kill her" [II,50]) and his guilt about the prospect of murder ("not. . . to kill her" [II, 50]).

Ultimately Clyde is unable to commit the act impelled by his own aggression. According to Lewis, it is common for "experiences of guilt and shame . . . to fuse with each other, especially when feelings are acute."[32] And indeed Clyde's feelings at that moment of death are at their most acute. The novel, however, closes with resolution: Clyde is found "guilty" and executed. In Clyde's character, guilt appears ultimately to be a more potent force than shame. Clyde punishes himself: He leaves such an obvious trail of incriminating evidence that he does not need an external avenging father. He has internalized his own father and then destroyed him, when he kills not only his "wife" "in his heart" (II, 25), but also his child and himself. He is destroyed ultimately for an act that he did not commit but which he had intended. The Bible preaches that sin "in [the] heart" (Matthew 12:31) is the same as committing the act. Ironically but with the logic of a fierce poetic justice, Clyde is destroyed by standards as unremitting and otherworldly as his father's.

Given the fate of such a shame-filled son, how did Dreiser escape such a curse himself? That is, why was *he* not a permanent victim of the shame instilled by his own father? Why was *he* not always crippled or at least deeply inhibited by his family's shame? In his fictions *Jennie Gerhardt* and *An American Tragedy*, Dreiser shows what can happen to shame-filled children of a shaming father. In his nonfictions, he shows the struggles against that "dragon" that beset him. But one other trait of his shame-filled characters is their inarticulateness. Shame psychologists suggest that one of the earmarks of shame is wordlessness, the inability or unwillingness to come forth, to unburden oneself of that which needs to be healed.[33] One of the remedies is expression, articulation of underlying feelings that are most secret and most concealed. One of the unique features of family systems therapy is that people bring in various members of their families who then *talk*. Dreiser creates families in which he is the only one who talks. In portraying shame, voluminous Dreiser may well have exorcised much of his own.

Notes

1. I want to express special gratitude to Florian Stuber for his careful reading of this essay. His many suggestions for editorial changes

were particularly helpful. I am also indebted to Albert Ashforth and Madelyn Larsen for their many thoughtful comments.

2. The University of Pennsylvania edition of *Jennie Gerhardt*, with its restoration of some 16,000 words cut by the Harper and Brothers editors in 1911, provides much material that amplifies on the theme of shame, the subject of this essay. See Theodore Dreiser, *Jennie Gerhardt*, The University of Pennsylvania Dreiser Edition, ed. James L. W. West III (Philadelphia: University of Pennsylvania Press, 1992). All subsequent references in my text (*JG*) are to this edition.

3. My focus is on shame in men, and, thus, in this regard, it is a gender study. Usually when we think of gender studies, however, we think of feminist or women's studies. And many feminist scholars have argued against the necessity of *men's* studies at all because they think so much of the curriculum already fulfills that function. But I disagree. I believe to understand women's and men's issues and the degree to which we can find commonalities and differences between them, a male gender perspective can be elucidating, especially when a psychonalytic approach is taken. However psychoanalytic criticism is not free from controversy either and this presents a dilemma. In this essay, I will make distinctions between the "psyche" and the "analysis" camps of psychoanalysis.

For an excellent discussion of the current status of gender studies, including men's studies, see Eve Kosofsky Sedgwick, "Gender Criticism," in *Redrawing the Boundaries,* ed. by Stephen Greenblatt and Giles Gunn (New York: Modern Language Association, 1992), pp. 271–302.

4. Theodore Dreiser, *An American Tragedy* (New York: Boni and Liveright, 1925), I, 7; emphasis added. All subsequent references in my text (*AAT*) are to this edition.

5. This word "mortification" is one of the many such words regarding shame restored in the University of Pennsylvania Press edition of *Jennie Gerhardt.*

6. There have been a number of excellent biographical/critical studies that have called attention to Dreiser's early traumatic sense of shame. Particularly see Volume One of Richard Lingeman's recent critically acclaimed biography, *Theodore Dreiser: At the Gates of the City, 1871–1907* (New York: Putnam's Sons, 1986). In Chapter 3, "The Damndest Family," and Chapter 4, "Her Wandering Boy," Lingeman traces Dreiser's enduring sense of shame to his impoverished childhood in Terre Haute and, especially, in Sullivan, Indiana, where he lived on the "wrong side of the tracks" with his scandal-ridden family. Among others, also see William Swanberg's *Dreiser* (New York:

Charles Scribner's Sons, 1965), Donald Pizer's *The Novels of Theodore Dreiser: A Critical Study* (Minneapolis: University of Minnesota Press, 1976), Richard Lehan's *Theodore Dreiser: His World and His Novels* (Carbondale: Southern Illinois University Press, 1969), Ellen Moers's *Two Dreisers* (New York: Viking, 1969), and Philip Gerber's *Theodore Dreiser* (New York: Twayne, 1964). In *The Novels of Theodore Dreiser*, Pizer, for example, perceptively discusses Dreiser's use of his "autobiographical imagination" in the creation of *An American Tragedy.* Pizer refers to the "prologuelike nature of the opening vignette" in terms very similar to the ones used at the opening of this essay. He suggests that "Dreiser's memory of the immense handicap imposed upon him by his own 'peculiarly nebulous, emotional, unorganized and traditionless' family, and in particular his memory of a father whose primitive religiosity made him incapable of fighting the battle of life . . . " contributed to the creation of the novel. (Quotation from Pizer, pp. 209–10.)

I agree that his "autobiographical imagination" helped Dreiser write *An American Tragedy* and other of his novels especially those in which the characters are so shame driven. My contribution in this essay is to situate Dreiser's autobiographical imagination in a psychoanalytic context of shame. I suggest that some of most powerfully rendered fictional creations are projections of intrapsychic struggles and that his internal monitoring system of shame, guilt, and pride can be traced back in part to his overzealous father, who unrealistically demanded that his children live by otherworldly standards. In Dreiser, these internalized demands found if not resolution at least expression through re-creation in the written word.

7. Michael Kerr, "Chronic Anxiety and Defining a Self," *Atlantic Monthly* (September 1988): 35–58. (Quotation, p. 35.)

8. *Ibid.*, p. 35.

9. Carl Whitaker and T. Malone, *The Roots of Psychotherapy* (New York: Brunner/Mazel, 1981). (Quotation, p. xxi.)

10. See Meredith Skura, "Psychoanalytic Criticism," *Redrawing the Boundaries*, pp. 349–73.

11. Although Murray Bowen asserts that individuals derive their behavior from their family systems, I do not categorically accept this position. There may be many other factors that contribute to an individual's behavior outside the family system, including genetic and environmental influences. See Murray Bowen, *Family Therapy in Clinical Practice* (New York: Jason Aronson, 1978). (Quotation, p. 472.)

12. Kerr, p. 41.

13. Samuel Osherson and Steven Klugman, "Men, Shame, and Psychotherapy," *Psychotherapy* 27 (Fall 1990): 327–39. (Quotation, p. 327.)

14. William James, *The Principles of Psychology* (New York: Henry Holt, 1890).

15. A shame-bound family, according to psychologists, results from "a self-sustaining, multigenerational system of interactions with a cast of characters who are (or were in their lifetime) loyal to a set of rules and injunctions demanding control, perfectionism, blame and denial." Adherence to such a code of conduct inhibits the formation of authentic intimate relationships, they state, and "promotes secrets and vague personal boundaries, unconsciously instills shame in the [individual] family members, as well as chaos in their lives, and binds them to perpetuate the shame in themselves and in their kin." See Merle Fossum and Marilyn Mason, *Facing Shame: Families in Recovery* (New York: Norton, 1986). (Quotation, p. 8.)

16. Osherson and Klugman, p. 327.

17. Osherson and Klugman, pp. 328, 332.

18. See the discussion of Dreiser's womanizing in the body of and in note five of the introductory essay to this book, pp. ix–xix.

19. Theodore Dreiser, *Dawn* (first unpublished typescript), the Dreiser Collection, Charles Patterson Van Pelt Library, University of Pennsylvania, ch. LX, 554; emphasis added. All subsequent references to the *Dawn* typescript (typescript) are to this edition. I have often chosen to quote from one of the typescripts rather than from a published edition of *Dawn* because the typescripts are more revealing and frank about Dreiser's own feelings of rage, humiliation, and sexual shame.

20. Lingeman, p. 38.

21. In the typescript of *Dawn*, Dreiser says that by the time he was old enough to remember, in many ways the "war" was over between his father's religious zealotry and his mother's dreamy paganism, and that his mother had won, for the battle had been about the older boys. It is helpful to keep in mind Dreiser's perspective as the penultimate child and son. He came relatively late in his parents' lives and thus lived in the aftermath of much of the struggle. But clearly, the "war" was resurrected when Dreiser's sisters became pubescent and to Dreiser's father, "shameless hussies."

22. My discussion of male-based shame could be more fully developed in light of the complexities. For instance, an infant's early recognition of differences between himself and his mother can be shame producing. The process of "disidentifying" with mother and iden-

tifying with father can also serve a part in this male shame-based drama. In a family context such as Dreiser's in which his father was physically and psychologically absent much of the time, Dreiser too must have struggled with the shame of identifying with a father perceived as rejecting, disinterested, and himself inadequate. Clearly Dreiser's relationship with his father is ambivalent and complicated. See Osherson and Klugman, p. 327.

23. Fossum and Mason, p. 92.

24. Quoted in Lingeman, p. 70.

25. Theodore Dreiser, "Theodore Dreiser," *Household Magazine* (November 1929), typescript, the Dreiser Collection, Charles Patterson Van Pelt Library, University of Pennsylvania, p. 2.

26. Helen Block Lewis, *Shame and Guilt in Neurosis* (New York: International Universities, 1971), p. 30.

27. For instance, Martha understands the family "curse" as "structural weaknesses" that led to defeat of almost all the family members: "Martha had always been a little ashamed of her family, after she became old enough to discover its structural weaknesses, and now, when this new life dawned, was anxious to make the connection as slight as possible. She barely notified the members of the family of the approaching marriage—Jennie not at all, and at the time of the actual ceremony only wanted Bass and George because they were doing fairly well. Gerhardt [her father!], Veronica and William were not included and noticed the slight. Gerhardt was not for comment any more. He had had too many rebuffs. Veronica was resentful. She hoped that life would give her an opportunity to pay her sister off" (*JG* 239–40).

28. To some, Elvira Griffiths would appear to be outside the spectrum of shame for she is obviously respected by those who know her and repeatedly described as a woman of "force and earnestness" (I, 5–6), "the strongest in the family—so erect, so square-shouldered, defiant—a veritable soul pilot in her cross-grained . . . way" (III, 215) who nonetheless was without "any truer or more practical insight into anything" (I, 10) than Asa. However, one of the dynamics that creates and maintains shame in a family, regardless of the character of its individuals, is the requirement that those who are dependent live up to standards beyond their own ability. And, like her husband, she not only lives by such standards but inculcates them into her children and preaches them to the world.

29. Like Asa, Dreiser's father was "wholly unconscious of the danger to his sons and daughters in a too strict interpretation of a rule of

living": "he was all for church going, money earning and saving—in rags if necessary—a strictly self-denying attitude of mind and body" (typescript, *Dawn*, ch. IV, 28). But "even my mother (largely because of past religious oppression), looked upon father as an old fogy, a tyrant, a numbskull, and whatever else you choose, He (*sic*) was always trying to repress his children and hold them back, they—not my mother exactly but the others—said. He knew nothing of life as they knew it—which was entirely true" (typescript, ch. XLI, 335).

30. Fossum and Mason, p. vii.

31. Again, at this stage, Dreiser must have drawn on his own father, who after the death of his wife was at his most bereft: John Paul, Sr. was "an interesting illustration of a beaten or psychically (*sic*) depressed man and hence one who could not bring himself to enter upon any other contest with the world . . . " (handwritten, *Dawn*, ch. XXXII, unnumbered page after p. 272).

32. Helen Block Lewis, *Shame and Guilt in Neurosis*, p. 267.

33. A key to defusing shame is to develop ways to talk about it, connecting words with feelings. Many men do not realize or understand what they are experiencing as shame. One patient described it: "You feel as if you're fragmenting, coming apart, when you feel confused." The connection between anger and shame can be made more manifest. As another said, "ok, so when I feel threatened, I attack" (Osherson and Klugman, p. 333).

Lacanian Equivocation in *Sister Carrie, The "Genius,"* and *An American Tragedy*

Leonard Cassuto

Anyone who has read any general criticism of Theodore Dreiser will recognize one of its reigning clichés: that the vitality of the master's characterizations overcomes the prose in which he renders them. It is a measure of his success that it remains a fresh enterprise to ask why this is so. In the protagonists of *Sister Carrie, The "Genius,"* and *An American Tragedy*, Dreiser depicts a pitched battle of ideas and urges of the mind. The author considers not only *how* his characters react to the environment and chance, but (crucially) he ponders *why* they respond as they do. The result is a complex, conflicted view of consciousness: a model that virtually describes modern psychoanalysis—though it largely antecedes it.[1]

Freud and Dreiser share a model of human behavior based on conflict. They show in different ways the myriad implications and essential difficulties lying behind the phrase, "I want." Put simply, Dreiser's protagonists do not know what they want or why they want it. Desires assert themselves on the consciousness of Dreiser's characters, shaping and directing it. Ellen Moers calls Clyde Griffiths "the Everyman of desire,"[2] but accepting this description hardly serves to simplify *An American Tragedy*. Desire has many faces in the work of Dreiser; ultimately, it is responsible for identity, the way that characters see themselves, and the way that we see them. In the following pages I will investigate the engine of desire that drives Dreiser's novels forward. This complex force gives rise to the psychological depth of characterization and persistent ambiguity that characterizes Dreiser's best fiction.

This ambiguity of Dreiser's has been explored in other contexts, but almost never psychoanalytically. Lee Clark Mitchell compares Hurstwood at the safe to Silas Lapham contemplating bankruptcy in William Dean Howells' *The Rise of Silas Lapham* and points out that the latter seems a moral agent in charge of his fate, while Hurstwood (faced with somewhat similar circumstances) appears out of control. Gordon O. Taylor anticipates this insight in his study of the fictive depiction of thought: "[T]he mental experience which interests Dreiser most is sub- or semi-conscious. . . . "³ Mitchell's analysis of character is based on moral philosophy as it relates to the formation of the self.⁴ I would argue from a psychoanalytic perspective that the different ways that Lapham and Hurstwood deliberate arise from different views of the self: how Dreiser and Howells define consciousness. For Howells, Lapham exists, and therefore Lapham decides. For Dreiser, the ingredients of a decision are more varied, mixing together into a turbulent, conflicted state of imperfect awareness. To Mitchell, Hurstwood's inconclusiveness and uncertainty about the source of his intentions result in the lack of "an integrated self."⁵ A psychoanalytically oriented response would be, "Who has a perfectly integrated self anyway?"

This brief discussion shows that Dreiser's model is – despite its partial antecedence to Freud – a thoroughly modern one. His view is grounded in conflict that originates in competing desires. He portrays desire compounded by its own long repression (as seen, for example, in Hurstwood's deeply unsatisfying life during the years before the action of *Sister Carrie* begins).

Given the congeniality of Dreiser's art to psychoanalytic criticism, it is surprising indeed that there is so little of it, even given the dominant social focus of most naturalist criticism.⁶ Why has psychoanalysis been so largely ignored in Dreiser's case? Although Dreiser's fiction has recently begun to receive some generally based (and valuable) psychological attention, psychoanalytic treatments of his work are still scarce. Excluding studies of historical influence, two Freudian readings stand out from an otherwise sparse field.⁷ A quick examination of them will shed some light on the question of why there has not been more psychoanalytic Dreiser criticism.

In the first and only psychoanalytic study of The "Genius," Richard B. Hovey and Ruth S. Ralph see Dreiser's Eugene Witla in the thrall of the maternal superego, persuasively showing how his nine affairs (three in each section of the novel) reveal a gradually increasing need to be caught and reprimanded by a mother figure.⁸ The pleasure principle, they say, competes with the desire to be punished. This argument (to which I will return) highlights an important aspect of Dreiser's characters: they have very active unconscious faculties which scheme and speak beneath the often troubled surfaces of the characters' personalities. Compare Eugene's conscious and unconscious machinations to those of Frank Norris's McTeague, for example, where there is only the threat of pain—which is simply at odds with the pleasure principle.

Terry Whalen offers a more comprehensive interpretation of the workings of psychoanalytic ideas in Dreiser's fiction, suggesting that the author's sense of tragedy is Freudian in its emphasis on the embattled ego.[9] Concentrating on *Sister Carrie* and *An American Tragedy*, Whalen sees the basic Freudian image of the ego under siege from social strictures and inner urges as the source of Dreiserian tragedy. To Whalen, Dreiser's Freudian view holds more than a simply fatalistic or deterministic vision of the human drama. For example, his reading of the safe scene in *Sister Carrie* focuses on Hurstwood's embattled, "endangered" ego, whose inefficiency eventually leads him to ruin—a more complex vision, says Whalen, than mechanistic philosophy can provide. Clyde Griffiths, says Whalen, is powerless, caught between status and sex, a "pitiful victim" whose destiny ultimately results from the undomesticated power of his id.

Although a worthy signpost toward rich sources for future inquiry, Whalen's own argument finally dead ends, for having located the problems of Dreiser's two most famous tragic protagonists in their weak egos, he "solves" the psychological equation of the characters. However, the simplicity of the solution (the "poor ego" as the source of all difficulty) contains more than a hint of brute force, of irregularly shaped pegs pushed into perfectly round holes. For example, Whalen sees Clyde as "little more than a blend of id-inspired dreams of sexual bliss and culture-inspired dreams of material success by the time he is working in Lycurgus."[10] This reading finds no place for Clyde's basic sensitivity (noticed by Pizer and others).

Consider also Clyde's need for acceptance. His materialistic dreams arise at least partly from this basic desire. As a "soul that was not destined to grow up,"[11] Clyde requires the approval that any child does. His dreams of wealth, prosperity that will make him an adult in his own eyes, must flow from his superego as well as from his comfort-loving id. If Clyde were simply a creature of desire, he would have been a far better criminal, more cold blooded in planning and execution. His ineptitude deserves closer study, arising as it does from both his mixed feelings for Roberta and his consciousness of the law, along with its moral basis. Whatever its strength or weakness, Clyde's ego is at bottom conflicted. He knows the difference between what he has and what he wants, but he also knows, both consciously and unconsciously, something of the cost of gaining his desires. There is more to Clyde than first meets the psychoanalytical eye.

With an eye on this critique, I venture an hypothesis to explain the paucity of psychoanalytic criticism of Dreiser's novels: it is because everything appears so simple at first glance.[12] In *An American Tragedy*, one could put forth an equation for the crime that covers everything neatly, so neatly that it is suspicious. Such an equation starts with Clyde's unhappy, humiliation-filled childhood and proceeds "inevitably" to its consequences of murder and retribution. Clyde's Efrit takes its place as a crudely dramatized id that overcomes Clyde's weak ego. Accenting it all are Clyde's crudely symbolic dreams. It is a neat package; there does not seem to be much to add. One can break down *The "Genius"* and *Sister Carrie* similarly. Hovey and Ralph portray Eugene as a servant alternately of the pleasure principle and the maternal superego: one can say that his ego is no match for these two. Carrie can be viewed in this way as a victorious id trampling her own ego on the way to a success unencumbered by conscience, realizing her dreams of wealth and comfort. And inversely, we have already seen Whalen argue that Hurstwood is an ego at sea without sail.

This little exercise shows how easy it is to see Dreiser's characters as having strong ids and weak egos. In fact, it is too easy. Because of the enduring critical attention that they have received over the years, it is fair to expect that Clyde, Eugene, Carrie, and Hurstwood be composed of more than elementary oppositions. If Dreiser's novels were that simplistic, no one in the age of Freud would want to read them.

This kind of formulaic thinking ignores what Shoshana Felman calls "the textuality of the text."[13] Her solution is the "implication" of psychoanalysis and literature, offering a wide variety of possibilities "not necessarily to recognize a *known*, to find an answer, but also, and perhaps more challengingly, to locate an *unknown*, to find a question."[14] Felman is describing a different kind of psychoanalytic literary criticism, one which celebrates complexity and equivocation rather than reducing the text to one of a few possible variations of Freud's triadic organization of the mind. Such a task demands a new, or at least altered, methodology, which she finds in the psychoanalysis of Jacques Lacan.

Why complicate the issue by bringing Lacan into it? The attractiveness of Lacan to a project like this lies in Lacan's focus on the ego, and his deemphasis of the mechanistic aspects of Freud's thinking. By refusing to reduce desires to drives, we can, by adopting a Lacanian perspective, attempt to analyze the conflicting wants and alienations of Dreiser's characters as a confused (and often confusing) mixture of conscious and unconscious desires that are not the products of biological drives as such. "For Lacan, anatomy is not equivalent to destiny."[15] This pronouncement describes the dynamic between chance and determinism in Dreiser's work, carried through to the psychological realm.

The Lacanian ego is not situated in an objective psychological reality: it is positioned relative to other subjective phenomena, based on the subjective phenomenon of language that shapes and conveys it. "Diagnosing" Dreiser's characters as having weak egos, Lacan would say, labels them rather than analyzes them. To Lacan, we all have weak egos in a certain sense: every one of us has an ego defined against our own early narcissistic tendencies. We locate ourselves at the end of a series of alienations from these. Using Lacan's ideas, we can better understand the individual peculiarities of Dreiser's invented egos and release their interpretation to embrace the ambiguity of Dreiser's vision of the individual's predicament in society.[16]

Because Lacan conveys his ideas in a dense, difficult prose style that is meant to evoke the complexities of his subject, a brief summary might help at this point.[17] For Lacan, the ego comes into being during the mirror stage, named for the process by which the infant comes to distinguish its own image in the mirror.[18] In the early stages of development, the child perceives no boundary between itself and its mother. Seeing itself makes the child simultaneously aware that it is not its mother; the ideal, seamless unity is lost and the child's individual ego comes into being. The ego thus emerges from denial, the loss of unity with the mother. Desire to recover this unity forms the basis for the unconscious (the desire of the Other). Preventing the desired union is the presence of the father, which has a name: the word "no." This first "no" signals the simultaneous birth of language along with denial of desire. The word "no" takes its place as the first law, the first restriction from the outside. This drama of loss, Lacan's version of Freud's Oedipal conflict, takes place in what he calls the Symbolic realm, which offers a means of conveying the activity of the Imaginary, where desire (and the unconscious) originate.

Language mediates, then, but it is itself the product of desire; its coming into being is tied to the unconscious. The expression of want (language) is identified with the wanting thing. Part of the subjective foundation of identity formation, language is therefore to Lacan a highly subjective construction. The unconscious is thus identified inextricably with and through language, leading to Lacan's most famous, oft-repeated insight, that the unconscious is structured like a language.[19]

So the self is borne of the fundamentally subjective frustration of want; language is tied inextricably and self-referentially to that formation and its expression. Lacan renders the child's identification with the father (following alienation from the mother) in the linguistic terms that govern his work: one signifier (identification with the father) replaces another (the desire for the mother), inserting itself in its space on the signifying chain.[20]

The unconscious is structured like a language; it speaks in signifiers. But like language, it is murky, not always speaking straightforwardly or consistently. When one signifier substitutes for another, Lacan calls this a metaphor. Symptoms are studied as metaphors and are detected by the close study of the structure of the signifying chain.[21] In this examination of the structure of the chain, Lacan is especially attentive to repetition, for through repetition the analyst can study linguistic patterns and variations. Repetition compulsion (which, says Freud, lies beyond the pleasure principle, as part of the death instinct) is very important in Lacan's linguistic model: he needs the slight differences from one iteration to another to identify the discourse of the unconscious. This emphasis on form (the structure of the chain, not necessarily the content of the signifier [that is, the signified]) has as its goal the location of contradiction and loss, "the truth of the subject." With this truth comes "the peace that follows the recognition of an unconscious tendency."[22]

This peace domesticates aggressivity, Lacan's loose reinterpretation of Freud's death drive, a destructive force powered by the energy of the ego's want. Aggressivity, which Lacan represents with images of the fragmented body, provides the force behind repetition compulsion.[23] When the symbolic (linguistic) realm cannot contain it, it expresses itself in the concrete realm of the Real in the form of symptoms. These can be directed towards the self or (because of the potential for displacement of one signifier by another) at others as well. Thus, a crime can be viewed as an irruption of aggressivity (from the imaginary realm), an expression of the energy of want in an act against another. This model, more flexible than Freud's death drive, will allow for a reconsideration of acts such as Hurstwood's theft and Clyde's murder, where self-destructive urges are displaced along the signifying chain.[24]

Lacan leaves us with a portrait of an untrustworthy, complicated ego that is anything but weak. It is torn, divided, and confused, trying to recover a unity it will never know again. Ungrounded in any objective reality, fraught with unresolvable contradictions, it is the product of alienation, always questing after an-Other that it can never know.

Given the self-absorption of Dreiser's characters, Lacan's focus on narcissism at the root of ego formation requires a look at the Freudian concept that precedes it. In "On Narcissism: An Introduction," Freud describes "two fundamental characteristics: megalomania and diversion of . . . interest from the external world—from people and things."[25] Like Lacan, Freud postulates a primary narcissism in everyone as part of childhood development (88). In an adult, however, the condition exists when "the libido that has been withdrawn from the external world has been directed to the ego" (75).

Of Dreiser's creations, the autobiographical Eugene Witla of *The "Genius"* is one of the most prominent narcissists (a designation he shares with Frank Cowperwood, the self-absorbed hero of *The Trilogy of Desire*). Eugene's ego-energy is directed inward, toward himself; his passion is not love, for he is consistently self-centered in his affairs. His maternal superego fixation suggests an unresolved problem, while his repeated affairs (a telling repetition compulsion) represent a continuing attempt at fulfillment of a need that is sometimes emotional, and also—when he breaks down—physical. At the end of the book, we see Eugene as a committed parent and a born-again artist. But Freud says that child care, though selfless in its way, is a transparent attempt to recapture childhood narcissism (91). If being in love is the highest state of object-libido (76), Eugene's loves certainly bear examination. So do Clyde's, and Carrie's, and Hurstwood's.

Eugene's love is anything but selfless. His passion for Suzanne is more of a personal triumph, getting her to love him after he has inwardly shrugged off his qualms and surrendered to his sexual desire for her. He never thinks about their future except as a rose-tinted fantasy, nor does he consider the feelings of anyone else involved. His past treatment of Ruby and Angela displays a similar dearth of consideration. Clyde Griffiths's love for Sondra likewise lacks any sort of sacrificial mentality: he would never give up the chance to rise in social standing for the chance to be with her because her status is what attracts him in the first place. His feelings for Roberta are more complicated, but they originate in a similar narcissistic desire for sexual gratification. Likewise, Hurstwood is sufficiently self-absorbed to kidnap Carrie. As for

Carrie, her libidinal energy is primarily directed not at people, but rather at money, which is described through her eyes in loving terms throughout *Sister Carrie*.[26] She looks back to her former poverty, but never to her former lovers.

Offering an insight into the artistic representation of narcissism, Freud says that

> [G]reat criminals and humorists, as they are represented in literature, compel our interest by the narcissistic consistency with which they manage to keep away from their ego anything that would diminish it. (89)

This is a way of saying that criminals fascinate us because they lack a superego that would stop them from doing the things they do. Freud here pictures a criminal in control, unencumbered by socially motivated distress. This profile fits Eugene, though his action is technically antisocial rather than illegal. Eugene feels throughout *The "Genius"* that he is special, that he should not be bound by social convention. A textbook example of a narcissist, he is in perpetual revolt against the "censoring agency" of the ego-ideal (as Freud first called the superego [96]). But Freud's portrait hardly describes Hurstwood or Clyde, who are both tortured wrongdoers. Consequently, let us qualify our observation to say that these two characters may have narcissistic tendencies, but are not full-blown narcissists by virtue of the significant force of their consciences. Ironically, Dreiser's criminals have a more developed sense of conscience than he gives to his fictional representation of himself.

To Freud, love counteracts narcissism. A person who loves (in psychoanalytic terms, one who makes another the object of one's own libidinal energy) forfeits part of his narcissism, and is therefore humbled. To restore the balance of ego-energy, a lover needs to be loved in return. Dreiser's characters consistently direct their libidinal energy away from people, with the result that it can only be satisfied from within. Consider Carrie, who loves money, which can never love her back. Perhaps this is why she sits rocking at the novel's end, needing to make a commitment to art—or maybe to people. Hurstwood loves Carrie (though possessively), but Carrie cannot or will not return it. Carrie's commitment to money means that Hurstwood's need cannot be satisfied—which has to figure in his decline. Eugene loves only beauty, which is fleeting in its human form, but which cannot return his love in its more permanent incarnations. So he bounces from love object to love object. Clyde loves status, which he does not have, and which can never reciprocate his passion. His unfulfilled need contributes to his insecurity and indecision.

These narcissistic portrayals suggest egos that try to be too strong. The characters have in common a lack of fulfillment in love, which—says Freud—creates an emotional need, a space to be filled. The loves of Eugene, Clyde, Carrie, and Hurstwood extend from narcissistic self-love. They all need to love and be loved in return, but their clumsy mishandling of this need helps to account for their defectiveness in other areas.

Lacan's image of an aggressive, narcissistically motivated ego offers a way into these characters, a means of negotiating their psychic labyrinths. Aggressivity expresses the ego's unconscious need to unite with the unconscious Other. This need for integration provides insight into the struggles of Dreiser's protagonists. Carrie, Hurstwood, Eugene, and Clyde are forever lacking and seeking. The result is, among other things, improperly channeled aggressivity, where the unconscious act takes the place of the word in a group of notably nonintrospective personalities.

We can identify aggressivity through the examination of repetition compulsion, which is rife in *Sister Carrie*, *The "Genius,"* and *An American Tragedy*. The characters in these novels repeat themselves *all the time*, and almost never with understanding.[27] The frequency of repetition motifs in Dreiser's fiction makes it an especially rich field for Lacanian exploration. Dreiser's repetitions nearly always arise fortuitously, but they also owe something to compulsions, or tendencies, in the characters. The doubling in *An American Tragedy* has already been extensively documented in pursuit of nonpsychological critical goals.[28] To cite just two examples, Clyde's liaison with Roberta parallels the one he has with Hortense Briggs in the first part of the novel, and also echoes the pregnancy and abandonment of his sister Esta. When he refuses to swim to the drowning Roberta, the scene reenacts one from the first section in which he flees from an auto accident. Hovey and Ralph show how *The "Genius"* splits into three patterned cycles of three affairs each. Eugene's affair with Suzanne is only the most spectacular and consequential of many such amorous adventures. In *Sister Carrie*, Carrie's liaisons with Drouet and Hurstwood have strong similarities, most notably the way she seems to drift into each one. Hurstwood's courtship of Carrie is the culmination of many such dalliances he has had before the narrative begins.[29]

Aggressivity in the novels invariably sweeps the performers of the actions along in its destructive wake, giving it a more classically Freudian cast. Recall that aggressivity originates "beyond the pleasure principle."[30] Again, the value of this idea to understanding the motivations of Dreiser's protagonists is estimable. Hurstwood's theft is a bumbling escapade; we can see in his wavering (and, in the police presence in the back of his mind) a desire to be *un*successful, to correct his course. "I wish I hadn't done that," he says to himself after the theft. "That was a mistake."[31] Even so, he goes on to kidnap Carrie. His entire subsequent decline makes his original judgment of his act into a self-fulfilling prophecy that reaches its nadir in his suicide, the ultimate act of self-destruction.

Clyde's murder of Roberta has self-destructive elements as well. Though not a great intellect (criminal or otherwise), he is hardly such an idiot that we should believe his crude getaway plan is the best that he is capable of. There is a part of Clyde that wants — even needs — to be caught. His conflicted self emerges during the crime. Right after refusing Roberta's gesture and striking her, he reaches for her, "half to assist or recapture her and half to apologize for the unintended blow" — a blow which arose an instant earlier from the momentary surrender to "a tide of submerged hate" (*AAT* 492). Clyde's wants cross in cerebral space and get tangled up: his desire for the good life is threatened by Roberta's pregnancy, which has itself arisen from his sexual desire. Overlaying the situation is his pity for Roberta, in which his desire reaches outside of himself to preserve an essential regard for her.[32] The universal, instinctive sense of right that Dreiser describes as Hurstwood ponders the open safe in *Sister Carrie* is also at work in Clyde, and it cannot allow his criminal inclinations unfettered reign. His Efrit, or "darker self," is by definition only a part of him. If it held full sway, he would simply have brained Roberta with the camera as he originally planned.

As for *The "Genius,"* Eugene's cruelty to his wife Angela stands out as what Lacan would call an imago of aggressive intent. However, Hovey and Ralph show how Eugene repeatedly passes up opportunities to sleep with Suzanne, and how he all but invites her mother and his wife to find out about their affair. Mr. Colfax, Eugene's sharp-tongued boss, points out to him that it would have been smarter to deflower Suzanne first and negotiate later.[33] But Eugene's refusal to plan, a persistent lapse in his makeup that Colfax is not the first to notice, leads in this case (as in the others) to exposure and defeat. Since the autobiographically inspired Eugene is arguably the most intelligent of Dreiser's creations, we must question this curious, increasingly self-destructive resistance of his.

It lies, I think, in the death drive itself, which expresses the contradictions and alienations of being. Lacanian psychoanalysis holds that this self-destructive energy comes not from the id, which according to Freud's metaphor is the seat of instincts, but from a tightly convoluted ego whose energy does not benefit from the self-knowledge which might defuse or redirect it. Freud sees a separation between "repressed" and "repressing," but Lacan brings them together and makes them part of each other. Repressed material comes into view through repetition. The repetitions I just described are not exactly the same, nor should we expect them to be. Repetition, says Lacan, does not mean reproduction.[34] If we study the repetitions as chains of signifiers and look for the differences from one occurrence to the next, we can locate the "unreadable" element, the discourse of the unconscious. Aggressivity, as a correlative of narcissistic identification, is tied from its inception to the original desire for union with the mother. The mirror stage, the "narcissistic moment" of libidinal frustration normally followed by normative sublimation,

> allows us to understand the aggressivity involved in the effects of all regression, all arrested development, all rejection of typical development in the subject, especially on the plane of sexual realization, and more specifically with each of the great phases that the libidinal transformations determine in human life, the crucial function of which has been demonstrated by analysis: weaning, the Oedipal stage, puberty, maturity, or motherhood, even the climacteric. (*Ecrits* 24–5)

We should first recall that all of the Dreiser protagonists under discussion have problems associated with sexual relationships (difficulties in "sexual realization").

Now consider all of the trouble that Dreiser's protagonists have with their mothers. Clyde essentially turns his back on his mother to try and ascend the social ladder, an ascent governed by secular values. After his arrest he does not want to face his mother, and so he wires that she is not needed (*AAT* 619, 624). When she arrives after his conviction, his feelings are equivocal, even in his own dire need:

> his troubled intricate soul not a little dubious, yet confident also that it was to find sanctuary, sympathy, help, perhaps—and that without criticism—in her heart. (*AAT* 748)

Although Clyde eventually surrenders to his mother completely, it is clear from his feelings before he sees her that he does so with unarticulated misgivings, born of his early alienation from her.

Complicating Eugene's tangled relations with the mother figures in his life is his avoidance of his own mother, a negligence so complete that his wife is the one who writes the letters to her in Illinois. He visits his home only once, after he has broken down and is clutching at any possibility of rejuvenation. But even that one time is more than Carrie sees her mother, who vanishes from *Sister Carrie* following Carrie's "gush of tears" at her mother's parting kiss on the first page of the book. Hurstwood also turns his back on a mother figure (in the form of his domineering wife) in favor of Carrie, who is much younger. Mothers stand out by omission in all three novels. Their children repress them.

But we cannot consider the mother without the father: each is a vertex of the primal triangle. The metaphoric replacement of desire for the mother by identification with the father is Lacan's linguistic rendering of the first act of repression. Through this process, the father becomes identified with the law, a fact of special significance for the analysis of Clyde and Hurstwood, and also for Carrie and Eugene, who flout social norms, a different kind of law.

Clyde's father is an unexplained, vague presence in his life. Only Clyde's mother commmunicates with Clyde after his arrest and attends him after his conviction; the son never asks about his father. The elder Griffiths, with his rigidly fundamentalist notions, is absent. In other words, Clyde has broken the law, and its first symbol has become invisible. In Clyde's father's only comment to reporters after Clyde's conviction, he says "He had never understood Clyde or his lacks or his feverish imaginings . . . and preferred not to discuss him" (*AAT* 743). Even when Clyde is in jail, struggling to understand his strong impulses and desires, he considers that his mother, uncle, cousins and the minister attending him do not seem troubled by such urges, but, significantly, he does not compare himself to his father (*AAT* 785). In place of Clyde's biological father steps the Reverend MacMillan. MacMillan's assumption of the paternal role proves disastrous for Clyde, as the cleric denies forgiveness to his surrogate child. Thus, Dreiser literally enacts the identification of the father with the law in the Oedipal equation. MacMillan's rejection of Clyde is a final defeat at the familiar site of past repression.

Hovey and Ralph minimize the presence of fathers in *The "Genius,"* but this judgment needs revision. Eugene finds them in his bosses, and evades them with the same regularity with which he invites confrontation with his surrogate mothers. Among Eugene's father figures are the art dealer M. Charles, and then later (and more importantly) Mr. Kalvin, the wise and benevolent head of his Philadelphia company, whose knowledge of Eugene is greater than Eugene's own and whose advice is always good. The aforementioned Hiram Colfax finally gives Eugene a comeuppance, dismissing him from his job when his affair with Suzanne threatens to become a scandal. In addition, we should not overlook Eugene's natural father, and also his father-in-law Jotham Blue, whom he loves dearly but nevertheless allows to slip from his circle. Jotham's fate is typical of Eugene's male mentors. He lets these men recede from view, usually as silently as possible.

Carrie's father lives only in recollection. Because he does not accompany Carrie to the train station, we never see him. He comes into view later, however, as the focus of the most important of her conscious memories in the novel. She sees men working on the streets, and reflects:

> Toil, now that she was free of it, seemed even a more desolate thing than when she was part of it. She saw it through a mist of fancy—a pale, sombre half-light, which was the essence of poetic feeling. Her old father, in his flour-dusted miller's suit, sometimes returned to her in memory, revived by a face in the window. A shoemaker pegging at his last, a blastman seen through a narrow window in some basement where iron was being melted, a bench-worker seen high aloft in some window, his coat off, his sleeves rolled up; these took her back in fancy to the details of the mill. She felt, though she seldom expressed them, sad thoughts upon this score. Her sympathies were ever with that under-world of toil from which she had so recently sprung, and which she best understood. (*SC* 108)

We see Carrie's artistic sensitivity here (the narrator remarks upon her tenderness and the delicacy of her feelings in the continuation of this passage). More important, Dreiser shows us the source of her deepest empathy. This loving memory suggests, among other things, that Carrie did not leave Columbia because of ill will toward her absent father, but absent he remains. For all we know, he may even be dead. Why does Carrie reflect so little about him? Dreiser shows her turning away from her own history, the only possible source of her own understanding of her unconscious self.

Lacan calls this "foreclosure." Because of it, Dreiser's characters overflow with aggressivity that harms both themselves and others. It persists because they show an alarming resistance to seeking its cause. Instead, they unconsciously repeat their actions, with ever more serious consequences. In healthy people, says Lacan, "Subjective experience must be fully enabled to recognize the central nucleus of ambivalent aggressivity...," a core exposed through repetition.[35] In other words, one must learn the truth of one's own unconscious through one's own personal history. Psychoanalysis, Freud's great practical contribution, uses "the talking cure" as a way to expose the workings of the unconscious. It thus becomes, in Felman's words, *"a life usage of the death instinct* — a practical, productive use of the compulsion to repeat."[36]

Dreiser's characters invariably run from this sort of recognition, and so desert the possibility of self-discovery. His descriptions of repression anticipate Freud. Witness Carrie:

> [S]he had not the mind to get firm hold upon a definite truth. When she could not find her way out of the labyrinth of ill-logic which thought upon the subject created, she would turn away entirely. (*SC* 71)

And Eugene, who refuses to delve into his feelings for Angela: "[H]e did not permit himself to realize just what that meant — to take careful stock of his emotions" ("*G*" 159). Clyde, of course, is Dreiser's most overtly repressed character, a tangle of unacknowledged emotions that are so tightly locked out of his consciousness that they cloud his mind and even pain his body at times. For example:

> [S]o disturbed was he by the panorama of the bright world of which Sondra was the center and which was now at stake, that he could scarcely think clearly. Should he lose all this for such a world as he and Roberta could provide for themselves — a small home — a baby, such a routine work-a-day life as taking care of her and a baby on such a salary as he could earn, and from which most likely he would never again be freed! God! A sense of nausea seized him. (*AAT* 414)

Clyde's reaction recalls Freud's famous case studies of hysterical paralysis, where repression has serious physical consequences. Lacan also speaks of the unconscious being detectable in the body as well as in language and memory.[37]

Dreiser's protagonists willfully ignore the unconscious at their own peril. The incessant and insatiable desires that we see in them are merely the tip of the iceberg, the end of a chain of signifiers that has pushed the original desire beneath the surface of consciousness. But the conscious tip still connects to that underwater ice mass, linking that unconscious want to its conscious substitute. We see this link in Eugene: his belief that the artist is special and so can do anything he likes is very much a conscious one, while his sexual inconstancy (which he sees as an exercise of his specialness), coupled with the need to rebel against authority (symbolized by his mother and father figures), sends its roots down to his unconscious narcissism.

Clyde Griffiths certainly wants to be rich. But why? For what? To satisfy whom? Clyde never tries to track this desire down into himself—he will not admit to what Dreiser points to: that his childhood humiliation has marked him, that the taunting he received because of his poor evangelistic background has shaped his wants. His occasionally incisive views of other people contrast with a strikingly poor perspective of himself. In Lacanian terms, his longing for riches and status is a metaphor for another, deeper, undefined longing.

Dreiser's tacked-on ending to the 1900 edition of *Sister Carrie*, though described with some justification as drivel, suggests that Carrie is a seeker who won't look into herself:

> Oh, Carrie, Carrie! Oh, *blind* strivings of the human heart. . . . In your rocking-chair, by your window, shall you *dream* such happiness as you may never feel. (*SC* 369; emphasis added)

Carrie's verbal and emotional reticence leads to something of a superficial existence: she chases her dreams without "reading" them, and therefore without reading herself. She is as devoid of introspection as any character in fiction, even for a writer like Dreiser, who created many characters with a similar reluctance to explore their own longings. For Carrie, wants are always dreams, products of an unconscious which she actively (that is, consciously) refuses to explore.

Her active refusal supports Lacan's pronouncement that "the ego represents the centre of all the *resistances* to the treatment of symptoms."[38] This is very much the case with Hurstwood, Eugene, and Clyde as well as Carrie. Their repression leads to destructive behavior that springs from the unconscious, the seat of identity, contradiction, and alienation.[39] Aggressivity operates within constraints, says Lacan. He ties it to neurosis in the context of social living and its discontents. But the balance can be hard to maintain. In a frequently quoted speech from *Jennie Gerhardt*, Lester Kane speaks for many of Dreiser's protagonists in lamenting that, "The best we can do is hold our personality intact."[40] Such is the difficulty in maintaining an integrated self. When the accommodation between the symbolic and the imaginary breaks down and the latter can no longer be contained, aggressivity operates out of control. We see the results in the thieving, philandering, even murderously negligent behavior of Dreiser's protagonists.

Such compulsive behavior is almost never accompanied by self-reflection in Dreiser's narratives. In Hurstwood's case, "The true ethics of the situation never once occurred to him, and never would have, under any circumstances" (*SC* 193). Clyde's blow is "accidentally and all but unconsciously administered" (*AAT*

493). Eugene, though clearly the most reflective character under consideration here, is no champion of introspection, either:

> [His physical passion] seemed to overcome him quite as a drug might or a soporific fume. He would mentally resolve to control himself, but unless he instantly fled there was no hope, and he did not seem able to run away. He would linger and parley, and in a few moments it was master and he was following its behest blindly, desperately, to the point almost of exposure and destruction. ("*G*" 172)

The narrator later describes him as "a rudderless boat in the dark" ("*G*" 286).

"To bring the subject to recognize and name his desire," says Lacan, "this is the nature of the efficacious action of analysis."[41] This psychoanalytic tenet offers especially compelling insight into Dreiser's characters, for they are especially reluctant to name their desires, partly because they usually do not even know what they are. Carrie's "voice of want" never stills, for example. Her deepest desire is repressed, with a series of signifiers inserted in its place. What she wants is an unspeakable, unreadable thing, a part of the unconscious discourse of the Other, about which we can only speculate.

"Analysis" of other Dreiserian creations has yielded similarly equivocal results. When we examine Dreiser's art psychoanalytically, we find the sources of desire not only in the culture that surrounds them — a main focus of current criticism — but also buried deep in the personal unconscious, at the end of an increasingly obscure trail of signifiers. We see only the top signifier, the first link of the chain, but its direction is important: the chain points into the characters' unarticulated pasts.

Tracing the chain backwards, I have highlighted some of the patterns of alienation, repetition, and resultant aggressivity inherent in Dreiser's portraits. My point has been to identify areas of ambiguity, gaps, losses: sites of repression that trail back into the subjects' personal histories. Following Lacan, I have sought the unconscious by examining what is missing as well as what is there. When something is repressed, it becomes unreadable — but it leaves a trace in the form of whatever has replaced it on the signifying chain. To illustrate the effect of the unreadable means moving away from comprehensive readings of encrypted absolutes. As a way to read American naturalist literature, this perspective provides a source of multiplicity and indeterminacy on the level of individual personality. As such, it represents an important alternative to the socially oriented, culturally contextual readings that have predominated in the criticism of the literature of the period.

This "implication" of Dreiser with psychoanalysis will, I hope, invite further psychoanalytic readings of Dreiser's canon. Such analysis is clearly not a question of isolating psychological "problems" to be "solved," but of locating structural interrelationships, matrices of desire that combine in unpredictable—that is, nonteleological—ways. To treat Dreiser's complicated psychological portraits as "poor egos" in distress cuts down on the possible variations in their behavior. The contribution of Freud is better served in naturalist criticism by readings that allow for the diversity, unpredictability, and complex past of the divided mind.

Lacan emphasizes the psychoanalytic ambiguities. So does Dreiser. In their blind strivings after desire, the motivated acts of Dreiser's characters are signifiers, but the signified has been censored. Actions and speech are thus ambiguous, "unreadable." Therefore, to reduce them to the sum of one or two psychic vectors is to deny the ambiguity of the signifying act, and of the discourse of which it is a part. The equivocal depth of Dreiser's characters lies in their conflicting wants originating in their pasts, and cutting different ways into their presents. Lacanian analysis embraces this ambiguity, depth and complexity of the striving of the ego. It gives a density to behavior that does justice to Dreiser's deeply layered fictional personalities.[42]

Notes

1. Dreiser first read Freud's work around 1914–1915. In 1931, at a dinner honoring Freud on his 75th birthday, Dreiser said in his speech:

   I shall never forget my first encounter with his *Three Contributions to the Theory of Sex*, his *Totem and Tabu*, and his *Interpretation of Dreams*. At that time and even now every paragraph came as a revelation to me—a strong, revealing light thrown upon some of the darkest problems that haunted and troubled me and my work. And reading him has helped me in my studies of life and men. . . .

   See Theodore Dreiser, *A Selection of Uncollected Prose*, ed. Donald Pizer (Detroit: Wayne State University Press), p. 263.

2. Ellen Moers, *Two Dreisers* (New York: Viking, 1969), p. 228.

3. Gordon O. Taylor, *The Passages of Thought: Psychological Representation in the American Novel* (New York: Oxford University Press, 1969), p. 13. Taylor is most concerned with the representation of

moral analysis. Though psychological, his perspective is decidedly not psychoanalytic.

4. Lee Clark Mitchell, *Determined Fictions* (New York: Columbia University Press), ch. 1.

5. *Ibid.*, p. 17.

6. American naturalist literature — Dreiser's work included — is currently being examined by a new generation of critics as a literature of social (as opposed to psychological) concerns, especially those pertaining to the marketplace. For an overview of this body of work, see Eric Sundquist's "The Country of the Blue," his influential introduction to *American Realism: New Essays* (Baltimore and London: Johns Hopkins University Press, 1982), pp. 3–24. A recent example of such analysis is *Bodies and Machines* (New York and London: Routledge, Chapman and Hall, 1992), in which Mark Seltzer focuses on the nexus between the natural and the social/cultural, describing a system of "relays" between opposing forces. This continuous opposition creates a dynamic tension that he broadly terms "the miscegenation of nature and culture." In the case of Dreiser, Seltzer is concerned with the way that desire is expressed in the marketplace. Seltzer's argument is sweepingly synthetic, challenging, and persuasive; the characters in the stories scarcely matter to him, except as they illustrate the larger scheme. I think that Dreiser's complex protagonists particularly merit individual attention.

7. An excellent influence study has already been done by Ellen Moers, augmented by the work of Donald Pizer. In *Two Dreisers*, Moers documents Dreiser's discovery of Freud and his incorporation of Freudian ideas into *An American Tragedy*, while Pizer's analysis in *The Novels of Theodore Dreiser: A Critical Study* (Minneapolis: University of Minnesota Press, 1976) extends the historical frontier through the study of Dreiser's drafts and holographs. Though he does not engage in full-blown psychoanalytic readings, Pizer's exigesis is informed in places by Dreiser's Freudian influences.

Dreiser has lately begun to get his due as a novelist of character as well as social texture. In "Dreiser and the Naturalistic Drama of Consciousness," *Journal of Narrative Technique* 21 (1991): 202–11, a recent essay focusing on *Jennie Gerhardt*, Donald Pizer argues that one of Dreiser's distinguishing features is the way that he depicts consciousness in concrete terms. Two psychologically oriented critical voices of significance are those of Barbara Hochman and Thomas P. Riggio. In her work on Dreiser (and also Norris and Wharton), Hochman has approached realist and naturalist fiction foremost as complex storytelling about complex characters (see "A Portrait of the

Artist as a Young Actress: The Rewards of Representation in *Sister Carrie*," in *New Essays on SISTER CARRIE,* ed. Donald Pizer [New York and Cambridge, England: Cambridge University Press, 1991], pp. 43–64). And in an important essay in the same volume, Riggio calls for recognition of Dreiser as a "psychological realist" ("Carrie's Blues," pp. 23–41; Quotation, p. 25). Riggio's psychological reading of Carrie interprets her actions against the complex background of her mind.

8. Richard B. Hovey and Ruth S. Ralph, "Dreiser's *The "Genius"*: Motivation and Structure," *Hartford Studies in Literature* 2 (1970): 169–83.

9. Terry Whalen, "Dreiser's Tragic Sense: The Mind as 'Poor Ego'," *The Old Northwest* 11 (1985): 61–80.

10. *Ibid.*, p. 71. Traditional Freudian methodology of the sort that Whalen uses actually offers insight into *Jennie Gerhardt* — the anomaly in Dreiser's fictional canon. Jennie's balanced ego (nearly unique among Dreiser's protagonists) strikingly contrasts with the dominant appetites of her lover Lester and the social stricture embodied by her father. See Leonard Cassuto, "Dreiser's Ideal of Balance" (forthcoming in *Jennie Gerhardt: New Essays on the Restored Text,* ed. James L. W. West III [Philadelphia: University of Pennsylvania Press, 1995]).

11. Theodore Dreiser, *An American Tragedy* (New York: New American Library, 1964), I:169. Future page citations refer to this edition, and will be given parenthetically within the text. *An American Tragedy* was first published in 1925.

12. I would further suggest that the lack of psychoanalytic Dreiser criticism can be traced to the abundance of deterministic criticism of his work. The general reluctance to scrutinize the characters in his stories as "possible persons" is, I think, a result of the long-running debate on determinism that still centers on this group of texts; that is, it may be hard to perceive characters as having real psychological depth if they are seen to lack free will.

13. Shoshana Felman, *Jacques Lacan and the Adventure of Psychoanalysis* (Cambridge and London: Harvard University Press, 1987), p. 48.

14. *Ibid.*, pp. 49–50.

15. Sherry Turkle, *Psychoanalytic Politics* (New York: Basic Books, 1978), p. 75.

16. Dreiser did not want to be constrained by Freudian determinism, either. Pizer relates how Dreiser revised *An American Tragedy* in order to keep it from becoming a Freudian tract (*The Novels of Theodore Dreiser,* pp. 213–4).

17. My summary of Lacan's theory of ego formation and the unconscious is informed and aided (one might say, "implicated") most notably by those of Shoshana Felman (*Jacques Lacan and the Adventure of Insight* [Cambridge and London: Harvard University Press, 1987], Sherry Turkle (*Psychoanalytic Politics*), and Ellie Ragland-Smith (*Jacques Lacan and the Philosophy of Psychoanalysis* [Urbana and Chicago: University of Illinois Press, 1987]).

18. The mirror stage does not depend on the presence of a literal mirror; the important thing is that the infant comes to distinguish the presence of an-Other, and thereby realizes its own existence.

19. See, for example, "The agency of the letter in the unconscious or reason since Freud" (Jacques Lacan, *Ecrits*, trans. Alan Sheridan [New York and London: Norton, 1977], p. 147).

20. Felman, *Adventure of Insight*, p. 65. Philip Rieff (among others) documents Freud's frequent analogies of himself to Copernicus and Darwin (*Freud: The Mind of the Moralist* [Chicago and London: University of Chicago Press, 1959; 3d ed. repr. 1979], pp. 24, 76, 398, 401). Felman describes the Copernican comparison eloquently: "Just as Copernicus discovers that it is not the sun that revolves around the earth but the earth that revolves around the sun, so Freud displaces the center of the human world from consciousness to the unconscious" (*Adventure of Insight*, p. 64). Freud saw himself in an intellectual line with Copernicus and Darwin, with the contributions of all three serving to remove the human being from the center of things. Felman's reworking of Freud's Copernican metaphor is revealing: "In Lacan's explicitly and crucially linguistic model of reflexivity, there are no longer distinct centers but only contradictory gravitational pulls" (65).

21. See Lacan's "Function and field of speech and language in psychoanalysis," (*Ecrits*, p. 51), and "The agency of the letter in the unconscious . . . " (*Ecrits*, p. 175).

22. Lacan, "The Freudian Thing," (*Ecrits*, p. 118).

23. These "elective vectors" include "castration, mutilation, dismemberment, dislocation, evisceration, devouring, [and] bursting open of the body" (Lacan, "Aggressivity in Psychoanalysis," [*Ecrits*, p. 11]).

24. Freud also allowed that the death drive could be directed towards others, but in his view, its primary focus is the self.

25. Sigmund Freud, "On Narcissism: An Introduction," trans. James Strachey, *The Standard Edition of the Works of Sigmund Freud* (London: Hogarth, 1953–1974), Vol. XIV, pp. 73–102. (Quotation, p. 74.) Further quotations will be given parenthetically within the text.

26. This observation covers the 1900 published edition of *Sister Carrie*; the recently published "unexpurgated" University of Pennsylvania Press edition reveals more sexual desire on Carrie's part.

27. Dreiser's protagonists repeat without gaining mastery, which often makes the repetition appear imposed from without (especially in the case of *An American Tragedy*). This offers a context for the preponderance of teleologically deterministic readings of Dreiser.

28. Richard Lehan, *Theodore Dreiser: His World and His Novels* (Carbondale: Southern Illinois Press, 1969) and Lee Clark Mitchell, *Determined Fictions,* have authored the best, most comprehensive discussions of repetition and doubling in *An American Tragedy*, both in support of deterministic arguments.

29. The unexpurgated edition of *Sister Carrie* documents Hurstwood's affairs more unflinchingly than the version originally published. Dreiser portrays him as periodically unfaithful, a regular visitor to meeting places of ill repute.

30. See Freud, *Beyond the Pleasure Principle* (*Standard Edition,* Vol. XVIII, pp. 3–64. Lacan's rereading of *Beyond the Pleasure Principle* does not revise content the way, for example, his mirror stage moves the Oedipal trauma back further in infancy than Freud originally placed it; the difference in this latter case is largely one of emphasis. Lacan's focus on the form of the discourse (the structure of the signifying chain) leads to his close study of repetition and broader reading of the death drive.

31. Theodore Dreiser, *Sister Carrie* (New York and London: Norton, 1970; 1st ed. repr. 1900), p. 194. Future citations refer to this edition, and will be given parenthetically within the text.

32. Buttressing this point is the sympathy that mixes with Clyde's other contradictory feelings when he sees Roberta's house for the first time. Though she is pregnant by then and Clyde wishes to be rid of her, his reaction (communicated in indirect discourse by the narrator) to this "lorn, dilapidated realm" is full of pity for her, even as he fears that this fate could be visited upon himself (*AAT,* pp. 426–7).

33. Theodore Dreiser, *The "Genius"* (New York: New American Library, 1981), p. 644. Future citations refer to this edition, and will be given parenthetically within the text. *The "Genius"* was first published in 1915.

34. Lacan, *Four Fundamental Concepts of Psychoanalysis*, trans. Alan Sheridan (New York: Norton, 1978), p. 50. Lacan studies the structure of repetition compulsion very closely in his "Seminar on the

Purloined Letter," trans. by Jeffrey Mehlman, in *The Purloined Poe*, ed. John P. Muller and William Richardson (Baltimore and London: Johns Hopkins University Press, 1988), pp. 28–54.

35. Lacan, "Aggressivity" (*Ecrits*, p. 21).

36. Felman, *Adventure of Insight*, p. 139.

37. Lacan, "Function and Field" (*Ecrits*, p. 50).

38. Lacan, "Aggressivity" (*Ecrits*, p. 23).

39. *Ibid.*, p. 11.

40. Theodore Dreiser, *Jennie Gerhardt* (New York: Penguin Books, 1989), p. 401. The passage is the same in the restored edition of the novel edited by James L. W. West III (Philadelphia: University of Pennsylvania Press, 1992), p. 392.

41. Jacques Lacan, *Seminaire II* (Paris: Seuil, 1978), p. 267; quoted in Felman, *Jacques Lacan and the Adventure of Psychoanalysis*, p. 131.

42. I wish to thank Dr. Gary Rosenberg of the Philadelphia Academy of Natural Science for his aid and insight in the preparation of this essay.

On Language and the Quest for Self-Fulfillment: A Heideggerian Perspective on Dreiser's *Sister Carrie*

Paul A. Orlov

During the 1970s and 1980s, the ideas and methods of philosopher Martin Heidegger on hermeneutics increasingly influenced the work of many critical theorists in literary studies. My interest in Heidegger's writings, however, centers not on the hermeneutical methodology they reveal for interpreting texts, but on the thematic content that some of them offer as an innovative basis for extended readings of various modern American literary texts. In particular, I am concerned with the ways that Heidegger's ideas on "authenticity" and "inauthenticity" within the ontological inquiry "into the question of the meaning of Being" in his masterwork, *Being and Time* (1927),[1] provide a unique paradigm for a critical approach to the fiction of Theodore Dreiser. In the rather limited scope of the present discussion, I hope to give a suggestive illustration of one facet of this approach, while tracing a Heideggerian perspective on the relation between "language" and the quest for self-fulfillment in *Sister Carrie* (1900).

It is initially worth noting that traditional misconceptions about Dreiser (his purely naturalistic worldview, his own weaknesses as a thinker, and—above all—his supposed lack of fictional artistry) would seem to make him an improbable novelist to be discussed in terms of concepts drawn from a major twentieth-century philosopher such as Heidegger. Moreover, there can be little doubt that Dreiser, who was not especially well read in philosophy, never studied *Being and Time*;[2] and given the chronology, he obviously could not have heard of it when he wrote *Sister Carrie*. But much recent criticism has finally recognized the complex vision and artistic merits of Dreiser's novels. And just as some criticism (for example) has applied psychoanalytic concepts to the works of Hawthorne—who could not have read the writings of Freud—and by doing so has shed new light on his art, it is surely valid to use various Heideggerian concepts, despite Dreiser's unfamiliarity with them, in interpreting his fiction. In fact, this interdisciplinary approach to Dreiser's famous first novel can help disclose new meaningfulness in the literary text.

In Heidegger's *Being and Time*, the human existent is by nature uniquely an ontological creature, ever engaged in the process of defining itself as it (also) discovers and discloses Being and the beings in the world. (Remarkably, Heidegger's description of human existence makes no use of the terms "man" or "woman," or references to "people." Rather, to signify the special ontological role and nature of human beings as that place or "clearing" in which Being discloses itself, the philosopher uses the term *"Dasein"* — literally in German, "being-there.") The meaning of things or even truth itself can be disclosed only when and as long as Dasein, which is essentially disclosedness, *is* (*B and T,* 269). But *how* Dasein understands the disclosure of the things and beings it encounters in its individual "Being-in-the-world" depends on the nature of its sense of the meaning of being a Self. And this sense or mode of existence may be either "authentic" or "inauthentic."

The assumption underlying the entire enterprise of *Being and Time* is made explicit at many points in the philosophical text — that "authenticity" is much more a potential than an actual state for Dasein in day-to-day existence. For to be in the "authentic" mode, Dasein must "project" itself in terms of "primordial" thought — comparable to the thinking of "fundamental ontology" most intensely embodied as well as expressed in Heidegger's work — making possible the genuine disclosure of Being and truth. For Heidegger, it must be stressed, rejection of all forms of subjective metaphysics that have made the *transcendens* a super-thing existing beyond our world or have given anthropomorphic conceptions of it, means that Being "is" in fact "no-thing," though it is certainly the transcendent and Absolute. Indeed, as John Macquarrie, a major authority on Heidegger who served as cotranslator of *Sein und Zeit* into English has stated (1968), "He is careful never to formulate the question of the meaning of Being in the form 'What is Being?', for to ask this question would be to imply that Being 'is' a 'what', a thing or substance or entity."[3] Yet while it is essential to note the sharp distinction Heidegger makes between Being and beings/entities, and his insistence on "authentic" Dasein's eschewing of concern with "things" and the thinking of thinghood — to anticipate a point crucial to the link I will seek to illuminate between the philosopher's vision and Dreiser's in the novel — it will suffice here to conceive of Being as broadly analogous to the transcendent principle of thought and existence. As I shall also show, there is relevance for a reading of the story of Carrie Meeber in Heidegger's equation of Being with both ultimate or ideal truth and Beauty. Such disclosure of Being rarely occurs in everyday existence, however, for Dasein is too often caught up instead in "calculative" thought, preoccupied with beings for their own sake. In this mode, explains the philosopher, one sees entities and even other people as *things* to be mastered or defined — and related to — merely by their practical ("ready-to-hand" or instrumental) use, and thus lives "inauthentically."

This central aspect of the contrast between "authentic" and "inauthentic" ways of being — and of discovering the meaning of *other* beings — immediately relates to part of Heidegger's view of life that will make *it* useful in an approach to *Sister Carrie*. In its everyday state, the human individual, Dasein, responds to the things he/she encounters in terms of what they are "good for" and understands the self and his/her world with reference to practical concerns alone. But (human) Others that Dasein is "with" in the world are to be distinguished sharply from those entities that can be appropriately encountered in this "ready-to-hand" manner. And in the "inauthentic" state Heidegger describes, Dasein loses sight of this — in the process threatening to reduce others and (thus too) the self to the status of "things" — as an especially insidious component of a distorted way of understanding oneself, the world, and relationships. (That this insight in *Being and Time* has intriguing pertinence to Dreiser's first novel can be anticipated from the fact that so many recent studies of *Sister Carrie* have stressed the work's vision of the commodification of life.[4])

Heidegger finds that one crucial, baneful influence causing "inauthentic" Dasein thus to exist in a distorted manner — often misunderstanding its own genuine possibilities, the "meaning" of the world it discovers, and the nature of truth — is its immersion in the values, attitudes, and pursuits of that "crowd" of Others he calls "the They." Using this expressive term, Heidegger explains at length that "inauthentic" Dasein so surrenders its true selfhood in assuming the viewpoints and values of the many that it fundamentally loses itself (the "I," as it were) and becomes absorbed in a way of being aptly termed "the they" (*B and T* 164–6). As we shall see, recognition of a striking parallelism between "the they" described by Heidegger affecting Dasein and the American society (drawn by Dreiser) shaping Carrie's life as an aspiring individual helps make the philosopher's ideas a new lens for illuminating the novel.

The Heideggerian analysis of "inauthenticity" in *Being and Time* is an especially provocatively pertinent source for insights into the worldview in *Sister Carrie,* because the philosopher is tacitly criticizing the way we live now in a modern age of increasing technology and commercialism and of decreasing personal identity. (Although Heidegger asserts that "inauthenticity" is Dasein's common, everyday state and that his account of it is not meant to be taken pejoratively, distinguished interpreters of his thought have agreed that just as the philosopher's term "fallen" for this way-of-being suggests, it is unmistakably a sharp criticism of the mode of modern living that "they" foster.)[5] Heidegger's discussion of the everyday world in which "they" prevail describes various major facts of life in an industrialized mass society: alienation, anonymity within the "crowd," an obsession with things (with an attendant tendency to reduce others and oneself to a form of thinghood), an emphasis on appearances, the loss of true self, the dehumanizing advance of forms of mechanization, and — particularly important for the present discussion — the lack of genuine communication and communion among people. Comparably and significantly, in *Sister Carrie* Dreiser depicts an emerging modern American society, which is ever more marked by the same facts and effects, at a key point in its development (the 1890s) between the Gilded Age and World War I. Radically shaped by the rise of industrial capitalism and urbanization, this society brought forth a way of being, according to Eric Sundquist's nice summary (1982), in which "the market becomes the measure of man himself" and (as any gap between "inherent values and their external representation . . . dissolves") the "inner values of the spirit are drawn outward until they appear at last to merge with the *things* from which one cannot be distinguished and without which one cannot constitute, build, or fabricate a self."[6]

The language of this summation of the world of "American realism" — a world captured in works such as Dreiser's novel published in 1900 — again clearly points to the potential usefulness of Heidegger's account of an "inauthentic" state as a critical analogue. Such a parallelism suggests, along with the diverse "facts" in American life at the turn of the century that prompted Dreiser to write what he would describe as "a picture of conditions,"[7] a societal context confirming that *Being and Time* contains a view of human experience that can be instructively compared to the novel's study of its characters' ways of being. Of course, in saying this much, I am making some implicit assumptions about the relation between the "real" world (at a given time period in our nation's history) and fiction "about" it that perhaps need to be addressed explicitly before I proceed. For obviously, many recent literary studies have questioned our traditional assumptions about the nature of (supposedly objective) "reality," about the meanings of literary texts, and about the significance of one's use of such terms as "realism" or "realistic" to privilege some texts as documents presumed to have socio-historical value. And while the purposes and scope of this discussion clearly do not allow for detailed consideration of these complex, important issues, my attempt to validate the approach to *Sister Carrie* — as a "reading" based on premises about both Heidegger's and the novel's representations of the "real" modern world, and about Dreiser's intentions to critique the values of that society in which his heroine seeks selfhood — demands at least a brief response to such challenging questions, abroad in today's critical climate, that might seem to make my approach problematic.

Among the works of theory and criticism that have raised such questions, presenting very new perspectives on how literary texts in general take meaning and on what specific texts can safely be said to signify, are some of the "new historicist" studies. And since one of these — Walter Benn Michaels' *The Gold Standard and the Logic of Naturalism* (1987)[8] — has become so influential and controversial, and opens with a discussion of *Sister Carrie* directly opposed to some of my most emphatic ideas about the novel, it is a work warranting some focus here as a sample (implied) challenge to the bases for my critical enterprise. Michaels had originally written the essay "*Sister Carrie*'s Popular Economy" (which became his first chapter) not just from "admiration" for the novel, but also ("especially") "out of irritation with those critics who read it as an indictment of American culture" reflected in the career of Carrie as portrayed by Dreiser (*GS* 17). Because I affirm and even embrace just that critical stance which Michaels found so irritating (as a mis-reading of the text), it is worthwhile trying to get — briefly yet bluntly — at the origin of our conflicting outlooks on a literary work we both admire. Seeing the story of Carrie through the new historical lens of theories and ideas on capitalism, consumption, and desire, Michaels argues that — quite to the contrary of the view so many readers of the novel, including the present writer, have held — the "power of *Sister Carrie* . . . derives not from its scathing 'picture' of capitalist 'conditions' but from its unabashed and extraordinarily literal acceptance of the economy that produced those conditions" (*GS* 35). A crucial point behind this assertion is his claim that critics have (misguidedly) "managed to convince themselves of Dreiser's fundamental hostility to the burgeoning consumer economy he depicts" by mis-taking as the novelist's own ideas those given to the character Ames, whom Carrie finds so critical of materialistic values and goals just as she achieves what most define as "Success" in New York (*GS* 41–2). But crucial to his argument, too, it seems to me, is Michaels' *own* ironic, unexamined tendency to assume that the vision and values of Carrie — so devoted to the "ideals" of consumerism and so certain that happiness will follow from total "desire" for such ideals — are to be taken for, simply identified with, those of her creator! Perhaps this telling trouble with the argument in *The Gold Standard* results in part from the fact that, as senior Dreiser scholar Richard Lehan has observed (1991), "while Michaels spends a great deal of time talking about capitalism and desire, he spends very little time contextualizing these matters."[9] Indeed, a careful reading of *Sister Carrie* supports the assumption shared by so many readers that key distinctions need to be made between Carrie's view of her experience and Dreiser's. For as Amy Kaplan has stated (1988) in writing about Dreiser and other artists of "American realism," they "do more than passively record the world outside; they actively *create and criticize the meanings, representations, and ideologies of their own changing culture.*"[10] Just so, I approach *Sister Carrie* by assuming that it is a "realist" work with its author's implicit commentary on his culture and society, and that in ways which Heideggerian ideas on "inauthenticity" help to reveal, Dreiser in fact dramatizes the dire consequences for the seeking self in a realm of rampant materialism and its gods.

Now one of the reasons that the application of a Heideggerian perspective to a reading of *Sister Carrie* becomes intriguingly meaningful is because of some striking parallels between Dreiser's and Heidegger's views on Beauty and the nature of human communication/relationships. In Heidegger's terms, the individual Dasein living "inauthentically" as a "they-self" misunderstands its genuine possibilities and the nature of Being in the world; this in turn has crucial implications for an individual's pursuit or apprehension of Beauty (an idea vitally important to Dreiser's characterization of Carrie), since Heidegger explicitly identifies Beauty with Being:

> To be beautiful means — in Greek as well as German — to shine, gleam, and blaze forth, to appear in the light, to be revealed in one's essential nature, to be disclosed in one's true Being. Beauty is disclosure. That is why Being and beauty belong together. . . . Beauty, Being, and Truth are but so many names for the same thing: original disclosure.[11]

With its own humanity reduced to thinghood and blinded to such true disclosure of Beauty and Being by the prevailing values and views of "the they" (the mass society), the "inauthentic" individual is led astray from his/her own genuine, ideal possibilities. And these Heideggerian concepts provide a pertinent and meaning-ful means of understanding Dreiser's portrait of his protagonist in the novel, as she seeks self-fulfillment through her response to and quest after Beauty in both the spectacle of the city and the world of the theater—each suggestively shining brightly with lights. Influenced (in effect) by the "crowd" around her, Carrie acquires distorted impressions of what to value and (accordingly) how to define both others and herself in her unfolding quest—fed by her inherent desire for Beauty—for self-fulfillment. It is finally the relevance of the philosophical context of "inauthen-tic" being (so applicable to Carrie's confusion over her goals in light of her society's materialistic values) that makes important some key similarities between Heidegger's and Dreiser's ideas on "language"—more basically, on communication and the nature of relationships[12]—in relation to the disclosure of truth and the understanding of self in human experience.

The opening scene of the novel immediately begins to show how even the moments of potentially genuine "self-and-world dis-closure" in Carrie's life are tinged with the gilded hues of the false "ideals" her society offers her as ways of defining herself and of pursuing Beauty. In her encounter with Drouet on the train, Car-rie finds "something satisfactory in the attention of this individual with his good clothes," as he describes the "magnificence" of the city she is approaching (*SC* 5). Meanwhile, she is "of interest to him from the one standpoint which a woman both delights in and fears" (*SC* 5). Their conversation is superficial and basically im-personal, yet we learn that there "is much more passing [between them in the scene] than the mere words indicat[e]" (*SC* 5). For Dreiser explains that

> . . . words are but the vague shadows of the volumes we mean. Little audible links, they are, chaining together great inaudible feelings and purposes. Here were these two, bandying little phrases, drawing purses, looking at cards, and both unconscious of how inarticulate all their real feelings were. Neither was wise enough to be sure of the working of the mind of the other. He could not tell how his luring succeeded. She could not realise that she was drifting, until he secured her address. Now she felt that she had yielded something—he, that he had gained a victory. Already they felt that they were somehow associated. (*SC* 6)

These comments by the novel's narrator on the nature of com-munication interestingly invite comparison with Heidegger's views on language. Drawing a key distinction between the language of people's ordinary "inauthentic" state[13] and that of an "authentic"[14]

Being-in-the-world, Heidegger first describes the former (the language of "inauthenticity") as merely "everyday talk" (*Gerede*):

> In talk, everything is understood because everyone moves on the same level of generality without trying to get to the foundations of what is being talked about. Communication is no longer a problem, since no one really attempts to appropriate what is communicated. Almost everything is self-evident and one cannot fail to understand anything, because understanding is not attempted but presupposed. In talk, understanding is more or less disrooted, it is a public good belonging to everyone and no one, and communication occurs on the ambiguous level of the everyday, public, generally known, common-sense "real world." (*H, B, & T* 29)

The flow of words between people is so easy that it glibly obscures, or omits the expression of, individuals' underlying attitudes and purposes; such common "talk," which falsifies the essential meaning of life, is an appropriate medium of communication for a world living on the surface of things—whether described analytically by the philosopher or dramatized by the novelist. Dreiser's authorial statement about "words" quickly suggests that his novel similarly questions the meaningfulness of "everyday talk" and significance of speech per se in scenes of important action.

On the one hand, his characters use and misuse language in ways that illustrate the nature of *Gerede*: Hurstwood's relationship with each patron of Fitzgerald and Moy's is based on his skill (as the title of Chapter V says) in "the use of a name" (or formula of address) in response to the person's socioeconomic "rank." And in the "personal" relations shown between Sven and Minnie Hanson, Mr. and Mrs. Hurstwood, Drouet and Carrie (later on) in Chicago, and then Carrie and "Wheeler" in New York, we see people who converse, but do not truly *communicate*, with each other. On the other hand, scenes throughout the novel show the unimportance of words in instances of profoundly personal illumination for Carrie and of genuine understanding between her and others and her world. Although we shall have to return soon to the problematic nature of this theme conveyed by Dreiser, these parts of the novel—explicable in terms of the forms of communication which Heidegger calls "Discourse"—*seem* to further her development and quest as a self.

According to the philosopher, "discourse"—the language of "authenticity"—is "a meaningful articulation of Being-in-the-world as disclosed in 'finding' (oneself-in-the-world) and [in genuine] 'understanding'" (quoted in *H, B, & T* 29). This language of "authenticity" is by no means dependent on words: In silences as well as in speaking and listening, it "manifests the existential openness of coexistent ontological beings toward each other" (quoted in *H, B, & T* 29). As Heidegger sums it up in *Toward Language,* "The essence of saying is the saying of Essence" (quoted in *H, B, & T* 133). Thus the essential function of any form of language (or communication) is to express a disclosure of Being.[15] Because talking often obscures the way to true understanding, a communication without words may best conduce to such disclosure. Indeed, pertinently, the philosopher sees the fundamentally wordless creation of art as one of the most striking illustrations of "discourse." Heidegger notes a special affinity between the artist's responsiveness to Beauty—which is itself tantamount to a disclosure of Being—and "authentic" experience's openness to Being. The inspiration of the artist makes him/her one who is unusually attuned to Being; as she "creates" a work of art, Beauty and Truth come to light through her.[16] So the essence of art is disclosure, and artistic expression—which originates largely in silence and needs no words in several of its forms—is exceptionally well suited to be an "authentic" medium of "language." And in view of Carrie's artistic nature and aspirations, as well as her eventual ascent to stage stardom (ironically) in a nonspeaking role, the relevance of these philosophic ideas to Dreiser's fictional design is readily suggested.

It becomes evident that a theory of "language" akin to Heidegger's underlies the action in *Sister Carrie*. Dreiser's own ideas about often wordless communication are quite appropriate in a work depicting relatively inarticulate characters and dramatizing "primitive" kinds of experience related to his on-going artistic attempt to get at the core of Life's meaning. And one can easily see the potential relevance of the concept of "discourse" to the story of Carrie herself. In the opening chapter, as she begins wonderingly discovering the city, she is (indirectly) termed by the narrator a "genius with imagination" (*SC* 6), whose whole developing life will be portrayed as a passionate pursuit of Beauty derived in great part from her artistic instincts and needs. Years later, led by that pursuit into the world of the theater, Carrie becomes a remarkably successful "actress," in Ames's analysis, because the silent "expression in [her] face" represents and discloses what her audience senses as its true, "natural . . . longing" (*SC* 356)—its most fundamental feelings.

With a skepticism like Heidegger's about the value of "talk" as a vehicle for the "truth" of Being, Dreiser asserts that words "are, as a rule, the shallowest portion of all the argument. They but dimly represent the great surging feelings and desires which lie behind. When the distraction of the tongue is removed, the heart listens" (*SC* 88). This authorial viewpoint clearly underlies Dreiser's presentation of his protagonist and of the other characters in their urban world of desires, from the opening scene onward: here the communication between Carrie and Drouet on the train, like "discourse," begins (as Heidegger puts it) to "manifest the existential openness of [these] coexistent ontological beings toward each other" as they *show* an "openness" to the discovery of each other that has little to do with their conversation. Even though their "real feelings" are "inarticulate," they come to an implicit understanding that makes them feel "somehow associated" and that forms the basis for their subsequent relationship (*SC* 6). Behind the surface of their words, their unvoiced feelings – of material/aesthetic desire on her side, of sexual desire on his – "speak" very eloquently to each other, creating the incipient bond between them. Since Carrie's "heart listens" with great intensity to her desires, she is especially sensitive to all that *apparently* communicates "the saying of Essence" in her life. Just a few observations filtered through the alembic of her imagination suffice to "tell" her a volume of things about "who" Drouet is and what he may mean to her: "The purse, the shiny tan shoes, the smart new suit, and the air with which he did things, built up for her a dim world of fortune, of which he was the center. It disposed her pleasantly toward all that he might do" (*SC* 6).

Now the novel's opening scene obviously starts the process (linked to her travel to the city and all its new possibilities) of Carrie's pursuit of self-discovery, realized desire, and essential Beauty. But as I have hinted previously, Dreiser portrays her unfolding quest in a manner to which the Heideggerian perspective may meaningfully be applied, revealing as he does (from the outset) the problem of whether the nature and course of Carrie's experiences are "authentic" or "inauthentic." In fact, the novel increasingly discloses that both the particular aims she pursues and the way she relates to others and her world in the process of that pursuit, subvert even the most "authentic" desires and moments she has with key qualities of "inauthenticity."

Both the reference to the "dim world of fortune" in the opening scene and the scene's first suggestion of the precise *way* in which Carrie reacts toward Drouet start conveying this theme. In a well-known essay on her growth through a process (pertinently) of largely "inarticulate" experiences, Julian Markels claimed decades ago (1961) that Carrie's "consciousness of her identity does not precede, but arises out of, the ebb and flow of her experience. And this makes us feel that only by submitting to this ebb and flow, only by being loyal and responsive to each of her facts as it presents itself in turn, may [she] attain her identity."[17] More recently, writing about Carrie's unique talent for "representation" — of her responsiveness to others and to beauty, and of desire itself — Barbara Hochman has suggested (1991) that in Dreiser's view, "representation implicitly facilitates not only human interaction but 'being' as such."[18] Yet while these observations have some validity — as Carrie's experiences result in a process that *generally* enhances and individualizes her "being" — it is much less certain than these critics suggest whether she *genuinely* "attains" her identity. For many of the "facts" to which she is "responsive" in the initial encounters with the city, and the man (Drouet) partly symbolizing it for her, at once distort her sense of her identity and purposes; the "possibilities" toward which it/he points her will ultimately undermine her search for self-realization and fulfillment in their materialistic lure. At the same time, perils for Carrie's pursuit of "authentic" being and individual fulfillment are implied, from the very start of her quest for "success" in the urban world, by the paradoxical fact that this world's materialistic values encourage her to achieve selfhood through extreme imitation of *others*.[19]

Of course, the aspects of her experience to which she responds are a function of the nature of her longings, and these are summed up well by Sheldon Grebstein (1963):

> The only passion or urge which Dreiser does grant Carrie is the urge, as much sublime as sensual, for nice things. Early in the narrative he sets forth Carrie's chief motivation: 'She realized in a dim way how much the city held — wealth, fashion, ease — every adornment for women, and she longed for dress and beauty with a whole heart.' This synthesis of aestheticism and materialism — the yearning for beauty, and the expression of the yearning . . . is integral to the novel as well as to Dreiser's total conception of character. . . . [20]

Yet it is crucial that we understand the implications of this "synthesis" of motives underlying all of Carrie's actions, for the "expression of the yearning [for beauty]" that predominates in her life is ultimately incompatible with her "yearning for beauty" (in Heideggerian terms, ideal Beauty) itself. For the "aestheticism" referred to here and most central to Carrie's theatrical artistry is undermined by the materialistic values her society so strongly encourages her to absorb and to confuse with it. And it is the conflict between the materialistic and artistic facets of her nature

(I hope to show) that makes Carrie a complex character and finally frustrates her pursuits.

Just as Heidegger's analysis of "inauthenticity" would make us expect, Dreiser's depiction of his fictional heroine shows that her distorted aims about what to seek (in Grebstein's summary, "nice things") induce her to define others and her relationships with *them* in a distorted manner. A narrative comment in the novel's third paragraph immediately makes it clear that Drouet is less a person to Carrie than an initial embodiment of the seductive city that offers so much she desires: "The city has its cunning wiles, no less than the infinitely smaller and more human tempter. There are large forces which allure with all the soulfulness of expression possible in the most cultured human. The gleam of a thousand lights is often as effective as the persuasive light in a wooing and fascinating eye" (*SC* 1). Here the phrase "the soulfulness of expression" implies the importance of nonverbal communication of essential meanings that the city and its emblematic "human tempter" have for the seeker after beauty in her discovery of its suggestive "thousand lights." Yet by the closing portion of the opening chapter, as we have seen, Carrie has begun identifying all of the aesthetic possibilities of the city with the material fulfillments that Drouet's clothes and money imply, and has thus begun seeing him as a symbolic "center" of "a dim world of fortune." That is, she responds not to him (as an individual), but to what he represents, which her longings make all-meaningful. This fact foreshadows at once the "ambassadors" motif central to the novel in its dramatization of relationships that, like those described in Heidegger's account of "inauthenticity," diminish the human significance of other people, reducing them (as "ready-to-hand" entities) to the status of instruments of one's selfish, practical purposes. Let us see how Dreiser uses the idea of "ambassadors."

This "ambassadors" motif, suggestive of a vision of human relationships similar to those marking the "inauthentic" mode of being, is manifestly a key part of Dreiser's design in *Sister Carrie*. Not only is it implied or described in various textual passages, starting with the one in Chapter I described above, but also several of the much-maligned chapter titles originally used in the novel focus explicitly on it: the titles of Chapters VIII, X, XII, XIII, and XXVI all refer directly to "ambassadors" or the related concept of "credentials" involved in the progressive pattern of Carrie's experiences.[21] Variations on the theme of "ambassadors" indicated through these titles suggest that her view of Drouet, and later Hurstwood, is fundamentally impersonal: as "ambassadors," Drouet and Hurstwood represent the experiential worlds Carrie wishes to enter. But her way of seeing them makes them not only symbols, but also instruments of power — her means of access to the realm which (as the title of Chapter XXXIII puts it) seems to be "the walled city" of "success." So from the standpoint implied by the title of Chapter XXIII, the men are the "ladders" (rendered objects or things by an "inauthentic" outlook) by which she can climb to that place of eminence: once she has accepted Hurstwood's "credentials" and has quarreled with Drouet, the drummer becomes (merely) "One Rung Put Behind" her. And in a related vein that further widens the significance of the "ambassadorial" theme, the titles of several other chapters (XVI, XVII, XXVI, XXXVII, XXXVIII) imply Carrie's perception of these men as (equivalent to) "gates" through which she needs to pass to get inside that "walled city." Both her way of relating to these men and the eventual ironic disillusionment resulting from the pursuits based on it find their final summation in the novel's epilogue: "Drouet, Hurstwood; the world of fashion and the world of stage — these were but incidents. Not them, but that which they represented, she longed for. Time proved the representation false" (*SC* 368).

Although I am getting a bit ahead of my discussion here, it is helpful to outline the pervasiveness in the novel of the "ambassadors" theme, which is expressive of the "inauthentic" relationships Dreiser portrays, as a foundation for explaining his treatment of "language" in Carrie's problematic "progress." Words are of limited importance in the scenes between her and each of her "ambassadors" not only because she understands what his "credentials" communicate symbolically, but because she is incapable of understanding him personally: that is, each "ambassador's" way of using language, which expresses the nature of his personality, has no intrinsic significance for her, since his *personal* identity does not truly interest her. What Drouet and Hurstwood (and later, in a very different sense, Ames) say only has meaning for her as it relates to her possibilities of "success," reflecting their ambassadorial qualities for her. And all of this fits the warped logic of a world in which "love and friendship" have little "reality" because "almost everything turns on money" and "personal relationships are inseparable from commodity relationships."[22] These ideas, as well as his views of "language" akin to Heidegger's, appear to underlie Dreiser's presentation of characters and scenes.

Although my main focus, like the novel's, is on Carrie, it is important to stress that her "inauthentic," instrumental way of relating to others is rampant in the world of the novel — characterizing *most* of the relations in her society, based as they are on materialistic motives. It will be recalled that Heidegger explains there is neither "authentic" communication nor genuine communion between people in an "inauthentic" existence derived from overinvolvement in appearances and the values of materialism.[23] And the individual Dasein, having had his or her human dignity subverted by an obsession with things, improperly treats (human) Others rather as if *they* are things and have "the kind of Being which belongs to equipment ready-to-hand. . . . " For we know that Dasein "approaches the world teleologically, discover[ing] beings in terms of its own ends" (*H, B, & T* 25) with respect to "what they are 'good for' in its Being-in-the-world" — and we find that "they" regard human beings, in the same way, as instruments. In sum, Heidegger indicates that individuality and relationships are perverted in an age inducing an unconscious "fall" into thinghood: "Everydayness takes Dasein as something ready-to-hand to be concerned with — that is, something that gets managed and reckoned up. 'Life' is a 'business,' whether or not it covers its costs" (*B and T* 336). This view of the human condition clearly corresponds to Dreiser's, in his fictive study of characters whose lives spent in search of material "success" as a means to happiness, neither "cover" their "costs" nor contain genuine relationships.

With a vision of the modern age's effects similar to the philosopher's, Dreiser reveals relationships throughout *Sister Carrie* that are rife with misunderstandings and manipulative motives, as those involved in them think of other people as "possibilities" for themselves. Drouet is shown capable only of shallow liaisons aimed at diversion and sexual pleasure. Hurstwood's loveless marriage is based merely on a preservation of appearances and a joint possession of goods; he and his wife do not truly *share* anything, care about each other, or even communicate (in authentically personal terms), and tellingly raise a daughter who will marry only for money. In his relationship with Carrie, Hurstwood first deceives her about his marital status and romantic "intentions," then conceals from her the fact of his theft and the change in his social position (away from Chicago), and finally ceases to care for her or even converse with her except with regard to their common *economic* problems. Meanwhile, Carrie keeps her thoughts and rocking-chair dreams to herself while living with men whom she sees impersonally as symbols — symbols of social worlds to which they can give her access and which seemingly offer higher possibilities for a life of "success." Personally committed only to the dreams she pursues and the stage roles she plays, Carrie, caught in the perpetual quest for more and other, is ever the "anticipatory self" (as Philip Fisher has pointed out [1982]) whose "emotional substance" of "desire, yearning, and a state of prospective being" finds its apt "cultural symbol" in the "notion of acting. . . . "[24] Giving herself to each man in a physical sense alone, she withdraws from him once he is no longer materially useful, as if his role in the drama of her life has abruptly ended. At the end of the novel, her life of luxury and Hurstwood's death in poverty, for all their outward contrast, equally manifest the profound aloneness of ways of being based on "inauthentic" relations with others.

Against the background of the foregoing focus on the way the novel as a whole exposes distorted relationships caused by the values in a materialistic American society, Dreiser's peculiarly Heideggerian treatment of "language" in crucial moments within his heroine's evolving quest for fulfillment can be fully understood. The opening scene's ideas on "language" and on Drouet's potential "ambassadorial" value for Carrie are greatly extended by the luncheon scene in Chapter VI: during this scene arising out of their chance encounter in downtown Chicago at the point, months later, when a discouraged Carrie has lost her first job and appears about to be forced to retreat from the city whose magnetic attraction has totally seduced her, Drouet attains his full "ambassadorial" status in her life through some profound—yet peculiar—communication. Considering the dramatic importance of the scene to the design of his plot, Dreiser minimizes the part that dialogue plays in it to a remarkable degree. While Drouet "chatter[s] on at a great rate, asking questions, explaining things about himself, [and] telling her what a good restaurant" they are in, his loquacity is reported rather than shown, suggesting its limited effect on the action being presented. Carrie, meanwhile, merely smiles a great deal; she does almost no talking, and when she *does* speak to reply to a question, her answers are monosyllabic or absurdly terse:

> "What have you been doing?" he went on. "Tell me all about yourself. How is your sister?"
>
> "She's well," returned Carrie, answering the last query.
>
> He looked at her hard. "Say," he said, "you haven't been sick, have you?"
>
> Carrie nodded.
>
> "Well, now, that's a blooming shame, isn't it? You don't look very well. I thought you looked a little pale. What have you been doing?"
>
> She told him. (*SC* 45)

And so it goes throughout the scene. Nevertheless, they soon "c[o]me to an understanding of each other without words" (*SC*

46); and the manner in which they do so strikingly illustrates a kind of "discourse."

As Kenneth Lynn has pointed out (1957), in *Sister Carrie* the "characters' longings for material objects have a unique animation; not even Scott Fitzgerald talked about money the way Dreiser does. . . . Expensive clothes and jewels are hungered after by his characters with such an intensity that their desire actually seems to breathe life into what they seek. . . . "[25] When read against the background of the Heideggerian view of language, the lunch episode shows why and how Carrie's desire for things even enables them to "speak" to her. While Drouet is talking to her, she is busy thinking that he "must be fortunate. He rode on trains, dressed in such nice clothes, was so strong, and ate in these fine places" (*SC* 45–6). The "dim world of fortune," of which she had imagined him to be "the center" in their initial meeting, now appears clearly visible, as Carrie looks at the restaurant to which he has taken her and hears him invite her to the theater. Having earlier been "disposed . . . pleasantly toward all that he might do" before her arrival in the city, she is naturally far more "captivated" by him at this time when its life has been revealed — and yet remained all but closed — to her. And under these circumstances, she studies Drouet as if he is a book of revelation about possibilities for herself that he may offer.

In illustrating the way a work of art "authentically" discloses Being, Heidegger analyzes a painting by Van Gogh of a pair of peasant's boots, mere objects unlocated in any spacial context, to make them a kind of "authentic" communication: "All the strands of a peasant's life are gathered within [the boots], woven into a fabric and exposed to sight. This is the world in which these boots belong [suggesting the diverse details of the peasant's everyday existence that the philosopher 'sees' in the boots]. . . " (quoted in *H, B, & T* 92). The philosopher's perspective on the painting is meant to convey that the most outwardly commonplace things have a deeper significance that reveals itself to eyes gifted with insight, like those of the "artistic" Carrie. Being open to the message of Beauty, she scrutinizes Drouet in the same manner as Van Gogh studied the boots and as Heidegger perceives the painting. Just as the boots "gather in themselves the whole world" of the peasant, exposing it to sight for the painter and philosopher, so do the clothes and trappings of the drummer manifest his "whole world" to her, making him an alluring symbol of the city. Even Drouet's gleaming rings acquire a fresh importance when seen in the light of the idea of language as "disclosure," for they nearly speak to Carrie as he cuts the meat for her. The light reflected from the rings into her eyes originates in his own "radiant presence," and that presence is composed of the clothes and money he displays, the restaurants and theaters he frequents, and the complete optimism he exudes. Thus his rings articulate the meaning of his whole way of being—and tell her, along with his eyes, that his world can be hers as well:

> Drouet looked at her and his thoughts reached home. She felt his admiration. It was powerfully backed by his liberality and good-humour. She felt that she liked him—that she could continue to like him ever so much. There was something even richer than that, running as a hidden strain, in her mind. Every little while her eyes would meet his, and by that means the interchanging current of feeling would be fully connected. (*SC* 46)

Of course, the "hidden strain" in her mind is the idea that she can become his mistress, and would wish to do so in order to enjoy the effects of "his liberality" to the full. For at this first key turning point in her life in the city, Carrie has begun to realize, in Amy Kaplan's shrewd phrasing (1988), "the absurdity of the notion of 'earning your bread'" in a realm of extreme consumerism, "and the greater importance of having 'something which the world would buy'"—and that "she has only her self to sell . . . " (*SCAR* 143). Thus toward the close of the scene, the narrator states that "the influence [Drouet] was exerting was powerful. They came to an understanding of each other without words—he of her situation, she of the fact that he realised it" (*SC* 46).

It is at this moment, significantly, that he verbalizes the proposition that had been eloquently implied by his rings and other trappings: he offers to help her with his money. And her brief show of indecision about accepting the offer ends as soon as he strikes the "key-note" by referring to her need for clothes (*SC* 47): this reference "speaks" to Carrie's deepest feelings, like the passionate plea of a lover, by reminding her of his crucial "ambassadorial" value. This leaves her completely susceptible to Drouet's advances—of cash and gifts. And so the luncheon scene (from which she emerges holding the two ten dollar bills she has accepted from him) is a symbolic "seduction" that tacitly confirms Carrie's (imminent) acceptance of a role as Drouet's mistress in exchange for the materially enhanced ways of being all his money can give her.

With subtleties of craft of a kind for which he is too seldom given credit, Dreiser suggests the complex implications of this episode in Carrie's life—merging aspects of "authenticity" and "inauthenticity," so to speak — prefiguring her eventual ironic discontent with "success" in the very moments when it points toward the start of her personal growth and ascent to that golden goal. It is first worth noting that the scene's significance as a symbolic "seduction" and as implicit commentary on the peculiar nature of human relationships, is underscored by the telling limitation of the physical contact shown. For at the "climax" of this unusual "seduction" scene, the one sensation Carrie experiences is the feel of Drouet's greenbacks in her hand.

> He pressed her hand gently and she tried to withdraw it. At this he held it fast, and she no longer protested. Then he slipped the greenbacks he had into her palm, and when she began to protest, he whispered:
> "I'll loan it to you — that's all right. I'll loan it to you."
> He made her take it. She felt bound to him by a strange tie of affection now. They went out, and he walked with her. . . . (*SC* 47)

From a conventional point of view, the "tie of affection" between them is indeed "strange."   But it is a perfectly natural basis for a relationship in the world of *Sister Carrie*, where material "success" is a beacon that guides people as they judge themselves and respond to others — in fact causing the quest for selfhood to become an endless emulation of *others* and the "things" that *define* them.[26] The fact that Dreiser makes the transfer of money the reason for the only physical contact in the scene, and infuses that transfer with a kind of sexual excitement,[27] subtly conveys his intention to suggest how essentially impersonal personal relations become under the influence of modes of being based on false values.

And Dreiser's depiction of the close of the scene is rich with related, understated meanings.   When Carrie walks out of the restaurant with Drouet, clutching the greenbacks she has not yet examined, she has tacitly agreed to become his mistress, yet what concerns her is not her prospective lover himself, but the symbolic nimbus that gives him importance.   So as soon as she is alone (the narrative seems to imply), she stops, opens her hand, and looks down at her palm to find out the full meaning of her experience: "The money she had accepted was two soft, green, handsome ten-dollar bills" (*SC* 47). This fictional moment curiously resembles that of the "epiphany" at the end of James Joyce's "Two Gallants" (in *Dubliners* [1914]), in which Corley opens his hand in the lamplight to reveal the shining gold coin that discloses to his "disciple" — and more fully, to the reader — the nature of his character and the significance of his meeting with the young woman.[28] Like the "epiphany" closing Joyce's story, the final sentence of Dreiser's "luncheon" scene directs a sudden, brilliant spotlight on the essential meaning of the whole episode that has been presented, offering a twofold revelation in the process. For Carrie herself, the "discovery" of the money in her hand sums up everything that Drouet has "told" her about himself and her future "possibilities" with him. The sensuous adjectives suggest the way all her feelings throughout the encounter have been focussed on his expressive surface identity: the *good-looking* Drouet has proved both his attractiveness and his readiness to *act* handsomely toward her by giving her the bills that are "handsome" like him and "soft" as the tender emotions he has (thus) aroused. At the same time, the revealing last sentence *formally* illustrates for the reader the idea of language as a disclosure of "essence" already dramatized by the scene, amplifying the scene's thematic point with respect to Carrie's incipient development as a person. For in part, her responsiveness to Drouet's enticements shows her genuine grasp of both the realm of beauty that he symbolizes and the maturing mode of being toward which *his* world leads the way. *However,* too, in picturing her reaction to the money as the episode ends, Dreiser heightens our awareness of the fact that she may too easily mistake the tangible signs of wealth for the inner enrichment she seeks as well. And all the emphasis on externals and material things in this scene marks the very moment providing promise of self-realization for Carrie, with ironic signs of threats to her true selfhood *from* the seductive realm of "commodity fetishism, of the life of objects that consumes the life of the human beings who produce and consume them."[29]

This idea of the insidiously "inauthentic" elements within the profound communication genuinely (in part) furthering Carrie's self-discovery and pursuit of her possibilities, is additionally emphasized by a pair of structural devices Dreiser uses to conclude the crucial episode. First, the moment of illumination and apparent promise Carrie experiences at episode's end (in the final sentences of Chapter VI) is immediately commented on in an ominous way (suggesting her subsequent confusion of values in the search for Beauty) by the title of Chapter VII—"The Lure of the Material: Beauty Speaks for Itself." And then, revealingly, this new chapter begins with commentary on "the true meaning of money," in which the narrator notably says of Carrie that a person possessing "her order of mind would have been content to be cast away upon a desert island with a bundle of money, and only the long strain of starvation would have taught her that in some cases it could have no value" (*SC* 48). Here we have clear foreshadowings of the unfulfilled end of Carrie's quest for self-realization and Beauty at the point of that quest's seemingly auspicious start.

Once the novel has implied that the "seduction" is complete and that Carrie is sleeping and living with Drouet, Dreiser quickly and carefully intrudes upon the action with the authorial commentary on moral questions (in the opening portion of Chapter X) aimed at influencing the reader's response to this unconventional picture of a perhaps-not-pure-enough maiden. And parts of this commentary so pivotal to the design behind the controversial "picture of conditions" in *Sister Carrie* are very pertinent to my interpretive purposes. Dreiser begins this much-discussed section of the novel by stating, "In the light of the world's attitude toward woman and her duties, the nature of Carrie's mental state deserves consideration. Actions such as hers are measured by an arbitrary scale. Society possesses a conventional standard whereby it judges all things" (*SC* 68). In the ensuing passages, he begins developing from a *different* "scale" and an *un*-conventional "standard" of "judgment" a perspective on the "moral" import of Carrie's actions—a perspective which (however upsetting it was to the "genteel" readers who initially later made the novel a notorious failure) crucially contributes to our awareness of the work's Heideggerian outlook. Having announced his intent to seek "to evolve the true theory of morals" (*SC* 69), the narrator depicts his protagonist facing a dilemma with serious philosophical implications: "She looked into her glass and saw a prettier Carrie than she had seen before; she looked into her mind, a mirror prepared of her own and the world's opinions, and saw a worse. Between these two images she wavered, hesitating which to believe" (*SC* 70). What is at stake here in Carrie's self-assessment, after she has exchanged her feminine "virtue" for pretty clothes and other comforts, is not only the "moral" status of her behavior, but also—as the subsequent references (by the narrator) to the conflicting messages within her of "the voice" of "conscience" and the "voice of want" suggest—the meaning of her experience with regard to the "language" of "authenticity" or "inauthenticity" it involves.

Now to a certain extent (the Heideggerian analogue would suggest, at this turning point in her story), Carrie is becoming "authentically" herself by listening to the "voice of want" rather than to that of conscience. Dreiser intends us to see that her new condition does not constitute a "fall," as the "world's opinion" asserts, but, on the contrary, a rise: her actions toward Drouet (and subsequently, in a parallel manner, toward Hurstwood) lead to her growth as a person by giving her a heightened awareness of the possibilities of her nature and the world. The same conduct which the "voice of conscience" condemns, proves conducive to her progress toward the discovery of Beauty's manifestations of Itself in the world and the development (once Drouet chances to introduce her to the realm of the theater) of her individuality as an "artist." Thus it is only by *ignoring* the dictates of her "average little conscience" (*SC* 70) that Carrie can genuinely be herself. And to the extent that it actually enables her to "understand" the Beauty in life and to achieve an "authentic" way of being, her conduct, conventionally considered evil, is in fact *good*. In sum, Carrie is a "moral" person in a sense which the account of conscience in *Being and Time* helps to explain: the "voice of want" that guides her actions is rather like the "authentic" conscience described by Heidegger: it calls to her from within, disclosing to her what she ought to be and how she can become her true self.[30]

Conversely, the voice that says she is "immoral" falsifies her nature as an individual, for it distinctly resembles the conscience of "inauthentic" Dasein. Heidegger observes that this "everyday" conscience "is simply the voice of society, or the *superego*, in Freud's terminology. It reflects the conventions that 'they' have adopted. So this everyday conscience is neither authentic itself nor conducive to an authentic existence. It is just another way in which 'they' stifle and dominate the individual, and take away his own possibilities from him" (*MH* 32–3). Similarly, the conscience which would deny Carrie the possibilities she has in her liaison with Drouet "represent[s]" (says Dreiser) "the world, her past environment, habit, convention. . . . " In other words, it purports to be "the voice of God" but in fact merely expresses "the voice of the people . . . " (*SC* 70). So neither the prescription nor the proscription of acts by the voice of conscience is personally meaningful to her, and her transcendence of the averageness the voice advocates is tantamount to an escape from the tyranny of "the they" to the freedom of true self-discovery.

Yet, at the same time, her apparent escape from the influence "they" exert is undermined in an intensely ironic manner. For all the unconventionality of her conduct from the standpoint of morality, Carrie's life is essentially governed by the "voice" of the conventional world: *what* she desires reflects the values of her society, even if *how* she pursues her desires does not. Thus ironically, "they" taint her "aesthetic" idealism by making her wish for material wealth, while she is in the process of disregarding "their" moral ideals. One fact suggesting this irony in the scene I am discussing is Carrie's consultation of her mirror, for as various critics have noted, mirror symbolism in her story is identified with an extreme concern about clothes, imitation of others, and the *images* of "success."[31] Also, as Dreiser's comments in Chapter XI clearly suggest, the "voice of want" that frees her for *self-*realization by silencing the complaints of conscience too often turns into a voice which conveys to her a misleading message of its own:

> Carrie was an apt student of fortune's ways—of fortune's superficialities. Seeing a thing, she would immediately set to enquiring how she would look, properly related to it. Be it known that this is not fine feeling, it is not wisdom. The greatest minds are not so afflicted. . . . Fine clothes were to her a vast persuasion; they spoke tenderly and Jesuitically for themselves. When she came within earshot of their pleading, desire in her bent a willing ear. The voice of the so-called inanimate! (*SC* 75)

Here it is clear that the "voice" of things communicates to Carrie an essentially "inauthentic" set of goals. In listening to this voice of "inanimate" things, she mistakes "fortune's superficialities" for the true substance of Beauty. The "persuasion" of "fashion" is a Jesuitical influence indeed, for it directs her mind of "fine feeling" to desires that gradually debase her nature and delude her about how to *be*: lured by the loveliness of appearances, she begins to tend too much toward fulfilling the wants of the flesh but neglecting the needs of her spirit—a key theme to which the novel will cause us to return.

Directed by her desires toward this self-enhancing yet subtly self-defeating mode of being, Carrie soon discovers Hurstwood as an "ambassador" offering her still greater possibilities. And Dreiser's presentation of Carrie's response to the "resort" manager's wooing is informed by a similarly Heideggerian slant on the relation between language and being/Beauty. Once she has been Drouet's mistress for a time, has learned from experience the degrees of wealth and splendor the city offers, and has begun observing the distinctions (in taste and status) between the drummer and his more prestigious "friend" Hurstwood, Carrie becomes receptive to the manager's flattering attentions. In Chapter XII —having thus been emotionally prepared for these new events and being left alone during one of Drouet's sales trips—Carrie sees both the mansions of the rich and the richly attired Hurstwood as entrancing possibilities for her ever-yearning self. And the way in which the novel depicts her discovery of these related seductive influences further implies Dreiser's idea of the unimportance

of words in moments of experience crucially meaningful for a
sensitive, seeking individual.

First Carrie takes (with her neighbor Mrs. Hale) an afternoon
buggy ride to look at the lamplit mansions along the North Shore
Drive, where she discovers with discontent a world higher (and
presumably happier) than her own:

> She was perfectly certain that here was happiness. If she could but
> stroll up yon broad walk, cross that rich entrance-way, which to
> her was of the beauty of a jewel, and sweep in grace and luxury
> to possession and command—oh! how quickly would sadness
> flee; how, in an instant, would the heartache end. She gazed and
> gazed, wondering, delighting, longing; and all the while the siren
> voice of the unrestful was whispering in her ear. (*SC* 86)

With this "voice" communicating to her, she returns home and
characteristically sits in her rocking chair, "sad beyond measure,
and yet uncertain, wishing, fancying" (*SC* 87). Then suddenly,
while she is rocking and dreaming of the magical realm of beauty
she has glimpsed, Hurstwood appears—as if summoned up, genie-
like, by the (magical) "lamps of the mansions" (described by part
of the title of Chapter XII).

With Drouet absent and in her mood of unfulfilled yearning,
Carrie is totally susceptible to the appeal of a new experience; and
by becoming the voice of that appeal during his unexpected visit,
the manager takes full advantage of her mood. Just as was the case
in the opening and lunch scenes involving Drouet, there is a sharp
discrepancy between verbal action and the underlying emotional
"action" in this episode of "seduction." The words spoken by
Hurstwood throughout the scene are largely unimportant, for they
are casual and confined to impersonal topics. Nevertheless, he
eloquently makes what seems to Carrie (as the latter part of the
chapter's title highlights) a true "ambassador's plea":

> In this conversation she heard, instead of his words, the voices
> of the things which he represented. How suave was the counsel
> of his appearance! How feelingly did his superior state speak for
> itself! The growing desire he felt for her lay upon her spirit as
> a gentle hand. She did not need to tremble at all, because it
> was invisible; she did not need to worry . . . because . . . She
> was being pleaded with, persuaded, led into denying old rights
> and assuming new ones, and yet there were no words to prove
> it. (*SC* 88–9)

Throughout this scene of mostly wordless wooing, Hurstwood uses
his eyes a great deal to make his case to Carrie: like the man-

sions' lamps which earlier glowed with a "mellow radiance" for her (*SC* 86), his eyes now "radiate an atmosphere which suffuse[s] her being" (*SC* 88). Significantly, the only words Hurstwood speaks to emphasize the message conveyed by his glances and his impressive clothes, are those in which he asks her (with seeming clairvoyance) if she has ever seen the houses along the shore drive! Appropriately and perceptively, his question quickly leads him to remark on her evident unhappiness and dissatisfaction (*SC* 89). That this "seduction" scene based on a language akin to what Heidegger terms "discourse" has established a genuine (if distortedly self-serving) understanding between her and the manager is clear, since just two days later—in their drive on Washington Boulevard—Hurstwood receives a kiss from Carrie symbolically confirming her prospective acceptance of his "credentials" as her new "ambassador." And so the stage is set for their subsequent relationship, pointing toward her quest for new forms of beauty and self-realization in the ultimate urban world of New York, especially in its seductively glamorous theatrical world.

Precipitating Hurstwood's desperate resolve to possess Carrie (that soon results in his tricking her into traveling to new places with him) and preparing for her later work in the New York theatrical realm, Carrie's role in the Elks lodge production of *Under the Gaslight*—for which Drouet, playing a "witless Aladdin" to her most grand wishes, recruits her—marks a crucial moment in the novel's tracing of the course of its protagonist's pursuit of self and "Success." Before she receives this chance to play a part in the famous melodrama, Carrie has been readied for the role by attending various stage productions with one or both of the men toward whom she has actually been enacting, quasimelodramatically, her unconventional parts (as a "waif amid forces" becoming a "knight of today," in the language of the titles of Chapters I and VI). In seeing several plays, she has become enchanted by the brightly illuminated, luxurious world of the theater—with its dramas of desire that in one sense seem larger than life, yet in another[32] seem quite continuous with those realities of the urban realm which most inspire Carrie's imaginings. Further, in being involved in her distorted relationships with Drouet and Hurstwood, she has cultivated a talent for role-playing that corresponds to her own desire-driven search for self so dependent upon her trying out or wishing to imitate other "parts" in the social scene. In fact, Philip Fisher, in his interesting reading of the novel (1982), sees "acting" as an apt symbol and metaphor for its world of selfhood based on costume-like clothes, shifting "roles," and above all a notion of "acting" (in the life of Carrie) that "involves primarily . . . not deception but practice, not insincerity but installment payments on the world of possibility" ("Acting" 269). Thus does the narrator comment, at the point when Drouet suggests she participate in the play, "She was created with that passivity of soul which is always the mirror of the active world" (*SC* 117). As the revealing allusion to the "mirror" figure reminds us here, the course of her experiences leading up to this theatrical opportunity—based on both sartorial and more subtle imitations of others in her efforts to create her "self"—has already prompted her to display "the first subtle outcroppings of an artistic nature, endeavouring to re-create the perfect *likeness* of some phase of beauty which appealed to her" (*SC* 117).

Now as this latter remark by the novel's narrator indicates, the world of the stage to which her one night in *Under the Gaslight* introduces her, will reveal to Carrie an ultimate path for pursuit of (a "perfect likeness of") Beauty and a fulfilled sense of self. Unfortunately for Carrie, however, this path is even more destined to disillusion her than the one leading her from one human "ambassador" to another. For while it may be the case, as one critic suggests, that "acting" in *Sister Carrie* "draws its moral meaning not from a world of true and false but from a dynamic society where all are [socioeconomically] rising or falling" ("Acting" 264), it is surely true that the epistemological and ontological meaning that Carrie finds in the formalized realm of acting entails falsehood to which her self falls prey. As Dreiser's description of her responses to the backstage ambiance at the theater makes clear, she approaches this realm too trusting in its possibilities:

> Since her arrival in the city many things had influenced her, but always in a far-removed manner. This new atmosphere was more friendly. It was wholly unlike the great brilliant mansions which waved her coldly away, permitting her only awe and distant wonder. This took her by the hand kindly, as one who says, 'My dear, come in.' It opened for her as if for its own. She had wondered at the greatness of the names upon the bill-boards, the marvel of the long notices in the papers, the beauty of the dresses upon the stage, the atmosphere of carriages, flowers, refinement. Here was no illusion. Here was an open door to see all of that. She had come upon it as one who stumbles upon a secret passage, and behold, she was in the chamber of diamonds and delight! (*SC* 128–9)

That the *partly* "authentic" disclosures of a way of being and finding Beauty which the stage world will give her are also riddled with essential elements of "inauthenticity" that will frustratingly misdirect Carrie's quest is implied by the intensely ironic view she has—"Here was no illusion"—of a world so intrinsically illusory in its nature and purposes. And this passage further foreshadows the disillusionment her stage success will later bring her in New York, by suggesting — through all its references to material splendor and goals — how Carrie is confusing the Beauty her spirit seeks with some of its more gilded appearances, "diamonds" (so to speak) with genuine "delight." All the material fulfillments envisioned in this prophetic passage will eventually be hers because of a stage career, of course, without bringing Carrie the contentment (and "spiritual" satiation) she seeks.

Given both the "inauthentic" core and false assumptions for their relationship and the fact that her liaison with him will eventuate in her life on stage, it is very appropriate that Hurstwood is moved to greatest desire for Carrie (and to desperate deeds to obtain her) by the impact of multilayered illusion — seeing Carrie Meeber, pretending to be Drouet's wife, calling herself the actress Carrie Madenda, impersonating Laura, the romantic heroine (whose loving, devoted nature is so unlike her own) in *Under the Gaslight*. In further parody of the stage melodrama, Hurstwood is soon driven to the melodramatic actions of his "theft" of his employers' money and his "abduction" of Carrie from Chicago through trickery, leading to Carrie's new role as "Mrs. Wheeler" in New York. And this role, soon played off against Hurstwood's steady decline (and loss of "ambassadorial" status for her), points toward the final phase of Carrie's search for selfhood emblazoned with success and Beauty — a phase in which her encounters with Ames importantly reveal the self-defeating sources of that search.

As soon as Carrie meets Ames through her New York neighbor Mrs. Vance, it is evident that he is meant to be a spokesman for Dreiser — a character/commentator valuably contributing to the novel's illumination of its heroine's problematic pursuit. Presented as a studious man with technical expertise, rather intellectual, appreciative of the fine arts, culturally more refined and less hedonistic than the men Carrie has met before, Ames (with his patently symbolic name) aims to educate her (at a new turning point in her life) regarding values. In the process, due to his quite different nature and his lack of seductive or manipulative motives toward her, Ames — it should be noted — communicates to Carrie in a language (potentially "authentic") causing her to consider, for a change, some *questions* of value in her life. That is, as June Howard has put it (1985), Ames's "analytical perspective" enables him not just to "represent" some "qualitatively different . . . aspirations" to Carrie, but in fact to begin "to explain aspiration itself to her" (*Form and History* 108). For his views clearly summarize those of Dreiser, articulating in the text a critical commentary on the way of living engendered by the materialistic society she unquestioningly accepts. On the evening of their first encounter, Carrie and Ames accompany the wealthy Vances to dinner at the famous Sherry's, where (as the title of Chapter XXXII indicates) Ames plays the role of Daniel—acting as "A Seer to Translate" while the others enthusiastically enjoy "The Feast of Belshazzar" (as the first part of the title proclaims it). If Carrie sees Sherry's as an Aladdinish spectacle of lights, jewels, and fine clothes, and reacts to it with the fervor of her response to the "magical" theatre, Ames shrewdly perceives the shallowness of the restaurant's illusion of grandeur. The episode makes it clear that Ames is a true individual whose way of being liberates him from all the opinions and customs held sacred by those caught up in conventionality. And the fact that Ames voices his criticisms of the life of "inauthenticity" at Sherry's reflects careful staging on Dreiser's part, for that "wonderful temple of gastronomy" (*SC* 233) perfectly represents all that New York and society as a whole call "Success."

When Carrie arrives at the sumptuously showy restaurant, she feels like a devoutly religious person who has arrived at a magnificent cathedral to worship: "In all Carrie's experience she had never seen anything like this. . . . There was an almost indescribable atmosphere about it which convinced the newcomer that this was the proper thing. . . . Here was the splendid dining-chamber, all decorated and aglow, where the wealthy ate. Ah . . . what a wonderful thing it was to be rich" (*SC* 233–4). While she sits nearly swooning with delight in looking with admiration at every portion of the place, her response is quickly contrasted with Ames's: offering what is meant as a corrective vision of the scene, he comments to her on the "shame" of such ostentation and wasteful expenditure, as people misguidedly "pay so much more than these things are worth" (*SC* 235–6). Later in their dinner conversation, as they discuss the most fundamental topic in the novel—the question of the underlying worth of wealth—"seer" Ames gives his most incisive "translation" of the evening:

> "I shouldn't care to be rich," he told her, as the dinner proceeded. . . . "not rich enough to spend my money this way."
>
> "Oh, wouldn't you?" said Carrie, the, to her, new attitude forcing itself distinctly upon her for the first time.
>
> "No," he said. "What good would it do? A man doesn't need this sort of thing to be happy."
>
> Carrie thought of this doubtfully. . . . (*SC* 237)

This moment in the episode is an ironic prelude to the last stage of her journey of self-discovery, in which she will ultimately learn from experience that money, equated with power in so many ways,[33] is powerless to give her true happiness. What Ames communicates to Carrie here, of course, is not just a Veblenesque critique of "conspicuous consumption," but a message meant to guide her way of seeking value and beauty in life. And since Carrie's stage career subsequently becomes the means by which she pursues those precious goals (conceived as wealth and happiness entwined with the aspiration to "act"), it is apt that the last part of her talk with Ames occurs in the theater to which the Vances take them, hinting at the effect on her "artistic" spirit of her most materialistic aims.

In the final part of the episode, in the theater, Ames's role as a guide to Carrie's future is symbolically completed. For after having called her materialistic "ideals" into question, he now helps to inspire anew in her a theoretical *artistic* idealism. In fact, a few of his words at the theatre imprint an ideal upon her memory that will trouble her long afterward.

> During the acts Carrie found herself listening to him very attentively. He mentioned things in the play which she most approved of—things which swayed her deeply.
>
> "Don't you think it rather fine to be an actor?" she asked once.
>
> "Yes, I do," he said, "to be a good one. I think the theatre a great thing."
>
> Just this little approval set Carrie's heart pounding. Ah, if she could only be an actress—a good one! This man was wise—he knew—and he approved of it. If she were a fine actress, such men as he would approve of her. (*SC* 238)

Unfortunately, from the very outset of Carrie's pursuit of selfhood and "success" as an actress, this ideal becomes subverted by her emphasis on her career as a self-projection in economic terms,[34] rather than (as the view of Heideggerian "authenticity" would urge) toward true individuality and a "disclosure" of beauty. Thus a few years later, after she has achieved the first "success" of her stage career as a well-paid chorus line leader in a comic "ballet," Carrie has her memory of Ames's words jarred by a parallel experience. Accompanying some "friends" from her theatrical company to dinner at Delmonico's, she suddenly recalls the evening with the Vances and Ames:

> It was the Sherry incident over again, the remembrance of which came painfully back to Carrie. She remembered Mrs. Vance . . . and Ames.

At this figure her mind halted. It was a strong, clean vision.
He liked better books than she read, better people than she
associated with. His ideals burned in her heart.

"It's fine to be a good actress," came distinctly back. What
sort of an actress was she? (*SC* 293)

She asks herself this question uneasily, for she already knows
that she is not what he meant by "a good actress," despite being
"popular" and "successful."

Ames's ideals may "burn" in Carrie's "heart" (at least in that
part of it dedicated to an artist's desire for transcendent experiences of Beauty), but not sufficiently to cure her of her longing
for material "success" and its manifestations of the beautiful. For
if, as Mark Seltzer suggests (1992), Carrie becomes a stage star
(by the novel's close) who, "not unlike" Henry Adams's "Virgin
. . . represents" (as a vehicle of deepest feelings) a "'medium' and
'carrier' of force," it is also always sadly true that for her, "the
representation of desire" is equated with "the desire for representation in consumer culture. . . . "[35] Thus she unwittingly makes
the mistake of letting her desire for money shape the course of
her career in the theater. And when she has become rich and
famous in her stage role as the frowning Quakeress, her experience illuminates a further ironic sequel to her acceptance of
Ames's ideals. She started her quest for a place on the Broadway
stage with the thought that Ames had inspired: "If she were a
fine actress, such men as he would approve of her." Yet during
her performances as the frowning Quakeress, it is obvious that
the men who "approve of her" are not at all like Ames — and
that the approval they offer is very different from the aesthetic
appreciation he meant: "As she went on frowning, looking now at
one principal and now at the other, the audience began to smile.
The portly gentlemen in the front rows began to feel that she
was a delicious little morsel. It was the kind of frown they would
have loved to force away with kisses. All the gentlemen yearned
toward her. She was capital" (*SC* 326). "On stage Carrie truly
is 'capital,'" as Amy Kaplan shrewdly observes (1988), "for her
looks and her sexuality become a valuable commodity" (SCAR
157). But she is so elated by the achievement of her worldly aims
of wealth and applause that she fails to see how she is prostituting
her talent and distorting the ideals of Ames: "Success had given
her the momentary feeling that she was now blessed with much
of which he would approve" (*SC* 354). Only during their chance
meeting at Mrs. Vance's apartment does Carrie (lauded by so
many, like "the they") become truly aware of what Ames thinks

of a theatrical career like hers: after learning that she still has not gone into serious plays, "[H]e look[s] at her in such a peculiar way that she realize[s] she ha[s] failed" in his eyes (*SC* 354).

Another way in which this scene shows Ames speaking, in effect, a "language" of values and ideals for the "artist" that is very unlike Carrie's — and opposed to hers quite as "authenticity" is to "inauthenticity" in Heidegger — is revealed in his response to her very status as a "star" or celebrity. Dreiser tells us bluntly that "[a]s a matter of fact, her little newspaper fame was nothing at all to him. He thought she could have done better, by far" (*SC* 354). And this idea intriguingly invites connection to Heidegger's discussion of another effect of "inauthentic" ways of being, in his work *An Introduction to Metaphysics* (1953).[36] A further reason why the "inauthenticity" described by Heidegger (in *Being and Time*) can usefully be compared to the misguided ways of being Dreiser depicts in *Sister Carrie* is that it includes a trust in and emphasis on *appearances*. Both its obsession with the world of things and its faith in the way "they" publicly interpret existence indicate "inauthentic" Dasein's extreme externality. Analogously, Dreiser's people live *for* externals and *by* the way everything looks to society, as we have seen. Carrie judges her own and others' identities in terms of the clothes they wear, the possessions they have, the appearance they present in society. To her, as to "inauthentic" Dasein, who one is seems equivalent to what one *appears* to be. And *An Introduction to Metaphysics* explains some more implications of these facts in a way that proves pertinent to our understanding of Carrie's false goals in her acting career.

In this later philosophic work, Heidegger notes that while the difference between Being and appearance initially seems clear — involving "the real in contradistinction to the unreal" — this familiar distinction is actually "another of the many worn-out coins that we pass unexamined from one hand to another in an everyday life that has grown flat" (*An Intro.* 98–9). He explains that there is a hidden unity of being and appearance which the ancient Greeks recognized, and shows how their thought stressed that inner connection, by giving an etymological analysis of the words for "being" and "appearing" in their language (*An Intro.* 100–2). Truth and being involve *unconcealment*, the disclosure of that which manifests itself by appearing, so for the Greeks, who were (in Heidegger's view) "authentically" attuned to Being, "appearing belonged to being, or more precisely . . . the essence of being lay *partly* in appearing" (*An Intro.* 102–3). After pointing out that Being "gives itself an aspect" when it comes to light, Heidegger demonstrates etymologically that the Greek word for "aspect" or "regard" *(doxa)* also meant "fame" and "glory" when the "regard" in question was a distinguished one. Thus he establishes the fact that the Greeks equated glory or grandeur with the disclosure of the truth of Being (*An Intro.* 102–3). And because appearances *partly* conceal the truth, the Greeks were perpetually compelled to wrest Being from appearance and to preserve it against appearance (*An Intro.* 105, 109). Indeed, he cites *Oedipus Rex* as a splendid illustration of the Greeks' passion for the disclosure of Being: the play dramatizes a struggle between appearance (concealment and distortion) and unconcealment (Being and truth), evincing the protagonist's (and Sophocles') persistent will to probe appearances (*An Intro.* 106–7).

But as humanity has forgotten about Being and "fallen" into "inauthenticity," asserts the philosopher, the meaning of appearance has degenerated into mere seeming and opinion. And Heidegger might well adduce the story of Carrie to show how an "inauthentic" modern age is mirrored in its literature, just as he cites a work of Greek tragic poetry as an expression of experience in an age of "authentic" Dasein. When people form and live by opinions (as "they" do), they are concerned not with the aspect of what shows itself, but with their views of it; in this situation, since a view about appearances may have no support in the thing itself, seeming usurps the place of truth (*An Intro.* 104). For example, the "glory" which the Greeks associated with an understanding of Being has become for modern man "nothing more than celebrity and as such a highly dubious affair, an acquisition tossed about and distributed by the newspapers and the radio—almost the opposite of being" (*An Intro.* 103). Thus Carrie becomes a highly publicized "star" (and even ludicrously receives marriage proposals from male admirers, based just on her stage fame and image), but remains uncertain about who she truly *is* and what real fulfillment *means*. And Heidegger's contrast between "appearing" and "seeming" helps to cast light on the reasons for Ames's indifference to Carrie's "celebrity" in judging her theater "art," and—more importantly—for Carrie's failure to achieve an artistic oneness with a sense of Being (and thus Beauty), amidst the ironic "success" of a career that yields her all the rewards a mass audience ("they") value. Providing a different helpful analogue pertinent to the causes for Carrie's unsatisfying "success" in the theater-world is Howard Horwitz's account (1991) of Emersonian idealism as a challenge to materialism. Analyzing "The Transcendentalist," Horwitz finds in Emerson's essay the idea that the "idealist" manages to avoid "[m]istaking representations of things for the things themselves" and so to avoid victimization by "'illusions of sense'" — contrary to the conduct toward which the "materialist" is prone in apprehending "values." Instead, the "idealist, intuiting the true grounding of sensual representations in consciousness, can discern in phenomena 'the laws of being.' . . . " (*By the Law* 64–5) This idea further throws into perspective the false premises about value making Carrie a victim of materialist "illusions."

Most tellingly, Dreiser uses Ames during that character's last chance encounter with Carrie (when she has become a wealthy stage celebrity) to offer an explicit commentary on the source of her dawning disillusionment as an artist and seeking individual. Prior to the meeting at Mrs. Vance's, Carrie has already begun to experience the emptiness of her "success": initially thrilled by her sudden fame and large salary's fortune, she thought, "The one hundred and fifty! the one hundred and fifty! What a door to an Aladdin's cave [of all delightful wishes fulfilled] it seemed to be"; yet almost at once, she "conceived of delights which were not" (*SC* 334) and started realizing, in lonely discontent, "what gold will not buy" (as the title of Chapter XLIV puts it). These incipient feelings of hers serve as an ironic prelude to Carrie's encounter with Ames (in Chapter XLVI) in which he gives an important analysis of both the origins of her artistic potential and the way she is misusing it in an essentially "inauthentic" manner. While urging her to abandon the popular, profitable realm of stage comedy for more serious theatrical work, Ames tells Carrie of the significance of her sad eyes and mouth:

> "Well," he said, as one pleased with a puzzle, "the expression in your face is one that comes out in different things. You get the same thing in a pathetic song, or any picture which moves you deeply. It's a thing the world likes to see, because it's a natural expression of its longing."
>
> Carrie gazed without exactly getting the import of what he meant.
>
> "The world is always struggling to express itself," he went on. "Most people are not capable of voicing their feelings. They depend on others. That is what genius is for. One man expresses their desires for them in music; another one in poetry; another one in a play. Sometimes nature does it in a face — it makes the face representative of all desire. That's what has happened in your case." (*SC* 356)

She characteristically interprets this idea in a selfish way, seeing her "look" as a "creditable thing," until Ames adds incisively: "That [gift from nature] puts a burden of duty on you. It so happens that you have this thing. It is no credit to you — that is, I mean, you might not have had it. You paid nothing to get it. But now that you have it, you must do something with it" (*SC* 356).

As the language of finance ("credit" and "paid") here hints, Carrie is misdirecting the talent given her by her "face representative of all desire" by *using* it to desire merely materialistic "success" in superficial comic shows approved by the uncritical crowd. Instead, as he goes on to tell Carrie, she should "turn to the dramatic field" to make her potential talents truly "valuable to others" (*SC* 356). And Ames cautions her that only by doing so — by adapting her art to unselfish purposes — will she enable her "powers" to "endure": "You have this quality in your eyes and mouth and in your nature. You can lose it, you know. If you turn away from it and *live to satisfy yourself alone*, it will go fast enough. The look will leave your eyes. Your mouth will change. Your power to act will disappear" (*SC* 356; emphasis added). The part Ames plays as analyst in this key passage underscores the novel's theme of the self-thwartingly insidious implications for Carrie's pursuit of fulfillment through her "art," in her selfish, material values. In giving her his crucial advice, Ames tries to be a different sort of "ambassador" for Carrie, pointing her toward a more "authentic," fulfilling sphere of experience; yet she remains unable to pursue his ideals or take this advice because seductive "success" leads to "inactivity and longing" when so much "comfort [is] about her" (*SC* 357).

Ames's comments to Carrie in their encounters heighten the novel's illumination of the sad irony involved in her pursuit of fulfillment through her "art," that its very sources — defined by the values motivating the pursuit — are selfish and materialistic, and thus "inauthentically" misguided. One of the basic ideas informing *Sister Carrie* is that things in the material world have an importance transcending their own particular "values" because ideal Beauty manifests itself (in part) through them. And this very Dreiserian idea clearly underlies the story's tracing of ways in which Carrie genuinely realizes and develops her self, as well as her "artistic" instincts, by responding to the realm of things. But in the novel as a whole, Dreiser suggests, like Heidegger, that man/woman ought not to be *solely* or *essentially* concerned with the realm of money and material objects in which his/her everyday life necessarily (and to a degree, beneficially) involves him/her. Like the account of the "they-self" in *Being and Time*, the story of Carrie discloses the fact that an excessive interest in appearances and possessions leads the individual astray from an authentic understanding of her being, distorting her view of Beauty in the process. Just as Heidegger's ideas on the connection (or even oneness) of Beauty and Being emphasize, there are particular perils for self-realization in the "inauthentic" mode for a person motivated by aesthetic desires and aims: the materialistic world in which Carrie finds herself and begins to develop her personality misleads her in ways which steadily corrupt the purity of her nature as an "artist." Her life on stage, in this regard, expresses the theme of the conflict between the artist's integrity and commercial motives — a key theme to which Dreiser would return in his highly autobiographical novel, *The "Genius"* (1915). At the same time, the philosophical perspective on her experience revealed by Heidegger's ideas helps to reinforce Dreiser's vision — contrary to what seems to me the surely mistaken view of the matter in Michaels' *The Gold Standard* (1987)[37] — that Carrie's ultimate unhappiness derives not from the depth or insistence of her desires, but from their misdirection toward false ends.

Carrie's quest is unfortunately destined to leave her sadly unfulfilled — no matter what paths it takes or how outwardly successful she is in it — despite the diverse essential moments of her openness to authentic possibilities for her growth and advancement of self. For in the ironic worldview of the novel, Dreiser depicts a society (analogous to the modern world of excessive materialism and "calculative" thinking described in *Being and Time*) in which the individual too readily falls prey to the influence "they" have — thus losing herself in "inauthentic" or false possibilities. Likewise, in the world Dreiser portrays, excessive emulation of others' images of "success" and other possibilities for being makes the "characters always seem to be in pursuit of something that commodities promise but never quite deliver, because they seek in things around them an image of themselves" (*SCAR* 149). Just so, the Carrie seeking Beauty with an artist's instincts confuses the means toward *partial* revelations of it (material possessions, scenes, pleasures) with the end itself: deluded by her world's distorted values into expecting to find the ideal materialized before her, she is constantly seeking something (to borrow a phrase from Fitzgerald) commensurate with her capacity for wonder: "Every hour the kaleidoscope of human affairs threw a new lustre upon something, and therewith it became for her the desired — the all. Another shift of the box, and some other had become the beautiful, the perfect" (*SC* 107). But Heidegger's philosophy makes it clear that Beauty/Being can, in fact, never be fully apprehended, for they are always partly concealed as well as revealed — even in "authentic" moments of illumination.

Similarly, if she were sufficiently aware and articulate, Carrie could well describe the nature of her experiences in the words of

Dreiser's explicitly philosophical poem, "Protoplast," from *Moods* (1926):

> My error consists,
> If at all,
> In seeking in mortal flesh
> The Likeness
> Of what
> Perhaps
> Is Eternal.
> I have turned to you,
> And you are not the one.
> And to you,
> And within my possession
> My very hands,
> You have faded,
> Or changed. . . .
> . . .
> My error,
> If at all,
> Has been
> In seeking in mortal flesh,
> A substance that is not flesh.[38]

Especially in the crassly commercial world in which Dreiser places her, Carrie's desire for ideal Beauty must inevitably remain thwarted by the ironic limits of the possibilities presented to her—of the very people and things shadowing it forth to her overly materialistic self.

In the novel's epilogue, as she still sits "rocking and dreaming," Dreiser sums up the pattern of Carrie's experiences against the backdrop of this vision of her pursuing "authentic" possibilities (of an artistic self attuned to Beauty) that are undermined by the material means "inauthentically" defining them for her:

> Chicago dawning, she saw the city offering more of loveliness than she had ever known, and instinctively, by force of her moods alone, clung to it. In fine raiment and elegant surroundings, men seemed to be contented. Hence, she drew near these things. Chicago, New York; Drouet, Hurstwood; the world of fashion, the world of stage—these were but incidents. Not them, but that which they represented, she longed for. Time proved the representation false. (*SC* 368)

To Carrie herself, the worlds of "fashion" and "stage" seem quite inseparable—which is essentially why neither of them makes her truly "contented": because of her divergent desires, she is unable either to enjoy wholeheartedly the former (symbolizing the misguided materialism in her life) or to dedicate herself ascetically to the latter, with an idealism (of devotion to art itself and its value to *others*) about the "good" actress' work so troublingly suggested to her by the aptly named Ames. Listening to what finally proves to be the "inauthentic" language of the materialistic world around her, Carrie becomes victimized by that "tragic pattern of inner defeat" described by Blanche Gelfant (1954) as the core of experience of the urban dreamer for whom even "success" means failure—a pattern based on mistaken sublimating of desire for beauty into one for wealth, and on the "incompatibility between spiritual desire and materialistic goals."[39] In the last analysis, Carrie is trapped—as the suggestive title nearly given the novel [40] underlines—between the conflicting demands of "The Flesh and the Spirit." And because her "spirit" becomes tainted by her corporeal desires, Carrie's personal and professional lives unfold (as Heidegger's ideas have helped to illuminate) in a manner that delimits her relationships, deludes her about her needs, and so finally debases her potential artistry as an actress, and fulfillment as a self.

Notes

1. Martin Heidegger, *Being and Time*, trans. John Macquarrie and Edward Robinson (1927; New York and Evanston, Ill: Harper and Row, 1962), p. 21; all subsequent references in this essay (*B and T*) are to this edition.

2. For information on Dreiser's reading of philosophical works, the best sources are Robert H. Elias, *Theodore Dreiser, Apostle of Nature*, rev. ed. (Ithaca, N.Y.: Cornell University Press, 1970), pp. 27, 38, 80–2, 148, 231, 240, 287; W. A. Swanberg, *Dreiser* (New York: Charles Scribner's Sons, 1965), pp. 60–1, 109, 444; Ellen Moers, *Two Dreisers* (New York: Viking, 1969), pp. 73–4, 136–44, 184, 243–4, 259, and 341; and Richard Lingeman, *Theodore Dreiser: At the Gates of City, 1871–1907* (New York: Putnam's Sons, 1986), pp. 52–3, 63, 69, 72, 129, 132–3, 144, 146–7, 235, and 331.

3. John Macquarrie, *Martin Heidegger* (Richmond: John Knox Press, 1968), pp. 4–5; all subsequent references to this work are cited (*MH*) from this edition.

4. Among many such recent studies, especially enlightening discussions are to be found in Philip Fisher, "The Life History of Objects: The Naturalist Novel and the City," in *Hard Facts: Setting and Form in the American Novel* (New York: Oxford University Press, 1985),

which includes material reprinted from his earlier essay cited in note 24 below; June Howard, *Form and History in American Literary Naturalism* (Chapel Hill: University of North Carolina Press, 1985), esp. pp. 41–50, 99–102, 106–11, and 149–51; and Amy Kaplan, "The Sentimental Revolt of *Sister Carrie*," in *The Social Construction of American Realism* (Chicago: University of Chicago Press, 1988). I will return to these studies later in more specific references.

5. Two particularly persuasive arguments establishing this point, which is so central to an understanding of Heidegger's treatment of "inauthenticity," are offered by Thomas Langan and John Macquarrie—both highly respected authorities on the philosopher's work. See Langan, *The Meaning of Heidegger: A Critical Study of an Existentialist Phenomenolgy* (New York: Columbia University Press, 1959), p. 227, and Macquarrie, p. 26.

6. Eric Sundquist, "Introduction: The Country of the Blue" in his valuable volume *American Realism: New Essays* (Baltimore: Johns Hopkins University Press, 1982), p. 11; emphasis added.

7. This famous phrase occurs in the transcript of an interview with Dreiser conducted by Otis Notman in 1907, reprinted in Donald Pizer, ed., *Sister Carrie* (New York: Norton, 1970), p. 475. All subsequent page references to the novel in my discussion are cited from this authoritative reprint (SC) of the original edition (1900) of the work, which has by no means been supplanted as the version scholars should study by the new (1981) "Pennsylvania Edition."

8. See Michaels, *The Gold Standard and the Logic of Naturalism: American Literature at the Turn of the Century* (Berkeley: University of California Press, 1987); all subsequent references cited are to this edition (*GS*).

9. Quoted from Richard Lehan, "*Sister Carrie:* The City, the Self, and the Modes of Narrative Discourse," in *New Essays on SISTER CARRIE*, ed. Donald Pizer (Cambridge and New York: Cambridge University Press, 1991), p. 78. Lehan offers a very detailed analysis and critique of Michaels's entire approach to Dreiser on pp. 77–9.

10. See Kaplan, p. 7, emphases added; all subsequent references to her book are cited parenthetically as (*SCAR*).

11. Quoted from Laszlo Versenyi, *Heidegger, Being, and Truth* (New Haven: Yale University Press, 1965), p. 94; all subsequent references to this key work on Heidegger are cited as (*H, B, & T*).

12. For purposes of my discussion, as I have begun implying but should here make it clear, I am focusing on "language" not as an abstract

function of human consciousness or as technical linguistic ability, but as (crucially) an interrelational phenomenon. As Terry Eagleton's succinct synthesis of key ideas of Mikhail Bakhtin will help quickly to suggest, I am concerned with language – in my whole Heideggerian perspective and my analysis of *Sister Carrie* – in a Bakhtinian sense. For as Eagleton points out, "Bakhtin shifted attention from the abstract system of *langue* to the concrete utterances of individuals in particular social contexts. Language was to be seen as inherently 'dialogic': it could be grasped only in terms of its inevitable orientation towards another." In fact, since the Russian philosopher and literary theorist saw all language as involving many values, individuals, social groups, and societal interests in conflict, he reached a conclusion analogous to the implicit view of language's significance in the human drama that I am seeking to highlight in Dreiser's novel: "Language . . . was a field of ideological contention," for Bakhtin, "not a monolithic system; indeed signs were the very material medium of ideology, since without them no values or ideas could exist." See Eagleton, *Literary Theory: An Introduction* (Minneapolis: University of Minnesota Press, 1983), p. 117.

13. For Heidegger's extensive comments on this "language" of everyday Dasein, see *Being and Time*, pp. 167 ff, 212 ff, and 335 ff.

14. Heidegger discusses the language of "authenticity" in *Being and Time*, pp. 270 ff.

15. The most concise, accessible account of this aspect of Heidegger's thought is in Versenyi, p. 133.

16. An especially helpful discussion of this idea is in Versenyi, pp. 99–104.

17. See Julian Markels, "Dreiser and the Plotting of Inarticulate Experience," *The Massachusetts Review* II (Spring 1961): 431–48; reprinted in Pizer, ed., *Sister Carrie*, pp. 527–41. The quotation here is from p. 533 of Markels' essay in the Norton edition reprint.

18. See Barbara Hochman, "A Portrait of the Artist as a Young Actress: The Rewards of Representation in *Sister Carrie*," in Pizer, ed., *New Essays on SISTER CARRIE*, p. 56.

19. More extensive, intriguing discussions of this theme of the paradoxical search for selfhood through imitation of others in *Sister Carrie* are presented by Rachel Bowlby, *Just Looking: Consumer Culture in Dreiser, Gissing, and Zola* (New York and London: Methuen, 1985), pp. 62–3 ff, and Alan Trachtenberg, "Who Narrates? Dreiser's Presence in *Sister Carrie*," in Pizer, ed., *New Essays on SISTER CARRIE*, pp. 108–9.

20. See Sheldon N. Grebstein, "Dreiser's Victorian Vamp," *Midcontinent American Studies Journal*, IV (Spring 1963): 3–12; reprinted in Pizer, ed., *Sister Carrie*, pp. 541–51. I am quoting here from p. 549 of the reprinted version of Grebstein's essay.

21. The titles of these key chapters in the novel are, respectively, as follows: "Intimations by Winter: An Ambassador Summoned," "The Counsel of Winter: Fortune's Ambassador Calls," "Of the Lamps of the Mansions: The Ambassador's Plea," "His Credentials Accepted: A Babel of Tongues," and "The Ambassador Fallen: A Search for the Gate." While the title of the first of these chapters pertains to Drouet in his "ambassadorial" value for Carrie, the others trace the course of her relations with Hurstwood—from her discovery of him as the "ambassador" to an experiential realm superior to the one Drouet offered, to her eventual abandonment of the ex-manager in New York. (While not all editions of *Sister Carrie* preserve the chapter titles Dreiser originally used in writing the novel, the Norton edition that I am using as the basis for my discussion—considered the most authoritative scholarly reprint of the first edition text—contains these thematically suggestive titles.)

22. Quoted from Lehan, p. 69.

23. For Heidegger's full explanation and analysis of this matter, see *Being and Time*, pp. 165, 210–24.

24. These ideas are from Fisher's essay, "Acting, Reading, Fortune's Wheel: *Sister Carrie* and the Life History of Objects," in Sundquist, *American Realism: New Essays,* p. 263; all subsequent references to Fisher's excellent, important discussion are cited as ("Acting").

25. Quoted from the "Introduction" to Lynn's edition of the novel (New York: Holt, Rinehart, 1957), pp. xiv-xv.

26. For other recent interesting discussions of these and related ideas on *Sister Carrie*, though from quite different perspectives than mine, see Sundquist, "Introduction: The Country of the Blue," p. 21; Kaplan, *The Social Construction of American Realism*, pp. 148–9; and Howard Horwitz, *By the Law of Nature: Form and Value in Nineteenth-Century America* (New York: Oxford University Press, 1991), pp. 136–7, references to which are hereafter cited as (*By the Law*). Horwitz explicitly discusses the idea of "emulation" in the novel in relation to Veblen's concept of the "emulative self," on pp. 136–8, in a cogent way.

27. This idea is developed in a detailed reading of the scene by Ellen Moers, in her essay "The Finesse of Dreiser," *American Scholar* XXXIII (Winter 1963–1964): 109–14; reprinted in Pizer, ed., *Sister*

Carrie, p. 565. My viewpoint here is partly indebted to Professor Moers's fine discussion of the whole episode in the novel on pp. 564–6.

28. See James Joyce, *Dubliners* (1914; repr. Harmondsworth, England: Penguin Books, 1966), p. 58.

29. This incisive quote is from June Howard, *Form and History in American Literary Naturalism,* p. 42; all subsequent references are cited as (*Form and History*).

30. The nature of "authentic" conscience is described fully in *Being and Time,* pp. 312–48; there is also a helpful comment on this matter in Macquarrie, p. 32.

31. Especially pertinent observations on the significance of mirror symbolism in the novel, can be found in Bowlby, pp. 61–2; and Trachtenberg, p. 108.

32. Several critics have explored this idea of the connection (or odd sense of continuity) of the urban and theatrical worlds in the novel, in their rather different ways. See Bowlby, pp. 62–5; Howard, pp. 149–50; and Fisher, "Acting, Reading, Fortune's Wheel," especially pp. 262–5 and 268–70.

33. While many critics have naturally noted the importance of money as power in the fictional world of Dreiser, an interesting view of this theme occurs in Harold Kaplan, *Power and Order: Henry Adams and the Naturalist Tradition in American Fiction* (Chicago: University of Chicago Press, 1981), pp. 85–99.

34. This idea finds further development in Fisher's *Hard Facts: Setting and Form in the American Novel,* p. 130, where he intriguingly suggests, "The city mediates between and models the larger society, once that society is understood as an economy, and the individual, once that individual is understood as a career, a self-projection. This world of ambition and possibilities favors a strong capacity for dreaming and often creates a confusion between dreaming and lying since both are forms of impatience with the present." Seen against the background of the very different sort of self-projection (ontological and utterly personal) exhorted by Heidegger for "authentic" Dasein, these ideas on the peculiar "career" and self-exploration in *Sister Carrie* help cast further light on the distinctly "inauthentic" nature of experience in the work's world.

35. See Mark Seltzer, *Bodies and Machines* (New York and London: Routledge, 1992); the former quotation is from p. 30, the latter from p. 186, note 9.

36. See Martin Heidegger, *An Introduction to Metaphysics*, trans. Ralph Manheim (1953; repr. New Haven: Yale University Press, 1959); all subsequent references to this work are cited as (*An Intro.*).

37. Writing on what he calls "*Sister Carrie's* Popular Economy," in *The Gold Standard and the Logic of Naturalism*, Michaels argues that the crux of Carrie's story is the *quantity* of her desires: he asserts that the "model" Ames offers her for dealing with desire most contentedly is "an economy of scarcity, in which power, happiness, and moral virtue are all seen to depend finally on minimizing desire." In this "model" mistakenly viewed as Dreiser's, claims Michaels, "Wringing our hands over far-off things can serve only to perpetuate discontent; the Amesian ideal is satisfaction, a state of equilibrium in which one wants only what one has" (p. 35). But in making this argument, because of his total absorption in his "new historicist" theories on forms of "economy" in turn-of-the-century American society— and his minimal focus on the actual text of *Sister Carrie* (or on Dreiser scholarship on the work) as fictional art—Michaels completely overlooks or disregards the issue of the *quality*, the nature of Carrie's desires. And as my essay as a whole and countless other commentaries on the novel and Dreiser's worldview suggest, it seems emphatically clear and crucial that Carrie is disillusioned and discontent because she wants the *wrong* things and expects from them an impossibly idealized state of being and fulfillment, *not* because she wants what she does not have (in some general respect, as Michaels' argument implies throughout). As I argue in my discussion and as Michaels conveniently fails to notice, Ames talks with Carrie about the *objects* of her desire—not the mere fact of its intensity or ongoing presence within her—in their important encounters in the text.

38. This is merely an excerpt from Dreiser's usefully relevant poem (very straightforwardly didactic like all his poetry) "Protoplast," found on pp. 247–9 of the original edition of *Moods: Cadenced and Declaimed* (New York: Boni and Liveright, 1926).

39. See Gelfant, *The American City Novel* (Norman: University of Oklahoma Press, 1954), pp. 69, 70; for Professor Gelfant's full, excellent account of this insidious pattern of experience so pertinent to Carrie's life, see pp. 21–4, 63–94.

40. My sources here are a xerox of the original contract for the novel that I obtained from the Dreiser Collection at the University of Pennsylvania (Van Pelt) Library, and Donald Pizer's note, on p. 436 in the Norton edition of the novel. It should be noted that the title "The Flesh and the Spirit" appears (from the evidence of the handwriting) to have been suggested by someone at Doubleday, Page

rather than Dreiser himself. But Dreiser's own use of the same motif in his chapter titles, several of which stress it—in Chapters XX, XXI, XXII, XXIII, XXVIII, XXXVII, and (by implication) XLVII— highlights this theme as essential to the work, focusing on the crucial split in Carrie's experience and in her conflicting goals.

Squandered Possibilities: The Film Versions of Dreiser's Novels

Lawrence E. Hussman

No American novelist has excited the interest of so many legendary filmmakers as Theodore Dreiser. Among the directors drawn to his works have been the highly acclaimed "auteurs" D. W. Griffith, Eric von Stroheim, Sergei Eisenstein, Joseph von Sternberg, and William Wyler. George Stevens won an Academy Award for his direction of *A Place in the Sun*,[1] his adaptation of *An American Tragedy*.[2] Yet for all of the attention Dreiser has received from Hollywood's brightest creative minds, none of the four film projects that finally transferred his work to the screen have satisfied his reading aficionados. Nor is it likely that even Eisenstein's scenario for *An American Tragedy*,[3] had it actually been filmed, would have made the apologists for the written Dreiser word entirely ecstatic. Is their disappointment and degree of demand warranted or do they expect too much of a medium they just do not understand? Has a first-rate picture authoritatively based on a Dreiser book yet been put on celluloid?

Any attempt at a satisfactory answer to these questions must be prefaced by a working definition of authenticity in adaptation and a suggested evaluation standard for the subgenre. No agreement about these matters exists among novelists, directors, or critics in either art form. Indeed, even the pronouncements of individual commentators are often maddening in their contradictions.

At one end of the spectrum are those writers, literary critics, literature scholars, and readers who insist that any moviemaker adapting a great canonical work must follow that textual source as slavishly as humanly possible. Few opinions rile film critics more than this one. Such a view, by their lights, demeans the art of cinema, denies its differences from other media, and deflates the director's creative role. In radical response to what they view as the outrageously restrictive view of these arrogant bookworms, some film critics move to the other end of the spectrum and grant the moviemaker carte blanche to twist the text to their hearts' content. This stance, taken for obvious reasons by many directors themselves, has caused a number of celebrated battles between Hollywood and novelists.

Two recent discussions neatly illustrate the troubling tension between the filmmaker's theoretical freedom and his accountability. Writing in *The New York Times Book Review* in 1990, Molly Haskell betrays the film critic's characteristic impatience with the literary world's perceived half-learning.[4] Haskell believes "the fact that a fine adaptation might be one that is freely reimagined rather than faithful to its source is a concept little understood by custodians of literature." Yet later in the same essay, she denies "that an adaptation should be judged entirely on its merits as a film and without reference to the work on which it is based" (36). Just how the debts to sources acknowledged in Haskell's analysis are to be paid by filmmakers who faithlessly "reimagine" remains less than clear. The same contradiction occurs more subtly in the extended television interview given by Orson Welles just before his death in 1985.[5] The director rejects the idea that his adaptations of literary works owed any special allegiance to their authors. Yet later in the interview, Welles expresses continuing "bitterness" over the mutilation of *The Magnificent Ambersons* by others intent on giving it an upbeat reworking. Particularly galling to him was the substitution of a happy ending that utterly violated the integrity of "the story." Of course, one is forced to conclude that Welles was embittered more by the "reimaginative" rape of his screenplay than by the rapists' simultaneous assault on the Booth Tarkington novel that inspired the film. But this case should serve to remind us that any viable definition of authenticity in adaptation must measure both the original author's vital interests and the filmmaker's degree of freedom.

One of the more provocative propositions concerning adaptation is formulated in Keith Cohen's essay (1977) about Eisenstein's cinematic plans for *An American Tragedy*.[6] Cohen argues that transferring any novel to film becomes "a truly artistic feat only when the new version carries with it a hidden criticism of its model or at least renders implicit (through a process we should call 'deconstruction') certain key contradictions implanted or glossed over in the original" (245). Few would argue that a work of literature could be adapted for film with deconstruction of the text as the primary goal, but surely such a theory is too narrow to cover more than a few actual cases. After all, it stands to reason that the vast majority of directors who adapt for serious artistic purposes are drawn to works they admire, not to those with which they wish to quarrel. This is not to say, however, that there is no legitimate room for *interpretation* of the literary text. The very process of turning written language into visual images, even though those images are accompanied by spoken language, necessitates interpretation. The more complex the literary source, the more varied the possible interpretations. In the case of Eisenstein's scenario for *An American Tragedy*, as I will maintain presently, the great director did not subvert his source, as Cohen appreciatively argues, but merely subjected it to a legitimate interpretation. In fact, Dreiser approved of Eisenstein's scenario and denounced as subversive von Sternberg's film treatment of *An American Tragedy*.[7] The key to legitimacy in film adaptation, however, must involve limiting interpretation to ideas, beliefs, and attitudes for which there is some evidence within the source text or in other of the source author's closely related works.

Because most complex novels achieve structural tension through the clash of ideas about which their authors are undecided or even tortured, the resulting ambiguity offers the filmmaker considerable intellectual discretion in adaptations. Since making movies of Dreiser novels is the subject of this essay, a word or two about the latitude offered potential filmmakers by other "naturalistic" texts might prove useful. Naturalists are thought to be among the most doctrinaire of literary artists. Consider, however, the varying possibilities offered for filmic interpretation even by Stephen Crane's intellectually rigorous short story "The Open Boat." Two hypothetical directors might produce equally "artistic" and equally "authentic" film versions of the story even if one centered on the grim deterministic engine of cosmic indifference which the men in the boat are powerless to counter, while the other produced a tribute to the freely willed heroism of the bonded group that finally saves all but one of its members. Most naturalistic novels are considerably more complicated than "The Open Boat." They offer, therefore, a fertile field for "contradictory" yet legitimate cinematic treatment. And most often it is the filmmaker's ideological, political, or otherwise vested perspective that dictates the treatment of source materials in any adaptation. This should not surprise, since the source author's own ideology almost always dictates his or her approach to the subject, as contemporary literary critics such as Walter Benn Michaels[8] and Amy Kaplan[9] have demonstrated.

As much as we might agree about the extent of the filmmaker's freedom to interpret in adaptation, however, that agreement does not help us judge the relative appropriateness or success of the end product. And film criticism supplies us with few helpful guidelines. Cinema scholar Louis Giannetti gives a typical treatment to adaptations by dividing them into three categories: loose, faithful, and literal.[10] His breakdown avoids value judgments, as no qualitative differences are imputed to the three categories. With some amplification, however, his scheme might further our evaluation of Dreiser on film. By a loose adaptation, Giannetti means one that is based on "only an idea, a situation, or a character ... taken from a literary source, then developed independently" (329). The example he cites is Kurosawa's *Throne of Blood*, which both retains and alters plot elements from Shakespeare's *Macbeth* while transferring the action to medieval Japan. We might argue that such a treatment is legitimate, whatever its cinematic quality, because it does not purport to be more than it is. Kurosawa did not call it *MacBeth*, after all, or even *MacShogun*. But we should add a note of caution about the "loose" designation. Film adaptations are suspect when passed off as facsimiles of literary texts though they alter important elements so capriciously that the source author's ideas are seriously diluted, distorted, or destroyed. The most infamous example of a fraudulent adaptation is the 1930 version of *Moby Dick*, in which Ahab kills the whale and takes a bride.[11] We might consider as an example of a film marred by intermittent illegitimacy the NBC television treatment of *The Old Man and the Sea*.[12] Hemingway's relatively insignificant young tourists, whose only role in the novel is to comment on Santiago's catch from a restaurant window, become major characters in this treatment, and the old man is given a daughter who nags him to retire. Not even the bravura performance of a marvelous mechanical marlin could make up for these two ill-advised departures from the book. Judgment of such loose adaptations will depend on where the films locate over a continuum embracing works roughly ranging from Kurosawa's to the 1930 *Moby Dick*.

The movies in Giannetti's second category, faithful adaptations, "attempt to recreate the literary source in filmic terms, keeping as close to the spirit of the original as possible" (330). For our purposes, this "faithful" category needs to be subdivided into at least two subcategories — successful and unsuccessful. Here judgment must be based both on how justifiable the interpretation of the source text turns out to be and how effectively the filmmaker has used the conventions of his medium to transform that interpretation into a work of art in its own right. Moreover, I would also suggest a third subcategory to be called "superior." This designation would be reserved for those few films that manage the source material so that the complexity of the novelist's vision is preserved rather than "interpreted out" by emphasizing only one or two strands of it. In our hypothetical film of the "The Open Boat," a superior treatment would focus on the debate between determinism and free will implicit in the Crane text. An actual film adaptation which achieves the kind of superiority I am describing is Ken Russell's *Women in Love*, an intricate masterpiece that actually clarifies some of D. H. Lawrence's ideas.[13]

Giannetti applies his third category, the literal adaptation, almost exclusively to filmed versions of plays (331). But even these are rarely "literal," because cameras are seldom if ever left at long shot to merely record a play. Certainly when film adaptations of novels are called literal, as von Stroheim's forty-two reel *Greed*[14] based on Frank Norris's *McTeague*[15] sometimes has been, they are simply mislabeled.

All five of the Dreiser screen projects discussed in this essay (including the unfilmed Eisenstein scenario) represent, to a greater or lesser degree, faithful adaptations. With the critical system outlined above in mind, let us now judge the strength of their interpretation and the quality of their art.

By far the most promising project dedicated to filming a Dreiser novel was never completed. Subsequent to the enormous popular success of *An American Tragedy*, Dreiser's publisher Horace Liveright sold the film rights to Lasky's Famous Players (later Paramount). For four years no action was taken to bring the novel to film. In 1930 Lasky arranged for the brilliant Soviet director of the silent montage classics *Battleship Potemkin*[16] and *Strike*,[17] Sergei Eisenstein, along with several of his associates, to come to Hollywood. Eisenstein was interested in the American movie industry because its pioneering breakthroughs in sound technology had left the Russians, who were concentrating on camera and film systems, decidedly behind the curve. One of the properties offered Eisenstein was *An American Tragedy*.

Dreiser could not have asked for a more respectful, sympathetic, or understanding director. Eisenstein regarded the novelist, whom he had met during Dreiser's trip to Russia in 1927, as a "live Himalaya." *An American Tragedy* he thought "a work which has every chance of being numbered among the classics of its age and country."[18] The reverence the Russian team felt for the text when they began to formulate plans for the scenario was summed up years later by Ivor Montagu, Eisenstein's assistant screenwriter.[19] Montagu, who attributes "immense power" and "majesty" to the book, also indicates the responsibilities to such a source that ought always to be acknowledged. The Russian team was not dealing with a minor work that had "no claim to act as more than a springboard when adapted for another medium." Their source was a major one, and so they must "reflect the quintessence of the book" and endeavor at all costs to avoid any angle that might "pervert its content" (Montagu 114–6). If Montagu's transcription of motivations is accurate in this regard, the deconstruction of Dreiser's text was the furthest thing from Eisenstein's mind. But this is not to say that the several implicit quarrels that developed among critics over the director's *interpretation* of Dreiser were not justified.

Eisenstein's most controversial interpretive decision was to find Clyde Griffiths innocent in the death of Roberta Alden. The director's verdict, which flowed logically out of his Marxism, provided his scenario with a center around which all of the action and symbolism would revolve. To Eisenstein, the American capitalist system had thrust the "characterless" Clyde into irresistible temptation. Then "invoking morality and justice," it had executed him (Eisenstein, "An American Tragedy" 113). In order to establish Clydes's essential innocence, Eisenstein planned to apply a technique that he believed would revolutionize the way movies were made, namely sound montage. The director, whose storied command of diverse subjects included an encyclopedic knowledge of world literature, had for some time been fascinated by the interior monologue as practiced to "absolute literary perfection" by Joyce and Larbaud. He believed that of all the arts, and especially as opposed to the theater where O'Neill's *Strange Interlude* showed the impotence of that genre to do so, cinema could render stream of consciousness most convincingly (121).

The crucial point in *An American Tragedy* where sound montage could serve to establish the whole meaning of the movie was, of course, the scene on the lake to which Clyde has taken Roberta, intent on killing her. Two voices struggle for dominance in Clyde's mind. One, introduced earlier when Clyde stumbles on a newspaper article recounting an accidental drowning, becomes the film's equivalent of the novel's Efrit who urges him to do away with Roberta. The voice in the scenario begins as a "whisper from afar" that "gradually creeps up till it forms the word: 'KILL'" (Eisenstein, Alexandrov, and Montagu 286). This voice dominates Clyde's thoughts until he has executed his ruse and lured Roberta into the boat. Now the first voice, an "echo of his dark resolve," insists "Kill-kill" but is joined by a second that cautions "Don't kill-don't kill" (Eisenstein, Alexandrov, and Montagu 293). This second voice articulates what Dreiser called in the novel Clyde's "chemic revulsion against death."

As the boating scene plays out, the "kill" voice becomes "harder and insistent," but is eventually subdued by the "don't kill" voice which "grows and tenderly supplants the other." Clyde sits in the boat, his face "wild with misery" after his intense inner struggle, and Roberta sympathetically comes toward him. When he pulls away from her in his repugnance, his camera accidentally hits her and she falls back. Clyde moves to help her but he upsets the boat, tossing them both into the water (Eisenstein, Alexandrov, and Montagu 294). These actions parallel those in the novel scene. But in portraying Clyde's and Roberta's struggle in the lake, Eisenstein and Dreiser differ slightly. In the novel, Clyde has time to think through the situation before Roberta sinks under the surface for the third time. He realizes that by a stroke of incredible luck an accident is about to accomplish what he had originally intended and so he elects not to save the thrashing woman, partly in fear she will drown him and partly to be rid of her. Then, with the remembrance of Roberta's drowning cries as a spur, he begins immediately the tortuous assessment and reassessment of possible guilt that drive the rest of the novel. In the Eisenstein scenario, Clyde makes an abortive attempt to save Roberta but she sinks below the surface. Then he prepares to dive down after her. These actions are meant to further exonerate him, though the scenario preserves a portion of the novel's complex vision when Clyde "stops, and hesitates" rather than diving for Roberta (Eisenstein, Alexandrov, and Montagu 294). In adding to Clyde's motivational profile the intention of taking action to save Roberta while preserving the novel character's failure to do so, Eisenstein inadvertently illustrated the tension between his Marxist agenda and his perceived obligation to Dreiser. He could, after all, have sent Clyde diving repeatedly but unsuccessfully for Roberta and still have operated within the parameters of the novel's plot.

Eisenstein's presumption of Clyde's innocence represents a legitimate perception of the novel which, in fact, invites its readers to choose among optional interpretations. Dreiser had been led into such an intellectual tangle by his study of the Gillette case on which *An American Tragedy* was based that he could not decide himself how to assess Clyde's guilt. The attempt to explore all the possibilities became so exhaustive that Eisenstein could rightly describe the novel as an "epic of cosmic veracity" admitting of "any point of view in relation to its theme, like the central fact of nature herself." Here Eisenstein put his finger on the core of Dreiser's achievement in this expressive masterpiece. Although the novelist had begun the book with the intention of making it a vehicle for his deterministic thought, his immersion in the facts of the actual case on which it is based served to bewilder him, to render his preconceptions speculative, and to broaden his vision beyond the confinement of ideology. Eisenstein's objective, on the other hand, was to bring to the screen version "some well defined psychological standpoint and direction" (Eisenstein, "An American Tragedy" 110). But such a narrowing could very well have the negative effect of insuring against the kind of multifaceted treatment I have argued to be superior.

In fact, when Eisenstein discussed the central issue of Clyde's innocence, he himself used language that confuses rather than clarifies. His interpretation of the novel would center on a protagonist "driven to commit murder by social conditions," for instance. At another point he refers to "the murder itself" as the "climax of the tragedy" (Eisenstein, "An American Tragedy" 112). But how can Clyde be innocent if the novel is about a murder? Later in the same discussion, the director speaks of Clyde as a "pawn in the hands of a blind destiny," a reading that further discounts free will. Then he argues that Clyde's inability to drown Roberta "actually was a change of heart," in other words, an act of volition. At one point he invokes the specter of the "inexorable course of laws" as an emanation from an indifferent "cosmic principle," but at another indicts the "by no means blind political intriguers" (Eisenstein, "An American Tragedy" 116–7). Eisenstein's Marxism apparently blinded him to these lapses in logic. And that blindness in turn deflected him from matching the complex vision of the novel. Dreiser's approval of the director's ideologically purer and simpler scenario probably owed some of its enthusiasm to his own leftward political drift following the loss of his profits from *An American Tragedy* in the stock market crash. (Even Dreiser's own responses often reflected his politics.) But the novelist's outlook became irreversibly more complex through the experience of researching and writing *An American Tragedy*. His subsequent ambivalence concerning the efficacy of capital punishment and his new openness to previously scorned religious explanations of life, among other changes, testify to this evolving complication.

The most questionable change of Dreiser's text in the Eisenstein scenario involves the role of Clyde's mother. The director disliked what he called the "halo of martyrdom" the novelist assigned her. She works ceaselessly in the novel to extricate Clyde from his predicament. Such "sacrificial sublimity," Eisenstein sneered, downplayed "the absurd religious dogmatism" she had substituted for meaningful child rearing (Eisenstein, "An American Tragedy"

117). The director corrects this fault by making her the agent of Clyde's ultimate betrayal. In his cell on death row, Clyde confesses to his mother that he had wanted to kill Roberta though he could not finally do so. When later she has the chance to plead his case to the governor himself, she is asked: "Can you, Mrs. Griffiths, can you from the bottom of your soul tell me that you believe him innocent?" (Eisenstein, Alexandrov, and Montagu 339). She remains silent and so, in Eisenstein's words, delivers Clyde "into the jaws of the Christian Baal," thanks to her religion's "sophism as to the equality of action in thought and action in deed" (Eisenstein, "An American Tragedy" 118). Eisenstein's decision here may actually have had something to do with dramatic economy as well as his antipathy to Christianity. Sending Clyde's mother off to the governor's mansion allows the director to eliminate altogether Reverend McMillan, the compassionate minister introduced late in the novel. But the banishment cost Eisenstein another opportunity to transfer a layer of Dreiser's complexity to film. In the novel, the minister sees the governor but cannot vouch for Clyde's innocence. Mrs. Griffiths betrays her son in the scenario because of what Eisenstein believed to be a simple-minded religious principle. In the novel, McMillan fails Clyde because his initial rigidly religious certainty has given way to tortured self-doubt brought on by his immersion in Clyde's confusing case.

Whatever opportunities for Dreiserian complexity Eisenstein forfeited in his Soviet simplification of *An American Tragedy*, he did not fail to exhibit technical mastery of the medium once he settled on a political approach to the material. But, alas, Eisenstein's scenario, the most promising of all the vehicles designed to transfer Dreiser to the screen, never was filmed. Once it was completed, the director submitted it to Paramount executives Jesse Lasky, Myron Selznik, and B. P. Schulberg. All of them seemed terrifically impressed, but Schulberg still worried that the director's decision to absolve Clyde of guilt constituted "a monstrous challenge to American society."[20] Predictably, Lasky announced days later that Paramount's agreement with Eisenstein was at an end (Montagu 120). The Russian genius went off to film in Mexico. After a decent interval, Paramount contracted *An American Tragedy* to screenwriter Samuel Hoffenstein and the renowned Austrian director, Joseph von Sternberg.

Von Sternberg had decided to provide Paramount with something closer than the Eisenstein scenario to what it wanted, namely "a straight detective story" (Eisenstein, *Notes* 105). But it would be a detective story devoid of the element of mystery that marks most examples of the genre — not a "whodunit" but a "hedunit." In keeping with the moralistic preoccupation the Austrian director had displayed in his earlier Marlene Dietrich vehicles, including *The Blue Angel*,[21] von Sternberg believed that Clyde was clearly guilty of murder. Of course, von Sternberg's legitimate interpretation of *An American Tragedy*, which might have satisfied Dreiser six years earlier, could not please him in 1931 thanks to his leftward political trajectory in the interim. To the Dreiser of the 1930s, Hoffenstein's script had turned Clyde into a "scheming, sex-starved drug store cowboy."[22] To show his ire, the novelist sued Paramount over this reduction of complexity.

Von Sternberg's strategy would center on the elimination of the novel's "sociological elements," which in the director's mind were "far from being responsible for the dramatic accident with which Dreiser had concerned himself."[23] (Interestingly, von Sternberg calls the central event an "accident" even though his film finds Clyde guilty of murder.) Following his judgment, downplaying "sociological elements," von Sternberg decided to eliminate the Griffiths' mission background and take up the story only after Clyde is working at the Green-Davidson. But just after the opening credits, the film starts sending signals that might lead an audience in a direction quite different from the one von Sternberg intended. Superimposed over the image of a stone thrown into water by an unseen hand, a symbol that appears at each turning point, von Sternberg's dedication heralds "the army of men and women all over the world who have tried to make life better for youth." Such a sentiment seems to imply possibilities for improvement through sociology of the kind that sees the Clydes of this world as victims rather than sinners. Furthermore, the film's early scenes tend to reinforce the idea that Clyde is more acted upon than acting. At the bell captain's bidding, for example, he escorts a middle-aged woman and her daughter to their suites as the film opens. The daughter drapes herself across a bedroom doorway so as to make Clyde brush against her, an obvious come-on. But Clyde coolly resists her advance. Once out of the room and clutching the girl's extravagant tip, he is cajoled by a chambermaid insisting he join the party of revelers whose drunkenness will lead to the fateful auto accident that evening. Not only does Clyde hesitate about the party, but also he rebuffs the chambermaid's sexual groping. During the party scene itself, he is obviously quite drunk yet indifferent to the young woman's overheated petting. Later at his uncle's factory, he supervises a floor full of apparent nymphomaniacs while remaining markedly aloof. As he circulates among the work tables, he is ogled brazenly and incessantly by the women, who have perfected the art of simultaneous collar stamping and vamping. Critic Barrie Hayne writes that von Sternberg's Clyde is "eager to sow his wild oats."[24] Andrew Sarris weighs in more portentously that the film focuses on "the dilemmas of desire which torment men and women eternally."[25] But there is precious little evidence for the first assertion and the second seems only to apply to the women in the picture. Sondra, for example, played by Frances Dee, seems more interested in bedding Clyde than vice versa.

These early scenes that paint Clyde far less the lecher than the "lechee" tend to muddle his motivation and cloud von Sternberg's message once his protagonist meets Roberta. The audience might well be led to wonder what she offers that her more willing coworkers do not. Maybe the answer lies in the ludicrous scene wherein Clyde succumbs to his desire and plants three successive kisses on her mouth while her eyes widen more and more disbelievingly. Judging from her reaction, as opposed to the frank worldliness of the other women, we might logically conclude that Clyde has singled out for his attentions the only reluctant virgin in the Griffiths factory. This could be a striking dramatization of the Dreiserian given that we want most what is most difficult to get. But Clyde seems genuinely in love with Roberta, a circumstance that could solidify the audience's impression that he is fundamentally virtuous.

Once Clyde begins to lure Roberta, however, his character undergoes what must strike an audience as an illogical change. He browbeats her for an invitation to her room and when she resists he sulks petulantly for days until she relents. But immediately after he seduces Roberta, he meets Sondra for the first time and begins preening himself for a society role. Soon he devotes all of his time to the rich beauty, while the poor one waits forlornly for word from him. These scenes are part of von Sternberg's attempt to evoke sympathy for Roberta, winningly played by Sylvia Sidney, as it lessens empathy for Clyde. When he finally faces Roberta's pregnancy and her demands for marriage, Clyde tries stalling tactics until the fateful moment when he concludes a call to her from a store's pay phone. Walking out to the street, he encounters a newsboy hawking the evening edition with its lead story about a double drowning. Von Sternberg designs this scene so that the audience's remembrance of it will incriminate Clyde later. First he directs Phillips Holmes, the actor who played Clyde, to achieve a maniacal facial expression as the idea of drowning Roberta insinuates itself. Second, Clyde visualizes the overturned boat and his hat floating on the water, the exact duplicate of the drowning scene a few film minutes later. This ploy links Clyde's intention and enactment. Moreover, von Sternberg eliminates the intense inner dialectic Eisenstein transcribed in his "Kill-Don't Kill" sound montage. The von Sternberg film's crucial drowning scene itself pays only lip service to its source. Clyde tells Roberta that he had intended to do away with her but has changed his mind. When, however, she is accidentally tossed into the lake, he makes less than a split second move toward her before heading resolutely to the shore. If this flagrant display of self-absorption should prove inadequate to convince the audience of his guilt, the film's final scene settles the matter. In it Clyde confesses to his mother that he could have easily saved Roberta.

The last third of von Sternberg's film is devoted to Clyde's trial and its brief aftermath. Here again the director stacks the deck against his protagonist. District attorney Mason, played histrionically by Irving Pichel, delivers a convincing opening argument for Clyde's guilt. So convincing that Clyde's attorneys immediately "reassure" him that at the most he will get twenty years. During Clyde's testimony, his lawyer Jephson urges him to outline his mission background for the jury, but von Sternberg denies the audience access to this narrative of extenuating circumstances by cutting to later moments in the trial. Even the filming of the courtroom undermines Clyde in the eyes of the audience. Behind him throughout his lawyer's examination, framed by a window, an enormous tree looms in front of a church steeple. One huge, gnarled limb dominates the set during Clyde's testimony, and as the defense concludes its unpersuasive examination, an altered camera angle reveals a thick, rope-like vine trailing from the tree. Even the curtain cord suspended from the window frame is tied in a large hangman's knot.

On cross examination, Mason successfully elicits from Clyde a pastiche of obvious lies, a program of would-be deception unlike anything in the novel and so damning that even the defense attorneys are swayed. Toward the end of Mason's performance, Jephson whispers to his partner Belknap: "It must have been that he did kill her." Belknap's reply clinches it: "I wouldn't be a bit surprised." Von Sternberg also undercuts Clyde's mother's staunch support of her son. The director does allow her a brief sociological explanation of Clyde's actions when she visits him on death row. But her excuse that he had not been given "the right start" might be misinterpreted, because she is played by actress Lucille LaVerne less like a devoted mother than a demented one, or at least one three-quarters-of-a-bubble off plumb. The final courtroom scene, in fact, includes one sequence that makes no sense whatsoever. Von Sternberg has Clyde and his mother smile rapturously at each other just as his sentence is being imposed. Far from dramatizing for the audience what Sarris sees as the moment when Clyde attains self-knowledge and releases his repressed feelings, the interchange more likely convinces viewers that the son has joined the mother somewhere over the edge (34).

Evaluations of von Sternberg's *An American Tragedy* have run the gamut from high praise to ridicule. Barry Hayne, in an essay comparing the Eisenstein, von Sternberg, and Stevens versions, finds the Austrian director's product "ultimately most successful in conveying [the novel's] essential virtues." According to Hayne, this success derives from the director's focus on the internal world of Clyde's psyche, a region of cold, unfeeling passivity (146). But, aside from the fact that Dreiser would have rejected out of hand such a pejorative gloss of his character's mental makeup, the film fails to deliver essential insight into why von Sternberg's Clyde turns out as he does. Since the audience sees so little of his blighted background and never gets a sense of his urgent early material and sexual desires as Dreiser so elaborately documented them, it can only guess at some kind of unexplained psychopathology. Harry S. Potamkin doubtless had such a consideration in mind when his contemporary review of the film complained that it displayed no "process" and that its "unit structure lacked thematic motivation."[26]

Robert Penn Warren later dismissed the film as a mixture of "bathos, dishonesty, and total confusion."[27] Two of the three specifications in Warren's indictment hold water. The bathetic elements are most blatant in the trial scenes, in which von Sternberg often pursues melodramatic effects. Beyond the confusion created by Clyde's tepid sexuality, other botched elements include several that are important conceptually. An example of the latter is the inclusion of a scene featuring a vendor hawking peanuts and popcorn to the crowd pushing into the courthouse for the trial. The film audience might logically assume that such a scene was meant as a negative commentary on the American judicial system. Indeed, Dreiser had employed similar devices to make the trial seem like a circus for that very reason. But the director's scene has no logic. Since von Sternberg's Clyde is patently guilty and is found so in short order, the system obviously works well. But bathetic and confused as the film assuredly is, Warren's charge of dishonesty misses the mark if by it he means to include von Sternberg's decision to find Clyde guilty. Such a verdict is no more dishonest than Eisenstein's "innocent by means of capitalist insanity" plea. Each is a legitimate reading of an open-ended text, though neither duplicates that text's rich philosophical ferment.

In the case of the von Sternberg version, many of the novel's thematic strands are included, but they are not intellectually integrated. The Austrian director created the confusion that Robert Penn Warren laments rather than reproducing the complexity of the source text because he did not effectively "reimagine" his material in the light of his ideological perspective.

Nearly two decades later, Dreiser's novel inspired an adaptation by another prominent director, George Stevens. In 1947 he began planning to put on film an updated version with its accusatory title intact. But this was the time of the House UnAmerican Activities Committee's growing influence and Stevens felt obliged to water down the novel's unwelcome message about the national life. In this case it was the political climate rather than the director's own ideology that colored the character of the adaptation. The direction in which Stevens' serial revisions were heading can be seen in the new title he first substituted for Dreiser's, namely *The Lovers.* His final decision to call the 1951 film *A Place in the Sun* reestablished Clyde (renamed George Eastman and played by Montgomery Clift) as its focal point, but kept clear of any indictment of society. Through Steven's reformulation, George became more sympathetic. Roberta (now called Alice Tripp and played by Shelley Winters) changed from a sweet, small-town girl to a whining nag. Sondra (given the name Angela Vickers and played by eighteen-year-old Elizabeth Taylor) was transformed from an airhead into a loving goddess. The affair between George and Angela was to become the emotional core of the film.

In at least one way, *A Place in the Sun* transcends both the Eisenstein scenario and the von Sternberg film as adaptation. Stevens successfully dramatizes George's sex drive, that ruling passion defining Clyde as it does all of Dreiser's male protagonists. From the film's first scene in which the hitchhiking George stops to admire a billboard bathing beauty with pneumatic breasts, no doubt about his first principle can be entertained. With the mission background and the auto accident eliminated, George finds himself thrust immediately into the affluent Eastman social circle. His first visit to his uncle's mansion provides a chance meeting with Angela, and Clift gives Taylor an unanswered look that smolders with sexual desire. Taylor comes across on screen as something like Dreiser's ersatz-religious-feminine icons Suzanne Dale of *The "Genius"*[28] and Berenice Fleming in *The Cowperwood Trilogy*,[29] too beautiful to touch. Not to George, however. Thanks to Stevens' direction of Montgomery Clift, George's attraction to Angela comes off as overwhelmingly physical. Downplaying

George's blighted background and social-climbing ambitions also reinforces the sexual motivation.

George's libido stays on display throughout the early scenes leading up to his affair with Angela. When his cousin gives him a tour of the Eastman business, which Stevens converts into a swimsuit factory, George swivels around at one point to admire a model posing in the design department. When he enters the boxing room where he will work as foreman, several girls proffer appreciative whistles. Unlike the curiously neutered Clyde of the von Sternberg film, George responds, focusing on the smiling Alice Tripp. When George and Alice meet by accident later at a movie theater, the kissing couples around them further stimulate his need and the relationship is launched. Despite intervening glimpses of Angela, George urges Alice to submit, finally succeeding after he rushes into her room to quiet the radio she had accidentally turned up through her opened window.

A promotion at the factory and invitation into the Eastman social circle caps George's success with Alice. When Angela approaches him out of obvious attraction at the first society party he attends, the two quickly become involved, successive scenes of their enraptured dancing charting the course of their intimacy. Meanwhile, Alice informs George of her pregnancy and begins the programmatic shrewishness designed to irritate the audience as much as her would-be husband. Shelley Winters' Academy Award performance helped Stevens realize his unhidden agenda of building sympathy for George in his ultimate choice of Angela over Alice, a necessity given the novel's recasting as a love story. As if the physical disparity between Winters and Taylor were not sufficient to do the job, Stevens has Clift call Winters "Al." Interestingly, Clift objected to Stevens' and the actress' interpretation of her role because, in the actors judgment, it was too "downbeat, blubbery, irritating" to render George's attraction to her comprehensible. In fact, Clift's overall conception of the film seems at odds with Stevens' given the actor's gut feeling that Eastman is an "essentially unsympathetic" character.[30] Actually, Stevens makes him more sympathetic than does the novel or the other film versions in a variety of ways. Certainly George displays none of the callous cruelty of von Sternberg's Clyde in dealing with the pregnancy, for example. Instead, he comes across as genuinely concerned about Alice's well-being until his predicament drives him to consider doing away with her.

After Alice's long but unsuccessful abortion interview with a moralizing physician, George returns to his room and listens to a news broadcast highlighting reports of Labor Day weekend auto accidents and drownings. In a close-up sustained for several seconds, Clift's face registers recognition of a possible way out, but Angela provides specifics for his plans later during an intimate moment at Loon Lake. She tells George about a couple's drowning there and the fact that the man's body had never been recovered, a revelation that sets up the film's climactic scene. George considers and apparently rejects the idea of drowning Alice as they drift on Loon Lake. Then Alice paints a verbal picture of their scrimping and saving future life together that is so depressing the audience might be forgiven for hoping he will kick her overboard and hold her under for the rest of the film. But Stevens fudges the last moments of the take. Alice mistakes George's tortured appearance for evidence of a physical illness and when she lurches toward the front of the boat to help, he stands up and tosses them both into the water. Their thrashing is recorded by a distant camera shot that disallows judgment of Clyde's action. When Stevens zooms in sufficiently to reveal a figure in the water, we recognize George swimming ashore.

The trial scenes in *A Place in the Sun* differ markedly from von Sternberg's. In the Stevens film, George tells the truth on the witness stand but is incriminated by a cascade of circumstantial evidence. He soon finds himself awaiting execution on death row. Stevens measures his protagonist's guilt in the film's final scenes. Surprisingly, given his recalibration of the source narrative to this point, the director's verdict echoes von Sternberg's, not Eisenstein's. Unlike either of the older directors, however, Stevens introduces Reverend McMillan at the end of his film and the task of assessing George's responsibility for Alice's death falls to the minister. In the penultimate cell block scene, George wonders how he can decide if he deserves to die in the electric chair. McMillan responds that one point holds the answer—when George was in the water with Alice, was he thinking of her or Angela? George's silent discomfiture speaks volumes. McMillan then articulates what the condemned prisoner now presumably sees: "In your heart it was murder, George." The prominent place given this scene clearly invites the audience to share McMillan's judgment of George. In the novel, Clyde realizes that had Sondra been the one thrashing helplessly in Loon Lake, or even the attractive Roberta of the previous summer, he would have made more of an effort to save her. But this realization is just one passageway in a labyrinth that fails to lead him toward insight into his share of the guilt. Stevens extracts this one filament from the tapestry of tortured self-examination that makes the last scenes of *An American Tragedy* great literature and uses it to tie up the loose ends of his film. That he misses an opportunity to recreate the marvelous ambiguity of the novel is nowhere more apparent than in his characterization of McMillan. The novel's "strange, strong, tense, confused, merciful and too after his fashion beautiful soul; sorrowing with misery, yearning toward an impossible justice" becomes the smugly certain appraiser of George's actions in the film (Dreiser, *An American Tragedy*, II, 371).

Stevens' puzzling personal verdict pronouncing George a murderer barely beats the final flap of the film spool. It can be looked at in at least two conflicting ways. On the one hand, an unfriendly critic might perceive it as a lapse into the sort of incoherence that mars von Sternberg's version of the novel. After all, Stevens has rigged a number of things inducing viewers to withhold harsh judgment of George while they vicariously participate in his romance with Angela. (George's earlier kindness to Alice even when nagged, Angela's beauty and verve juxtaposed to Alice's frumpiness and torpor, the distant camera location during the drowning scene, etcetera.) From this dissenting point of view the film finally looks confession magazine formulaic, its last minute moral tacked on to its questionable content to placate conservatives. But a more sympathetic critic might be intrigued by Stevens' implication of the audience in George's crime. After all, probably even most women viewers of *A Place in the Sun* tend to sympathize at least somewhat with George facing Alice in the boat, given Angela's magnetic appeal. What the picture accomplishes may be a masterstroke of manipulation worthy of Hitchcock whereby we confront our own darker selves. Might not we be pushed to murder if confronted by similar temptations?

There are many other aspects of the film to stimulate both Stevens' admirers and his detractors. Among the admirable is the opening scene in which the hitchhiking George is passed by Angela's speeding white Cadillac convertible and picked up by a ragged man driving an ancient black Ford truck. It makes for a most effective shorthand rendering of the boy's outsider status. Stevens captures the spirit of Dreiser's sexual politics by suggesting in various ways that George is thinking of Angela even while pursuing Alice, including a ubiquitous VICKERS sign flashing outside his apartment window. And in an inspired moment during the scene when George and Angela first meet in the billiards room at the Griffiths mansion, his uncle steps in and insists the boy call home. While Clift sheepishly explains to his mother at the mission he is being a good boy, a playful Taylor grabs the phone and tells the worried woman George is with her. Stevens could not have succeeded better at making explicit the resistless attraction George feels for the careless life of the rich as opposed to the drab world of his own background.

On the other hand, a number of small and more serious flaws mar *A Place in the Sun*, especially in its final stages. Some of these mistakes might be overlooked if committed by a filmmaker less conscious of detail. But Stevens invited the closest scrutiny by insisting that he was "one of those directors who believes every element that goes into a picture affects the viewer, although the viewer may not realize the impact of tiny minor things" (quoted in Bosworth 183). An amusing slipup occurs in a late scene in which Taylor, worriedly awaiting word concerning her lover's fate, sits on a couch framed by a wide window. Just outside the window the violent wind, obviously produced by a machine, nearly bends the saplings in the foreground double while not a pine needle in the forest beyond so much as quivers. More damaging is the bizarre way in which Stevens pretties up Dreiser's prison scenes. In place of the novel's death row, described after the author's visit to Sing Sing as a monument to "human insensitiveness" and "destructive torture" demanding a thousand deaths of its victims, Stevens invents a penitentiary more like a country club (Dreiser, *An American Tragedy*, II, 352). Flower baskets adorn the cell block and the inmates enjoy a continuous serenade from a songbird. The explanation sometimes offered that these amenities were forced by Stevens' concern over possible criticism from right-wing Congressmen fails to persuade. Surely not even they would have objected to a more realistic portrait of prison conditions. But the most telling of Stevens' offenses to the novel has Angela visiting George in his cell for a tender goodbye. No single facet of the film more clearly demonstrates how thoroughly Stevens' adaptation diminishes its source. The scene has its place, flowing as it does out of the director's emphasis on the novel's love story, but how impoverished that emphasis looks compared to Eisenstein's or even von Sternberg's.

I have tried to demonstrate that neither Eisenstein's scenario nor the two adaptations of *An American Tragedy* realize the novel's full potential for cinema. Each unnecessarily narrows the range of the book's vision. Each fails because of impinging ideologies transcended by Dreiser in the novel. As for the other two film versions of Dreiser novels, *Jennie Gerhardt* and *Carrie*,[31] the former fails solely for artistic reasons and the latter for both artistic and ideological reasons, as I will seek to demonstrate.

Dreiser sold Paramount the rights to *Jennie Gerhardt* in 1932.[32] Despite his previous trouble with the studio, his dealings this time were relatively agreeable. A minor flap developed with producer Schulberg over Dreiser's right to approve the script, which the novelist had neglected to ensure while acting as his own agent. But all was smoothed over when the movie, directed by Marion Gering, appeared the following year and Dreiser pronounced it "moving" and "beautifully interpreted" (quoted in Swanberg 406).[33]

Jennie Gerhardt, the movie, does copy most of the novel's characters and situations with a surface fidelity.[34] From the directly lifted opening scene (Jennie and her mother scrubbing the steps of a posh hotel staircase), the Gerhardt family's poverty is front and center. Jennie's rescue from the underclass, first by Senator Brander and then by Lester Kane, forms the backbone of the film's plot. The moral outrage of Jennie's father and the gossipy Gerhardt neighbors over the heroine's relationship with Brander is made manifest in two telling scenes. In the first, two women discuss the wristwatch Brander has given Jennie and in the second old Gerhardt smashes it in a fit of righteous rage. Gossip hounds Jennie throughout the film as it does in the novel, and Lester's ultimate decision to embrace respectability leads to the tragic conclusion.

The most important departure from the book in Gering's film involves Jennie's character. Sylvia Sidney in the title role comes across as much more sophisticated and self-possessed than her saintly counterpart. She projects very little of the almost pathologically giving nature of the novel's heroine. In this isolated instance, the filmmaker actually improves on Dreiser. For this, the few moviegoers who saw *Jennie Gerhardt* in the 1930s and the fewer who have seen it since should be grateful. Even Hollywood's legendary sentimentality could not easily equal the simpering emotion of this novel, Dreiser's weakest. But Gering squanders the gain in characterization on several ill-advised attempts at leavening a deadly serious story with comic relief. One unaccountable scene features a would-be Romeo's inept attempt to win a girl on a park bench. If this prefiguring of a "Laugh-In" blackout does not lighten the load sufficiently, there are several chuckles added to Jennie's and Lester's tour of Europe. But the most striking deficiency of the film qua film is its choppy editing. The superabundance of scenes gives it an episodic quality that its few virtues cannot make up for. In the last analysis, the picture earns the disregard into which it has fallen.

Paramount released William Wyler's *Carrie* in 1952.[35] Some commentators employ its historical context (HUAC's heyday) to account for the movie's missing social criticism. Whatever the merits of that argument, Ruth and Augustus Goetz's screenplay certainly leaves a great deal to be desired as a vehicle for adaptation in most other ways. Radical changes in Carrie's character alone suffice to render the film nearly unrecognizable to the novel's admirers. Jennifer Jones projects little of the dreamy longing and unfulfillment that mark the book's heroine as so quintessentially American, the spiritual precursor of characters as diverse yet typical as Fitzgerald's Gatsby, Updike's Rabbitt, and Didion's Maria Wyeth. Nor did the script allow Jones to exploit the book Carrie's status as American fiction's first fully developed material girl, dazzled by department store jewelry counters and turned on more by the cut of men's clothes than by the protoplasm beneath the cloth. In a scene particularly revealing of the screenplay's errant trajectory (by Dreiser buffs' standards), Hurstwood accidentally burns one of his last presentable suits with an iron and Carrie cannot understand why he gets so upset. Carrie, the book character, could never be so uncomprehending of such a sartorial tragedy.

Assuming that the Goetz team and Wyler were perceptive readers who did not simply misconstrue the novel, their intention in rounding off the edges of Carrie's character looks akin to Stevens' in turning Dreiser's careless Sondra into the committed Angela of *A Place in the Sun*. Like that film of the previous year, Wyler's is primarily the story of two lovers more romantically portrayed than those in the source text, designed to win over an audience. In *Carrie's* case, the distance between the novel and the film is widest in the closing scenes. Whereas the Carrie of the novel gives a perfunctory bill or two to the down-and-out Hurstwood, who petitions her at the stage door, and then soon forgets him in the flush of her success, Wyler's heroine responds to the former bar manager's predicament with a rich overflow of sympathy. In fact, she welcomes him back into her life and utters a line unthinkable in the novel: "Let's take what comes." Such a distinctly generous act, even though her sympathetic side has been nurtured by Bob Ames, would be beyond the character in the novel. But it is perfectly in sync with Wyler's Carrie because Ames is missing from the movie, along with Carrie's internal debate that Ames stimulates concerning getting or giving as potential paths to secular salvation. By the end of the novel, readers know Carrie to be a cross-fired compound of self-absorbed longing and latent compassion. By the end of the movie, the audience sees her just as she appears throughout, a simple-hearted helpmate closer in character to Dreiser's Jennie. Leaving out the inner conflict which constitutes the heart of the novel cost Wyler any chance at the kind of enhancing ambiguity I have been describing as characteristic of the best adaptations.

Another opportunity missed by Wyler to the detriment of his film involves the short shrift he gives to the novel's urban scenes. Dreiser endows Chicago, and to a lesser extent New York, with a life of their own. Seen mostly through Carrie's eyes, the city emerges in the novel as a vibrant marketplace of modern man's desire objects, resistlessly alluring. Unaccountably, Wyler reduces rhapsodic descriptions of Chicago to one inspired street scene and the film's action in New York takes place almost exclusively inside. The director's long take technique was not well suited to the task of bringing the urban scene alive. Had Eisenstein undertaken an adaptation of *Sister Carrie*, he might have effectively used montage to suggest the city's infinite promise. Unfortunately, Wyler's talky, downbeat, darkly photographed *Carrie* might be better titled *A Place in the Gloom*.

Another problem with Wyler's adaptation has a good deal to do with the political atmosphere in Hollywood at the time. Though the director professed admiration for *Sister Carrie's* "intense feeling" about "abject poverty during the triumph of American capitalism," one gets little sense of social outrage from the film. Editors made more and more cuts in it and even eliminated the actual filming of Hurstwood's suicide to ease Paramount's worry over showing "an American in an unflattering light."[36] Whatever punch the filming originally packed was left on the cutting room floor and the remaining reels depict a tragedy wrought by violations of what one critic calls "suburban" mores — especially marital respectability.[37] But questions about the depth of Wyler's own sensitivity to his source material can also be raised. The controversy that attended the director's casting of Laurence Olivier as Hurstwood conjures up one such question. The reviewer Bosley Crowther, in a contemporary piece, alludes to unidentified parties who regarded Olivier as a "perilously chancy choice."[38] Wyler regarded Olivier, however, as eminently suitable. The reason is clear. The director later described Dreiser's Hurstwood as "very sophisticated and cultured," a view for which there is little evidence (quoted in Madsen 306). The dapper manager of the novel knows a few current plays but his interests center on the gossip of the bar scene and Carrie. Wyler's conception of Hurstwood's sophistication comes closer to Dreiser's Ames, or at least to the Ames the novelist tried unsuccessfully to flesh out. Consequently, Olivier, though his relatively pompous presence dominates the movie, fails to recall the original Hurstwood. Actually, the only inspired bit of casting in the film features Eddie Albert as Drouet. His gaseous, duplicitous travelling salesman, mouthing the refrain "Drouet's the name, charm's the game," perfectly captures the novel's "merry, unthinking moth of the lamp" (63).

Unfortunately, Albert's performance cannot save what Axel Madsen calls the "violently sentimental version of Dreiser's tale" (306).   Wyler's preoccupation with Hurstwood's fall and near total neglect of Carrie's rise typifies the sentimentality. (As does the director's decision to tug at the audience's heart strings by making Carrie pregnant with Hurstwood's child which she loses, a miscarriage in more ways than one.) In fact, Dreiser corrected his own inappropriate focus on Hurstwood at the conclusion of the novel by adding a coda about Carrie to the typescript. (The holograph ends with his suicide. The film ends with his decision to kill himself.) In redirecting the reader's attention to his heroine, the novelist attended to what Wyler chose to ignore, namely the fact that the book in question was called *Sister Carrie*, not *Brother Hurstwood*. Actually, Wyler and others at Paramount had been concerned about the title, dropping the "Sister" for fear the public would shun it as the story of a nun.   Ironically, the film, so mistakenly called "memorable" by Dreiser's psychologist niece, Vera,[39] has been overshadowed by the late horror opus of the same name featuring another "Sister," Sissy Spacek.[40]

For the reasons I have set out in this essay, none of the versions of Dreiser's novels so far filmed have approached their source texts in complexity of vision, not to mention force of feeling. The two adaptations of *An American Tragedy* and Wyler's *Carrie* fail in part because of ideological or narrow political considerations and in part for artistic reasons.   None achieves the range of Dreiser's novels. Gering's *Jennie*, on the other hand, does not measure up solely because of artistic incapacity. Only Eisenstein's scenario for *An American Tragedy* promised a superior treatment. But even it, thanks to the Russian director's Marxist template, decreases the dimensions of the source material. The general lack of enthusiasm displayed for these films by Dreiser's votaries is understandable. A fully realized adaptation would recreate the profound tensions that structure any given Dreiser novel just as they trouble our own lives. It would explore in depth crucial questions about the limits of individual and societal responsibility, about desire and its discipline, about the beauty and cruelty of life, about all the conflicts that Dreiser exploited to become in C. P. Snow's view the last of the great American storytellers.[41] We can only hope that a new generation of filmmakers appreciates and does not squander the possibilities Dreiser's books offer.

Notes

1. *A Place in the Sun.* Dir. George Stevens. With Montgomery Clift, Elizabeth Taylor, and Shelley Winters (Paramount, 1951).

2. Theodore Dreiser, *An American Tragedy,* 2 vols. (New York: Boni and Liveright, 1925).

3. Eisenstein, Sergei M., G. V. Alexandrov, and Ivor Montagu. *"An American Tragedy*: Scenario," in *With Eisenstein in Hollywood* by Ivor Montagu (New York: International, 1967) pp. 208–341. (Quotation, p. 286.)

4. Molly Haskell, "Is It Time to Trust Hollywood?" *New York Times Book Review* January 28, 1990: 1ff.

5. Orson Welles, Interview. *Stories from a Life in Film* by Leslie Megahy (BBC in association with Turner Broadcasting, 1989).

6. Keith Cohen, "Eisenstein's Subversive Adaptation" in *The Classic American Novel and the Movies,* ed. Gerald Peary and Roger Shatzkin (New York: Ungar, 1977), pp. 239–56.

7. *An American Tragedy.* Dir. Joseph von Sternberg. With Phillips Holmes, Sylvia Sidney, and Francis Dee (Paramount, 1931).

8. Walter Benn Michaels, *The Gold Standard and the Logic of Naturalism.* Berkeley: University of California Press, 1987.

9. Amy Kaplan, *The Social Construction of American Realism* (Chicago: University of Chicago Press, 1988).

10. Louis Gianetti, *Understanding Movies,* 3d ed. (Englewood Cliffs: Prentice-Hall, 1982).

11. *Moby Dick.* Dir. Lloyd Bacon. With John Barrymore and Joan Bennett (Warner Brothers, 1930).

12. *The Old Man and the Sea.* Dir. Jud Taylor. With Anthony Quinn, Gary Cole, and Patricia Clarkson (NBC Television, 1990).

13. *Women in Love.* Dir. Ken Russell. With Alan Bates, Oliver Reed, and Glenda Jackson (Brandywine Productions, Dist. United Artists, 1970).

14. *Greed.* Dir. Eric von Stroheim. With Gibson Gowland, ZaSu Pitts, and Jean Hersholt (MGM, 1925).

15. Frank Norris, *McTeague* (New York: Doubleday, Doran, 1928).

16. *Battleship Potemkin.* Dir. Sergei Eisenstein. Sailors of the Red Navy, Citizens of Odessa, and Members of the Proletkut Theater, Moscow (First Gosinko, 1925).

17. *Strike*. Dir. Sergei Eisenstein. With Maxim Straukh and Grigori Alexandrov (Gosinko, 1924). (Quotation, p. 109.)

18. Sergei M. Eisenstein, *"An American Tragedy," Close Up* 2 (June 1933): 109–24.

19. Ivor Montagu, *With Eisenstein in Hollywood* (New York: International, 1967).

20. Sergei M. Eisenstein, *Notes of a Film Director* (London: Lawrence and Wishart, 1954). (Quotation, p. 98.)

21. *The Blue Angel*. Dir. Joseph von Sternberg. With Emil Jennings and Marlene Dietrich (UFA, 1931).

22. Theodore Dreiser, *The Letters of Theodore Dreiser*, 3 vols., ed. Robert H. Elias (Philadelphia: University of Pennsylvania Press, 1959). (Quotation, 2:510.)

23. Joseph von Sternberg, *Fun in a Chinese Laundry* (New York: Macmillan, 1965). (Quotation, p. 46.)

24. Barrie Hayne, "Sociological Treatise, Detective Story, Love Affair: The Film Versions of *An American Tragedy*," *Canadian Review of American Studies* 8 (1977): 131–53. (Quotation, p. 148.)

25. Andrew Sarris, *The Films of Joseph von Sternberg* (New York: Doubleday, 1966). (Quotation, p. 34.)

26. Harry S. Potamkin, "Novel Into Film: A Case of Current Practice," *Close Up* 8 (December 1931): 267–79. (Quotation, pp. 272–3.)

27. Robert Penn Warren, *Homage to Dreiser* (New York: Random House, 1971). (Quotation, p. 166.)

28. Theodore Dreiser, *The "Genius"* (New York: John Lane Company, 1915).

29. Theodore Dreiser, *The Trilogy of Desire* (New York and Garden City, N.Y.: Harper and Row, John Lane Company, and Doubleday, 1912, 1914, 1947).

30. Patricia Bosworth, *Montgomery Clift* (New York: Bantam, 1978). (Quotation, pp. 133–4.)

31. Theodore Dreiser, *Sister Carrie* (Philadelphia: University of Pennsylvania Press, 1981).

32. Theodore Dreiser, *Jennie Gerhardt* (New York: Harper, 1911).

33. W. A. Swanberg, *Dreiser* (New York: Charles Scribner's Sons, 1967).

34. *Jennie Gerhardt*. Dir. Marion Gering. With Sylvia Sidney and Edward Arnold (Paramount, 1933).

35. *Carrie*. Dir. William Wyler. With Laurence Olivier, Jennifer Jones, and Eddie Albert (Paramount, 1952).

36. Axel Madsen, *William Wyler* (New York: Crowell, 1973). (Quotation, pp. 299, 306.)

37. Carolyn Geduld, "Wyler's Suburban Sister: Carrie 1952," in *The Classic American Novel and the Movies*, ed. Gerald Peary and Roger Shatzkin (New York: Ungar, 1977) pp. 152–64.

38. Bosley Crowther, "The Screen in Review," *New York Times*, July 17, 1952: 20.

39. Vera Dreiser, *My Uncle Theodore* (New York: Nash, 1976).

40. *Carrie*. Dir. Brian DePalma. With Sissy Spacek, Piper Laurie, and William Katt (Paul Monash for United Artists, 1976).

41. Charles Percy Snow, "A Conversation With C. P. Snow," by Robert Moskin, *Saturday Review World* April 6, 1974: 20ff.

Carrie's Library: Reading the Boundaries Between Popular and Serious Fiction

M. H. Dunlop

Theodore Dreiser's *Sister Carrie* (1900), like any other surviving late-nineteenth-century fiction, stands in literary history surrounded by innumerable ghostly presences of now-unread fictions, many of which may once have far outrun the survivor in popularity and sales. Complex evaluative processes that lift one fiction into cultural durability, at the same time relegate dozens of its contemporaries to the rubbish heap. The boundaries between the surviving and the lost exercise continuing historical power even though the real nature of those boundaries loses definition over time – and in fact seems to lose visibility along with the vanished fictions themselves. Any mining operation into the underground world of lost popular literature will reveal numerous substrata: there are levels at which there can be no hope of "rediscovering" a text, levels through which no effort at eccentric evaluation can guide an investigator, and levels crammed not only with trash – i.e., readable junk – but with genuinely unreadable discarded objects.

At every level of the search, terminology is a problem. During the last two decades critics and literary historians have attempted to define the boundaries between literary strata; the terms employed in the effort constitute the boundaries drawn but often do so without illuminating them. In his far-ranging study of the popular arts in America, Russel Nye made a series of distinctions between "popular" and "elite" art forms: popular art is "aimed at a wider audience," is sensitive to sales, and is "more consciously adjusted to the median taste"; it is the product of cultural consensus and further consensus is its target.[1]

Establishing such a split between the popular and the elite closes off views of what might differentiate the material on either side of the split or of what might connect those materials were there no gulf between them. Moreover, the cultural-consensus view has faded, and the remainder of Nye's distinctions, while still operative in the minds of many critics and historians, are being vigorously denied by others. Gerald Graff, for example, denies the "illusion that mass culture is the democratic expression of the people, as if mass culture were not owned and operated to suit private interests."[2] Finally, the ideas that popular literature can serve as a window opening directly onto a view of "median taste" or that popular fictions can be differentiated from serious fictions on the basis of audience suffer from lack of solid historical evidence about readers. Away from inferences about the audience for popular fiction, the field of popular literature has been internally differentiated by formula—what John G. Cawelti defines as "a combination or synthesis of a number of specific cultural conventions with a more universal story form"[3] and connected among themselves on the bases of how they reflect the culture from which and into which they emerged. Considerable significant analysis of popular fiction along these lines already exists.[4]

It is apparent that of the terms available for defining the subject—"good," "art," "original," "serious," "elite," "durable," "surviving," and "canonical" on the one side, and "popular," "transient," "formula," "junk," "trash," "rubbish," "noncanonical," and "lost" on the other—all seem to be misnomers. No pairing of terms can accurately convey the difference between one century-old text that (regardless of its reception at the moment of publication) has remained in print and is studied seriously and another century-old text that (again regardless of its initial reception) is now unread, physically vanished, and historically invisible. In complex fact, the two texts may be divided from each other by certain standards of literary quality, by matters of production and distribution, and by the demands of an ever-changing marketplace for fiction. To attempt to study two or more such texts alongside each other involves not only a struggle with inadequate taxonomic terminology, but also an effort of retrieval whose difficulties should not be overlooked.

The case to be examined here involves just four roughly contemporaneous texts and arises from a single scene in *Sister Carrie* that assembles a group of lost popular fictions in the context of a work long since established as serious. The difficulties of the retrieval process have been erased by the sharp-eyed Dreiser himself. By embedding specific popular fictions of the time in *Sister Carrie*, Dreiser opened for questioning the boundaries that divide the lost popular items from the durable text in which they appear as counters in a drama of urban taste exchanging.[5]

In *Sister Carrie*, chapter 32,[6] the fashionable Mr. and Mrs. Vance, Hurstwood and Carrie's New York City apartment house neighbors, invite Carrie, who is alone for the evening, to accompany them to dinner and the theater; also present is Bob Ames, a young engineer from Indianapolis who is cousin to Mrs. Vance. Dining at Sherry's, whose "gorgeousness and luxury" (223) Carrie has not previously experienced during her two years in New York, the foursome carries on a conversation about money and its uses, which then shifts into remarks on recent fiction. Mrs. Vance judges Albert Ross's *Moulding a Maiden* (1891)[7] to be "pretty good," but Bob Ames finds it "nearly as bad" as Bertha M. Clay's *Dora Thorne* (1883),[8] a novel that Carrie had previously "supposed that people thought . . . very fine" (236–7).

It is interesting to note that in the University of Pennsylvania's "restored" *Sister Carrie*,[9] Mrs. Vance's opening topical reference to Albert Ross and his novel is gone, and in its place she mentions E. P. Roe's *The Opening of a Chestnut Burr*,[10] published in 1874; the rest of the conversation continues unchanged through the comparison to *Dora Thorne*. Pennsylvania's editors note the change from Ross to Roe without comment on the effects their "restoration" of the Roe reference have had on the simple sense of the scene, how it relates to the publication dates of the novel mentioned, or whether they are aware of any differentiating boundaries between Albert Ross and E. P. Roe (Penn 334, 569).

It is at such points in the study of popular fiction that the formulaic distinctions mentioned earlier become important. E. P. Roe's *The Opening of a Chestnut Burr* is pious fiction, with a religious conversion at its center and a disaster—in this case a shipwreck—its vehicle; in formula it is identical to Roe's earlier bestseller, *Barriers Burned Away* (1872), which employed the Chicago fire as its vehicle. Bertha M. Clay's *Dora Thorne* (1883) is sentimental fiction, concerned with class differences, romantic love, and family ties. Albert Ross's *Moulding a Maiden*—sixth in his "Albatross" series—is urban sensationalism centered on money, power, and sex; its plot revolves on deception.[11]

In effect, the Pennsylvania edition of *Sister Carrie*, when it replaced the Ross–Clay comparison with a Roe–Clay comparison, replaced not simply one novel with another but one fictional world with another—and, furthermore, made hash of the dinner scene at Sherry's. First, on the level of surface realism it is apparent that the fashionable Vances would hardly be validating their inside status ("They're all the rage this fall" [231]) by discussing a seventeen-year-old pious book such as the Roe novel, nor would Vance, as he remarks, have seen it "discussed in some of the papers" (236).

Mr. and Mrs. Vance are consumed by—and consuming in—the present, in a world to which Roe's pious formula is irrelevant. Within just a few pages in Chapter 32, the Vances consume or discuss consuming pearl-buttoned gloves, shoes with patent-leather tips, the shirtwaists at Altman's, circular serge skirts, asparagus, oysters, olives, turtle soup, several bottles of wine, a DeMille play at the Lyceum—and the latest Albatross novel. Second, on the linguistic level, Bob Ames's judgment that *Moulding a Maiden* is "nearly as bad" as *Dora Thorne* makes good conversational sense only if Ames is comparing a recent popular success to an older one, an 1891 novel to an 1883 novel. Bob Ames impresses Carrie as an educated person whose every remark illuminates, who is familiar with the contemporary scene and able, at the same time, to make discriminations within it. Thus his comparative judgment of two novels should not expose him to Carrie, Mrs. Vance, or the reader as ignorant of how to construct a comparison.[12]

Now to the greater matter—the effect of the formulaic choices involved in the scene. The dinner party at Sherry's involves four fictional characters discussing two popular fictions in the absence of a fifth and very important character—Hurstwood—and inside the containing fiction of *Sister Carrie* itself. Two specific popular formulas, the sentimental and the urban sensational, operating within the context of the naturalistic, work to connect the pairs of characters who have read them, to offer alternate versions of the still-linked careers of Carrie and Hurstwood, to introduce potentially conflicting views, and to echo *Sister Carrie*'s own main concerns. Moreover, within the scene, the Albert Ross and Bertha M. Clay novels raise questions about the use the characters make of the popular print world and its force within their culture.

Albert Ross's *Moulding a Maiden*, set in New York City and Paris, connects its two readers, Bob Ames and Mrs. Vance. Money is at its core; any reader opening the novel first encounters the author's note bragging that although he has been accused of every possible fault as a writer, no one can dispute his sales figures. A reader thus assured of possessing a salable commodity can begin the story of Rosalie, a young girl equipped with three competing legal guardians of very different social attitudes, three Pygmalions to one Galatea. One of the guardians is, unknown to Rosalie, actually her mother; she wishes to mold Rosalie along conventional and pious lines. Another, Stanley, a Wall Street hustler whose business ethic is dubious, insists on raising Rosalie as a model of physical fitness, indifferent to personal adornment and devoted to exercise. The third, Lysle, is a painter uncompromised by the sale of a single painting; although Lysle seems as virtuous as Elsie

Dinsmore, he uses his turn at "molding" Rosalie to introduce her to a version of the Paris demimonde.

Moulding a Maiden transports into the dinner conversation at Sherry's a confusion of ideas about sex, money, clothes, art, personal deception, and gender roles. Its consecutive "moldings" of Rosalie echo Carrie's progression from Drouet to Hurstwood to (possibly) Ames, and the career of Stanley the businessman, who suffers loss of place and is forced to flee, echoes the career of George Hurstwood. In Albert Ross's world, however, fortunes are as easily recouped as lost, and Stanley is eventually reestablished in Argentina. Everyone is in motion in Ross's novel, its human material is entirely fluid, and its characters' personal loyalties and desires continually reshape themselves. No character in *Moulding a Maiden* is allowed the information he or she needs in order to act knowledgeably; thus struggles for personal power—especially the guardians' struggle over Rosalie—are decided by money. Albert Ross's "maiden" is molded by whoever controls her money at any point in the novel. When she is finally released into control of her own money, she spends it, undramatically and without thought or interest, on clothes and jewels. The novel's tensions thus dissipated, it winds down in a rapid series of rescues, reversals, unmaskings, and marriages.

Bob Ames and Mrs. Vance are cousins and are further bonded by the "cousinship" of having read *Moulding a Maiden*. Mrs. Vance indicates that she would not be uncomfortable in Albert Ross's fluid money world, and when her cousin Ames, his stomach full of Sherry's expensive cookery, opines that he would not care to be rich, he asserts his further cousinship with Ross's artist-character Lysle, the painter wealthy enough to refuse to sell his work. Regardless of what a reader thinks of Bob Ames, Carrie sees him as "wiser" (237) than the absent Hurstwood, a man who certainly would not share Ames's sentiments on money. Ames, who looks like a bit of a hypocrite when placed in the context furnished by *Moulding a Maiden*, thinks little of the novel and even less of *Dora Thorne*, the novel that bonds him with Carrie.[13]

The formula and concerns of *Dora Thorne* are distinctly different from the deliberately titillating material of *Moulding a Maiden*. In *Dora Thorne*, set in the English and Italian countryside, Ronald Earle, a noble young English painter whose surname is already a title, stoops from his station to marry the simple and beautiful Dora, daughter of his father's lodgekeeper. Eventually Ronald, disowned, flees with Dora to Italy where they live a secluded life of mild deprivation until Ronald's successful society portraits begin to draw him into social circles where the socially uneasy and apparently ineducable Dora cannot function. Dora bears twins, acquires a noble and beautiful rival for Ronald's affection, and suffers nervous collapse. The novel trails on through succeeding generations of romantic disasters and doomed marriages, with love-at-first-sight the governing device.

Dora Thorne drops onto the dinner table at Sherry's a set of polarities alien to *Sister Carrie*'s world; beauty and virtue versus social class and breeding. After raising these opposites, however, *Dora Thorne* evades them, dissolves its own conflicts, and lodges all its surviving characters in a glowing world of wealth and privilege, a world where, as James D. Hart remarked in his discussion of similar fiction, "what was seen was ordered better and what was not seen did not exist."[14] Not one of *Dora Thorne*'s verities— the happy virtuous poor, the cultivated tastes of the wealthy, the separated family members longing to be reunited—is observable in *Sister Carrie* or in the glittering paid-for world of Sherry's where Bob Ames judges the novel to be "bad" (236).

Dora Thorne's success in the 1880s, one can surmise, grew out of its alignment with the late-nineteenth-century American fascination with royalty and titles, a recurrent phenomenon in American culture that is reinforced when the group goes from dinner at Sherry's to see a DeMille–Belasco play titled *Lord Chumley*.[15] What *Dora Thorne* may have offered to Carrie, who read it "a great deal in the past," was the chance she longs for more than once in the novel, the chance to "suffer the pangs of love and jealousy amid gilded surroundings" (228). Otherwise *Dora Thorne*'s assertion that inherited social place is of primary value and should be clung to at any cost is sheer irrelevance in Carrie's world. Both popular novels—the sentimental and the sensational—present women in submissive, even helpless, roles. *Dora Thorne* is insistent on the point that its example of "magnificent womanhood . . . never troubled her head about 'woman's rights'" but was content to be "a good and gentle wife" (400–1). Neither feminism nor good-wifehood has truly constituted one of Carrie's choices.

A further potential connection raised in the scene at Sherry's by the Ross and Clay novels is the possibility that in those novels Mrs. Vance and Bob Ames have unknowingly read versions of Carrie's life. Carrie has, like Dora Thorne, run off with a man who thereby lost everything; like *Moulding a Maiden*'s Rosalie, she has moved through consecutive relationships, each of which influenced her desires. It is as if Ames and Mrs. Vance know Carrie's past though she has concealed it from them. Carrie herself did not "wholly enjoy" (78) the Bertha M. Clay version of her life but has not read the Albert Ross version in which she rescues the fallen Hurstwood figure from the poverty and disgrace that results from his theft but does not marry or live with him. Ames, interestingly, judges the sensational Ross version of her life to be "nearly as bad" (237) as the sentimental Clay version.

If both popular fictions give Carrie a part to play, they have a still further function in the scene at Sherry's of making oblique comment on the absent figure of Hurstwood, offering alternate versions of his past and future and suggesting that he might survive could he find fictional life in a sensational or sentimental novel rather than in a naturalistic one. Like Stanley in *Moulding a Maiden*, Hurstwood appropriates another's money and must flee; like Ronald Earle in *Dora Thorne*, Hurstwood conducts a socially inappropriate romance and must flee. Again like Ronald Earle, who comes to think that "Dora enjoyed herself more at home than in society, consequently he left her there" (104), Hurstwood in New York City "felt attracted to the outer world, but did not think [Carrie] would care to go along" (222). While Ronald Earle repents of his mistake, Hurstwood keeps repeating his.[16]

Stanley and Ronald are both saved by generous women and regain their lost social places, but Carrie has only nine dollars to offer Hurstwood in their final encounter, at which point his place has been long since permanently lost. On another level, Hurstwood's views on the indisputability of profits are identical to those expressed by Albert Ross in his note to his readers, wherein Ross beats off his critics with the club of his sales figures. Similarly, back in Chicago in conversation with Drouet, Hurstwood dismissed the seriousness of Caryoe's gout with "Made a lot of money in his time, though, hasn't he?" and deflected Drouet's question about the medium Jules Wallace's possible fraudulence with "Oh, I don't know . . . he's got the money, all right" (35, 37).

When the three novels are considered together, they form a conversation on two topics of concern: personal choice and art. In *Sister Carrie*'s dinner scene at Sherry's, it is Mr. Vance who carries the weight of personal choice. Mr. Vance leads the way into Sherry's (the temple of consumption), he orders (makes consumer choices) for the entire party, and then he continues "studying the bill of fare, though he had ordered" (233–6). By contrast, in *Dora Thorne* the choices are polarized—the dark or the fair, the noble or the lowborn; *Moulding a Maiden* similarly polarizes its choices between the artist and the businessman, seclusion and society. In *Sister Carrie*, however, the characters, provided with no such polarities, must choose within categories of narrowly differentiated items: " . . . soup at fifty cents or a dollar, with a dozen kinds to choose from; oysters in forty styles and at sixty cents the half-dozen . . . " (234). The enormous range of commodities in every category from soup to gloves to plays to housing—and the absence of clear guides to choice—creates a drama of opportunity and confusion far more difficult for Mr. Vance and the others to see their way through than are the worlds of polarized or forced choices offered in *Moulding a Maiden* and *Dora Thorne*.

The three novels link up again over the subject of art—what it is, how to view it, whether to sell it, and what it is worth. Art has a certain mystique in *Dora Thorne* and *Moulding a Maiden*. Ronald Earle of *Dora Thorne* paints society portraits that idealize—even mysticize—their subjects. For Ronald, however, art functions as a means of reentry into the social circles from which his marriage and his reduced circumstances have removed him. In contrast, Lysle, the prosperous painter of *Moulding a Maiden*, refuses to compromise his art by selling the nude portraits many wish to buy. In both novels, public interest in painting focuses on speculation about the painter's relationship with his subject—then and now an exploitable point. Both novels link art to women's appearance and to sexual secrets; neither can justify the sale of a painting except by the artist's poverty, and neither sees any separation between a painting and its subject. To sell one is to sell out the other.[17]

In *Sister Carrie*, where there are neither painters or paintings, art is securely lodged in the arena of personal adornment. *Sister Carrie* erases the artist/subject/artifact triad of *Dora Thorne* and *Moulding a Maiden*; in *Sister Carrie* the individual is at once artist, canvas, and subject, and the skills of the artist are bent upon the self. Carrie yearns over the gorgeous results this version of art can produce, over the actress whose "dresses had been all that art could suggest" (229). The view is explosive in its candor; it makes a direct connection between art and personal appearance, a connection that is not gender specific and that is practiced not only by Carrie and Mrs. Vance, but also by Drouet and Hurstwood.

Crosscutting among the three novels reveals that the world of *Moulding a Maiden* constitutes a parallel to *Sister Carrie*'s world; *Dora Thorne*, on the other hand, seems to parallel the elements of the theater world within *Sister Carrie*. Crosscutting also reveals that neither of the popular fictions can stand alone; their limitations are very great. Although it is amusing to find canon-busters telling the *New York Times* that the choice between the canonized and the uncanonized is "no different from choosing between a hoagy and a pizza,"[18] in fact the popular fictions examined here do not mix their ingredients in a way readily comparable to *Sister Carrie*.

Individually, nineteenth-century popular fictions can seem mysterious and unreadable, only achieving understandability when grouped with others — for each of them is backed by dozens or hundreds of others like itself — or when linked to a fiction that can stand alone. Popular fictions are embedded in cultural concerns, but as narratives they operate so as to conceal the seriousness of their concerns. The narrative development of *Moulding a Maiden*, for example, becomes progressively disconnected from the development of the novel's core subjects, and the novel's resolutions complete the disconnection. In this feature *Moulding a Maiden* is not unusual but typical; it is such jarring disconnection that can give popular fiction its apparent lack of depth or texture, its insubstantiality, its nearly irresistible drive toward trivializing itself.

Even when one has had Theodore Dreiser to do the difficult work of selecting the popular fictions to be examined, the intertextual connections that emerge resemble shadows that generate further shadows and back up into even greater shadows. *Dora Thorne* is a distorted shadow of a mobile society that occasionally yearns to be immobilized in a clear-cut social hierarchy; *Moulding a Maiden* is a flickering shadow of a society's unresolvable tensions over wealth, identity, and character. Both fictions shadow the plot, characters, and concerns of *Sister Carrie*. It becomes apparent that popular fictions function in the national conversation not as vigorous participants but as flitting presences. They pose topics — money, power, sex, status — and then race away from them into uncontrolled plot development and a furious drive toward the door-slamming ending. Approachable enough in formulaic groups, as individual fictions they are elusive; while their inconclusiveness is total in all but plot matters, it is not an inconclusiveness that is readily pursued or discussed, unlike the highly arguable inconclusiveness of *Sister Carrie*.

From another point of view, however, studying popular and serious fiction together has a notable effect of erasing any boundary that might be posed by authorship. The authors of the two popular fictions examined here are shadows behind pseudonyms used as selling points — "the Albatross Series," "the new Bertha M. Clay Library" — and, in Clay's case, as cover for a group of writers. Bertha M. Clay was originally an acronymic pseudonym invented for Charlotte Mary Brame or Braeme (1836–1884), who wrote perhaps twenty novels under that name; *Dora Thorne* was probably the last. Because the pseudonym was too popular to expire with its bearer in 1884, Brame's daughter began to write as Bertha M. Clay. Eventually the pseudonym passed into the control of the publisher Street & Smith; there a dozen male writers—including John Russell Coryell and Frederick Merrill Van Rensselaer Dey of Nick Carter fame—produced enough Bertha M. Clays to meet demand. In the 1890s, Street & Smith's standard back-of-the-book advertising asserted that the novels "are not sold in dry-goods stores, are returnable, and Newsdealers should be sure to have a complete stock."[19]

For Dreiser, who also had at one time worked as an editor at Street & Smith, both Albert Ross and Bertha M. Clay were representative of, were indeed the very apotheosis of popular fiction, and he regularly used them as reference points in discussing the subject. In 1921, criticizing a "democratically inclusive" list of 242 American writers assembled for the new Department of American Literature and Civilization at the Sorbonne, Dreiser demanded to know why the list contained the names of Eleanor H. Porter, Zane Grey, and Harold Bell Wright, but not those of Albert Ross and especially Bertha M. Clay:

> I know that in speaking this revered name I'm really speaking of Messrs. Ormond and George Smith of that redoubtable bulwark of American literature and intellectuality, the firm of Street & Smith of New York. But what of it? Are they not her inventors and patentees? We know so. In including her name an asterisk would have to lead to a footnote reading "George and O. G. Smith, inventors. The following writers have written on salary the books credited to this very celebrated name." But still is the name not fully representative of American intellectuality and literary interest and taste? What American author has been more widely consumed? She is certainly "one of our largest authors," invented and patented or otherwise.[20]

Between 1876 and 1928, twenty-seven different publishers issued titles under the name Bertha M. Clay. Six novels were translated into other languages. Bertha M. Clays appeared in fourteen different series ("The Primrose Series," "The Sweetheart Series") and eleven different "libraries." One series was named after the long-departed Charlotte Mary Brame, and a series and two libraries were named after Bertha M. Clay. A single Clay might be issued under as many as three different titles; some stayed in print as long as forty-four years. Street & Smith's New Bertha M. Clay Library, a paperback series begun in 1900, stretched to more than four hundred numbers. Eighty-eight Bertha M. Clays survive—an *oeuvre*, though whose we do not know; nor does anyone yet know what cultural shifts five decades of Bertha M. Clays might reveal, nor what connection they might bear to fiction contemporaneous with them. Liberated from specific authorship and also generally from publication dates, existing under a variety of titles, Bertha M. Clays are nearly free-floating formulas.

It is clear that Dreiser's decades-long attack on Bertha M. Clay constituted an effort to draw a boundary between his work and that of Clay and Ross. Although it has been suggested that serious literature may "draw nourishment" from the popular,[21] such is not necessarily the case; one might just as well see certain levels of popular fiction as drinking at a not-inexhaustible pool of cultural material at least some of which Dreiser himself wanted to draw on: money, emptiness, disconnectedness, affectlessness. And although a mocking Dreiser proposed that in a "democracy" of literature — especially in an American Studies program — Bertha M. Clay could not be ignored, he was nonetheless aware, as is a reader today, that the Clay and Ross fictions he tossed onto the dinner table at Sherry's are antidemocratic, class conscious, and sentimental, and that their readers were not participants in a web of popular democratic ideas and art but accomplices to profit-making fiction factories. The presence of the Clay and Ross novels in *Sister Carrie*, however, allows Dreiser to indicate a certain view of his characters' cultural situation, allows a reader to read his readers, and allows his characters to express subtleties of self-disgust that their situations and communicative abilities would not otherwise allow them.

The available evidence suggests that in *Sister Carrie*'s dinner scene at Sherry's, Dreiser was aiming neither at popular taste nor at writers who aim at actual popular taste; his target was instead the role that the fiction factories — whether individual factories like Albert M. Ross or corporate factories like Street & Smith — played in the creation of popular taste for anonymously produced multiples that such naive readers as Carrie Meeber think must be "very fine" (237) because they are very ubiquitous. Every waiter in every restaurant scene in *Sister Carrie* judges every diner's choices to be "very good"; likewise the fiction factories offered a limited menu of "very good" choices to be consumed. From this angle no such thing as "the popular taste in fiction" exists: instead consumers of fiction choose from a limited range of consumable texts and very probably find the choice considerably more troubling than would be the choice of a pair of shoes or a preparation of oysters at Sherry's. Consuming the bestseller apparently functions not to validate the reader's taste but to cast doubt on that taste and to cast shadows over the life and real experience of the reader — as *Dora Thorne* does over Carrie's experience.[22] To eat an oyster is at least to have an experience, but to read a Bertha

M. Clay is to be alienated from one's experience and from what might have been one's own taste. Substituted for that taste is the dubious feeling that one ought to have liked something that one did not much like but that many others have also thought they ought to have liked. It is theoretically possible that no reader ever liked *Dora Thorne* at all and that nothing whatever can be learned about popular taste from its popularity.

As Theodore Dreiser represents it in *Sister Carrie*, the function of what is called popular fiction is to form popular taste along the lines of whatever fiction is producible in multiples. The Bertha M. Clay—which always concerns an experience called "love" that effectively ends a woman's development and binds her forever to a bad choice made early in life—was a formula capable of being continually reproduced by numbers of anonymous writers. Rather than illustrating popular taste, illuminating a historical moment, or defining a sociocultural trend, a Bertha M. Clay locates its special power, as Dreiser shows, in its considerable ability to blow smoke in a reader's eyes.

Notes

1. Russel Nye, *The Unembarrassed Muse: The Popular Arts in America* (New York: Dial Press, 1970), pp. 3–4.

2. Gerald Graff, *Literature Against Itself* (Chicago: University of Chicago Press, 1979), p. 95.

3. John G. Cawelti, *Adventure, Mystery, and Romance* (Chicago: University of Chicago Press, 1976), p. 6.

4. To note but a few: Will Wright, *Six-Guns and Society* (Chicago: University of Chicago Press, 1975) and John G. Cawelti, *Adventure, Mystery, and Romance* are seminal studies of formula, Janice Radway, *Reading the Romance* (Chapel Hill: University of North Carolina Press, 1984) studies reader response to formula, and parts of Leslie Fiedler, *What Was Literature?* (New York: Simon and Schuster, 1982) analyze the long-range influence of a potent formula. Sally Allen McNall, *Who Is in the House?* (New York: Elsevier, 1981) takes a psychoanalytic approach to popular literature, and Diana Reep, *The Rescue and Romance* (Bowling Green, Ohio: Popular Press, 1982) analyzes popular conventions. Christopher Pawling, *Popular Fiction and Social Change* (London: Macmillan, 1984) and Jean Radford, *The Progress of Romance* (London: Routledge and Kegan Paul, 1986) bring together historical, political, and theoretical approaches to popular forms. These studies tend to treat popular fiction only, to treat it in terms of itself, and to view it in the framework of formula and

convention found suitable to it. About that framework the studies have little argument with each other. Rarely does one of them mix a durable canonical work into the study or attempt to examine the nature of the boundaries that separate literary strata.

5. Guy Szuberla, "Ladies, Gentlemen, Flirts, Mashers, Snoozers, and the Breaking of Etiquette's Code" *Prospects* 15 (1990): 169–96, offers the possibility of considering *Sister Carrie*'s intersection with the behavior modeling attempted by still another popular literature — street-etiquette fables of the 1880s and 1890s and their stock characters.

6. *Sister Carrie*, ed. Donald Pizer (New York: Norton, 1970). Page references in the text are to this edition.

7. Albert Ross, *Moulding a Maiden* (New York: Dillingham, 1891).

8. Bertha M. Clay, *Dora Thorne* (Chicago: M. A. Donahue, n.d.).

9. *Sister Carrie*, ed. John C. Berkey, Neda M. Westlake, Alice M. Winters, James L. W. West III (Philadelphia: University of Pennsylvania Press, 1981). Page references appear in the text with "Penn" immediately preceding the page number.

10. E. P. Roe, *The Opening of a Chestnut Burr* (New York: Dodd, Mead, 1874).

11. Cathy N. Davidson and Arnold E. Davidson, "Carrie's Sisters: The Popular Prototypes for Dreiser's Heroine," *Modern Fiction Studies* 23 (Autumn 1977): 396–407, predates the Pennsylvania edition's juggling of the popular fictions referred to in the dinner scene at Sherry's. The Davidsons examine similarities and differences between Carrie and the similarly positioned female characters in the Clay and Ross fictions but do not touch on the other participants in the dinner scene or on the role of popular fiction itself in the world of *Sister Carrie*.

12. Richard Lehan, "*Sister Carrie*: The City, the Self, and the Modes of Narrative Discourse," in *New Essays on SISTER CARRIE,* ed. Donald Pizer (New York: Cambridge University Press, 1991) offers further discussions of objections to Pennsylvania's "restored" *Sister Carrie* and moves toward the idea of a compromise edition (pp. 81–4). No compromise is possible in the case of the popular fictions examined here: the scene alludes to either one novel or the other, and there is a distinct loss of allusive complexity in the Pennsylvania version.

13. Clare Virginia Eby, "The Psychology of Desire: Veblen's 'Pecuniary Emulation' and 'Invidious Comparison' in *Sister Carrie* and *An American Tragedy*," *Studies in American Fiction* 21 (Autumn 1993): 191–208,

offers a most interesting rereading of Ames as a character who, far from encouraging Carrie not to desire, encourages her to stimulate desire in others. "The only engineering that we see Ames do," writes Eby, "is to lubricate the wheels of the economy of desire" (p. 196).

14. James D. Hart, *The Popular Book* (Berkeley: University of California Press, 1963), p. 183.

15. *Lord Chumley*, a drawingroom comedy, offers an American version of the English upper class beset by problems of love and debt. Class differentiation is accomplished by a variety of comic dialects. The play, a vehicle for the actor E. H. Sothern, had four separate runs at the Lyceum during the 1880s and 1890s.

16. Thomas P. Riggio, "Carrie's Blues," in Donald Pizer, ed., *New Essays on SISTER CARRIE* (New York: Cambridge University Press, 1991), points out that the stunning unfolding of Hurstwood's psychology could occur only under the conditions of the naturalistic novel and only in a context of inevitability (p. 24).

17. Barbara Hochman, "A Portrait of the Artist as a Young Actress: The Rewards of Representation in *Sister Carrie*," in *New Essays on SISTER CARRIE*, ed. Donald Pizer (New York: Cambridge University Press, 1991), discusses the artist's "need for encouraging feedback" (p. 58) in the context not only of Carrie's career as an actress but also in the career of Dreiser himself as writer. This need is absent from *Moulding a Maiden*'s view of the artist; in *Dora Thorne* it is represented as a need for a high-class social circle that offers not feedback but prurient interest and cash.

18. Houston A. Baker, as quoted by Joseph Berger, "U.S. Literature: Canon Under Siege," *The New York Times*, January 6, 1988, p. 12.

19. See Frank Luther Mott, *Golden Multitudes* (New York: Macmillan, 1947); Quentin Reynolds, *The Fiction Factory* (New York: Random House, 1955); and Raymond H. Shove, *Cheap Book Production in the United States, 1870 to 1891* (Urbana, 1937), for further detailed information on nineteenth-century fiction factories and their operations.

20. Theodore Dreiser, "Why Not Tell Europe about Bertha Clay," *New York Call* 24 (October 1921): 6.

21. Lawrence Buell, "Literary History Without Sexism? Feminist Studies and Canonical Reception," *American Literature* 59 (1987): 102–14. (Quotation, p. 112.)

22. Philip Fisher, *Hard Facts: Setting and Form in the American Novel* (New York: Oxford University Press, 1985), develops the idea that the world of *Sister Carrie* is an "anticipatory world" that "has as its

consequence a state of the self preoccupied with what it is not" (159). If *Dora Thorne* functions as one version of what Carrie is not, *Dora Thorne* assumes by that fact even greater depressive and alienating power in Carrie's life.

Sister Carrie's Absent Causes

James Livingston

In one of the original manifestos of the new literary history—of what has become the "new historicism"—Hans Robert Jauss distinguishes between literature as an invented order of ideas and history as an inherited order of events: "In contrast to a political event, a literary event has no lasting results which succeeding generations can avoid. It can continue to have an effect only if future generations still respond to it or rediscover it. . . ."[1] If he is correct, as I think he is, then we need to ask how and why certain generations respond to or rediscover past "literary events."[2] We need, that is, to ask what circumstances enable these discoveries, these "acts of historical solidarity," as Roland Barthes calls them; otherwise we have removed readers and critics (ourselves included) from the historical time in which we have already situated the textual objects of our inquiry.[3]

In this essay, I address the question of historical solidarity by asking a simpler one about *Sister Carrie*, Theodore Dreiser's first novel: why did the author situate a realist style within the apparently archaic form of romance? I suggest that as the political–economic groundwork of the modern subject, the "natural individual," seemed to dissolve in the 1890s, with the completion of industrialization and the emergence of a "credit economy," the finished characters posited by realism (and required by liberalism) became problematic if not unintelligible. The rediscovery of romance—the literary form in which the line between self and society cannot be clearly drawn—accordingly became possible, and perhaps necessary. In effect I claim that, when reworked by Dreiser and the other naturalists, the romance form accommodated the new "social self" specified by philosophers, jurists, and social scientists in search of an alternative to the morbid isolation of the modern subject. I then turn to the contemporary relevance of their reworking as a way of proposing that the decade of the 1890s is the origin of our own time.[4] In concluding, I suggest that Whitman's claim about Hegel ("only Hegel is fit for America") should be taken seriously, if only because Hegel's theory of the transitive subject, the discursive self, helps us to understand why we still recognize Carrie as our sister.[5]

I want to explain how and why Dreiser chose to be influenced by the very writers Howells sought to displace, and why we still respond to Dreiser's choice. So I need to begin by asking why certain authors, forms, and styles were not immediately accessible to Dreiser's generation—in other words, why they had to be rediscovered. An answer is to be found, I think, in the critical if not popular success of realism in the late-nineteenth century. William Dean Howells, for example, who championed realism on moral as well as aesthetic grounds, criticized the "intense ethicism" of the antebellum masters, who excelled not in the novel as such but in poetry and romance: "they still helplessly pointed the moral in all they did . . . they felt their vocation as prophets too much for their good as poets." From this standpoint, Hawthorne's fiction was quite similar to the extremity of romance in *Uncle Tom's Cabin*: "its chief virtue, or its prime virtue, is in its address to the conscience, and not in its address to the taste; to the ethical sense, not the aesthetical sense."[6]

The shortcoming of romance as form, according to Howells, was its inversion of the proper relation between incident and character. Unlike the realistic novels he wrote, the romance moved erratically along the surface of extraordinary events and allegorical figures, and thus never produced a recognizable individual about whom one could ask: given this character, what will happen? To this extent, romance lacked a citizenry that could grasp, or be obligated by, the moral law; hence its creators had to point the moral from outside the text, as authorial presence, rather than in and through their characters. The task of the novel, was, then, to create these recognizable individuals, these characters, so that the moral law became intelligible as an active dimension of real, everyday life—as the truth embedded in and inseparable from an aesthetic sensibility, a form, that faithfully represented real, everyday life. Only by accomplishing this task could the novel unify the real and the ideal, the "is" and the "ought," or, as Howells put it in 1887, the facts and the duties of humanity: "no one hereafter will be able to achieve greatness who is false to humanity, either in its facts or its duties. . . . [N]o conscientious man can now set about painting an image of life . . . without feeling bound to distinguish so clearly that no reader of his may be misled, between what is right and what is wrong . . . in the actions and characters he portrays."[7]

The difficulty here, Howells knew, was to create finished characters with enough interiority to grasp the nuances of the moral law. Unless they were finished in this respect, they could not exemplify the moral issue(s) from within the text, and so could not validate the "ethical sense" of readers by appealing to their "aesthetical sense." But if they were finished—if their identities were fixed—they could not deal with the novel circumstances and new options that rapid social change, the hallmark of modernity, normally produces. To such characters, the incomplete present in which real life is necessarily lived would appear defiling and dangerous: it would become the source of delusion and the site of dissolution. In Howell's first major fiction—the work that signifies his attempt to make it as a novelist, not as an arbiter of taste from his editorial position at *The Atlantic*—this difficulty is powerfully illustrated by the characters themselves. The following exchange takes place toward the end of *A Modern Instance* (1882), after Ben Halleck, who is in love with Bartley Hubbard's wife, has returned to the scene of his anguish (from which Hubbard has disappeared) and has tried to convince his perfectly priggish friend Atherton that he has to repress his forbidden desire:

> Halleck lay back in his chair, and laughed wearily. 'I wish I could convince somebody of my wickedness. . . . I suppose now, that if I took you by the button-hole and informed you confidentially that I had stopped long enough at 129 Clover street to put a knife into Hubbard in a quiet way, you wouldn't send for a policeman.'
>
> 'I should send for a doctor,' said Atherton.
>
> 'Such is the effect of character! And yet, out of the fulness of the heart the mouth speaketh. Out of the heart proceed all those unpleasant things enumerated in Scripture; but if you bottle them up there, and keep your label fresh, it's all that's required of you—by your fellow beings, at least. What an amusing thing morality would be if it were not—otherwise. Atherton, do you believe that such a man as Christ ever lived?'
>
> 'I know you do, Halleck,' said Atherton.
>
> 'Well, that depends on what you call me. If what I was— if my well Sunday-schooled youth—is I, I do. But if I, poising dubiously on the momentary present between the past and future, am I—I'm afraid I don't. And yet it seems to me that I have a fairish sort of faith. I know that, if Christ never lived on earth, some One lived who imagined him, and that One must have been a God. The historical fact oughtn't to matter.'[8]

This last remark seems to contradict Halleck's attempt to locate his self in the momentary present; for the historical fact of his well Sunday-schooled youth authorizes his belief in the possibility of genuine selfhood. But it is consistent with the fear of externality or otherness that characterizes his search for a groundwork of the moral law which, once discovered, will presumably secure his identity. From Halleck's standpoint, such externality takes two forms. It appears in space as the body, both his own ("out of the fulness of the heart," etc.) and that of Christ. The historical fact of the god-man's bodily presence on earth "oughtn't to matter," Halleck claims, as if the very existence of the body's particularity calls morality as such into question. Externality also appears as time itself, in the form of an incomprehensible relation between past, present, and future; so conceived, as irrational contingency, the order of events cannot, or rather should not, impinge on the order of ideas Halleck calls morality.[9]

Halleck's appeal to the past is nostalgic, then, since he immediately points out that past and present are incommensurable, and that the future is unbound. What remains is the dubious present. If it is momentary, as Halleck suggests, it is of course unknowable. But once we have decided there is no comprehensible relation between past and present, as Halleck has, we have in effect erased the boundaries between them and encouraged one to colonize the other. The pastness of the past, lacking representation in the here and now, will then give way before an imperial present in which everyone, from every time and place, is recognizable as the exemplar of an unchanged and unchanging "human nature." This present is eminently knowable, for it is the abiding present of the pure self who, as interiorized mind, as living abstraction, is undefiled by externality of any kind, and thus is not so much above as absent from history. Because this present is conclusive, closed, and complete, characters such as Halleck can inhabit it without losing themselves in it. It becomes the groundwork for their metaphysic of morality.

That Howells, like Halleck, believed "the historical fact oughtn't to matter" is made clear in his criticism as well as in his fiction. By the turn of the century, he was engaged in a rear-guard action against the new historical romances, in which the excesses of affect and incident effaced character altogether. His strategy was to defend the historical novels of Tolstoy and Twain against the historical romances. His defense rested, however, on the grounds that the former depicted the past not as commensurable with but as identical to the present, and thereby preserved the sanctions of the moral law in the present: "There [in *War and Peace*] a whole important epoch lives again, not in the flare of theatrical facts, but in motives and feelings so much like those of our own time, that I know them for the passions and principles of all times. . . . For a like reason [Mark Twain] is a true historical novelist because he represents humanity as we know it must have been, since it is humanity as we know it is." Howells concluded his defense by proposing a test of the truth of any fiction: "It is not by taking us out of ourselves, but by taking us into ourselves, that its truth, its worth, is manifest."[10]

Howells's obsession with "the moral law" as the cultural work of fiction should not be equated with narrow-minded prudery. Like every other serious writer of his time, he was attempting to confer meaning on a world that had only recently been desacralized, to find durable significance and purpose in lives that had only recently been liberated from the obligations and constraints of parochial communities. He was attempting, in other words, to illustrate the possibility of morality in the absence of all external authority, including the authority of God. This project required that he demonstrate the sovereignty of the self, yet not concede that morality is purely subjective and contingent, thus strictly a matter of individual preference or "taste." Like Kant, Howells posited a supersensible, extrahistorical realm of mind as a way of meeting both requirements. By taking us ever farther into this infinite present–"not by taking us out of ourselves, but by taking us into ourselves"–he hoped to grasp its truth.

But in such an interiorized realm of pure selves, desire has no place, or rather no function. For, as Hegel suggested, it is precisely desire that takes us "out of ourselves" into the forms of objectivity that realize ourselves: it implicates us in externality, drives us to identify with and become something we are not. Desire, in this sense, is the cunning of reason, the source and medium of the self construed as the "concrete actuality" of self-consciousness. Whitman demonstrated the proposition poetically, by constructing an autobiography of the discursive self that never ignores or represses the body, but instead treats its particularity – its insistent desires – as consistent with an ingredient in a movement toward new consciousness, new identity.

This discursive self goes underground after the Civil War, as the realism of Howells and Twain carries the day. But it erupts from the exhausted soil of American letters in the 1890s, in the form of literary naturalism. Art and philosophy are meanwhile revolutionized by the rediscovery of this same underground (wo)man.[11] Naturalism, like pragmatism, foregrounds the sensational, desiring body as the necessary and enduring condition of self-consciousness and selfhood. In doing so, it contributes to the inversion — or at least the interrogation — of stereotypes applying equally to women, workers, and African-Americans (e.g., that their complexity is physical, "natural," sensational, thus beyond the pale of reason, character, and political deliberation). This naturalist notion of selfhood as the effect of entanglement in externality enables a new, discursive model of personality that lives another underground (or rather apolitical) existence from the 1930s to the 1950s, when, in the absence of official apartheid and an institutionalized Left, it reshapes the languages of both popular culture and radical politics.

So the truth embedded in the old-fashioned idea that literary naturalists are vulgar Marxists — the truth that must be included in any reassessment of naturalism — is that they did grapple with the possibility of a correlation between entanglement in externality and external domination. They explored the same constraints on morality and freedom that had obsessed Howells, in other words, and yet remained equivocal about the effects of such constraints. The naturalists sought confirmation of this equivocal stance in the future, not in the present; but they wrote the history of that future by defining the archaic form of romance as their usable past, by adapting the style of realism to the formal properties and implications of romance.

The best way to illustrate these propositions is to examine the exemplary naturalist novel, *Sister Carrie*. Critics have noted that it contains many levels of writing, but have invariably concluded that it is a species of realism. The typologies of form found in the work of Howells, Northrop Frye, and Fredric Jameson — three unlikely allies — suggest, however, that it should be read as romance. According to Frye, whose argument recalls that of Howells, the "essential difference" between the romance and the novel as a type of prose fiction is the absence of characterization in the former. In the novel, the "characters are prior to the plot," and the question both author and reader address is "given these characters, what will happen?" Romance, by contrast, describes what happens to characters, "for the most part, externally." Jameson draws on Kenneth Burke and Martin Heidegger to enlarge Frye's account: "romance is precisely that form in which the worldness of the world reveals or manifests itself, in which, in other words, world in the technical sense of the transcendental horizon of our experience becomes visible in an inner-worldly sense." More concretely, "in romance the category of Scene tends to capture and to appropriate the attributes of Agency and Act, making the 'hero' over into something like a registering apparatus" of external change or movement. Hence romance heroes and heroines seem always to be "reaping the rewards of cosmic victory without ever having been quite aware of what was at stake in the first place."[12]

The other salient elements of romance are results of the absence of characters. As Howells noted, and as Frye emphasizes, romance plots extraordinary episodes discontinuously along a "vertical" axis. Its normal planes of existence are idyllic and demonic; or at least they are higher and lower than the everyday experience rendered "horizontally" in realistic novels. Frye also points out that romance is closer to the mythic world of "total metaphor" than is the novel, because the population of romance is identified with the mysterious externality that constitutes its field of heroic action. From this standpoint, romance becomes the form in which desire cannot be effectively disciplined, evaded, or sublimated. Its heroes and heroines are always being projected beyond themselves by the force of their desires—since we cannot ask what these characters will do, but only what will happen to them, there is no story to be told unless they are so projected—and yet the worldness of the world they register is immediate, particular, almost invasive: it is otherness writ large. In romance, accordingly, there can be no abiding present in which the moral law becomes intelligible by virtue of its internalization: there can be no promise of release from the alienation, the perception of division, that is projected outward as desire. In this sense, the privileged place of truth in romance cannot be found outside of time; it lies at the beginning and at the end of time. Indeed the utopian agenda of romance—the morality of this form—finally derives from the fact that its "characters" are not contained by their world; instead they somehow contain it. As Frye puts it, "the desiring self finds fulfillment that delivers it from the anxieties of reality by containing that reality."[13]

Now let us suppose that our three unlikely allies have accounted for the differences between romance and the realist novel. Based on this supposition, *Sister Carrie* is formally or structurally a romance. To begin with, the novel has no characters to speak of, as Julian Markels observed more than thirty years ago: "they do not make the story, the story manifests them."[14] Carrie, Drouet, and Hurstwood are "below the threshold of consciousness," and so we cannot at any point ask, given these characters, what will happen? These people are so inarticulate—so "vacant," to borrow Dreiser's favorite adjective for his heroine—that Agency and Act have almost no meaning in the novel. Their enclosure within the category of Scene is made explicit by their common source in the darkened theater that Carrie finds so appealing ("This new atmosphere was more friendly. . . . Here was no illusion."): it is here, and only here, that each of the leading characters comes alive, comes to recognize the objects of his or her desire, and resolves to have them.

Certainly Carrie is a perfectly tuned registering apparatus for the particularity, the worldness of her world. Here she is on Lake Shore Drive at about five o'clock in the evening:

> There was a softness in the air which speaks with an infinite delicacy of feeling to the flesh as well as the soul. Carrie felt that it was a lovely day. She was ripened by it in spirit for many suggestions. . . . Across the broad lawns, now first freshening into green, she saw lamps faintly glowing upon rich interiors. Now it was but a chair, now a table, now an ornate corner, which met her eye, but it appealed to her as almost nothing else could. Such childish fancies as she had had of fairy palaces and kingly quarters now came back. She imagined that across these richly carved entrance-ways, where the globed and crystalled lamps shone upon panelled doors set with stained and designed panes of glass, was neither care not unsatisfied desire. She was perfectly certain that here was happiness. . . . She gazed and gazed, wondering, delighting, longing, and all the while the siren voice of the unrestful was whispering in her ear. (94)

Markels also reminds us that *Sister Carrie* is organized around the kind of vertical axis usually found in romance. When our heroine loses her shoe factory job, for example, "Dreiser reverses direction again, leaving Carrie at the bottom and taking us to the 'top,' to witness a conversation between Drouet and Hurstwood in the 'truly swell saloon' of Fitzgerald and Moy's."[15] This reversible movement between higher and lower planes of existence is the narrative device by which we are forced to see, in vertical perspective, that Carrie's early career as a Chicago factory worker is the demonic parody of her later career as New York actress, and that Hurstwood's decline and fall in New York is the demonic parody of his "high life" in Chicago. That *Sister Carrie* is dominated by metaphors, as against more displaced, "horizontal," and representational similes, probably needs no emphasis beyond that provided by Walter Benn Michaels and Lester Cohen.[16] But it is worth noting that metaphors are foreign to the language – or level – of realism in the novel; they begin piling up only when Carrie's desire identifies her with the objects she does not but must have if she is to be herself. "She did not grow in knowledge so much as she awakened in the matter of desire," Dreiser notes as preface to the scene on Lake Shore Drive (94). And in fact

Carrie's awakening desire determines her entire itinerary. In this sense, her rise in the real world from factory worker to celebrity actress is a demonic parody of the rise of Silas Lapham, whose moral integrity is secured as a consequence of his escape from the delusions of desire. Thus we can safely assume that the "economy of desire" that animates *Sister Carrie* is at the very least inconsistent with the fear, or absence, of desire that regulates realism as Howells defined and practiced it.[17] We can accordingly claim either that the tradition of social realism is not broad enough to contain the novel, or that a more appropriate formal designation for it is romance.

But the point is not to reclassify Dreiser's first novel; it is instead to recognize that both sentimentalism and realism are parodied by the romance form in which they are contained and criticized. This "dialogical" combination defines any choice between these forms as fundamentally false or as irrelevant to the possibilities of American life and letters. To put this another way, the transition from rhetoric to style that *Sister Carrie* reenacts by the juxtaposition of sentimental and realist passages is mediated and criticized by the morality of the novel's form; but the peculiar morality of the romance form is itself criticized by the realistic inversion of its conventions. Thus the long-standing conflict between romance and realism is registered if not resolved in a fictional discourse that incorporates both without becoming either.

Surely the binary opposition of good and evil that Jameson defines as the "ideological core of the romance paradigm" is destroyed by Dreiser's use of realism.[18] Carrie's journey to the idyllic upper world, for example, begins with the loss of her virginity. Her sister Minnie narrates this crucial event in her dreams according to the traditional terms of romance, as a descent or fall that negates identity. But that Dreiser has nothing to say about it in his narrative capacity is emphasized by his answer to Carrie's question ("What is it I have lost?"): "Before this world-old proposition we stand, serious, interested confused . . . " (64–5, 74). The binary opposition of good and evil that Minnie's romance dream depicts vertically is presented as archaic, as an axis that will not intersect at any point with Carrie's rise through the real worldliness of her world. But if it is fair to say that the ethical binary at the core of romance is in this manner displaced by realism, it is also fair to say that the serious, interested, and confused voice of realism is at critical moments replaced by a language, or a level of writing, that is neither grotesquely sentimental nor starkly realistic. This is the siren whisper of romance, which awakens the inertial Carrie and projects her toward new desires and dreams. This is the voice, as heard in Chapter 12 on Lake Shore Drive, that disavows not the real, but realism.

But how do we explain Dreiser's novel use of the romance form? Why does he resort to it? In other words, what is naturalized in *Sister Carrie* that lay beyond the scope of realism? I would suggest three possibilities. First, the incomplete present in which real life gets lived is reinstated under the sign of romance. But this is only one way of saying that the relation between past and present is recast as a developmental or cumulative sequence, through which self-consciousness or reason is realized, not posited as a property of mind in the form of finished characters. Second, desire becomes the medium of that discursive process of realization, so that illusion and alienation, the fall into time and space — and desire — become the sources of identity, not the obstacles to it: personality, consciousness, and character are construed as the results of entanglement in, not release from, the tyranny of external circumstances given by the past. Indeed, Carrie's desire is the medium through which her memory is restored, her consciousness is awakened, her personality is constructed — the means by which she begins to look and sound, at the end of the novel, like a character in a novel. Her externalization, her immersion in or absorption by the "worldness" of her world, objectifies her particular subjectivity, that is, it eventually makes her self-conscious.

Dreiser concludes, in fact, where a realist novelist might begin, at the moment consciousness, hitherto "a kind of external relation," as William James would suggest in 1904, returns to itself. It is almost as if Dreiser were writing the prehistory of the novel as a narrative form or — what amounts to the same thing — of the autonomous individual as a plausible fiction. But *Sister Carrie* is even more deeply and perversely "historical" than this. For the point at which it concludes is not just the historical moment at which a realist novel might begin; it is also the moment of memory, of self-consciousness, at which the recorded history of the species does begin. History is not, then, an absent cause in, or simply absent from, the novel: it is inscribed throughout as the product of desire. That is why it first appears under the fantastic sign of romance: "Such childish fancies as she had had of fairy palaces and kingly quarters now came back" (94).

Third, the "chronotope" — the peculiar space–time — of the theater is recovered in and by Dreiser's use of the romance form.[19] To understand what is at stake here, we need to recall the special significance of the theatrical self in nineteenth-century American culture, particularly at mid-century. The most popular ritual in this culture was probably minstrelsy, the Yankee invention through which the desiring, sensational self was projected and objectified on stage in the form of the African-American. Minstrelsy was in some ways the ambitious stepchild of melodrama, which was less conclusive, less strident, about the choices it offered between home, hearth, and feminine virtue on the one hand, and market, money, and masculine worldliness on the other.[20] In any event, the theater as such foregrounded the new divisions and extensions of the self that had become possible and necessary under the regime of antebellum accumulation.

Within the receding household economy of agricultural subsistence and artisanal industrial production, there was no meaningful distinction to be drawn between economic function and domesticity as the foundation of personal identity, for there were no extrafamilial economic functions except those of incidental commerce, not production. When this economy finally gives way at mid-century (c. 1846–1857), the distinction can be grasped as impending historical disjuncture — as the terms of a choice — in the work of the popular women writers.[21] But where the market, or rather money, mediates all social relations and multiplies social roles, so that neither economic function (marketplace) nor domesticity (home) can serve as the foundation of personal identity, the self is divided, distended, and dislocated. This is the problem that seizes the imagination of practically every writer, popular or not, at mid-century.

Some writers treat it as an opportunity as well as a problem (those who treat it as both are our canonical writers). Whitman goes further than anyone else in treating it as such; his "lesson of reception" tends toward what we might justly criticize as pure tolerance. But Melville and Hawthorne also treat the dislocation of the self as something more (or less) than a threat to selfhood. And in their most self-conscious meditations on the romance form — *The Confidence Man* (1857) and *The Blithedale Romance* (1852) — they do so in explicitly theatrical terms. Both fictions are deadly serious parodies of minstrelsy in which the self cannot escape its theatrically objectified Other.

Melville kept reminding his readers that the demand for consistency of character in fiction was unrealistic: "is it not a fact, that, in real life, a consistent character is a rara avis?" Real-life experience could not serve as an independent body of fact by which readers could test characterization. For "no one man can be coextensive with what is." Moreover, the stuff of experience was accumulated unevenly because the field of experience — space and time — was perceived and assimilated as disjuncture, as heterogeneous, not as simple location on a continuum: "that author who draws a character, even though to common view incongruous in its parts, as the flying squirrel, and, at different periods, as much at variance with itself as the butterfly is with the caterpillar into which it changes, may yet, in so doing, be not false but faithful to the facts." Thus the implosive chronotype of the theater was crucial to the realistic depiction of real lives: "And as, in real life, the proprieties will not allow people to act out themselves with that unreserve permitted to the stage; so, in books of fiction, they look not only for more entertainment, but, at bottom, even for more reality, than real life can show. . . . In this way of thinking, the people in a fiction, like the people in a play, must dress as nobody exactly dresses, talk as nobody exactly talks, act as nobody exactly acts."[22] The masquerade of the confidence man was this theatrical negation — this preservation by annulment — of the apparent stability of real lives: nobody on Melville's stage is exactly who he says he is because everybody is playing his role(s) with sincerity. Every one is false in reality because unity itself is impossible.

Hawthorne, too, announced that his purpose was to "establish a theatre, a little removed from the highway of ordinary travel," where he might gain a "foothold between fiction and reality." Miles Coverdale, the narrator, describes his own part as "that of the Chorus in a classic play," but he is in fact the director whose questions provide motives and whose staging creates the triangles of desire that destroy the masquerade at Blithedale. He is also one of the actors in the drama: the more he narrates, the more roles he plays.[23] In his concluding confession, at the point we might expect some indication that the narrator is now beyond the narration, Coverdale divides and reinterprets himself again. "I have made but a poor and dim figure in my own narrative," he claims at the outset, "establishing no separate interest, and suffering my colorless life to take its hue from other lives." Then he cautions us: "The reader must not take my word for it. . . . " But then he promises closure: "the confession, brief as it is, will throw a gleam of light over my behavior in the foregoing incidents, and is, indeed, essential to a full understanding of my story." And finally he confesses, making his behavior incomprehensible except as the effect of a wholly externalized self, whose personality was the sum of roles derived from total identification with other members of the Blithedale community.[24]

By their manipulation of the theatrical chronotope specific to a nonrealistic narrative form — the romance — Melville and Hawthorne elucidate what Harold Bloom calls the American Sublime.

They use the "flare of theatrical facts," as Howells put it, to illuminate the discursive self, the transitive subject that discovers itself
by desiring, or becoming, an Other. By his recovery and revision
of the apparently archaic romance form, Dreiser reintroduces this
self into American letters—or rather he revives the chronotype
of the theater specific to romance as a way of foregrounding this
self.

I have already suggested that the theater is the site of characterization in *Sister Carrie*. Its centrality may be grasped once
we recognize that the second half of the novel is a theatrical
parody of realism. Hurstwood, for example, is literally absorbed
by the reality of the fugitive's life in New York. He becomes
anonymous—in effect invisible—by virtue of his lack of employment, status, and income. Ultimately, he has no place in the real
world except in the "grim, beast silence" of a "cold, shrunken,
disgruntled mass" (396). But this loss of self may be read, Walter
Benn Michaels has shown, as the result of his attempt to secure or
stabilize his new identity in and through the paradigmatic realist
text—the newspaper.[25]

Hurstwood's death is the immediate consequence, then, of
desire exhausted, or sublimated, by realism. The last time he
rouses himself from his deepening lethargy is at Broadway and
Thirty-Ninth Street, under a marquee featuring a life-size poster
of "Carrie Madenda," the star of the Casino Company. "'She's
got it,' he said incoherently, thinking of money. 'Let her give
me some.' He started around to the side door. Then he forgot
what he was going for and paused, pushing his hands deeper to
warm the wrists. Suddenly it returned. The stage door! That
was it." He is of course shoved roughly out the door; without
further ado, he reaches his "one distinct mental decision"—that
is, to kill himself (391–2). He has no money because he cannot
get into the theater: his representational resources are exhausted.
He is as good as dead. Carrie, meanwhile, has become a star, a
celebrity, "an interesting figure in the public eye," mainly because
she refuses to inhabit the realist text. The narrative movement
in which she acts as the feature player is backward, as it were,
in time and space—toward the older commercial city, away from
the antic brutality of industrial Chicago. But this is the formal
movement of the novel, too: as it moves "backward" toward
romance, it moves beyond realism. In short, it moves back into
the theater rebuilt by Hawthorne and Melville from materials
available through melodrama and minstrelsy.

Like Hawthorne and Melville, Dreiser questions the choices
that melodrama (and minstrelsy) authorized, without dismissing

theatrical time and space as the proper setting for the realistic
exploration of selfhood. In this sense, he draws on popular forms
to replenish the raw materials of novelistic signification, to broaden
his constituency outside as well as inside the text, among readers
as well as characters. But he does not do so uncritically. For the
middle ground between social and individual, public and private,
marketplace and home — the ground sanctified by melodrama and
staked out by Hawthorne in *The House of Seven Gables* — did not
exist for Dreiser.   He was aware that modernity in the form
of machine production had somehow invaded and reconstructed
every kind of social intercourse.   At least, it had destroyed the
local grounds, the familiar places, that once supported it.   As he
explained in a piece on Salem published in 1898:

> It is so modern in parts. Why, only a block from the now large
> and grimy railroad station, there stood in Hawthorne's time 'the
> town pump,' which gave forth such a dainty and inspiring rill of
> thought concerning its own vocation. Some seven trolley lines
> pass around that identical corner now! The very bowels of the
> earth from which it drew the sparkling liquid, have been torn out
> to make way for a smoky two-track tunnel, and steam cars now
> pass where once the darksome well held its cool treasure in store
> for man and beast.[26]

The earth itself has been hollowed out since Hawthorne's time,
Dreiser suggests; and so the middle ground available to the writers
of mid-century offered no foothold to modern writers. The world
"out there" — otherness writ large — had already moved, uninvited,
into the most familiar realms.

Carrie's immersion in commodity production (the shoe factory)
and circulation (the department store) registers this invasion, and
thereby announces that there is no choice to be made between
domesticity and marketplace because there is no escape from the
latter, not even for a young woman from the country.   Minnie, the only representative of Carrie's family, is the character
who dreams according to the older terms of choice established
by melodrama and mid-century sentimentalism (and who lives
according to the political–economic dictates of modernity). Carrie's worldly success, and her development as — or rather into — a
character, violate these very terms. Again, each voice parodies
the other.   But Carrie, who as an actress plays the roles allocated by melodrama, embodies the absence of domesticity in
her "real life" from the factory and then the stage.   There is
no escape, then, from the phenomenology of the market: it
cannot be displaced or dismissed as it was in the sentimental

literature or in the larger highbrow culture of the nineteenth century.

The question that follows – for us as for Dreiser – is whether the self can be known, or can make itself, in this discursive milieu, where money creates but also contests the possibility of meaningful signification, of relating particular and universal, of unifying material circumstances and intellectual inscription. The great theorist of the puzzle is Karl Marx. But the immediate implications of the same puzzle obsessed most Americans for most of the nineteenth century because, as Marc Shell points out, "America was the birthplace of the widespread use of paper money in the Western world." Paper money complicates, intensifies, and enlarges the puzzle of meaningful signification that the use of coinage creates first in antiquity, again in the twelfth century in Western Europe, and yet again in the seventeenth century. For the relation between the substantial thing – the use value of the commodity – and its sign is recast by the appearance and generalization of banknotes as an everyday medium of exchange: "While a coin may be both symbol (as inscription or type) and commodity (as metallic ingot), paper is virtually all symbolic."[27]

Now Americans used paper money as early as the seventeenth century. But they did not become obsessed with the money question as a problem of representation, in both aesthetic and political terms, until the middle of the nineteenth century, when the collapse of the household economy is registered and reinforced by the doubling of the number of banks and the volume of banknotes in circulation (c. 1846–1854). Hereafter, issues of money in every sense come not only to dominate political discourse, but also to invade, if not enrich, aesthetic discourse. These issues turn on the uses of money and the meanings of the self under conditions of capital accumulation – that is, under conditions that efface and reconstruct the inherited division between household and market.

Paper money, it must be emphasized, is not necessarily a threatening or deconstructive medium, so long as its ghostlike formlessness is contained and structured by material antecedents and objects at either end of its circuit – by specie in the bank vault and by use values in the shape of needed commodities. So long as the symbol remains reductive, in other words, and corresponds in theory and practice to real, substantial things, the problem of signification need not be, and is not, a pandemic crisis of representation. For at this level, money functions as mind or language functions under the sign of Enlightenment. It is strictly a medium of exchange, by which the correspondence between unlike things – the underlying unity of particular objects –

is realized, and the relation between outward existence and inner reflection is posited. Under such a monetary regime, production presupposes a certain level of consumption; money remains a means of exchange, an instrumental appearance that "fits" reality but is never mistaken for reality as such. The production of wealth or the creation of value is accordingly construed as a means to the end of reproducing a certain social–political type—that is, the self-determining head of household whose independence is guaranteed by his control of productive property and consequently of his own labor power.

Capital accumulation requires and enables a different monetary regime, for it makes the production of wealth in the abstract an end in itself. The multiplication of symbols, of weightless tokens of value without material referents, inherent limits, or external moorings, now becomes both method and object of goods production. Since production no longer presupposes a certain level of consumption, money can function as a "store of value," a floating signifier, a fund of potential claims on time and commodities. The mobility of property and the mobility of the self are, as J. G. A. Popock suggests, constituted by this monetary regime, which emerges in Europe two generations before it does in the United States (1780–1820 as opposed to 1840–1880).[28] So it is probably neither incidental nor accidental that the autobiographical agenda of romanticism—its insistence that mind and language are fundamentally creative, for example, and not instruments with which the artist copies the given structure of external reality—emerges in Europe and in the United States at the very moment that money is detached from its referential moorings by the advent of the accumulationist regime.

In the United States, at any rate, the debate over the definition and uses of money was, in effect, a debate over the conditions of selfhood or self-production. And the issues were not decided until the 1890s. By then, however, the value of substitutes for issues of currency, whether greenbacks, Treasury certificates, or national banknotes, was greater than the value of the outstanding currency. These substitutes took many forms, but among them were checks, drafts, bills, deposits, bank clearinghouse certificates, and, finally, securities listed on the stock exchange or contracts made through the produce exchanges ("futures"). Paper money was substantial stuff compared to these apparitions of "credit," many of which were never seen outside of the cities, perhaps even the larger cities with central reserve status in the national banking system (New York, Chicago, and St. Louis). In *Looking Backward* (1887), the utopian novel that reached a circulation of more than one million by the mid-1890s, Edward Bellamy summarized the "prodigious illusions"—the crisis of representation—that followed from this development of a credit economy: "Already accustomed to accept money for commodities, the people next accepted promises for money, and ceased to look at all behind the representative for the thing represented. Money was a sign of real commodities, but credit was but a sign of a sign."[29]

Meanwhile, the insular world of "real commodities" was colonized by modern advertising, which, like modern credit, referred less to any particular or substantial use values than to the imagined possibilities and unrealized desires that commodities signified as the apparatus of autobiography. Here were the rudiments of the language of demand that economists needed once they assigned the problem of the supply side to classical political economy. But advertising remained the delinquent stepchild of the new marginalist economics, even though these two relatives shared the hedonistic psychology and "subjectivist" bent of modernist discourse. It continued to speak the vernacular of desire, and ignored—or redrew—the boundary between fact and fiction by valorizing consumers devoted to immediate gratification. Modern advertising was then the nonrealist language of illusion in which everyday life appeared, that is, became, theatrical.

Carrie inhabits this commodified culture, this spectacle, wherein the suspension of disbelief is both necessary and impossible: "she drew near these things, Chicago, New York; Drouet, Hurstwood; the world of fashion and the world of stage—these were but incidents. Not them, but that which they represented, she longed for. Time proved the representation false" (397). But what exactly did these "incidents" represent? "If she wanted to do anything better or move higher she must have more—a great deal more" (362–3). More of what? Money, say the critics, in unison. But isn't Carrie "too full of wonder and desire to be greedy" (100)? What, then, is money to her? It does not represent substantial things, as if it were a medium of exchange: "Not them, but that which they represented, she longed for." It is an end in itself: "One of her order of mind would have been content to be cast away on a desert island with a bundle of money, and only the long strain of starvation would have taught her that in some cases it could have no value. Even then she would have had no conception of the relative value of the thing . . . " (51). Or rather the notthing, the insensible symbol that is money: it has no relative or referential value in this sense apart from its self-referential values. "She found, after all—as what millionaire has not?—that there was no realising, in consciousness, the meaning of large sums" (355). Symbolization, as such, is now detached from any substantial things; there are only signs of signs. In this sense, the worlds accredited in *Sister Carrie* and in modern advertising are animated by the same belief in the reality of illusion, appearance, and representation.

What then becomes of my claim that Carrie's character is ultimately credible? This is not a strictly empirical question — in other words, to answer it is not simply a matter of presenting the textual evidence. For behind it stands the larger question that dominates modern political theory, moral philosophy, and cultural criticism. I have already alluded to that larger question, and will now merely rephrase it: can the self be known — can character be constructed — through entanglement in the externality peculiar to market society? According to Ann Douglas, the answer provided by the women writers of the mid-to-late nineteenth century was "No," but not exactly in thunder, because they had already been excluded from the market and were carving out a sphere of morality and spirituality that was by definition outside that dynamic, "masculine" preserve. Douglas claims that the "feminization" of American culture — its odd detachment from the hurly-burly of American capitalism — was the result.[30] The subsequent failure of our culture (including our political culture) to come to grips with modernity as such is one corollary of "feminization" so conceived. This is a powerful and persuasive argument, but, as Douglas understands, it applies with special force to those who, in the twentieth century, would be critical of the culture and politics specific to modern capitalism. For if these critics assume at the outset that the market in its modern manifestations is by definition defiling, as did their "feminine" precursors, they cannot locate a source of resistance to or transcendence of capitalism that resides within a present determined by the development of capitalism. More to the point, they cannot acknowledge the possibility that selfhood and market, or character and capitalism, are compatible. The unintended implication of their ostensibly critical stance is, then, the validation of business as usual except in those spheres of life that have somehow remained impervious to the corrosive effects of capital accumulation.

A good example of this implication may be found in the recent critique of the "culture of consumption" elaborated by that unruly discipline called American Studies. One of the most sophisticated contributions to the critique is that of Jean-Christophe Agnew, whose study of the "consuming vision" of Henry James is simply brilliant. But in this study of James, Agnew notes that his analysis of consumer culture is "deeply indebted" to the theoretical work of William Leiss. Now, according to Leiss, "the striving for satisfaction . . . is an 'intensive' dimension of experience involving the internal disposition of a person," that is, it does not involve or require the extroversion and objectification of desire as the condition of articulating (knowing) the possible forms of satisfaction. Hence, the "intensive character of needing suffers in proportion to the sheer extensiveness of the search [for satisfaction] carried out among the almost infinite possibilities."[31] The normative principle of Agnew's critique is, then, the pure self whose internal disposition—whose subjectivity, character, etc.—is created and experienced not in, through, and as externalized desire for particular objects and others, but rather as release or abstention from the plentitude of possibilities circulating as commodities in the market. This is a self that can secure its identity and realize its own needs only by ignoring such circulation. In effect, therefore, the self as such is to be found only above and beyond the defiling realm of commodity production and distribution, where, according to Douglas, the women writers of the nineteenth century had already placed it, and, for that matter, where the realists would leave it. And in this crucial sense, the contemporary debate about the character(s) of the "culture of consumption" formally recapitulates the literary debate at the turn of the century, for both debates center on the predicates of self-discovery and determination under conditions defined by the ubiquity of the commodity.

Dreiser's unique position within these debates is incomprehensible unless we recognize that both the sentimental and the realist traditions engender and finally entail the unargued assumption that now animates the critique of the "culture of consumption"—that is, the assumption that there is a necessary contradiction between the development of capitalism and the development of character. Taken at face value, it inspires cultural critique on *ethical* grounds: to discover the genuine self is to reject capitalism. But it also undermines political critique (or action) on *historical* grounds: to discover the genuine self is to recover the transparency of precapitalist social conditions, or, failing that, to find an Archimedean point, a "clearing," outside of existing social relations—perhaps in the "culture of resistance" afforded by radical movements, perhaps in the "free social space" of the university. Future and past accordingly appear as fundamentally incommensurable because the ethical principle—the integrity of the self—does not seem to reside in or flow from the historical development of capitalism. In *Sister Carrie*, Dreiser turns the assumption into argument by entertaining the possibility that character is a consequence of capitalism. To that extent, he explores the possibility that the ethical and the historical are not antithetical, but commensurable and interlocking planes of narrative and analysis.

I emphasize "possibility," because the novel is ambiguous at every level. But let us see where Carrie stands. At the conclusion, we note first, she has become neither a man nor a wife. That she remains a single woman may seem wholly unexceptional. Yet the playful confusion over identity that characterizes both romance and theater before the twentieth century often led to reversals that did not so much question an allocation of roles according to gender as confirm it, by giving the disguised woman who penetrates the public realm of politics and markets all the attributes of a man. Carrie's identity is never fixed; but she is still on her own at the end and has not lost the "emotional greatness" that originally propelled her into the world of money, commodities, and the stage. Nor has she learned that she must have a husband. In fact she becomes more wary of men: "Experience of the world and of necessity was in her favour. No longer the lightest word of a man made her head dizzy. She had learned that men could change and fail" (343). After she leaves Hurstwood and moves in with her female friend from the chorus line, a member of the opera company "discovered a fancy for her." But Carrie "found herself criticising this man. He was too stilted, too self-opinionated. He did not talk of anything that lifted her above the common run of clothes and material success" (351).

She also becomes a reader of the novel, leaving behind sentimental romances such as *Dora Thorne* (246–50, 392–3). To that extent, Carrie fulfills the hopes of Howells: she becomes a recognizable character who grasps the nuances of the moral law (she acquires "character") insofar as she can identify with the population of the realist text, yet not confuse fiction and fact — a project that requires a certain cognitive distance, or abstraction, from both realms. But the novel that moves her, that suggests "how silly and worthless had been her earlier reading," is Balzac's *Père Goriot* (1835), which Howells of course deemed the worst novel ever written. It is not my purpose to account for Howells's loathing, or to interpret *Père Goriot*. Even so, we should note that Carrie's new reading habits indicate — but also animate — her new capacity for introspection as well as abstraction. The "plague of poverty" that had "galled her" before she drew a star's salary, for example (318), is now projected outward through the medium of Balzac's fiction. From her "comfortable chambers at the Waldorf," her roommate hopes for enough snow to go sleigh riding. " 'Oh dear,' said Carrie, with whom the sufferings of Father Goriot were still keen. 'That's all you think of. Aren't you sorry for the people who haven't anything tonight?'" (393).

Briefly, then, what made old Goriot suffer? In what Howells claimed to be the worst of novels, Balzac has rewritten the Faust legend, setting it in the Paris of 1819, and has cast Father Goriot as our Father, who is not in heaven. He is not there because he is on earth, trying to reestablish his presence among the living: "I shall go and come like a good fairy who makes himself felt everywhere without being seen, shall I not?" But the Devil (Vautrin) now rules the world—"there was nothing he did not know"—and, as Luther claimed, the Devil's word is money: Vautrin is the banker of the Parisian criminal underground. This Mephistopheles identifies Paris, where money rules society, not only as a cesspool—here he follows Luther's usage—but as Europe's version of America, where money determines everything, including personal identity. The question that Vautrin asks, in striking his bargain with Rastignac, the provincial law student, is "how are you to prosper if you do not discount your love," that is, if you do not cash in on your sentiments before they come due?[32] The student has no answer, for everyone, even Father Goriot, agrees that the "heart is a treasury" (69)—love, like paper money and credit, has value and confers success because, but only insofar as, it circulates and thereby organizes social intercourse as such.

So *Père Goriot* inhabits and articulates a world turned upside down by the power of money. It, too, is a demonic parody of sentimentalism, for it announces that the secret alliance enforcing the rule of money is forged between fathers and daughters (e.g., 68, 127, 175): they may occupy separate spheres—production/consumption, public/private, and so forth—but their agendas converge on the reproduction of capitalism. And yet it is not a strictly realist parody of sentimentalism. As Dreiser noted in an essay of 1896, "romance and realism blend and become one" under Balzac's narrative spell.[33] In *Père Goriot*, the peddler of realism, among other things, is the Devil. His proposed alternative to the secret alliance of fathers and daughters is the exclusively masculine preserve that he associates with the wilderness of the New World: only bachelorhood in the frontier forest, Vautrin implies, can disentangle men from the "effeminate age" defined by sentimentalism but enforced by capitalism (92–3, 130–1). In this sense, Natty Bumpo is the Devil's disciple. Rastignac is not because he does not rise above, or try to escape, the commodified world symbolized in and by the great city.

Neither does Carrie. She becomes a credible character not by ignoring or avoiding the illusions of the market and the theater—

not by heading for the territory where the self's integrity is guaranteed by keeping the Other in its proper place — but by identifying with what she is not, indeed by becoming a sign of the signs specific to the symbolic universe of the stage. To put this another way, it is precisely Carrie's fictionalizing (her dreaming, acting, and identifying with others who are not "real people") that makes her a character, because it eventually takes her beyond what is given and what she is at the outset. However, the sources and materials of that fictionalizing — her money, her roles, her reading — are themselves fictional, symbolic, or lacking substance in the real world. Like the money she derives from the roles she plays, the consciousness that makes her a character has no objective correlate.

Is it false, then? I have already tried to suggest that our answer will depend as much on our extratextual evidence and assumptions as on our reading of the text. In this case, the evidence and assumptions will be consequences of a theory of knowledge, a notion of the truth, a model of the self. Thus we can and should turn to the language of philosophy for help in deciding the question. But which language? On what grounds, for example, should we choose Hegel over Kant? My own view is that we do not have much of a choice because our first responsibility as intellectuals is to understand the relation between past and present — to explain, in other words, how past and present may be treated as commensurable, and thereby to explain why we are neither wholly determined nor simply unbound by the past. If these priorities are in order, we need a language that historicizes, that allows us to see extension in space and times as something other than irrational contingency or natural externality, and that accordingly allows us to periodize more philosophies without succumbing to relativism. And so we are driven willy-nilly toward Hegel.[34]

In any event, he does address the problem of false consciousness in a manner that is immediately relevant to the question at hand. "Truth and falsehood as commonly understood belong to those sharply defined ideas which claim a completely fixed nature of their own," Hegel notes in his preface to *The Phenomenology*, "one standing in solid isolation on this side, the other on that, without any community between them. Against that view it must be pointed out, that truth is not like a stamped coin that is issued ready from the mint and so can be taken up and used." The truth, in other words, works something like paper money, but even more like modern credit in the form of interest-bearing securities, which preserve the original principal when canceled. The truth implies the negation—the preservation by cancellation—of original principles.[35]

"Doubtless we can know in a way that is false," Hegel acknowledges: "To know something falsely means that knowledge is not adequate to, is not on equal terms with, its substance." But to identify falsehood in such terms would be to posit a correspondence between, a unity of, subject and object, or knowledge and its substance, which could, in turn, serve as the normative principle for the evaluation of any form of knowledge. "Yet this very dissimilarity is the process of distinction in general, the essential moment in knowing. It is, in fact, out of this active distinction that its harmonious unity arises, and this identity, when arrived at, is truth." We cannot say that truth is "an original and primal unity as such" unless we are willing to derive it from the supernatural principle called God. It cannot be both an identity that somehow subsists beyond time and the criterion by which the living specify falsehood in human knowledge.

> But it [this unity] is not truth in a sense which would involve the rejection of the discordance, the diversity, like dross from pure metal; nor, again, does truth remain detached from diversity, like a finished article from the instrument that shapes it. Difference itself continues to be an immediate element within truth as such, in the form of the principle of negation, in the form of the activity of the Self.

Hegel summarizes, and emphasizes the historicizing movement of his argument, by claiming that "the false is no longer false as a moment of the true."[36]

So the divisions and dislocations of the discursive self cannot be construed as deviations from the truth of selfhood, thus as falsehood; for they are the predicates of the attempt to realize the "harmonious unity" this self learns in time, in that attempt, to call the truth. They become not the proximate cause, but the enduring conditions, of identity in every sense. From that standpoint, the falsehoods, the illusions, the waking dreams in which Carrie posits herself are moments in the truth of the character she is becoming. From the same standpoint, Hurstwood's early admonition to Carrie—"Don't you moralise until you see what becomes of the money" (80)—is a warning to readers who are looking for the bottom line.

With that warning in mind, let me demonstrate how two radically different political readings of *Sister Carrie* can be reconciled, or rather contained, by another, and thus how Dreiser forces us to treat this novel as a durable good that cannot be "consumed" or discarded, but does not pretend to stand above or outside the commodified world it describes. In 1977, Sandy Petrey tried to explain what bad writing meant in *Sister Carrie*. He argued that the function of the realist passages Alfred Kazin admired was to subvert the sentimental discursions Leslie Fiedler detested. For Petrey, the "direct language capable of stating what industrialism meant" is the authentic language of the novel, because its blank realism invalidates the media of false consciousness—that is, the sentimental and melodramatic "linguistic forms which perpetuated myths." *Sister Carrie* belongs, accordingly, in the "great tradition of social realism" because it undermined the "ideologically significant myths" nourished by the sentimental tradition: it "made a certain way of lying so patent that it does not need exposure." In such perspective, Dreiser's "refusal to approve the new industrial order" is self-evident.[37]

In 1980, Walter Benn Michaels suggested that *Sister Carrie* could not be interpreted as a refusal to approve modern industrial capitalism. He argued that the novel's "economy of desire" identifies Carrie with an inexhaustible commodity lust—an "involvement with the world [of objects] so central to one's sense of self that the distinction between what one is and what one wants tends to disappear." The equilibrium and individual autonomy celebrated in the republican and realist traditions of the nineteenth century are explicitly repudiated by such an economy, which defines desire that is "in principle never satisfied" as the condition of life itself. By this reading, Dreiser's doubts about the new industrial order are rather less than self-evident. Indeed Michaels claimed that the "unrestrained capitalism" of the turn of the century receives an "unequivocal endorsement" in *Sister Carrie*. He concluded by suggesting that what is "arguably the greatest American realist novel" remains popular because it celebrates the commodity fetishism and psychological desublimation peculiar to twentieth-century capitalism.[38]

It seems that these readings converge only on the name they give to the novel's form—realism. And yet they agree that realism is not the only level of writing in the novel. For Petrey, the language of realism par excellence is found in the shoe factory scenes; for Michaels, that language is the "literature of exhausted desire and economic failure" which corresponds to Hurstwood's decline. They might also agree that *Sister Carrie* is not merely a realist novel, simply because Carrie's career does not follow the path anticipated in the shoe factory and traced in Hurstwood's decline. Ultimately, she moves out of the neighborhood naturalized by realism. In any event, the reading I have proposed can accommodate those of both Petrey and Michaels, for it acknowledges, but does not privilege, the novel's realist level of writing. To put this another way, my reading would suggest that *both* Petrey and Michaels are correct, because *Sister Carrie* is critical of industrial capitalism, but not from the Archimedean standpoint of a self that remains undefiled by the commodity form.

Michaels is not wrong, for example, to claim that *Sister Carrie* represents an "unequivocal endorsement" of modern capitalism, because the novel embraces and endorses History as such, as the antecedent necessity or reality that is beyond criticism. Even so, the ethical or utopian principle of romance remains. For after all is said and done, Carrie is not contained by historical reality; she contains it. And so she stands between, and perhaps embodies, the transcendent truths realized in the epoch of accumulation. She is living proof that freedom resides in necessity, in the historically determined "worldness" of the world. But she also acts on the principle of hope residing in the knowledge that true freedom lies somewhere beyond necessity, in the posthistorical redefinition of work as Play. Since she is in this sense both object and subject of History, her story required the representation of the historical from the standpoint of the ethical, or, more simply, realism in the narrative form of romance.

As Dreiser tells the story, Carrie becomes the "new woman" of the twentieth century, in whom we can see a transitive subject taking shape in the movement away from the familiar social norms and roles of the nineteenth century. But it is precisely the movement away from the familiar that casts Carrie as our *sister*, as the lead in a "family romance" from which domesticity is altogether lacking. In effect, then, we are just now catching up with Carrie. For we can now see that she stood at the same crossroad we have finally reached in our own thinking about the character(s) of postmodern society.

We know, for example, that there is no meaningful distinction to be drawn between appearance and reality in the consumer culture—the "political economy of the sign"—specific to late corporate capitalism. We also know that if there is a meaningful distinction to be drawn between self and society in this consumer culture, it is not to be deduced from the ontological priority of the "natural individual," the modern subject, the pure self. Self and Other(ness) are not indistinguishable; but they are indissoluble. To choose between them, or to assume that they are not contingent moments on a continuum but elements of an irresolvable contradiction, is to validate the dualism that petrifies every invidious distinction, including the kind that keeps the spheres of male and female separate. In *Sister Carrie*, Dreiser postpones the choice and interrogates the assumption by avoiding closure; like Whitman, he will not let us read for the ending. So he invites us to extend and complete his fiction, to make its rendering of the self a moment of truth we are still producing.

Notes

1. See Hans Robert Jauss, "Literary History as a Challenge to Literary Theory," *New Literary History* 2 (1970): 7–37. (Quotation, p. 11.) On the ironies of historicism across the curriculum, see, for example, Quentin Skinner, "Meaning and Understanding in the History of Ideas," *History and Theory* 8 (1969): 3–53; David Carroll, "The Alterity of Discourse: Form, History, and the Question of the Political," *Diacritics* 13 (1983): 65–83; Peter U. Hohendahl, "On Reception Aesthetics," *New German Critique* 28 (1983): 108–46; Fredric Jameson, "Marxism and Historicism," *New Literary History* 11 (1979): 41–73; Alasdair MacIntyre, "The Relationship of Philosophy to its Past," in *Philosophy in History* ed. Richard Rorty, J. B. Schneewind, Quentin Skinner (New York: Cambridge University Press, 1984), pp. 31–48; and Michael Sprinker, "The Current Conjuncture in Theory," *College English* 51 (1989): 825–31.

2. For evidence that our generation of critics has rediscovered the literary event called naturalism, see the Special Issue on Dreiser of *Modern Fiction Studies* 23, no. 3 (1977); Eric J. Sundquist, ed. *American Realism: New Essays* (Baltimore: Johns Hopkins University Press, 1982); Donald Pizer, *Twentieth-Century American Literary Naturalism* (Carbondale: Southern Illinois University Press, 1982); Philip Fisher, *Hard Facts: Setting and Form in the American Novel* (New York: Oxford University Press, 1985), pp. 6–7, 12–13, 20–1, 128–78; June Howard, *Form and History in American Literary Naturalism* (Chapel Hill: University of North Carolina Press, 1985), esp. pp. 41–50, 99–102, 107–111, 115, 150–1, 155; and Rachel Bowlby, *Just Looking: Consumer Culture in Dreiser, Gissing, and Zola* (London: Metheun, 1985), esp. pp. 1–65.

3. Since narrative forms are embedded in the history of writing, to retrieve one from the dustbin of literary usage, Barthes suggests, is "an act of historical solidarity." He elaborates on the point in a way that informs all subsequent literary historicisms: the choice of form, he claims, establishes a "relationship between creation and society," and entails a "literary language transformed by its social finality." Thus writing as such is "essentially the morality of form, the choice of that social area within which the writer elects to

situate the Nature of his language" (*Writing Degree Zero*, trans. A. Lavers and C. Smith [London: Cape, 1967], p. 14). So conceived, form is both a result and a definition of history. The choice of one over another is determined in the first place by availability, by the range of forms the history of writing has placed at the disposal of writers. But that choice defines the scope of what may be represented, without apology or explanation, as real, plausible, or consequential events — that is, it defines the historical or usable past, and so anticipates, or prepares us for, a certain future. Since modern fiction "is constructed in a zone of contact with the incomplete events of a particular present," as Mikhail Bakhtin insists, it necessarily opens onto a future, and indeed "begins to feel closer to the future than the past, and begins to seek some valorized support in the future" (*The Dialogic Imagination*, trans. C. Emerson and M. Holquist, ed. M. Holquist [Austin: University of Texas Press, 1982], 33, 26). The morality of form, I would then say, simply is this anticipatory arena where actuality and possibility, past and present, are allowed to collaborate on a history of the future. Hence to suggesst that form or genre should be treated as the "immanent ideology" or the "political unconscious" of fictional discourse, as Fredric Jameson does in *The Political Unconscious: Narrative as a Socially Symbolic Act* (Ithaca: Cornell University Press, 1981), is not to remint the reductionist coinage of base and superstructure; it is instead to suggest that *form* is to fictional discourse what *paradigm* is to nonfictional discourse — that is, an historically specific protocol that naturalizes an observable reality and constitutes a social relation between practitioners (writers) and their potential publics.

4. See John Higham, "The Reorientation of American Culture in the 1890s," *The Origins of Modern Consciousness*, ed. John Weiss (Detroit: Wayne State University Press, 1965), pp. 25–48. See also Charles Child Walcutt, *American Literary Naturalism: A Divided Stream* (Minneapolis: University of Minnesota Press, 1956; 2d ed. 1973). Walcutt's approach to naturalism is consistent with my more limited attempt to situate one of Dreiser's novels within the problematic of cultural change in the late nineteenth-century United States, for, in chap. 1, esp. pp. 10–23, he suggests (1) that the American Dream resides in the overthrow of the dualism centering in the antinomy of desire and reason (or body and mind), which animates the Western intellectual tradition as such, and which is codified in modern liberal psychology; (2) that the poetics of this Dream are most clearly articulated in what he calls the monism of transcendentalism — in what most of the rest of us would probably call the dialectics of the American Renaissance; (3) that American literary naturalism is an effort to get beyond the same fundamental

dualism, and thus may be construed as a major reinterpretation of the American Dream and a literary agenda that derives from the earlier Renaissance; (4) that naturalism, as the extremity of realism, is pervaded by a perceived contradiction between "optimism and pessimism, freedom and determination, will and fate, social reformism and mechanistic despair"; thus it is one manifestation of the "divided stream of transcendentalism" because it fails to reinstate the original "transcendentalist union of reason and instinct" (12, 15). Although Walcutt's subsequent readings of naturalist novels are not as provocative and insightful as this introductory argument, the book seems to me a brilliant success because it illuminates the cultural context within which the intellectual extremity of the naturalist literary agenda begins to make sense. My only criticism of Walcutt is that he does not take his own insights seriously enough. For example, on p. 22 he notes that "naturalism involved a continual search for form." If he is correct — and I think he is — it becomes necessary to explain and defend, not merely mention in passing, Frank Norris's seemingly bizarre claim to the effect that Romance is the necessary formal antidote to Realism under modern conditions (see Norris, *The Responsibilities of the Novelist* [1901; Garden City, N.Y.: Doubleday 1928], pp. 163–8).

5. See my *Pragmatism and the Political Economy of Cultural Revolution, 1850–1940* (Chapel Hill: University of North Carolina Press, 1994), Part 2, for a more detailed discussion of Hegel's role in the intellectual innovation of the turn of the century.

6. Howells, *Literary Friends and Acquaintances* (Bloomington: Indiana University Press, 1968), pp. 101–2. These remarks appeared originally in *Harper's Monthly* of November 1895, as "Literary Boston Thirty Years Ago." On Howells's prolonged struggle against romance, see Amy Kaplan, *The Social Construction of American Realism* (Chicago: University of Chicago Press, 1988), Chap. 1.

7. E. H. Cady, ed. *W. D. Howells as Critic* (Boston: Routledge and Kegan Paul, 1973), p. 100.

8. *A Modern Instance* [1882] (Bloomington: Indiana University Press, 1977), p. 361.

9. Halleck's positions on the relation between extension in space or time and the intelligibility of morality are essentially Kantian. See, for example, Immanuel Kant, *Groundwork of the Metaphysics of Morals*, trans. H. J. Paton (New York: Harper and Row, 1964), p. 125, and *Critique of Pure Reason*, trans. N. K. Smith (New York: Oxford University Press, 1965), pp. 313, 464–79 (A 318–19, 533–57).

10. Cady, *Howells as Critic*, pp. 310–11; cf. p. 102.

11. Again see my *Pragmatism and the Political Economy of Cultural Revolution*, Part 2.

12. Northrop Frye, *The Anatomy of Criticism* (Princeton: Princeton University Press, 1957), pp. 304, 105–6, 136–43, and *The Secular Scripture: A Study of the Structure of Romance* (Cambridge: Harvard University Press, 1976), pp. 47–53; Jameson, *Political Unconscious*, pp. 112-3; and *Howells as Critic*, pp. 81–3, 97–103, 299–313.

13. See Frye, *Anatomy*, p. 193, and *Scripture*, pp. 53–4; cf. Bakhtin, *Dialogic Imagination*, pp. 41–83.

14. Julian Markels, "Theodore Dreiser and the Plotting of Inarticulate Experience," *Massachusetts Review* 2 (1961): 431–48, reprinted in *Sister Carrie*, ed. Donald Pizer (New York: Norton, 1970), pp. 527–41. Cf. Walcutt, *American Literary Naturalism*, p. 191: "The movement of the novel does not depend upon acts of will by the central figures." I am using the Bantam paperback edition of *Sister Carrie* (New York, 1972), and will hereafter cite page numbers in the text.

15. Markels, "Inarticulate Experience," pp. 531–2.

16. Walter Benn Michaels, "*Sister Carrie*'s Popular Economy," *Critical Inquiry* 7 (Winter 1980): 373–90. Cf. Cohen, "Locating One's Self," p. 366: "The material world becomes the mirror of Carrie's personality."

17. See Michaels, "*Sister Carrie*'s Popular Economy," and Leo Bersani, *A Future for Astyanax* (Boston: Little, Brown, 1976), esp. Chap. 2.

18. See Jameson, *Political Unconscious*, pp. 113–9, for discussion of the ethical binary at the core of romance.

19. See Bakhtin's "Forms of Time and Chronotope in the Novel," in *Dialogic Imagination*, pp. 84–258.

20. See Daniel G. Hoffman, *Form and Fable in American Fiction* (New York: Oxford University Press, 1961), Chaps. 1–2; David Grimsted, *Melodrama Unveiled: American Theater and Culture, 1800–1850* (Chicago: University of Chicago Press, 1968); Nathan Huggins, *Harlem Renaissance* (New York: Oxford University Press, 1970), Chap. 6; and David R. Roediger, *The Wages of Whiteness: Race and the Making of the American Working Class* (London: Verso, 1991), Chaps. 5–6.

21. See Nina Baym, *Woman's Fiction: A Guide to Novels by and about Women in America, 1820–1870* (Ithaca: Cornell University Press, 1978), pp. 27–40, 45–50, 110–233.

22. Herman Melville, *The Confidence-Man* [1857] (New York: New American Library, 1964), pp. 75, 190.

23. Nathaniel Hawthorne, *The Blithedale Romance* [1852] (New York: Norton, 1958), pp. 27–8, 116; on Coverdale's direction of the play, see pp. 143, 146, 170–3, 176, 178, 206, 208, 236.

24. Hawthorne, *Blithedale Romance*, pp. 249–50.

25. Michaels, "Sister Carrie's Popular Economy," pp. 384–6.

26. On Hawthorne's attempt "to locate a point of intersection between home and marketplace," see Mark Seltzer, *Henry James and the Art of Power* (Ithaca: Cornell University Press, 1984), pp. 191–2. Dreiser's commentary from "Haunts of Nathaniel Hawthorne," *Truth* 17 (September 21–28, 1898), reprinted in Yoshinobu Hakutani, ed., *Selected Magazine Articles of Theodore Dreiser* (Rutherford, N.J.: Fairleigh Dickinson University Press, 1985), pp. 57–66. (Quotation, p. 58.)

27. See Karl Marx, *Capital: A Critique of Political Economy*, trans. Samuel Moore and Edward Aveling, 3 vols. (Chicago: Charles Kerr, 1906), 1: 141–2, and *Grundrisse: Foundations of the Critique of Political Economy*, trans. Martin Nicolaus (Baltimore: Penguin, 1973), pp. 141–74, 196–236; Marc Shell, *Money, Language, and Thought* (Berkeley: University of California Press, 1982), pp. 5, 19, 105–111, and *The Economy of Literature* (Baltimore: Johns Hopkins University Press, 1978), Chaps. 1–3; Lester K. Little, *Religious Poverty and the Profit Economy in Medieval Europe* (Ithaca: Cornell University Press, 1978), Chaps. 1–4, 10.

28. J. G. A. Pocock, "The Mobility of Property and the Rise of 18th Century Sociology," in *Virtue, Commerce, and History* (New York: Cambridge University Press, 1985), pp. 103–24; cf. William Reddy, *Money and Liberty in Modern Europe: A Critique of Historical Understanding* (New York: Cambridge University Press, 1987), Chaps. 3–4; and Marx, *Grundrisse*, pp. 223–6.

29. See my *Origins of the Federal Reserve System: Money, Class, and Corporate Capitalism, 1890–1913* (Ithaca: Cornell University Press, 1986), Chaps. 3–5, esp. pp. 90–4, and Bellamy's *Looking Backward 2000–1887* (New York: New American Library, 1960), Chap. 22, to which I was led by Howard Horwitz's brilliant essay, "To Find the Value of X: The Pit as Renunciation of Romance," in Sundquist, ed., *American Realism*, pp. 215–37. The quoted remark is attributed to Doctor Leete, the character who acts as the novel's interlocutor. He is Bellamy's witness at the birth of what Jean Baudrillard calls the "political economy of the sign," or the "third phase" of po-

litical economy, which not incidentally coincides with the rise of "monopolistic capitalism" or "finance capital." See *The Mirror of Production*, trans. Mark Poster (St. Louis: Telos Press, 1975), pp. 119–29.

30. Ann Douglas, *The Feminization of American Culture* (New York: Norton, 1977), esp. Chap. 2.

31. Jean-Christophe Agnew, "The Consuming Vision of Henry James," in Fox & Lears, eds., *Culture of Consumption*, pp. 65–100 and endnotes at pp. 221–5, esp. note 9, p. 222, where, having cited William Leiss, *The Limits to Satisfaction* (Toronto: University of Toronto Press, 1976), Agnew states: "The following analysis is deeply indebted to Leiss's work." My quotations are from Leiss, *Limits*, pp. 25, 90.

32. I am quoting from the Airmont edition of *Father Goriot* (New York: Airmont, 1966), pp. 166, 21, 133, 91–3, except at this last passage (94), where I have substituted my own translation from Honoré de Balzac, *Oeuvres Completes: La Comédie Humaine, Etudes de Moeurs: Scènes de la vie privée*, Vol. VI (Paris: L. Conrad, 1912–1940), p. 338; page references to the Airmont edition are hereafter cited in text.

33. Dreiser, quoted in Richard Lingeman, *Theodore Dreiser: At the Gates of the City, 1871–1907* (New York: Putnam's Sons, 1986), p. 235.

34. Cf. MacIntyre, "The Relationship of Philosophy to Its Past," in *Philosophy in History*, eds. Rorty et al., pp. 31–48.

35. G. W. F. Hegel, *The Phenomenology of Mind*, trans. J. B. Baillie (New York: Harper and Row, 1967), p. 98; cf. Marx, *Grundrisse*, pp. 221–36. I am adopting and adapting the ambitious argument of Shell, *Money, Language, and Thought*, pp. 126–50.

36. Hegel, *Phenomenology*, pp. 81, 98–9; the last passage quoted according to the translation by Shell in *Money, Language, and Thought*, p. 149.

37. See Sandy Petrey, "The Language of Realism, the Language of False Consciousness: A Reading of *Sister Carrie*," *Novel* 10 (1977): 101–13; cf. Cathy N. and Arnold E. Davidson, "Carrie's Sisters: The Popular Prototypes for Dreiser's Heroine," *Modern Fiction Studies* 23 (1977): 395–407, esp. 404 ff.

38. Michaels,"Sister Carrie's Popular Economy," 384–6.

Works Consulted

Ahnebrink, Lars. *The Beginnings of Naturalism in American Fiction: A Study of the Works of Hamlin Garland, Stephen Crane, and Frank Norris with Special References to Some European Influences, 1891-1903.* Cambridge: Harvard University Press, 1950.

Barker-Benfield, G. J. *Horrors of the Half-Known Life: Male Attitudes Toward Women and Sexuality in Nineteenth-Century America.* New York: Harper and Row, 1976.

Barker-Benfield, G. J. "The Spermatic Economy: A Nineteenth-Century View of Sexuality," in *The American Family in Socio-Historical Perspective,* 2d ed., ed. Michael Gordon. New York: St. Martin's Press, 1978.

Barth, Gunther. *City People: The Rise of Modern City Culture in Nineteenth-Century America.* New York: Oxford University Press, 1980.

Baym, Nina. *Woman's Fiction: A Guide to Novels by and about Women in America, 1820-1870.* Ithaca: Cornell University Press, 1978.

Beauvoir, Simone de. *The Second Sex,* trans. and ed. H. M. Parshley. New York: Vintage, 1974.

Bell, Michael Davitt. *The Problem of American Realism: Studies in the Cultural History of a Literary Idea.* Chicago: University of Chicago Press, 1993.

Bellow, Saul. "An Interview with Saul Bellow." *Publishers Weekly* 204 (October 22, 1973): 74.

Bersani, Leo. *A Future for Astyanax.* Boston: Little, Brown, 1976.

Block, Haskell M. *Naturalistic Triptych: The Fictive and the Real in Zola, Mann, and Dreiser.* New York: Random House, 1969.

Boone, Joseph, and Cadden, Michael. *Engendering Men: The Question of Male Feminist Criticism.* New York: Routledge, 1990.

Bowen, Murray. *Family Therapy in Clinical Practice.* New York: Jason Aronson, 1978.

Bowlby, Rachel. *Just Looking: Consumer Culture in Dreiser, Gissing, and Zola.* New York and London: Methuen, 1985.

Brandon, Craig. *Murder in the Adirondacks: An American Tragedy Revisited.* Utica, N.Y.: North Country Books, 1986.

Brod, Harry. *The Making of Masculinities.* Newbury, Calif.: Sage, 1987.

Budick, Emily. *Engendering Romance: Women Writing in the Hawthorne Tradition.* New Haven: Yale University Press, 1994.

Buell, Lawrence. "Literary History Without Sexism? Feminist Studies and Canonical Reception." *American Literature* 59 (1987): 102–14.

Bunner, R. F. "In the Old Pit Shaft" (Cartoon). *Life* 29 (January 7, 1897): 32.

Burgan, Mary A. "*Sister Carrie* and the Pathos of Naturalism." *Criticism* 15 (Fall 1973): 336–49.

Cady, E. H., ed. *W. D. Howells as Critic.* Boston: Routledge and Kegan Paul, 1973.

Camfield, Gregg. *Sentimental Twain: Samuel Clemens in the Maze of Moral Philosophy.* Philadelphia: University of Pennsylvania Press, 1994.

Carnes, Mark C. "Middle-Class Men and the Solace of Fraternal Ritual" in *Meanings for Manhood: Constructions of Masculinity in Victorian America*, eds. Mark C. Carnes and Clyde Griffen. Chicago: University of Chicago Press, 1990.

Carnes, Mark C. *Secret Ritual and Manhood in Victorian America.* New Haven: Yale University Press, 1989.

Carroll, David. "The Alterity of Discourse: Form, History, and the Question of the Political." *Diacritics* 13 (1983): 65–83.

Cawelti, John G. *Adventure, Mystery, and Romance.* Chicago: University of Chicago Press, 1976.

Chesler, Ellen. *Woman of Valor: Margaret Sanger and the Birth Control Movement in America.* New York: Simon and Schuster, 1992.

Chopin, Kate. *The Awakening.* New York: Bedford, 1993.

Church, Joseph. "Minnie's Dreams in *Sister Carrie.*" *College Literature* 14 (1987): 184.

Clawson, Mary Ann. *Constructing Brotherhood: Class, Gender, and Fraternalism.* Princeton: Princeton University Press, 1989.

Clay, Bertha M. *Dora Thorne.* Chicago: M. A. Donahue, n.d.

Cohen, Keith. "Eisenstein's Subversive Adaptation" in *The Classic American Novel and the Movies,* ed. Gerald Peary and Roger Shatzkin. New York: Ungar, 1977, pp. 239–56.

Cott, Nancy. "Passionlessness: A Reinterpretation of Victorian Sexual Ideology, 1790–1850." *Signs* 4 (1978): 219–36.

Craig, Alec. *Suppressed Books. A History of the Conception of Literary Obscenity.* Cleveland: World Pub., 1963.

Crowther, Bosley. "The Screen in Review." *New York Times*, July 17, 1952: 20.

Davidson, Cathy N., and Davidson, Arnold E. "Carrie's Sisters: The Popular Prototypes for Dreiser's Heroine." *Modern Fiction Studies* 23 (Autumn 1977): 395–407.

Degler, Carl L. *At Odds: Women and the Family in America from the Revolution to the Present.* New York: Oxford University Press, 1980.

DeGrazia, Edward. *Girls Lean Back Everywhere: The Law of Obscenity and the Assault on Genius.* New York: Random House, 1992, pp. 4–5.

Diamond, Irene, and Quinby, Lee, eds. *Feminism and Foucault: Strategies for Resistance.* Evanston, Ill.: Northwestern University Press, 1988.

Douglas, Ann. *The Feminization of American Culture.* New York: Norton, 1977.

Douglas, Emily Taft. *Margaret Sanger: Pioneer of the Future.* New York: Holt, Rinehart and Winston, 1970.

Dreiser, Helen. *My Life with Dreiser.* New York: World Publishing, 1951.

Dreiser, Theodore. *An American Tragedy.* New York: Boni and Liveright, 1925; New York: New American Library, 1964; New York: New American Library, 1981.

Dreiser, Theodore. *A Book about Myself.* Greenwich, Conn.: Fawcett, 1965.

Dreiser, Theodore. Commentary in "Haunts of Nathaniel Hawthorne." *Truth* 17 (September 21–28, 1898).

Dreiser, Theodore. *Dawn, His Autobiography 1: The Early Years.* Greenwich, Conn.: Fawcett, 1965.

Dreiser, Theodore. *Dawn* (First unpublished typescript), the Dreiser Collection, Charles Patterson Van Pelt Library, University of Pennsylvania.

Dreiser, Theodore. *A Gallery of Women,* 2 vols. New York: Horace Liveright, 1929.

Dreiser, Theodore. *The "Genius."* New York: John Lane Company, 1915; New York: New American Library, 1981.

Dreiser, Theodore. *Jennie Gerhardt.* New York: Harper, 1911; Cleveland: Dell Publishing, 1963; ed. Donald Pizer, New York: Penguin Books, 1989; The University of Pennsylvania Dreiser Edition, ed. James L. W. West III. Philadelphia: University of Pennsylvania Press, 1992.

Dreiser, Theodore. *The Letters of Theodore Dreiser,* 3 vols., ed. Robert H. Elias. Philadelphia: University of Pennsylvania Press, 1959.

Dreiser, Theodore. *Moods: Cadenced and Declaimed.* New York: Boni and Liveright, 1926.

Dreiser, Theodore. *Newspaper Days.* Philadelphia: University of Pennsylvania Press, 1991.

Dreiser, Theodore. *A Selection of Uncollected Prose,* ed. Donald Pizer. Detroit: Wayne State University Press.

Dreiser, Theodore. *Sister Carrie.* New York: Modern Library, n.d.; New York and London: Norton, 1970; 1st ed. repr. 1900; Philadelphia: University of Pennsylvania Press, 1981; Harmondsworth: Penguin Books, 1981, published by arrangement with the University of Pennsylvania Press.

Dreiser, Theodore. "Theodore Dreiser." *Household Magazine* (November 1929), typescript, the Dreiser Collection, Charles Patterson Van Pelt Library, University of Pennsylvania.

Dreiser, Theodore. *The Titan, Trilogy of Desire,* vol. 2. New York: Thomas Y. Crowell, 1974.

Dreiser, Theodore. *The Trilogy of Desire.* New York and Garden City, N.Y.: Harper, John Lane, and Doubleday, 1912, 1914, 1947.

Dreiser, Theodore. "Why Not Tell Europe about Bertha Clay." *New York Call* 24 (October 1921): 6.

Dreiser, Vera. *My Uncle Dreiser.* New York: Nash, 1976.

Dudley, Dorothy. *Forgotten Frontiers: Dreiser and the Land of the Free.* New York: H. Smith and R. Haas, 1932.

Eagleton, Terry. *Literary Theory: An Introduction.* Minneapolis: University of Minnesota Press, 1983.

Eby, Claire Virginia. "The Psychology of Desire: Veblen's 'Pecuniary Emulation' and 'Invidious Comparison' in *Sister Carrie* and *An American Tragedy.*" *Studies in American Fiction* 21 (Autumn 1993): 191–208.

Eisenstein, Sergei M. *"An American Tragedy."* *Close Up* 2 (June 1933): 109–24.

Eisenstein, Sergei M. *Notes of a Film Director.* London: Lawrence and Wishart, 1954.

Eisenstein, Sergei M., Alexandrov, G. V., and Montagu, Ivor. *"An American Tragedy*: Scenario" in *With Eisenstein in Hollywood.* New York: International, 1967, pp. 208–341.

Elias, Robert H. *Theodore Dreiser, Apostle of Nature,* rev. ed. Ithaca, N.Y.: Cornell University Press, 1970.

Ellis, Charles Edward. *An Authentic History of the Benevolent and Protective Order of Elks.* Chicago: by the author, a member of Lodge #4, 1910.

Felman, Shoshana. *Jacques Lacan and the Adventure of Insight.* Cambridge and London: Harvard University Press, 1987.

Fiedler, Leslie. "Dreiser and the Sentimental Novel," in *Dreiser: A Collection of Critical Essays,* ed. John Lydenberg. Englewood Cliffs, N.J.: Prentice-Hall, 1971.

Fiedler, Leslie. *What Was Literature?* New York: Simon and Schuster, 1982.

Fish, Stanley. *Self-Consuming Artifacts: The Experience of Seventeenth-Century Literature.* Berkeley: University of California Press, 1972.

Fisher, Philip. *Hard Facts: Setting and Form in the American Novel.* New York: Oxford University Press, 1985.

Fishkin, Shelley Fisher. *From Fact to Fiction: Journalism and Imaginative Writing in America.* Baltimore: Johns Hopkins University Press, 1985; New York: Oxford University Press, 1988.

Fishkin, Shelley Fisher. " 'Making a Change': Strategies of Subversion in Charlotte Perkins Gilman's Journalism and Fiction," in *Critical Essays on Charlotte Perkins Gilman,* ed. Joanne Karpinski. Boston: G. K. Hall, 1992.

Fossum, Merle, and Mason, Marilyn. *Facing Shame: Families in Recovery.* New York: Norton, 1986.

Foster, Hannah Webster. *The Coquette,* 1797. New York: Oxford University Press, 1986.

Foucault, Michel. "Afterword (1983): On the Geneology of Ethics: An Overview of Work in Progress," in *Michel Foucault: Beyond Structuralism and Hermeneutics,* by Hubert L. Dreyfus and Paul Rabinow. Chicago: University of Chicago Press, 1983.

Foucault, Michel. *The History of Sexuality,* vol. 1, trans. Robert Hurley. New York: Vintage, 1980.

Freud, Sigmund. *Group Psychology and the Analysis of the Ego,* 1922, trans. James Strachey. New York: Norton, 1959.

Freud, Sigmund. *The Standard Edition of the Works of Sigmund Freud,* trans. James Strachey. London: Hogarth, 1953–1974.

Friedman, Jean E., and Shade, William G. *Our American Sisters: Women in American Life and Thought,* 3d ed. Lexington, Mass.: D.C. Heath and Co., 1982.

Frye, Northrop. *The Anatomy of Criticism.* Princeton: Princeton University Press, 1957.

Frye, Northrop. *The Secular Scripture: A Study of the Structure of Romance.* Cambridge: Harvard University Press, 1976.

Geduld, Carolyn. "Wyler's Suburban Sister: Carrie 1952," in *The Classic American Novel and the Movies,* ed. Gerald Peary and Roger Shatzkin. New York: Ungar, 1977.

Gelfant, Blanche. *The American City Novel.* Norman: University of Oklahoma Press, 1954.

Gerber, Philip. " 'A Beautiful Legal Problem': Albert Levitt on *An American Tragedy.*" *Papers on Language and Literature* 27 (Spring 1991): 214–42.

Gerber, Philip. *Theodore Dreiser Revisited.* New York: Twayne, 1992.

Gianetti, Louis. *Understanding Movies,* 3d ed. Englewood Cliffs, N.J.: Prentice-Hall, 1982.

Glicksberg, Charles. *The Sexual Revolution in Modern American Literature.* The Hague: Martinus Nijhoff, 1971.

Goffman, Erving. *The Presentation of Self in Everyday Life.* Garden City, N.Y.: Doubleday Anchor Books, 1959.

Gordon, Linda. "Birth Control and Social Revolution," in *A Heritage of Her Own: Toward a New Social History of American Women,* ed. Nancy F. Cott and Elizabeth H. Pleck. New York: Simon and Schuster, 1979.

Gordon, Linda. *Woman's Body, Woman's Right: Birth Control in America.* New York: Viking Penguin, 1990.

Gordon, Michael, ed., *The American Family in Social-Historical Perspective,* 2d ed. New York: St. Martin's Press, 1978.

Graff, Gerald. *Literature Against Itself.* Chicago: University of Chicago Press, 1979.

Grebstein, Sheldon N. "Dreiser's Victorian Vamp." *Midcontinent American Studies Journal* IV (Spring 1963): 3–12.

Grimsted, David. *Melodrama Unveiled: American Theater and Culture, 1800–1850.* Chicago: University of Chicago Press, 1968.

Hakutani, Yoshinobu. *Young Dreiser: A Critical Study.* Rutherford, N.J.: Fairleigh Dickinson University Press, 1980.

Hapke, Laura. *Tales of the Working Girl: Wage-Earning Women in American Literature, 1890–1925.* New York: Twayne, 1992.

Harris, Marguerite Tjader. *Theodore Dreiser: A New Dimension.* Norwalk: Silvermine, 1965.

Hart, James D. *The Popular Book.* Berkeley: University of California Press, 1963.

Hartsock, Nancy. "Foucault on Power: A Theory for Women?" in *Feminism/Postmodernism,* ed. Linda Nicholson. New York: Routledge, 1990.

Harwood, W. S. "Secret Societies in America." *North American Review* 164 (May 1897): 617–24.

Haskell, Molly. "Is It Time to Trust Hollywood?" *New York Times Book Review* January 28, 1990: 1ff.

Hayne, Barrie. "Sociological Treatise, Detective Story, Love Affair: The Film Versions of *An American Tragedy.*" *Canadian Review of American Studies* 8 (1977): 131–53.

Hegel, G. W. F. *The Phenomenology of Mind,* trans. J. B. Baillie. New York: Harper and Row, 1967.

Heidegger, Martin. *Being and Time,* 1927, trans. John Macquarrie and Edward Robinson. New York and Evanston, Ill.: Harper and Row, 1962.

Heidegger, Martin. *An Introduction to Metaphysics*, 1953, trans. Ralph Manheim. New Haven: Yale University Press, 1959.

Higham, John. "The Reorientation of American Culture in the 1890s," in *The Origins of Modern Consciousness,* ed. John Weiss. Detroit: Wayne State University Press, 1965.

Hobson, Barbara Meal. *Uneasy Virtue: The Politics of Prostitution and the American Reform Tradition.* New York: Basic Books, 1987.

Hochman, Barbara. "A Portrait of the Artist as a Young Actress: The Rewards of Representation in *Sister Carrie,*" in *New Essays on SISTER CARRIE,* ed. Donald Pizer. New York and Cambridge, England: Cambridge University Press, 1991, pp. 43–64.

Hoffman, Daniel G. *Form and Fable in American Fiction.* New York: Oxford University Press, 1961.

Hohendahl, Peter U. "On Reception Aesthetics." *New German Critique* 28 (1983): 108–46.

Horwitz, Howard. *By the Law of Nature: Form and Value in Nineteenth-Century America.* New York: Oxford University Press, 1991.

Hovey, Richard B., and Ralph, Ruth S. "Dreiser's The *"Genius"*: Motivation and Structure." *Hartford Studies in Literature* 2 (1970): 169–83.

Howard, June. *Form and History in American Literary Naturalism.* Chapel Hill: University of North Carolina Press, 1985.

Howells, William Dean. *"Criticism and Fiction" and Other Essays,* ed. by Clara Marburg Kirk and Rudolf Kirk. New York: New York University Press, 1959.

Howells, William Dean. *Literary Friends and Acquaintances.* Bloomington: Indiana University Press, 1968.

Howells, William Dean. *A Modern Instance,* 1882. Bloomington: Indiana University Press, 1977.

Huggins, Nathan. *Harlem Renaissance.* New York: Oxford University Press, 1970.

Hussman, Lawrence E. *Dreiser and His Fiction: A Twentieth-Century Quest.* Philadelphia: University of Pennsylvania Press, 1983.

Hymowitz, Carol, and Wesman, Michaela, eds. *A History of Women in America.* New York: Bantam Books, 1978.

Jaeger, Clara. *Philadelphia Rebel: The Education of a Bourgeoise.* Richmond: Grosvenor, 1988.

James, William. *The Principles of Psychology.* New York: Henry Holt, 1890.

Jameson, Fredric. "Marxism and Historicism." *New Literary History* 11 (1979): 41–73.

Jameson, Fredric. *The Political Unconscious: Narrative as a Socially Symbolic Act.* Ithaca: Cornell University Press, 1981.

Janeway, Elizabeth. *Between Myth and Morning: Women Awakening.* New York: Morrow, 1975.

Janeway, Elizabeth. *Man's World, Woman's Place: A Study in Social Mythology.* New York: Morrow, 1971.

Jauss, Hans Robert. "Literary History as a Challenge to Literary Theory." *New Literary History* 2 (1970): 7–37.

Kant, Immanuel. *Critique of Pure Reason,* trans. N. K. Smith. New York: Oxford University Press, 1965.

Kant, Immanuel. *Groundwork of the Metaphysics of Morals,* trans. H. J. Paton. New York: Harper and Row, 1964.

Kaplan, Amy. *The Social Construction of American Realism.* Chicago: University of Chicago Press, 1988.

Kaplan, Harold. *Power and Order: Henry Adams and the Naturalist Tradition in American Fiction.* Chicago: University of Chicago Press, 1981.

Kazin, Alfred. "Introduction," in *Sister Carrie,* by Theodore Dreiser. New York: Penguin American Library, 1983.

Kazin, Alfred. *On Native Grounds: An Interpretation of Modern American Prose Literature.* New York: Harcourt, 1942.

Kennedy, David. *Birth Control in America: The Career of Margaret Sanger.* New Haven: Yale University Press, 1970.

Kerr, Michael. "Chronic Anxiety and Defining a Self." *Atlantic Monthly* (September 1988): 35–58.

Kimmel, Michael. *Changing Men: New Directions in Research on Men and Masculinity.* Cambridge: Unwin Hyman, 1987.

Lacan, Jacques. *Ecrits,* trans. Alan Sheridan. New York and London: Norton, 1977.

Lacan, Jacques. *Four Fundamental Concepts of Psychoanalysis,* trans. Alan Sheridan. New York: Norton, 1978.

Lacan, Jacques. "Seminar on the Purloined Letter," trans. by Jeffrey Mehlman, in *The Purloined Poe,* ed. John P. Muller and William Richardson. Baltimore and London: Johns Hopkins University Press, 1988.

Lacan, Jacques. *Seminaire II.* Paris: Seuil, 1978.

Langan, Thomas. *The Meaning of Heidegger: A Critical Study of an Existentialist Phenomenology.* New York: Columbia University Press, 1959.

Lears, T. J. Jackson. *No Place of Grace: Antimodernism and the Transformation of American Culture, 1880–1920.* New York: Pantheon Books, 1981.

Lehan, Richard. "Sister Carrie: The City, the Self, and the Modes of Narrative Discourse," in *New Essays on SISTER CARRIE,* ed. Donald Pizer. New York and Cambridge, England: Cambridge University Press, 1991.

Lehan, Richard. *Theodore Dreiser: His World and His Novels.* Carbondale: Southern Illinois University Press, 1969.

Lewis, Helen Block. *Shame and Guilt in Neurosis.* New York: International Universities, 1971.

Lingeman, Richard. *Theodore Dreiser: An American Journey, 1908–1945.* New York: Putnam's Sons, 1990.

Lingeman, Richard. *Theodore Dreiser: At the Gates of the City, 1871–1907.* New York: Putnam's Sons, 1986.

Litoff, Judy Barrett. *The Historian* 40 (February 1978): 235–51.

Little, Lester K. *Religious Poverty and the Profit Economy in Medieval Europe.* Ithaca: Cornell University Press, 1978.

Livingston, James. *Origins of the Federal Reserve System: Money, Class, and Corporate Capitalism, 1890–1913.* Ithaca: Cornell University Press, 1986.

Livingston, James. *Pragmatism and the Political Economy of Cultural Revolution, 1850–1940.* Chapel Hill: University of North Carolina Press, 1994.

Lydenberg, John, ed. *Dreiser: A Collection of Critical Essays.* Englewood Cliffs, N.J.: Prentice-Hall, 1971.

MacIntyre, Alasdair. "The Relationship of Philosophy to Its Past," in *Philosophy in History* ed. Richard Rorty, J. B. Schneewind, Quentin Skinner. New York: Cambridge University Press, 1984.

Macquarrie, John. *Martin Heidegger.* Richmond: John Knox Press, 1968.

Madsen, Axel. *William Wyler.* New York: Crowell, 1973.

Markels, Julian. "Theodore Dreiser and the Plotting of Inarticulate Experience." *Massachusetts Review* 2 (Spring 1961): 431–48.

Martin, Theodora Penny. *The Sound of Our Own Voices: Women's Study Clubs 1860–1910.* Boston: Beacon Press, 1987.

Marx, Karl. *Capital: A Critique of Political Economy,* 3 vols., trans. Samuel Moore and Edward Aveling. Chicago: Charles Kerr, 1906.

Marx, Karl. *Grundrisse: Foundations of the Critique of Political Economy,* trans. Martin Nicolaus. Baltimore: Penguin, 1973.

Matheson, Terence J. "The Two Faces of Sister Carrie: The Characterization of Dreiser's First Heroine." *Ariel* 11 (October 1980): 71–85.

Matthiessen, F. O. *Theodore Dreiser.* New York: W. Sloane Associates, 1951.

McNall, Sally Allen. *Who Is in the House?* New York: Elsevier, 1981.

McWilliams, Carey. *The Idea of Fraternity in America.* Berkeley: University of California Press, 1973.

Mencken, H. L. "Theodore Dreiser" in *A Book of Prefaces.* New York: Knopf, 1920.

Michaels, Walter Benn. "Critical Response III. Fictitious Dealing: A Reply to Leo Bersani." *Critical Inquiry* 8 (Autumn 1981): 165–71.

Michaels, Walter Benn. *The Gold Standard and the Logic of Naturalism: American Literature at the Turn of the Century.* Berkeley: University of California Press, 1987.

Miller, Nancy K., ed., *The Poetics of Gender.* New York: Columbia University Press, 1986.

Millett, Kate. *Sexual Politics.* Garden City, N.Y.: Doubleday, 1970.

Mitchell, Lee Clark. *Determined Fictions: American Literary Naturalism.* New York: Columbia University Press, 1989.

Moers, Ellen. "The Finesse of Dreiser." *American Scholar* XXXIII (Winter 1963–1964): 109–14.

Moers, Ellen. *Two Dreisers.* New York: Viking, 1969.

Moi, Toril. *Sexual/Textual Politics: Feminist Literary Theory.* London and New York: Methuen, 1985.

Montagu, Ivor. *With Eisenstein in Hollywood.* New York: International, 1967.

Mott, Frank Luther. *Golden Multitudes.* New York: Macmillan, 1947.

"The Myth of Womanhood: Victims," in *Woman and the Demon: The Life of a Victorian Myth,* by Nina Auerbach. Cambridge: Harvard University Press, 1982.

Norris, Frank. *The Responsibilities of the Novelist,* 1901. Garden City, N.Y.: Doubleday 1928.

Nye, Russel. *The Unembarrassed Muse: The Popular Arts in America.* New York: Dial Press, 1970.

Osherson, Samuel, and Klugman, Steven. "Men, Shame, and Psychotherapy." *Psychotherapy* 27 (Fall 1990): 327–39.

Pawling, Christopher. *Popular Fiction and Social Change.* London: Macmillan, 1984.

Peiss, Kathy, and Simmons, Christina. *Passion and Power: Sexuality in History.* Philadelphia: Temple University Press, 1989.

Petrey, Sandy. "The Language of Realism, the Language of False Consciousness: A Reading of *Sister Carrie*." *Novel* 10 (1977): 101–13.

Pizer, Donald. *Critical Essays on Theodore Dreiser.* Boston: G. K. Hall, 1981.

Pizer, Donald. "Dreiser and the Naturalistic Drama of Consciousness." *Journal of Narrative Technique* 21 (1991): 202–11.

Pizer, Donald, ed. *New Essays on SISTER CARRIE.* Cambridge and New York: Cambridge University Press, 1991.

Pizer, Donald. *The Novels of Theodore Dreiser: A Critical Study.* Minneapolis: University of Minnesota Press, 1976.

Pizer, Donald. *Realism and Naturalism in Nineteenth-Century American Literature,* rev. ed. Carbondale: Southern Illinois University Press, 1984.

Pizer, Donald. *Twentieth-Century American Literary Naturalism.* Carbondale: Southern Illinois University Press, 1982.

Pizer, Donald, Dowell, Richard W., and Rusch, Frederic. *Theodore Dreiser: A Primary Bibliography and Reference Guide.* Boston: G. K. Hall, 1991.

Plank, Kathryn M. "Dreiser's Real American Tragedy." *Papers on Language and Literature* 27 (Spring 1991): pp. 268–87.

Pocock, J. G. A. "The Mobility of Property and the Rise of 18th Century Sociology," in *Virtue, Commerce, and History.* New York: Cambridge University Press, 1985.

Potamkin, Harry S. "Novel into Film: A Case of Current Practice." *Close Up* 8 (December 1931): 267–79.

Radford, Jean. *The Progress of Romance.* London: Routledge and Kegan Paul, 1986.

Radway, Janice. *Reading the Romance.* Chapel Hill: University of North Carolina Press, 1984.

Ragland-Smith, Ellie. *Jacques Lacan and the Philosophy of Psychoanalysis.* Urbana and Chicago: University of Illinois Press, 1987.

Reddy, William. *Money and Liberty in Modern Europe: A Critique of Historical Understanding.* New York: Cambridge University Press, 1987.

Reep, Diana. *The Rescue and Romance.* Bowling Green, Ohio: Popular Press, 1982.

Reynolds, Quentin. *The Fiction Factory.* New York: Random House, 1955.

Richardson, Dorothy. *The Long Day: The Story of a New York Working Girl Told by Herself.* New York: Century Co., 1905.

Rieff, Philip. *Freud: The Mind of the Moralist,* 3d ed. Chicago and London: University of Chicago Press, 1979.

Riggio, Thomas P. "Carrie's Blues," in *New Essays on SISTER CARRIE,* ed. Donald Pizer. New York and Cambridge, England: Cambridge University Press, 1991, pp. 23–41.

Riggio, Thomas P. ed., *Dreiser-Mencken Letters: The Correspondence of Theodore Dreiser and H. L. Mencken, 1907–1945.* Philadelphia: University of Pennsylvania Press, 1986.

Riggio, Thomas P., ed. *Theodore Dreiser: The American Diaries, 1902–1926.* Philadelphia: University of Pennsylvania Press, 1982.

Roe, E. P. *The Opening of a Chestnut Burr.* New York: Dodd, Mead, 1874.

Roediger, David R. *The Wages of Whiteness: Race and the Making of the American Working Class.* London: Verso, 1991.

Rosenberg, Charles E. "Sexuality, Class and Role in 19th-Century America." *American Quarterly* 25 (May 1973): 131–53.

Ross, Akbert. *Moulding a Maiden.* New York: Dillingham, 1891.

Rotundo, E. Anthony. *American Manhood: Transformations in Masculinity from the Revolution to the Modern Era.* New York: Basic Books, 1993.

Rowson, Susannah. *Charlotte Temple,* 1791. New York: Oxford University Press, 1986.

Salmon, Lucy Maynard. *Domestic Service.* New York: Macmillan, 1897.

Salzman, Jack. *Theodore Dreiser: The Critical Reception.* New York: David Lewis, 1972.

Sanger, Margaret. *Margaret Sanger: An Autobiography,* 1938. New York: Dover.

Sanger, Margaret. *My Fight for Birth Control.* New York: Farrar and Reinhart, 1931.

Sanger, William. *The History of Prostitution: Its Extent, Causes and Effects throughout the World.* New York: Medical Pub., 1913.

Sarris, Andrew. *The Films of Joseph von Sternberg.* New York: Doubleday, 1966.

Schwager, Sally. " 'Harvard Women': A History of the Rounding of Radcliffe College." Ed.D. thesis, Harvard Graduate School of Education, 1982.

Sedgwick, Eve Kosofsky. *Between Men: English Literature and Male Homosocial Desire.* New York: Columbia University Press, 1985.

Sedgwick, Eve Kosofsky. "Gender Criticism," in *Redrawing the Boundaries,* eds. Stephen Greenblatt and Giles Gunn. New York: Modern Language Association, 1992, pp. 271-302.

See, Fred G. *Desire and the Sign.* Baton Rouge: Louisiana State University Press, 1987.

Seltzer, Mark. *Bodies and Machines.* New York and London: Routledge, 1992.

Seltzer, Mark. *Henry James and the Art of Power.* Ithaca: Cornell University Press, 1984.

Shell, Marc. *The Economy of Literature.* Baltimore: Johns Hopkins University Press, 1978.

Shell, Marc. *Money, Language, and Thought.* Berkeley: University of California Press, 1982.

Shove, Raymond H. *Cheap Book Production in the United States, 1870 to 1891.* Urbana, 1937.

Showalter, Elaine. *Sexual Anarchy: Gender and Culture at the Fin de Siècle.* New York: Viking Penguin, 1990.

Showalter, Elaine. *Speaking of Gender.* New York: Routledge, 1989.

Simmel, Georg. *The Secret Society,* trans. Albion W. Small. *American Journal of Sociology,* XI (January 1906).

Simmel, Georg. *The Sociology of Georg Simmel,* trans. Kurt H. Wolff. Glencoe, Ill.: Free Press, 1950.

Skinner, Quentin. "Meaning and Understanding in the History of Ideas." *History and Theory* 8 (1969): 3–53.

Smith-Rosenberg, Carroll. *Disorderly Conduct: Visions of Gender in Victorian America.* New York: Oxford University Press, 1985.

Smith-Rosenberg, Carroll, and Rosenberg, Charles. "The Female Animal: Medical and Biological Views of Woman and Her Role in

Nineteenth-Century America." *Journal of American History* 60 (Sept. 1973): 332–56.

Snow, C. P. "A Conversation with C. P. Snow," by Robert Moskin. *Saturday Review World.* April 6, 1974: 20ff.

Sochen, June. *Herstory: A Record of the Women's Past,* 2d ed. Palo Alto: Mayfield Publishing Co., 1982.

Sprinker, Michael. "The Current Conjuncture in Theory." *College English* 51 (1989): 825–31.

Sundquist, Eric J., ed. *American Realism: New Essays.* Baltimore: Johns Hopkins University Press, 1982.

Swanberg, William A. *Dreiser.* New York: Charles Scribner's Sons, 1965.

Szuberla, Guy. "Ladies, Gentlemen, Flirts, Mashers, Snoozers, and the Breaking of Etiquette's Code." *Prospects* 15 (1990): 169–96.

Taylor, Gordon O. *The Passages of Thought: Psychological Representation in the American Novel.* New York: Oxford University Press, 1969.

Thorne, Robert. "Places of Refreshment in the Nineteenth-Century City," in *Buildings and Society: Essays on the Social Development of the Built Environment,* ed. Anthony D. King. London: Routledge and Kegan Paul, 1980.

Tovo, Kathryn. "Rescue Homes at the Turn of the Century: The Berachah Home Experience," unpublished paper, University of Texas, Austin.

Tractenberg, Alan. "Who Narrates: Dreiser's Presence in *Sister Carrie,*" in *New Essays on SISTER CARRIE,* ed. Donald Pizer. Cambridge and New York: Cambridge University Press, 1991.

Trilling, Lionel. "Reality in America," in *The Liberal Imagination.* New York: Viking, 1950.

Turkle, Sherry. *Psychoanalytic Politics.* New York: Basic Books, 1978.

Van Horn, Susan Householder. *Women, Work, and Fertility, 1900-1986.* New York: New York University Press, 1988.

Versenyi, Laszlo. *Heidegger, Being, and Truth.* New Haven: Yale University Press, 1965.

von Sternberg, Joseph. *Fun in a Chinese Laundry.* New York: Macmillan, 1965.

Walcutt, Charles Childs. *American Literary Naturalism: A Divided Stream,* 2d ed. Minneapolis: University of Minnesota Press, 1973.

Warren, Robert Penn. *Homage to Theodore Dreiser: On the Centennial of His Birth.* New York: Random House, 1971.

Weedon, Chris. *Feminist Practice and Poststructuralist Theory.* Oxford: Basil Blackwell, 1987.

Welles, Orson. Interview in *Stories from a Life in Film* by Leslie Megahy. BBC in association with Turner Broadcasting, 1989.

Wertheimer, Barbara Mayer. *We Were There: The Story of Working Women in America.* New York: Pantheon Books, 1977.

Whalen, Terry. "Dreiser's Tragic Sense: The Mind as 'Poor Ego'." *The Old Northwest* 11 (1985): 61–80.

Whitaker, Carl, and Malone, T. *The Roots of Psychotherapy.* New York: Brunner/Mazel, 1981.

Winkler, Karen J. "Seductions of Biography." *The Chronicle of Higher Education,* 27 (October 1993): A6.

Woloch, Nancy, ed. *Early American Women: A Documentary History 1600-1900.* Belmont, Calif: Wadsworth, 1992.

Wolsterholme, Susan. "Brother Theodore, Hell on Women," in *American Novelists Revisited: Essays in Feminist Criticism,* ed. Fritz Fleischmann. Boston: G.K. Hall, 1982.

Zanine, Louis J. *Mechanism and Mysticism: The Influence of Science on the Thought and Work of Theodore Dreiser.* Philadelphia: University of Pennsylvania Press, 1993.

Ziff, Larzer. *The American 1890s: Life and Times of a Lost Generation.* New York: Viking, 1968.

Contributors

Nancy Warner Barrineau (Ph.D., University of Georgia, 1988). Published in *American Literary Realism, Thomas Hardy Journal, Dictionary of Literary Biography,* among others. Book in progress: *Theodore Dreiser's "Working Girls": Journalism to Fiction.* Assistant Professor, Communicative Arts, Pembroke State University.

Leonard Cassuto (Ph.D., English, Harvard University, 1989). Published in *Studies in Short Fiction, Prospects, American Literary Realism,* among others. Assistant Professor, English, Fordham University.

M. H. Dunlop (Ph.D., English, George Washington University, 1982). Author of *Sixty Miles from Contentment: Traveling the Nineteenth-Century American Interior.* Published in *American Quarterly, The Old Northwest,* among others. Associate Professor, English, Iowa State University.

Shelley Fisher Fishkin (Ph.D., American Studies, Yale University). Author of *Was Huck Black? Mark Twain and African–American Voices* and the award-winning *From Fact to Fiction: Journalism and Imaginative Writing in America.* Coeditor of *Listening to Silences: New Essays in Feminist Criticism.* Numerous articles and presentations, several articles in press, *Reconfiguring Jewish–American Identity: Literary and Cultural Essays in an Autobiographical Mode* in progress. Professor, American Studies and English, University of Texas, Austin.

Irene Gammel (Ph.D., English, McMaster University). Author of *Sexualizing Power in Naturalism: Theodore Dreiser and Frederick Philip Grove*. Published in *The Faulkner Journal, Canadian Review of Comparative Literature, Canadian Literature, Ariel: A Review of International English Literature*, among others. Assistant Professor, English, University of Prince Edward Island.

Lawrence E. Hussman (Ed.D., English, University of Michigan, 1964). Author of *Dreiser and His Fiction: A Twentieth-Century Quest* and *Counterterrorist*. Contributing editor, *Dreiser Studies* (1983–present). Designated textual editor, *The Bulwark*, for the University of Pennsylvania Press critical edition of the collected works of Dreiser. Published numerous articles on Dreiser and wrote the Foreword to *The Bulwark* (1973). Wrote reviews of Dreiser's *Notes on Life*, the Pennsylvania Edition of *Sister Carrie*, and Vera Dreiser's *My Uncle Theodore*. In progress: editing, with a foreword, *The Lust of the Goat Is the Bounty of God*, by Marguerite Tjader (a posthumous memoir by Dreiser's literary secretary) and *Frank Norris and His Fiction*. Professor, Wright State University.

James Livingston (Ph.D., History, Northern Illinois University, 1980). Author of *Accumulating America: Political Economy and Cultural Revolution, 1850-1920* and *Origins of the Federal Reserve System: Money, Class, and Corporate Capitalism, 1890-1913*. He has published essays on Shakespeare, Poe, and Disney's "Little Mermaid," among other subjects. Associate Professor, History, Rutgers University/New Brunswick.

Paul A. Orlov (Ph.D., English, University of Toronto, 1979). Dissertation: "Dreiser's Defense of the Self: A Reading of *Sister Carrie* and *An American Tragedy*." Author of *An American Tragedy: Distorted Definitions of the Self in Modern Fiction* (in progress). Published in *Modern Fiction Studies, Journal of Narrative Technique, American Literary Realism*, among others. Assistant Professor, English, Pennsylvania State University/Delaware County Campus.

Scott Zaluda (Ph.D., English, City University of New York, 1992). Published and delivered papers on Theodore Dreiser, Franz Kafka, and Billie Holliday. Assistant Professor, English, Nassau Community College.

Index